D0571853

THE CHESTER
MYSTERY CYCLE:
ESSAYS AND
DOCUMENTS

THE

chester mystery cycle

ESSAYS AND DOCUMENTS

R. M. LUMIANSKY

AND DAVID MILLS

WITH AN ESSAY,

"MUSIC IN THE CYCLE,"

BY RICHARD RASTALL

THE UNIVERSITY OF

NORTH CAROLINA PRESS

CHAPEL HILL AND LONDON

The publication of this work was made possible in part through a grant from the National Endowment for the Humanities, a federal agency whose mission is to award grants to support education, scholarship, media programming, libraries, and museums, in order to bring the results to a broad, general public.

Library of Congress Cataloging in Publication Data

Lumiansky, R. M. (Robert Mayer), 1913–
 The Chester mystery cycle.

 Bibliography: p.
 Includes index.
 1. Chester plays. 2. Mysteries and miracle-
plays, English—History and criticism. 3. English
drama—To 1500—History and criticism. I. Mills,
David. II. Title.
PR644.C4L85   822′.0516   82-1838
ISBN 0-8078-1522-5   AACR2

CONTENTS

PREFACE

SOME YEARS AGO the first volume of our edition of the Chester Cycle appeared;[1] a second volume providing Explanatory Notes, English Glossary, and Bibliography will be published under the same auspices as the edition. The present volume presents four essays about various aspects of the cycle, a conveniently regularized transcription of the documents that furnish information about the cycle's development and presentation, and an appendix concerning stanza-forms in the cycle. We are deeply grateful to Richard Rastall of the Department of Music, University of Leeds, for contributing the essay on the important specialist subject of music in the cycle.

References throughout the essays are to our edition. Speech Headings, Stage Directions, and Margin Directions within the Plays are abbreviated as SH, SD, and MD. We have used the same abbreviations for manuscript-designation that were used in our edition. They are, in chronological order:

M	Manchester Fragment; MS. 822. IIC2 15th century (?)
P	Peniarth 399 c. 1500 (?)
Hm	Huntington 2 1591
A	Additional 10305 1592
C	Chester Coopers' Guild 1599
R	Harley 2013 1600
B	Bodley 175 1604
H	Harley 2124 1607

Because of their similarity, as distinct from H, manuscripts HmARB are called the Group.

We are especially indebted to the staff of the University of North Carolina Press for its counsel and assistance during the editing and production of this book. For preparation of the typescript, we are also grate-

1. *The Chester Mystery Cycle*. London: Oxford University Press for the Early English Text Society, supplementary series 3, 1974.

ful to Barbara Henning, Catherine Rees, Joan Welford, Annette Butler, and Isabel Tupper. In addition, we wish to express our appreciation for helpful advice to Lawrence M. Clopper, who has contributed so importantly to the study of the Chester cycle.

RML
DM

THE CHESTER

MYSTERY CYCLE:

ESSAYS AND

DOCUMENTS

1.

THE TEXTS
OF THE CHESTER
CYCLE

THE PURPOSE OF THIS chapter is to evaluate the evidence for the text of the Chester cycle presented by the extant manuscripts. Editors such as Deimling, Greg, and Salter have undertaken such evaluation as part of the process of selecting a base text for their editions or projected editions. We did not adopt that procedure in selecting the Huntington manuscript as our base text, and the manner of our evaluation therefore differs somewhat from theirs. In particular, we do not wish to argue for the priority of a manuscript on the grounds that it may present readings that are older than those of other manuscripts, or that its readings are stylistically or semantically better than those of other manuscripts. We are concerned rather with the meaning that should be attached to the phrase "the Chester mystery cycle" and with the different interpretations of the phrase implicit in the texts of the different scribes. Since our aim differs from that of earlier editors, we have not in general attempted to discuss their evidence in this essay.

The data for the discussion are the text and variants in our edition. To reduce this material to manageable proportion we have concentrated on two aspects. The first is the general distribution of variants, which we have used particularly in our discussion of the extant manuscripts. In 1974 we published a series of statistical tables of variants in *Leeds Studies in English* under the title "The Five Cyclic Manuscripts of the Chester

Cycle of Mystery Plays: A Statistical Survey of Variant Readings." We there pointed out that the figures given related only to the spoken text; that they represented only "five-manuscript" variants; that they took no account of the nature of the variants; and that they represented the results of a survey made before the final text of the edition was published and might contain minor differences from the figures that would result from a survey based on that edition. We remain convinced that the figures offer a good general indication of manuscript features and alignments, and we have cited certain of these figures in the course of this discussion. Readers are referred to the article for full statistics.

The second aspect of the variants emphasized here is the presence of demonstrable errors in manuscripts. "Error" is difficult to establish, but we would distinguish the following:

1. Errors of stanza-form: For the cycle as a whole the eight-line Chester stanza, $aaa^4b^3aaa^4b^3$ or $aaa^4b^3ccc^4b^3$, is dominant, except where functional or textual considerations seem to have dictated a different form. Thus in most passages we can properly suspect error (a) when there are fewer than eight lines in a stanza; and (b) when the rhyme-scheme is other than that stated above. Error in rhyme may be particularly suspected when an obvious rhyming alternative exists to the nonrhyming form in a manuscript. We are less happy about using the number of stressed syllables as a criterion for error, since we find that the Chester cycle has no obvious iambic consistency and that different readers scan the same line in different ways, often with variations in the number of stressed syllables.

2. Errors of meaning: We suspect errors when the information given in one part of a play is inconsistent with information given in another part of the same play. We suspect errors when a grammatical construction cannot be analyzed according to accepted patterns of concord and syntax. We suspect errors when a form has no counterpart in standard dictionaries or is not recorded in an appropriate sense or usage. These several kinds of errors affect our understanding of the meaning of the text.

3. Errors of fact: The Chester cycle follows a given narrative line in which certain events must occur; in places, very close correspondence can be detected between the cycle and a given text (e.g., 21/310+Latin-58 and the Apostles' Creed). We suspect error where this conformity is markedly disrupted.

We have also taken account here of material in the "Textual Notes" and in the "Manuscripts" section of our edition in order to characterize the attitude of the scribes and to gain further information about the state of the exemplar(s) from which they copied. We provide a few examples of scribal practice and variations in order to characterize general scribal practices. Comprehensive exemplification and analysis are prohibited by the limitations of space, and in any case such a presentation seems to us to be less necessary in a discussion of the present kind than it would be in an attempt to evaluate the claims of each manuscript to serve as base text.

Finally, we have, so far as possible, tried to limit speculation about the "prehistory" of the cycle. We are not here concerned with the evolution of the Chester cycle, and we do not wish to postulate a series of "proto-cycles," each with its own "lost" manuscript(s). In this analysis we have tended to emphasize the role of the scribe in changing the text rather than to seek the source of error in a prolonged sequence of textual transmissions. We would not deny the possibility of lost manuscripts antedating the extant forms, but we prefer to concentrate our speculation upon two lost manuscripts only: (a) an Exemplar that transmitted errors to all extant manuscripts, and (b) a Pre-exemplar which did not contain those errors.

The Cyclic Exemplar

The extant cyclic manuscripts share a number of errors. The presence of these shared errors indicates that somewhere in the textual history of each manuscript there was a text that contained these errors and that this text was a shared feature of the transmission of the extant cyclic manuscripts. This text, for convenience, we call "the Exemplar." The errors within it presuppose a text, or perhaps a series of individual play-texts, that contained the "correct" version of the cycle. For convenience, we call this text or series of texts "the Pre-exemplar."

The shared errors in the extant texts may be divided into a number of different categories, each of which is exemplified below.

Errors Affecting the Rhyme-scheme of a Stanza

We have assumed that the "standard" Chester stanza contains eight lines, rhyming aaabaaab or aaabcccb. Occasionally a different stanza-form with different rhyme-scheme is used (see Appendix: Stanza-forms in the Cycle). We suspect error when the expected rhyme-scheme is not realized, and we feel confident of it where the rhyme-scheme can be readily restored by substituting a word of equivalent meaning, or by changing word-order within a line. This type of error is the easiest to detect and constitutes our firmest evidence, but because we can readily detect such errors it follows that individual scribes who thought about what they were writing could also detect and emend errors of this kind. Hence the list of "rhyme-errors" below represents a minimum—the errors shared by all extant cyclic manuscripts. Probably there are many other cases, in which one manuscript alone has the appropriate rhyme-word, where the Exemplar was in error and one of the scribes of an extant manuscript has corrected the error independently.

1/5–19, st. 2	*essention* 8 AR, *assention* B, *licentia* H for *essentia*
1/56–59, st. 6	*lighte* 57 ARB, *heighte* H for *lee*
1/94–101, st. 14	*mayne* 98 for (?) *meed*
2/233–40, st. 30	*alsoe* 239 for *als*
3/25–32, st. 4	*shutte* 31 HmR, *sutte* A, *shoote* B, *sit* H for *shit* (cf. *shutt* 24/194; *shitt* 12/149 HmB, *sutte* A, *shutt* RH)
3/277–84, st. 37	*fleete* 281 HmB, *flitte* ARH for *flette*
4/333–40, st. 43	*gryll* 340 HmARH, *sliere* B for *gright*
4/452–58, st. 59	*bade* 455 for *bede*
4/468–75, st. 61	*understand* 468 for *understond* *confounde* 475 HmARB, *underfonge* H for *underfo*
4/484–91, st. 63	*abyde* 491 for *abye*
5/89–95, st. 12	*beode* 92 Hm, *byde* A, *bydd* R, *bade* B for *bede*
5/168–75, st. 23	*cann* 174 for *conn*
5/208–15, st. 28	*seeke* 215 for *seeche*

5/248–55, st. 33	*gonne* 252 for *goe* (cf. H, IB/197)
5/372–79, st. 49	*performe* 375 HmRB, *fulfill* A for an unidentified alternative
5/444–51, st. 58	*borne* 447 for *bore*
6/381–88, st. 50	*mankynd* 388 for *mankyn*
6/691–98, st. 89	*maye* 694 for *cwene*
7/25–32, st. 4	*penyewrytte* 28 for *penyewortte*
7/145–48, st. 29	*live* 147 for *libbe*
7/193–97, st. 41	*little* 194 for *litt*
7/266–73, st. 52	*loynes* 266, 272 for *lendes*
7/424–27, st. 80	*forder* 425 Hm, *starte* A, *foder* RB, *founder* H for *fother*
7/567–75, st. 107	*stare* 567 for *starne*
7/617–20, st. 116	*child* 620 for *barne*
7/633–40, st. 118	*handes* 638 Hm, *thombes* AR, *hondes* B for *hommes*
8/205–12, st. 28	*give* 206 Hm, *geve* ARBH for *gie*
9/33–40, st. 5	*lesse* 36 for *lasse*
9/104–11, st. 14	*sayd* 108 for (?) *known*
9/152–59, st. 20	*saye* 156 HmAR, *said* B, *fayle* H for (?) *tell*
9/256–63, st. 33	*trayne* 259 HmARH, *trame* B for *traye*
10/305–12, st. 42	*areste* 308 - *peace* 312 HmABH, *om* R for an unidentified alternative
10/450–57, st. 60	*daye* 457 for *dayes*
11/151–58, st. 20	*harte* 154 - *blys* 158 HmBH, *blesse* AR for an unidentified alternative
11/191–98, st. 25	*hast* 198 for *hasse*
11/239–46, st. 32	*knowes* 240 for *knawes*
	have drawe 244 for *drawes*
	might knowe 246 for *knawes*
11/291–98, st. 41	*not* 293 HmRBH, *note* A for *non*
11/311–14, st. 44	*teene* 312 for *tyne*
12/113–20, st. 15	*so high* 113 for *on hight*
13/153–60, st. 21	*out* 156 - *waye* 160 for an unidentified alternative
13/197–204, sts. 27–28	*to have remission* 204 for (?) *to be free*
13/402–9, st. 56	*donne* 409 for *do*

13/458–65, st. 63	*beforne* 461 HmRBH, *before* A - *kneene* 465 Hm, *knye* A, *knee* RBH for an unidentified alternative
14/153–60, st. 20	*lesse* 154 for *lasse* *goe* 156 for *gon*
14/201–8, st. 26	*hand* 204 HmBH, *handes* AR - *founde* 208 HmARB, *fonde* H for *hond* 204 or *fand* 208
14/225–32, st. 29	*marchandize* 228 - *anoye* 232 HmARB, *anye* H for *marchandie* 228 or *anyes* 232
15/73–80, st. 10	*muste* 80 for *moste*
15/89–96, st. 12	*mankynde* 93 for *mankynne* *mynd* 95 HmRBH, *om* A for *mynne* *bodye* 92 - *evermore* 96 for an unidentified alternative
16/363–70, st. 48	*have* 363 for *han*
16A/169–76, st. 22	*man* 170 for *mon*
16A/185–92, st. 24	*beheight* 189 for *bethought*
16A/360–67, st. 47	*knowe* 367 for (?) *see* (cf. H, IC/8)
16A/368–75, st. 48	*hand* 372, IC/13 H for *hond*
16A/464–71, st. 60	*clyft* 466 HmAB, *clyst* R, *cleft* H (cf. IC/119) for *clight*
17/301–8, st. 39	*commonwealth* 304 for *commonweale*
18/82–89, st. 11	*donne* 85 - *stand* 89 for an unidentified alternative
18/90–97, st. 12	*understand* 95 for *understond* *hand* 96 for *hond* *lacke* 97 for (?) *wond*
18/98–105, st. 13	*tatch* 105 for (?) *tack*
18/138–45, st. 18	*found* 144 for *fand* (or *fond*, if *hand* 142, *stand* 143 are held to have rounded vowels)
18/170–77, st. 22	*band* 177, HmARH, *bond* B for *bend*
18/258–65, st. 33	*swoone* 264 HmRB, *soune* A, *sowne* H for *swow*
18/417–20, st. 55	*might* 419 for (?) *mercy*
19/72–79, st. 10	*lawe* 73 for *laye*
19/176–83, st. 23	*tree* 183 for *rood*

19/248–55, st. 32	*weeninge* 251 for *weene*
	see 255 for *seene*
21/271–78, st. 35	*man* 271 for *mon*
	can 273 for *con*
22/73–80, st. 10	*learne* 80 for *lere*
22/125–32, st. 17	*I will leave* 132 for *leave will I*
22/133–40, st. 18	*fortredde* 136 HmARH, *fortrade* B - *hye*
	140 for an unidentified alternative
22/245–52, st. 32	*tyme* 248 for *tome*
22/261–68, st. 34	*the daye of doome* 264 for *doomesdaye*
	dwell 268 for *stay*
22/317–24, st. 41	*even* 317 for *een*
23/41–48, st. 6	*found* 48, *om* R for *fand* (or *fond*, if *land*
	44 is assumed to have a rounded vowel)
23/249–52, st. 33	*lawe* 250 for *laye* (but cf. P)
23/333–40, st. 44	*feynde* 337 for *fynde* (but cf. P)
	wend 339 for *wind* (but cf. P)
23/341–48, st. 45	*deceaves* 344 for *beguiles*
23/410–16, st. 55	*raygnes* 415 for *ringes*
23/417–23, st. 56	*reprove* 419, *om* R for *repreve*
23/424–31, st. 57	*lawe* 431 for *laye*
23/699–706, st. 96	*releaved* 702 for *releave*
24/301–8, st. 39	*wond* 302 for *wand* (unless rounded
	vowels are assumed for *land* 301, *hand*
	303)
24/493–500, st. 63	*beheight* 498 for *behett*
24/549–56, st. 70	*righteous* 551 for *rightwise*
24/581–88, st. 74	*grynne* 583 for *grenne*
	brenne 588 HmRH, *brune* B, *om* A for
	breme
24/597–604, st. 76	*styrre* 601 for *stere*
	lure 603 for *lere*
24/613–20, st. 78	*grace* 620, *om* A for *fate*
24/701–8, st. 89	*truste* 703, *om* A for *triste*

The following errors occur in passages found only in H:

IA/32–39, st. 5	*be soe* 39 for *soe be*

IB/25–32, st. 4   *looke* 28 for *see*
IB/257–64, st. 33   *beheight* 259 for *betaught*
IC/85–92, st. 12   *vayne* 92 for *bone*

These errors attest a variety of doubts on the part of the scribe. In many cases—e.g., *hand* for *hond, lesse* for *lasse, tyme* for *tome*—"error" may seem to be too strong a term for what may be merely a formal variation or an acceptably imperfect rhyme. In other cases—e.g., *gonne* for *goe, borne* for *bore, donne* for *do*—the scribe was evidently unhappy with the morphology of his text. But in an interesting number of instances, the word itself seems to have caused him difficulty—words such as *essentia, lee, gright, underfo, seeche, lendes, fother, hommes, bethought, rood,* and especially *lay*. Sometimes a stylistic or semantic consideration seems to override the consideration of rhyme, as in *child, to have remission, I will leave, the daye of doome, vayne;* probably such considerations underlie those instances in which we cannot readily postulate an alternative. There is, however, no evidence of systematic revision in the examples here cited.

Other Errors Affecting the Structure of Stanza and Line

The "regular" Chester stanza contains eight lines. We therefore suspect error when an otherwise "regular" stanza contains more or fewer lines than eight. Examples are: 6/st. 29 (7), st. 69 (7); 10/st. 56 (9); 13/st. 11 (10), st. 16 (10), st. 19 (10), st. 30 (10), st. 32 (10); 15/st. 40 (6); 21/st. 20 (6); IA/st. 2 (7). A very frequent departure from the "regular" stanza is the single Chester quatrain—e.g., 4/st. 38, st. 48, st. 52; 5/st. 16, st. 22, st. 44, st. 59; 8/st. 24; 10/st. 11, st. 14; 13/st. 24, st. 27, st. 29, st. 66; 16A/st. 45; 17/st. 42; 18/st. 37, st. 45, st. 56; 19/st. 34; 22/st. 15; 23/st. 17, st. 31, st. 33, st. 50, st. 62; 24/st. 13; IC/st. 6. It is, of course, within the competence of an alert scribe to make good a single-line deficiency in a stanza, as we suspect the H-scribe often does, but it is much more difficult for him to supply a complete quatrain. At the same time, it is also tendentious to assume that the Exemplar is in error wherever it fails to conform to a preconceived notion of stanza-structure. Hence such stanzaic variations do not constitute a major evidence of error unless associated with other features. Some clear examples follow.

At 5/st. 12 the four MSS HmARB—hereafter "the Group"—have a seven-line stanza, lacking one c-rhyme. A comparison with IB/st. 8 indicates that the Group lacks a counterpart to IB/61, which has evidently been erroneously omitted. But a comparison both with H and with the biblical text indicates the extent to which the Group-version has garbled lines 90–92 in the same stanza. Stanzaic error is here associated with other forms of textual corruption.

At 6/73–96 st. 10 contains six lines, st. 11 eight and st. 12 ten. It is clear that the first two lines of st. 12 are in fact the last two lines of st. 10, and that st. 11 has therefore been erroneously inserted into the text, with corresponding stanzaic misdivision. Removing st. 11 restores regular stanzaic form to sts. 10 and 12 and produces continuity of sense. It is not clear where st. 11 belongs in the text, since it seems to stand outside the *Magnificat*; possibly it had been added alongside st. 10 and should precede or follow st. 9. Since no manuscript has noted this misplacement, it may be inferred that the misplacement was incorporated into the Exemplar text. Only R is troubled by the irregular stanza-lengths and seeks to rectify the error by misguidedly omitting 79–80 and 91–92.

In some instances the deficiency in stanza-form can be correlated with the absence of material that is present in a text that underlies the play. Thus, 13/177–80, st. 24, a quatrain, would require preliminary material corresponding to John 9/19; 13/251–56, st. 35, which lacks two c-rhymes, has no counterpart to Christ's final words in John 10/30, and the key word of that passage, *one*, would supply a c-rhyme; in 13/389–93, st. 54, the three lines missing from the second quatrain may correspond to John 11/26. Play 13 may, however, have presented particular problems in view of its opening stanzas; certainly, Christ's words in John 10/30 are used in the opening of the play, and it is possible that the equivalent lines in st. 35 had been canceled in the Exemplar or in the material that its scribe was copying so that there should be no duplication. 22/st. 15 should be seen in the context of 95–124; the comparison with its source, Zechariah 6/8, suggests that the absence of a quatrain may correspond to the omission of material.

A second and equally speculative "error" relates to the structure of the line. We have made no assumptions about the precise meter of Chester, declining to impose an iambic pattern upon the lines or to prescribe exactly how lines should be stressed. But we accept as general principle that in a Chester stanza, the b-rhyme lines will normally have three strongly stressed syllables and the other lines four. Thus, when a line does not conform to this general expectation, we suspect error. It is often possible to speculate about what should be omitted to reduce the number of stressed syllables in a line, but rarely about what should be added to increase the number. Examples of lines containing too many stressed syllables are: 3/104 (omit *all daye*); 6/722 (read *todaye* for *within this playe?*); 16/166 (omit one adverb in *hense awaye*); 16A/228 (omit *a mon*); 18/177 (omit *synfull*); 18/185 (omit *payne and*); 18/250 (omit *syr*, as ARH, and *nowe*); 21/326 (omit *fayre*); 22/4 (omit *will* or *I*); 22/264 (omit *to fall* or *daye of*, or read *doomesdaye* for *the daye of doome*); 23/457 (omit *eke the*); 24/548 (omit *that place*). Examples of lines with fewer than the expected number of stressed syllables are: 7/33, 34, 45, 123; 9/166; 10/180, 309, 310, 381; 12/107; 14/234, 393 (*to* perhaps omitted before *thee*); 16A/22, 37, 477; 19/182; 23/319, 354, 446, 450, 452; IB/135.

Again, evidence here is of doubtful value, since meter has a strongly subjective element, and different readers and scribes may read lines in different ways. It seems probable that many variants, and particularly variations in word-order, represent attempts by scribes to improve the meter and perhaps to move in the direction of an iambic base. At the same time, a comparison of different versions of the same line in the extant texts does suggest their occasional source in Exemplar errors.

A third, and particular, instance of stanza-error is purely formal. The fact that no manuscript has the correct arrangement of 1/sts. 2–4 strongly suggests that the Exemplar itself presented the wrong line-division. H seems to have recognized the error after st. 2. Possibly the Exemplar arrangement arose in the misinterpretation of some indicator of medial cæsura in the material copied.

Errors of Text and Structure

The Exemplar carried a number of lines that did not give good sense because of mistakes in the words. These errors of text are often picked up and corrected in one or more of the extant manuscripts, although the underlying erroneous forms can on occasion still be constructed (see below, pp. 49–57). But sometimes the errors pass undetected. At 2/39, for example, all manuscripts read *dayes three* for *daye three*. Although Balaam has only by then blessed the Israelites twice, the Exemplar read *thrye* 5/316 for *twye*, perhaps indicating that a third blessing, present in the biblical account and H, had been omitted in the Group-version without the consequent emendation of this line. At 5/364 the Exemplar-scribe misread *leve*, "leave," as *love*. It read *fynter* for *fymter* 7/27, and *giftes* for *gifte* 9/78. It had *them* 10/165 where *him* seems more appropriate. At 11/197 the Exemplar *in* is apparently an error for *and*. The biblical text suggests that Exemplar *as* 13/368 should be *that*. The broken construction at 19/2 suggests an Exemplar error in which a verb has been lost. *my* is required for the erroneous *his* at 19/213. At 21/112+Latin, *supervenientes* is an error for Vulgate *supervenientis*. At 21/129–30 the text departs so far from the source, *Veni Creator Spiritus*, that textual corruption in the Exemplar seems certain, although its source is not clear. *yf* 24/359 does not give sense and may represent an Exemplar misreading of $\flat^t$ = *that*. At 24/580+Latin, *ubi* seems to be an Exemplar error for Vulgate *ibi*.

A particular group of errors occurs in Play 18. At 18/17–20 Pilate seems to say that Tiberius sent Jesus to him, but it is probable that *he* 19 should read *they*, referring to the Jews. 18/41–8, st. 6 contains nine lines instead of the expected eight and seems to derive from a situation in which the stanza lacked 42 and was simply a continuation of Pilate's speech, uninterrupted by Cayphas; here the "error" is stanzaic, not textual, and arises from 41 being regarded as a question rather than a statement. Finally, Pilate's oath at 18/126 is wholly inappropriate and suggests a transmitted error of speech-ascription that is inadequately resolved in H.

A second, more significant, sort of error is the misplacing of material. Such misplacing often involves stage directions, suggesting that at some point in the transmission of the text these directions had been in a margin. One example is the building of the ark in Play 3. 3/96 makes it clear that the ark is then complete, but a SD after 96 in H suggests that the family thereupon begins to work on the ark, while HmARB have the equivalent SD after 112, following both the stated completion of the ark at 96 and also the dialogue of Noah and his wife at 97–112; the direction seems to suggest the action that should accompany Noah's words at 81–96 and would substitute appropriately for 80+SD. The confusion here may be related to the existence of possible alternative forms of the play, discussed below. At 10/192+SD and 10/256+SD there are equivalent instructions requiring the soldiers to depart for Bethlehem, following two equivalent speeches of farewell by the first soldier (185–92, 241–48); again, the duplication may have implication for the existence of alternative forms of the play. In Play 20, the action described in 96+SD seems prompted by Jesus' words at 54, and should therefore follow 56; the action of 56+SD corresponds to Jesus' words at 41 and should perhaps follow 40. And 23/686+SD is appropriate to 698 and seems to have been misplaced.

On other occasions the misplacement affects the structure of speeches and stanzas. At 8/374–81, st. 51 the speeches of the second and third kings have evidently been transposed, destroying the rhyme-scheme. At 21/137–52 there is a change in the usual order of speakers, some speakers are omitted, and the extant manuscripts attest some confusion—A omits Simon's speech and H erroneously places 137–40 after 152; the variations suggest the removal of a final two-speech stanza effected in the Exemplar in a confusing manner. At 23/633–44, sts. 84–85, 641–44 should follow 636 (as in P). Hm has evidently omitted a quatrain, present in ARBHP and required before 637–40. Either the Exemplar presented the material in the wrong sequence, or it presented it in a confusing fashion.

Finally, some plays demonstrate marked structural inconsistencies, such that major decisions have to be taken by a producer before the play can be performed at all. A particularly difficult series of problems is presented by Play 10, where the number of knights involved seems to vary from one part of the play to another—cf. 10/58, 226, 289, 350. At 226 the names of two different knights from the earlier scene are amalgamated to provide the name for one knight; *fellowes* 289 HmRBH suggests that there are by then more soldiers than the original two, and 350 may indicate as many as five people—four knights and the Doctor. A similar problem seems to arise at 10/325–36 about the women, for either four women are here involved, despite the SHs, or the play contains alternative versions (see below).

There are problems also associated with Play 11. A minor matter is the confusion that exists in the text about the number of birds to be offered by Mary—variously described as two doves or a turtle-dove, 132, and three birds in all, 140, whereas the biblical text requires two pigeons or two doves; even allowing that *a turtle*, 133, might be an Exemplar error for *turtles*, the problem of number remains. But a major difficulty occurs at 11/207–*Finis*, "Christ Before the Doctors," where the omissions of SHs, the breakdown of rhyme-schemes and syntax on occasion, and the general inconsequentiality of the dialogue in 206+SH–26 all suggest a confusion in the Exemplar. It would seem that a bridge-passage linking the episode to the preceding Purification has been much altered, leaving some features of a different version, some lines of difficult legibility or uncertain status, and two SHs omitted. It is possible to recognize some of the errors and problems by comparing the play in detail with analogues in other cycles. It may be noted that no speech has been assigned to the Third Doctor before 259 and that the Second Doctor speaks twice in one sequence, 247–50 and 255–58.

The Coexistence of Alternative Passages

It seems that in a number of instances the Exemplar contained passages whose content contradicted the content of other passages in the play. Although such instances may be regarded as errors in the manner of the structural errors of the preceding section, it is possible, and in several cases very probable, that the Exemplar contained alternative forms of the same play and that those responsible for the production of the cycle were required to decide which version was to be performed. Seven examples seem noteworthy:

3/81–112. As noted previously, these lines contain contradictions, in that the building of the ark is stipulated in 80+SD, described in 81–95, and said to be complete at 96; there is then a dialogue between Noah and his wife, 97–112, after which 112+SD requires Noah and his family to mime the construction of the ark. H has a Latin equivalent of 80+SD; it also has a Latin equivalent of 112+SD after 96, Noah's announcement that the ship is complete; and it therefore omits 112+SD after 112. Clearly 112+SD is appropriate after 80, since it merely amplifies the short SD at that point in all manuscripts and describes the actions of 53–80. And God's further request, 113ff., follows logically upon the completion of the ark. A wholly satisfactory play would result from the omission of 80+SD–112. What is lost in that omission is a scene containing two elements partially inconsistent with what has preceded. First, instead of the whole family being directly involved in the building of the ark (*Noe with all his familye* 112+SD), only Noah is responsible for the construction (*Noe beginneth to buyld the arke* 80+SD), a fact confirmed by his speech, 81–96. Second, the wife, previously cooperative, 65–68, shows sudden belligerence in a comic exchange with Noah, 97–112. These scenes present two possibilities for a producer. Whereas the stage directions call only for mimetic labor (*shall make a signe as though the wrought upon the shippe* 112+SD), Noah evidently constructs major features of the ark and identifies its shape. We may note in particular the emphasis upon the construction of the mast:

> Of this tree will I make a maste
> tyed with gables that will laste,
> with a seale-yard for eych baste   [89–91]

and recall the importance of the mast for the "Raven and Dove" scene: "Et erit in nave aliam columbam ferens olivam in ore, quam dimittet aliquis ex malo per funem in manibus Noe," IA/15+SD. Second, the producer has the possibility of exploiting a vein of comic antifeminism not predominant in other parts of the play apart from the entry of the wife into the ark (which is anyway much more restrained than in Wakefield, for example). It seems therefore that three explanations are here possible:

1. That the play was performed without 80+SD–112 (and, with the omission of the mast-mechanism; perhaps also without the "Raven and Dove" scene);

2. That Noah's construction of the ark with its preceding SD was included, so that the play included the Group's 80+SD–96 (and perhaps also the "Raven and Dove" scene). This created uncertainty about the status of the SD, which followed 80 under our first possibility and led H to include it after 96 (or rather before 113 in this version);

3. That the play included not only the events of our second possibility, but also the comic exchange of Noah and his wife, 97–112. Here again the status of the SD that followed 80 in our first possibility remained uncertain, and the Group-scribes therefore retained it after 112 (or rather before 113).

5/104–63. Balak's opening speech contains an obvious inconsistency. Having established his anger and fear of the Israelites and recognized the impossibility of defeating them in battle, 96–103, he goes on to argue that his best hope of vengeance is Balaam, 104–23. St. 16, 120–23, is a quatrain; it is completed in rhyme and sense by the order given by Balak to the knight, st. 22, 164–67. In 123–164, Balak begins another speech, for having established that his best hope is Balaam, he begins: "But yett I truste venged to bee with dynte of sword or pollicye" (124–25), calls for aid in battle from his pagan gods, and recounts the Israelites' previous victories. This second tirade has no counterpart in H's version of the play and clearly destroys the continuity of meaning, tone, and stanza in the speech as a whole. The "But yett I truste" would seem a probable continuation from 100–104—"Although it is useless to fight against them, I nevertheless intend to have vengeance." Hence 105–19 and 124–63 represent alternatives; the latter has been misplaced since both speeches should end with the composite stanza 120–23+164–67. The choice allows a producer to present Balak either as a politic pagan (105–19) or as the traditional figure of a ranting tyrant (124–63), flourishing his sword (143+SD, 151+SD B). Not surprisingly, H prefers the former, which is in keeping with the more restrained tone of the prophet play, with Balak the agent for providing Balaam, an uncriticized Gentile prophet by the end, with the opportunity for his Messianic prophecy. The tyrannical alternative would seem much more in keeping with the exemplary action of the Group-version, where Balaam is presented critically and the opponents of God are killed. The existence of these alternative speeches suggests that the Group had at this point the version found in H and an alternative but did not recognize them as alternatives.

6/185–240. Octavian's opening speech begins with an introductory description of himself, 185–208, which derives ultimately from the account in the *Mirabilia Romæ*; a comparison with that text suggests that the Exemplar here transmits an error at 187–88 based on a misreading and a misunderstanding of the material copied. The speech then continues with two stanzas of corrupt French, 209–17, which were evidently once meaningful and constituted an introductory address to a dramatic audience in Octavian's palace:

Segneurs, tous si assembles a mes probes estates!   [209]

After the French stanzas, the speech continues with a further introductory address, this time in more tyrannical terms:

Kinge, coysell, clarke, or knight,
saudens, senatoures in sight,
princes, pryest here nowe dight

and present in this place,
peace!   [218–22]

Octavian then briefly rehearses the authority he has exercised, to some extent duplicating the more subdued account of the opening stanzas. St. 29 is a seven-line stanza, a fact recognized by H, which leaves a line-space empty. The duplication of material is related to the fact that there are two stanzas of French in the middle of the speech. These are the only instances of French in mid-speech, as might be expected since French was evidently employed at the start of a speech to characterize a man of special power and noble rank. The fact that both the French stanzas and the following English stanza directly address an audience suggests that 209–40 was an independent speech, characterizing the tyrannical Octavian who seems suggested by the Late Banns. 185–208 would represent a rational pagan, able—unlike Herod—to understand the nature of godhead and to believe. It seems adequately to represent the *Mirabilia* and hence to be complete in itself. To regard the two speeches as mutually exclusive would avoid awkward inconsistencies and repetitions. The sole disadvantage would be that Octavian is identified for the audience by name at 193 only; no such identification occurs at 209–40. Both speeches lead logically to the decision to carry out the taxing at 241.

7/448–80. Having heard the angel's song, the shepherds themselves sing. After the song, the third shepherd suggests

Nowe wend we forth to Bethlem   [448]

and the shepherds follow the star until it stops and they see the stable:

Harvye, that good bene our happes
we seene—by our Savyour fonde   [462–63]

Then, however, the angel appears and gives the shepherds the explanation that follows the brightness and precedes the angelic chorus in Luke. He repeats the injunction:

To Bethlem nowe right   [468]

and Garcius concurs:

To Bethlem take wee the waye   [472]

and urges them all to sing as they go. At 480 the first shepherd describes the stable scene. The text is evidently contradictory. The shepherds twice decide to go to Bethlehem and twice arrive. Moreover, the angel's explanation is apparently divorced from its biblical context and placed in the inappropriate context of Bethlehem:

> Sheppardes, of this sight
> be ye not afright [464–65]

which can refer only to the sight of the angel himself, who is giving advice already unnecessary. Finally, it seems unlikely that there should be two occasions for "journey-songs" on the way to Bethlehem. Perhaps, however, two textual matters constitute the strongest evidence of alternatives here. First, the first shepherd at 436–39 proposes that they respond to the angel's song with a song of their own so that the angel may be induced to provide them with an explanation:

> that hee will lett us to bee kent [438]

which suggests a desire for information. This explanation should logically follow the end of the song, 447+SD, and would therefore explain how the shepherds know where to go and what to see at 448–63. Second, the normal speaking order is shepherds 1-2-3-*Garcius*; but in 436–51 it is 1-2-*Garcius*-3. It seems probable that 444–51 are mis-ascribed—that Tertius Pastor utters 444–47 and Garcius 448–51. If this was so, and the angel's speech, 464–71, followed 447, then the next speaker would be Garcius, either at 448–51 or at 472–79, in both cases proposing that the shepherds go to Bethlehem. The mis-ascription might well have something to do with the fact that at 471–79 Garcius also proposes a song, as in 444–47. The change of speaking order at 444–51 may therefore be connected with the coexistence of alternatives. (It will be noted that by this thesis a break in order would occur in 460–63 followed by 480, moving directly from third to first shepherd.) It seems to us logical, therefore, to propose that after 447+SD there should follow the angel's explanation, 464–71, and then either 472–79 or 448–63, leading to 480ff.

10/305–76. The two soldiers approach two women, the first knight challenging the first woman, 305–12, the second knight the second woman, 313–21. The second knight kills one of the children, 321–24, and the two women grieve, 325–36, beating the soldier. The first knight then kills the son of the first woman, who attacks him, 337–60, and the second kills the "son" of the second woman, 361–76+SD. The text shows some confusion. The second woman's child seems to have been killed at 322–24 (though the child may be that of the first woman, who grieves at 325–28); however, surely both children must be killed. Immediately, however, the episode is repeated, the children of the first and second women being killed by the first and second knights. A and R in particular seem uneasy about the text in this section. It is possible that 305–36 and 337–76 are alternatives—that the first woman's child is killed at 324–28 and, as the second woman joins in her frenzy, the second child is killed after 336, leading directly to 376+SD. But this is not the only possibility, for it is clear from the text that there must at this point be more than two soldiers involved in the massacre, so that the SHs may be misleading; the two soldiers involved in 336–76 may not be the same two that are involved in 305–36, and similarly the two women involved in the later scene may be different women from those in the earlier. The possibilities have to be evaluated in relation to the corruption within the text of 10 discussed above.

21/159–238. God's long speech before sending the Holy Ghost to the apostles presents a particular problem. At 153 *Lyttle God* takes up the prayer of the apostles and asks the *gloryous Father*, 153, to fulfil the apostles with grace, wisdom, and prosperity; *Deus*—appropriately designated *Deus Pater* by H—responds to *my Sonne*, 159, and in 159–74 promises to send down his *Ghoost*, 167, to confer wisdom and a determination to attain heaven. But at 175 God addresses the assembly of Heaven, the patriarchs and prophets redeemed from Hell, and the angels and archangels, justifying his action as part of his ongoing purpose for the redemption of mankind. In this justification, God the Father evidently has assumed the role of the Trinity:

But while I was in that degree
in yearth wonynge   [199–200]

and his reason for sending the Holy Ghost is now that the disciples are unstable. Finally, at 231–38 God announces his intention to send down the Holy Ghost. It seems unlikely that God could speak as Trinity having addressed Little God as God the Father. It also seems strange that two separate reasons for the dispatch of the Holy Ghost should be given and that the intention to send down the Holy Ghost should be repeated. The speech of Little God is an unusual six-line stanza. Possibly we have here two different accounts—an abridged account, whereby 152+SD–74 follow 152 and lead directly to 238+SD, and an extended account, whereby Deus, the Trinity, responds to the prayers of the apostles with his speech to the assembly of Heaven, 175–238, following directly upon 152. Some further support is perhaps given to this view by the margin SD in HmB after 152: "Christ must speake in heaven." This was evidently an addition to introduce the speech, notable because it would be unnecessary if the speech followed the present 158+SD, found in all MSS: "Tunc omnes apostoli contemplantes vel orantes quousque Spiritus Sanctus missus fuit"; but instead of the expected *Christus dicat*, we have *Deus dicat*. It would seem that this SD introduces a speech beginning 175 and that it was left unchanged when the alternative dialogue of Christ and God the Father was incorporated. The MSS carefully specify the speaker at 153–58 as *Lyttle God* HmB, *God the Sonne* A, *Jhesus* H—only R reads *Deus*; but no similar precision applies to *Deus* 158+SD, although H adds a SH, *Deus Pater*. Evidently *Deus* was the existing SD form and was felt to be adequate to the new function.

23/77–104. At 77–80 Antichrist announces his intention to raise the dead. Without doing that, however, he immediately speaks as if he is about to perform a further trick (*Nowe wyl I turne . . .* 81ff.), and then again says that he will raise the dead, to be followed by his own resurrection from the dead, 89–96. He then raises the dead, 97–104+SD. 81–96 are redundant to the passage and their omission would improve its structure. At the same time, it is difficult to see how these lines constitute an alternative, unless it is assumed that the kings require no introduction and the text could pass directly from 56+Latin to 81.

If it is accepted that at some points the Exemplar presented alternatives, by intention or error, it must also follow that a scribe might recognize the presence of these alternatives and exercise his right of choice. Although this must be a matter for further discussion in the following section, two specific instances should perhaps be raised here.

First, it seems usual for a play-cycle to begin with a definition of the godhead and an account of the Creation and Fall of the Angels. Chester begins with an appropriate Latin quotation:

Ego sum alpha et oo,
primus et novissimus.   [1/1–2]

which it tellingly takes up at the start of the final play:

Ego sum alpha et omega, I, primus et novissimus   [24/*Before* 1 Latin]

But this neat parallel of "first and last" as an aspect of the godhead and as a description of the two plays to which it serves as preface seems partly upset by the beginning of Play 2:

Ego sum alpha et omega, I, primus et novissimus

[2/*Before* 1 Latin]

Moreover, Play 1 recounts the events of the first day's creation, the separation of the bad angels from the good having a symbolic counterpart in the separation of light and darkness which completes the first day's creation, 1/290–301. Play 2 does not, however, begin with day 2, but returns to the point at which heaven and earth are made and recapitulates the events of the first day, 2/9–16. It would, in fact, be possible to begin the cycle with the second play and to ignore the Creation and Fall of the Angels—particularly since Satan explains who he is at 2/161–76. It is certain from the page numberings that Hm once included Play 1, but its removal at a later date might well suggest that an owner of the manuscript recognized that the cycle could as well begin with Play 2 as with Play 1, a decision perhaps helped by the absence of any Chester stanza from Play 1. Possibly when Plays 1 and 2 were performed in sequence, 1/st. 44, lines 290–97 and 2/*Before* 1 Latin were omitted to avoid the recapitulation.

A similar problem, but on a larger scale, exists in the appearance of Jesus to his disciples in 19/168–99 and 20/1–56. In both instances the disciples fear that Jesus may be a ghost, and he eats to dispel their fears. The two appearances are independently attested by the gospel narratives, but only one requires the confirmation by eating. Repetition is possible, but it seems probable that the effect of the repeated scene in Play 20 would lose something from its production in the preceding play and that the performers would not be happy at this possibility. Moreover, the doubt reported by Jesus at 20/1–8 would seem unfounded in view of the confirmations given in Play 19. It would seem likely, therefore, that only one version of the scene was played and that 20/1–56 would not normally follow the full production of 19.

THE EXAMPLES DISCUSSED ABOVE are errors attested by all extant manuscripts and they are errors that must therefore have been present in the cyclic Exemplar. They suggest that the Exemplar is derived from an earlier form of the cycle in which such errors did not occur. The errors are of various kinds, ranging from the errors of stanza, line, and text that could represent scribal miscopyings on a small scale to large-scale confusions that give contradictory information and attest a garbled text or perhaps on occasion a range of choices to be made before production. Certainly the Exemplar did not provide a "perfect playing-text" and may indeed actively have challenged scribes to exercise choice and judgment. Before we can proceed to characterize it more fully, therefore, it is necessary to consider how the scribes of the extant manuscripts may have used the Exemplar.

The Cyclic Exemplar and the Extant Manuscripts

The simplest assumption that we can make about the transmission of the extant texts, given the existence of a Pre-exemplar and a derived Exemplar, is that each manuscript derives directly from the Exemplar. This is not an unchallengeable assumption. Deimling postulated that H belonged to a different and older tradition from the Group; Greg postulated a descent from a common Exemplar, which required each extant manuscript to be a copy of a lost intermediary manuscript; Salter held that each play could have its own textual history and argued that in Play 16 MS A was a copy of Hm. These issues will be discussed further in considering the individual manuscripts, as will the undoubted relationship between A and R. Here we wish to argue from a selection of the evidence available that the extant manuscripts, at certain points, reflect the effect of different scribal choices from the possibilities included in the Exemplar. Our main intention is to further our understanding of the nature of the Exemplar and hence of the cycle that it contained. But in pursuing this argument, we believe that we are also producing some evidence to suggest that all scribes must have been working from a common Exemplar. For convenience at this stage, no account is taken of the single-play manuscripts M, P, and C.

Alterations had been made on the Exemplar text,
confusing the scribes of the extant manuscripts

In 4/468–75, st. 61, the b-lines do not rhyme in any manuscript. Rhyme is required with 471, "that the dyvell had brought us to"; 475 reads variously:

and death for to confounde HmAR
and death to confounde B
his death to underfonge H

From the H reading it is possible to propose that the rhyme-word should be *underfo* and that *confounde* HmARB is an alteration. If H had to supply a rhyme-form independently, it would not have supplied *under-fonge*, since that does not rhyme; either, therefore, it was copying a manuscript that read *underfonge* in error, or H miscopied (or was unable to read) the original rhyme-form in the Exemplar. Replacing *underfo* by *confounde* reduces the number of syllables in the line and changes the meter; hence in compensation HmAR have an additional syllable, *for*, which is not in H. That B also omits *for* seems to suggest that the status of *for* in B's Exemplar was uncertain, although in all other respects the line was that of HmAR. This would be consistent with the insertion of *for* in the Exemplar accompanying the change of *underfo* to *confounde*. *his* H would then represent an independent alteration.

At 10/378 HmAR have the metrically rough "You shalbe hanged the rowte," which BH "improve" by reading *all the*. In B, however, *all* is inserted above the line with a caret, probably indicating the Exemplar form and the circumstances that led to the rejection of the reading by HmAR and its acceptance by H.

At 12/249–56, st. 32 HmARB have an acceptable eight-line stanza, but H contains an additional line after 255. If a regular stanza is to result in H, a line must be omitted, but syntactically that line cannot be 255, and rhyme prevents its being 256. The obvious candidate is 253, "What writest thou, maister? Now lett me see" HmB (*me*] om AR), which appears in H written in a single-line space of its own and which merely duplicates 250, "What writest thou, if it be thy will." If that were omitted, the additional line in H would follow logically, not after 255 but after 254. But such an insertion is not syntactically possible in HmARB, which read (with a metrically rough 255):

Owt, alas that woe is mee!
For no longer dare I here bee,
for dread of worldly shame.   [254–56]

H, however, would read:

Owt, alas that woe is me!
I see my synnes so clearly

Here no longer dare I be
for fear of worlds shame.

It seems logical to suppose that H had the HmARB stanza before it, with
the additional line in the margin and an alteration to 255; and finding
255 altered, H assumed that the additional line must in some way be associated with 255. It therefore included all lines. A possible explanation
for the change may be seen in other H readings. At 254 H has the SH
Primus Jew; this SH would be inappropriate to the version in which 253
was omitted, but would be quite appropriate in a version in which 250
and 253, the same question, were spoken by different speakers. H then
includes a MD beside 258, which must replace 256+SD HmARB to
indicate that 257–64 are spoken by the second, not the first, Pharisee,
a reading perhaps more in conformity with the biblical text. Hence the
variants here suggest two different allocations of speeches, with the H-
version, drawing upon margin-notes, including the alterations.

At 14/214 the phrase *on everye waye* HmRB is required for rhyme and
meaning. H reads *on every syde way*, suggesting an uncanceled error,
perhaps resulting from the automatic writing of a common collocation
that the H scribe later noted. But it is possible that this error existed in
the Exemplar itself, for there seems no other reason why A should omit
waye completely in this line. If *syde* was the Exemplar-reading and *way*
a margin correction, H would give an accurate transcription, and A
would reflect Bellin's unease at the apparent compound *sydeway*.

An alteration of particular interest for the development of the cycle
and the state of the Exemplar seems to have been made to the Guild-
ascription of Play 16. The various ascriptions are to the Fletchers, Bowers, Coopers, and Stringers HmAR; to the Fletchers, Bowers, Coopers,
Stringers, and Ironmongers B; and to the Bowers, Fletchers, and Ironmongers H. The H-ascription covers Plays 16–16A, which are presented
as one play in H, whereas in HmARB 16A is ascribed to the Ironmongers. Since B shares the HmAR guild-ascription to 16A, the Ironmongers
should not be included in B's ascription to 16. It would seem probable
that the reference to the Ironmongers was inserted or canceled in the
Exemplar's 16/*Guild-ascription* to correspond to the absence or existence of a 16A/*Guild-ascription*. B misunderstood the alteration.

16/10 concludes with the words *thy postie powere* HmARB, but H,
clearly correctly, omits *postie*. Again, it would seem probable that the
Exemplar scribe had written *postie* in error and that this had been cor-

rected in the margin beside the line by *powere*. The cancellation had not been understood by HmARB, which retained the two words, but H understood what was intended.

At 16A/241 *lee* BH is to be preferred for rhyme to *leere* HmAR, but B originally wrote *dere*, suggesting that it had the form *leere* in front of it but misread it. It is therefore possible that the Exemplar read *leere*, but that the final *re* had been canceled or the form emended in some other way that only BH finally understood. Independent emendation by B and H is, however, also possible.

In HmRB, 17/57–72, sts. 8–9 are two Chester stanzas, but in H these become a single stanza by the omission of 61–64, a rephrasing of 66–68 to provide a new b-rhyme for 60, and the omission of 69–72. Although these facts might suggest two separate Exemplars, the omission of 66–69 in A, destroying the structure of st. 9, suggests that A was uncertain about these lines, an uncertainty most probably occasioned by the existence of two alternative versions of them. R corrects A's deficiency. The speech concludes in all versions with 72+Latin, although only the Group-version provides the sort of formulaic introduction here characteristic of the other speeches in this section:

Wherfore these wordes I doe rehearse
with honour unto thee   [71–72]

It seems probable that the Group represents the version in the Exemplar to which changes recorded in H were later added. An even clearer example in the same play is 17/253–54, Adam's two-line speech about the Penitent Thief. In HmAR this reads

And who ys this that comes here,
that lives with you in this manere?

but B adds the unconvincing line:

with crose on shoulder in this manner

which produces an irregular nine-line stanza. H, however, substitutes the added line in B for 254, where it is quite acceptable. Obviously all three lines were present in the Exemplar, with alternative versions of 254. HmAR accepted one version, H the other, but B erroneously reproduced both. Possibly the BH line was written underneath 254.

21/47 Hm is metrically "regular":

/   x / x /   x /
Wee assenten us theretyll

BH, however, read *us all*, thereby removing this regular sequence, but H restores regularity by omitting the verb inflection:

/   x /   x /   x   /
We assente us all theretyll

whereas B keeps the Hm inflection. AR read *all* for *us*, a change that has no effect on meter, but also adopt the H verb-form, which does disrupt meter:

/   x / /   x   /
We assente all theretyll

Although all the versions are acceptable, it seems probable that the Exemplar presented two possibilities—a verb inflection in *-en* with *us*, or an uninflected verb with *us all*. Hm and H correctly evaluated the different possibilities, but B combined the inflection with *us all* and AR rejected both inflection and *us*, suggesting that they took what was evidently an insertion, *all*, as a substitution.

At 21/301 AR have the required rhyme-word *dighte*; *drest* HmB seems to be a substitution. But the H-form *dreight* strongly disposes us to the belief that *drest* was an alteration to *dight* and that the H-form must have been influenced by that alteration (see further below).

At 24/348 H reads *a thousand sythes* for Hm's *a thousand tyme*, A's *a thousand tymes*; R does not have the stanza. B evidently had the H-form before it in writing the formally similar but semantically less appropriate *othes*. But after 340 Hm erroneously wrote out 341, 346, 347, and 348 and then, realizing the error, canceled the lines. In that transcription, Hm read *sythes* for *tyme*, indicating that it also had the H-form available. An alteration had obviously been made to the Exemplar.

The nature of the alterations described above varies. Some are evidently margin corrections of previous scribal errors, but others seem to have been alterations on the working text itself, with insertions and cancellations.

*The Exemplar-text contained notes in its margins
made by and/or for a producer*

There is no doubt that the Exemplar's margins contained production
notes. These seem to have been in English, instead of the Latin used for
SDs in most plays, and to offer some sort of guidance to the performer.
Sometimes the notes are a musical cue. Sometimes they are mere words
that indicate where an agreed action should occur—as, for example,
with the entries in Balak's speech, 5/96–164 (*florish* 111+, *caste up*
115+, *sworde* 143+) or Herod's speech, 8/161–212 (*staffe* 196+, *sword*
200+, *cast up* 204+). Sometimes they serve to suggest the mood to be
conveyed by the actor, as in 4/264+SD: "Isaack, fearinge leste his father
will slea him, sayth"; or 4/268+SD: "Abraham, comfortinge his sonne,
sayth." Sometimes they indicate specific gestures, as in 4/475+SD: "Here
lett the Docter kneele downe and saye"; or 7/52+SD: "Sitt downe."
Sometimes they simply reinforce cues, extending our awareness of what
is happening, as in 5/64+SD: "Here God appereth agayne to Moyses,"
which at once indicates what we may deduce already from the fact that
the next speech is by God, and also indicates that God must have left the
stage after his opening speech, 5/1–24, and now returns.

Some of the margin notes seem to serve the same function as SHs (e.g.,
4/459+SD—in the Hm text, but in B's margin, and omitted in ARH; or
6/356+SD), but perhaps have emphatic force, suggesting that it is precisely at this point and at no other that a certain action shall occur, as in
7/447+SD (English): "Here singe 'troly, loly, loly, loo.'" At times the
MDs may point to some change in the text, indicating the point at which
a particular insertion or omission should become operative. Thus, at
4/16, the MD reads: "Abraham, having restored his brother Loth into
his owne place, doth firste of all begine the play and sayth." The MD
indicates that (1) before the speeches in the play, some mimed act of
restoring Lot to his own place must be performed; (2) at this point the
play proper will begin as opposed to the opening two stanzas by Preco,
rightly characterized as a *Preface* in a MD to the left of *Before* 1 SH in B;
and (3) the next speaker is Abraham. The omission of 4/475+SD–*Finis*
in H, including the counterpart to the *Preface* (see below) may suggest
that the Messenger's speeches were an addition to or omission from the
text. The MD at 4/16 may therefore be drawing the producer's and
actors' attention to a change in the text as well as to the stage business
required.

The MDs presented problems for the scribes because they were clearly different in form, kind, and position from the SDs in the body of the text. The scribes had three possible courses of action—to retain them in the margin, to incorporate them into the text, or to omit them. Play 4 was evidently well supplied with SDs and MDs and provides a good illustration of the problems confronting the scribes. At 48+SD–112+SD the text contains ten SDs of considerable detail, which are all present only in HmB. AR omit 112+SD and R additionally omits 68+SD; H omits 64+SD, 68+SD, 80+SD, 112+SD, but has a further SD at 62+SD, which replaces the parenthetical Latin of 64+SH. All SDs tend to be in English in HmARB but in Latin in H; both forms were clearly available, for at 48+SD HmAB have two forms of SD, English and Latin, where R has the English form only and H the Latin form only—each evidently selecting one possibility from the two available in the Exemplar and transmitted by HmAB. B also has English and Latin forms at 72+SD and 88+SD, the English agreeing with HmAR and the Latin with H, again suggesting that both forms were available in the Exemplar. B sets its three Latin SDs in the body of the text but puts its English SDs in the margin. AR put all SDs in the body of the text. Hm puts seven SDs, including 48+SD (Latin), in the body of the text, and four SDs, (including 48+SD [English]) in the margin. H's seven SDs are distributed as four in the body of the text and three in the margin.

It seems probable that the Exemplar contained a number of MDs that are retained in their original position by B but transferred to the body of the text by HmAR. It also contained some Latin SDs that were glossed in English in the margin; here HmAR substitute the English forms and BH retain the Latin forms. H seems generally to have rejected the MDs, but at times the scribe seems to have considered them important, and he therefore "translated" them into Latin and incorporated them into the text, as at 56+SD, 96+SD, and 104+SD. The three SDs omitted by H are, in fact, unnecessary since their information can be deduced from the text.

The situation in Play 4 suggests, paradoxically, that it is not a necessary feature of a MD that it should appear in the margin of an extant manuscript, although its presence in the margin of one or more manuscripts is the only certain way of establishing its status as a MD in the Exemplar. But there are several instances of SDs in the cycle that have the form, terseness, and function of a MD without appearing in a margin—e.g.,

2/632+SD: "Cayne speaketh mornefullye," where the SD is obviously an instruction to the actor about the emotion to be conveyed (not a usual function of the standard SD); it renders the following SH redundant—the SH is omitted in A, and H omits the SD, which suggests that it may well have been marginal. Or 8/144+SD, where the first sentence, "Here the Messinger must goe to the kinge," is in the body of the text in all manuscripts, but the second, "Minstrells here must playe," is in the margin of HmB, incorporated into the text in AR, and omitted in H. The second sentence was clearly a MD, treated in accordance with the practice already noted by the scribes; but in a text where SDs at 48+SD, 64+SD, 84+SD are in Latin, and where the form of the first sentence is similar to that of the second, so that the playing of the minstrels seems to cover the movement of the Messenger, it seems unlikely that the first sentence should not also have been a MD. That sentence is presented in a Latin form in H.

This latter point leads to a second caveat—that MDs seem to have been in English, but the existence of a Latin form does not preclude the possibility of MD rather than SD. H clearly translated the MDs or substituted Latin equivalents. Thus at 8/96, the MD "Here the kinges ryse up" appears in the H margin as "Et surgit"; at 196 the MD *staffe* appears as *baculum*; and at 204 the MD *cast up* appears as *jace gladium*. A particularly good example of H's practice, confirming the fact that H had before it the MD of the Exemplar and not a different set of MDs, is provided by 8/381+SD: "The boye and pigge when they kinges are gonne," marginal in all manuscripts except B, which omits it. It is a characteristically cryptic MD, presumably suggesting that a boy should enter at this point carrying a flagon of wine in anticipation of Herod's request at 416–17; but H misunderstands *pigge* as an animal reference and renders the SD "Puer et nefrens cum reges discescerunt"—a reading only possible on the basis of the English MD of the Group.

Third, it is an unfortunate consequence of these MDs that they are likely to be overlooked or consciously rejected by scribes. H often ignores them unless they seem to have some reference to properties or actions. B seems to wish to enter them consistently, but sometimes overlooks them, as at 381+SD just noted. Other manuscripts similarly tend to incorporate them, sometimes at the expense of SDs, as noted in Play 4, but they too may make a mistake and neglect a MD. So, for example, only B has the MD *sword* at 5/151. At 16/326+SD HmB indicate that the crown of thorns is placed on Jesus' head; H conveys that information in a MD to 328; but AR omit any SD. H continues with a series of unique MDs beside 333 and 336, suggesting that there was a series of significant actions noted in the margins but ignored by the other manuscripts. Here H has accepted the MDs, HmB the one SD, and AR none. The MDs provide therefore very limited evidence of manuscript relationships. Moreover, their uncertain status may affect the attitude of scribes toward isolated MDs in plays after Play 8; the comparative infrequency of MDs from these plays in our extant manuscripts does not necessarily mean that there were no MDs in the Exemplar. A very significant instance occurs at 18, where B alone has, to the left of 212–15: "The 3 knights must say thes ii staves and com in at the right hand." St. 26 and its preceding SH have been misplaced in the Group at this point. The MD affirms that the speaker of the two staves (? = quatrains) is the third knight and should "enter" (presumably move forward from the right to join the others) as he says them. It seems possible that the MD represents some sort of indication to the actors that acknowledges that there is a problem about who is speaking. It certainly acknowledges that a movement is necessary here to match the movements required by SDs at 193+ and 201+. But without B there would be no indication of MD in the play and no suggestion that a problem was recognized.

There is good reason to believe that the MDs are additions to the text and were not, as it were, a supplementary set of notes made by the writer of the text to guide a producer. The example just cited suggests a problem in the Exemplar that may be acknowledged in the MD. But a clearer case is 4/88+SD, where the English SD assigns the following speech to Melchizedek HmARB, an ascription confirmed by the following SH ABH; but the Latin SD suggests no change of speaker in BH, and this does seem to be what is required, since the speech only gives sense if the speaker continues to be Abraham. B's Latin SD is quite explicit: "Tunc tradit equum oneratum sibi dicens," where *dicens* suggests that the speaker remains Abraham, in defiance of the English SD and SH in B; H, recognizing the problem, omits *dicens*, includes the *Melchesadecke* SH, but proposes a change of speaker back to Abraham at 93. The MD introduces an error that becomes incorporated into the text in HmAR and leads H to a number of textual alterations to accommodate the inconsistencies.

Finally, a difficulty with a MD is that it is written beside the text and its exact position may well be in doubt. Limited space was no doubt a reason for the cryptic nature of many MDs. But often it is not possible to be certain of the exact point in the text at which the MD should operate. Part of the difficulty at 4/88+SD seems to have been that the action there described relates to 93–96 of the following stanza, while the first quatrain of that stanza indicates that Abraham understands Melchizedek's gift.

It is unlikely that an Exemplar would contain cryptic MDs of the kind here discussed unless the text was a producer's text intended for performance. Indeed, the MDs raise at least the possibility either that the Exemplar was used as an acting text itself, or that it was a compilation of acting texts. The second possibility raises the wider issue of compilation, since the MDs are attested mainly for Plays 1–8; if, however, each company was required to supply a text of its play, it is possible that some would provide "clean copies" and others production copies with producers' margin notes. That perhaps we are dealing here with copies once made from the Pre-exemplar but subjected to subsequent modifications for successive productions before recall is an attractive postulation. And some force may be given to this argument by the fact that some MDs seem to point to alternatives in the Exemplar. We have noted the possible significance of 4/16+SD in this respect. Here may be added such instances as 4/475+SD, where the Doctor's final prayer and the Messenger's intervention are preceded by a MD that marks the point at which H's omission begins. More obviously, in the Group-version of 5/335+SD–6:

Here Balaham speaketh to Balaack: "Abyde a while"
BALAHAM
O Balaack kinge, abyde a whyle

the MD seems comically redundant in view of the following text; but does it mean "It is at this point that we must proceed with the version of the play in which Balaam says 'Abyde a while' rather than the other (H) version where the play ends with the Doctor's speech"? It is on such occasions that the production notes seem to impinge upon the area of textual criticism.

The Exemplar contained alternatives,
and scribes made different choices among them

The Exemplar seems to have incorporated a number of different versions of the cycle. Clear evidence of the changing status of sections of the text is provided by B's *truly restored* 13/229. *restored* is written between 229 and 229+SH, suggesting that it is not part of a line but was a margin note relating to a portion of text; it may be notable that 13/225–34, st. 32 is a ten-line stanza, suggesting that the text may be a little unusual at this point. But possibly one should distinguish between the alternatives that involve departure from the Pre-exemplar and those that involve a choice among the episodes for performance. The former allow us to argue for a preferred reading, but the latter do not.

Thus at 7/124 H has a stanza not in the Group but clearly necessary to sustain the usual sequence of speakers among the shepherds. This stanza should be assigned to *Primus Pastor*, but H merely reassigns 7/125–28 from *Primus* to *Secundus Pastor* as the order requires. B leaves a gap of about twelve lines after 124 and follows H in reassigning 125–28 to *Secundus Pastor*. B must have had the same Exemplar as H before him in order to leave the gap and make the new speech-ascription; but he seems to have been uncertain about the status of the H stanza. There is no obvious reason why the stanza should have been canceled or treated as an alternative form.

At 13/270 BH have a quatrain necessary to transform the stanzaic quatrains, sts. 37–39, into two Chester stanzas. It is impossible to demonstrate conclusively that these lines were in the HmAR Exemplar, but it seems possible that the content of the First Jew's challenge to Jesus:

thou, that art man as well as I,
makes thieself God here openly

could have given offense and been censored. AR simply copy the resulting lines, but Hm recognized that st. 37 had the irregular form aaba and transposed 271 and 272 to give a more acceptable form. One may compare the two additional stanzas that in H follow 16A/256, where, although the lines may not have been available to HmARB, it seems possible that they were excluded from the text because of their emphasis upon the elect position of the Virgin Mary.

Four of the episode-alternatives require special attention.

All versions of Play 7 indicate that there are shepherds' boys as well as the three shepherds and Trowle. Trowle's references to *my fellowes*, 208, and, more ambiguously, to *yee lades*, 195, strongly suggest the presence of colleagues other than, and younger than, the shepherds. In the confused passage of 7/443+SH ff. discussed above, the Group SD at 447+ SD does not specify the singers of Garcius's song (*Tunc cantabunt*), but H is very specific: "Tunc omnes pastores cum aliis adiuvantibus cantabunt hilare carmen." It seems probable that the *adiuvantibus* are the boys whose presence has already been suggested in the text and is demonstrated in the guild accounts. But it is then strange that H, which alone specifies the presence of the "helpers," lacks the scene of the presentation of gifts by the shepherds' boys at 7/596+SH–640. We have noted above clear indications of alternatives in 7/443+SH ff., and it seems certain that H either invented the SD because it felt that the shepherds' boys were necessary, or copied a SD rejected by the Group in favor of an alternative. It cannot be proved that H contemplated including the "Shepherds' Boys' Gifts" and later decided against it, but there is a suggestion that such an interpretation is possible.

Because the "Shepherds' Boys' Gifts" is found only in the Group, we did not discuss its internal structure above, but it may be noted here also that some alternative exists within the scene. Three boys speak at the start, and the third says that he will present last, 607–8, but in fact a fourth boy appears and comes forward last at 632+SH–40. The inconsistency here strongly suggests corruption of alternatives within the text. Compare further the discussion of the boys and their payments in chapter 3, "Music in the Cycle."

Second, H lacks the "Ale-wife Scene" that ends the Group-version of 17/276+SH–*Finis*. The scene itself, which has some implications for dating (see further below), could have been available to H. The only suggestion, albeit slight, is the guild-ascription to the Cooks in HmARB, which in H appears as the "Cooks and Innkeepers." The Early Banns specify the Cooks and Ostlers as the companies responsible, the Late Banns only the Cooks. There seems perhaps some point in specifying the Innkeepers if—as seems appropriate—they supplied the ale-wife. The variation in guild-ascription and in the inclusion or omission of the scene may reflect confusion by the scribes; either one specified Innkeepers and retained the scene or deleted Innkeepers and canceled the scene, but no manuscript contains this combination.

Third, the alternative existed of regarding the events of "Christ's Trials and Passion" as a single play, as in H, or two plays, as in the Group. The topic of priority, of whether our manuscripts derive from the amalgamation of two plays or the division of one, exercised Greg and Salter. To some extent we have already considered this question in discussing the origins of B's confused guild-ascriptions above. But a number of wider issues are raised by the situation in the manuscripts. It is clear that in the Group-version the colophon to Play 16 is designed to emphasize a division, and probably a departure from the usual format used in marking the end of one play from the start of the next. The colophon may well have taken the form found in R: "The End of this pagent is fynished in the next leafes following," which led to the confusion between *leafe* AB and *leafes* HmR, with A's attempt to give sense to the reading by substituting *begennan* for *fynished*. There is no number in the play heading to 16A, and nothing to identify the priests for the audience at its start. Hm, the only manuscript to specify play-numbers in the *Finis*-formulae for 16 and 16A, refers to both as *Paginae Decimae Sextae*. The internal evidence seems most readily to point to a division in the Exemplar of a single play. It should, however, be noted that the earliest record of the cycle suggests that in 1422 the "Trial and Flagellation" and "Passion" were two separate plays. Although this conflict of recension does not alter the evidence for a changed Exemplar, some resolution seems to be required. Either the internal evidence may be otherwise interpreted, or it may be accepted that the separate plays of 1422 underwent further processes of amalgamation (H) and subsequent division (Group). But for whatever reason, and by whatever process, the Exemplar demanded an editorial choice on the part of the scribes of the extant manuscripts.

This choice was merely a matter of division, not of material. But it was erroneously interpreted as a choice of material also by the Group, because the Exemplar contained the incomplete version of the episode of "Peter's Denial," 16/378+SH–94. This is out of place at the conclusion of the trials—it should appear in the dramatization of Jesus' inquisition at the High Priests' palace. It seems to have been on a piece of scrap paper that the Exemplar-scribe used as a divider. At the bottom of the leaf was space for at least the colophon, if not some of the concluding material of 16. But the scribe failed to cancel the fragmentary material above, perhaps believing that its irrelevance was obvious. H simply rejected this leaf and the alterations on the following leaf that marked the start of play 16A, but the Group copied it together with the *Finis*-formula.

The "Denial"-fragment is valuable evidence of the existence of episodes either excised totally from the Exemplar or omitted by all manuscripts as a possible choice. It is useful to combine its discussion with the fourth example of episodic alternative, the ending of 18 in RH, Appendix ID. Play 18 is obviously incomplete in HmAB, in that the dialogue between Mary Magdalen and the Angel has no sequel in those manuscripts. B ends at 424, HmA at 432, suggesting some uncertainty about the exact point at which the play ended. RH, however, continue with Christ's appearance to Mary Magdalen, to the women, and to Peter. The agreement of R and H here is unusual. As will be discussed later, R generally follows A but seems to have been checked against the Exemplar again. It seems therefore probable that the Exemplar contained the material in our Appendix ID, but that this represented a canceled ending to the play, suggesting that the ending was an alternative to some other form of the play. Possibly the alternative was an ending at either 368, with the Maries seeking Peter and rejoicing, or at 400, with the race to the tomb and Peter's affirmation of Christ's resurrection. The former would remove the awkward shift from the rejoicing Mary Magdalen to the doubting and sorrowful Mary Magdalen at 369–76, a shift resulting from the contradictory accounts in the synoptic gospels and John; but the latter is far closer spatially to the material in ID and might perhaps indicate that the scribe merely omitted to cancel a folio beginning at 400+SD. The confusion in HmA and B about the exact point at which the HmAB version should end strongly suggests that there was doubt about the point at which the cancellation began. And it is notable that B leaves the following recto blank and begins 19 on a verso page. This is one of only three instances of this practice, one of which is the start of Play 23 (which follows directly on Play 22), and the other significantly is the start of Play 3, where B has omitted 681–*Finis* of Play 2.

It seems impossible to demonstrate conclusively that where passages or episodes are found only in some manuscripts and not in others all the scribes had the passages before them. Yet the thesis is attractive and simple and seems to us to have enough circumstantial evidence to support its proposal. We believe, but can offer no evidence for such a belief, that in all cases of major divergence between the manuscripts, the divergence may be attributed to scribal choice inherent in the Exemplar. Thus, we would believe that the unusual practice of beginning Play 3 on a verso page by B suggests that B had available 2/681–*Finis* and chose to reject it; it represents the meeting of Cain with his parents, a self-contained episode. Similarly, we believe that the conflicting information of 4/*Before* 1 SD and 16+SD suggests that the opening speech of Preco was an alternative to beginning the play at 16+SD; it would follow that the corresponding concluding speech of the *Doctor* at 475+SD, together with the Messenger's intervention at 484+SD, were also alternatives, to be omitted when Preco's opening was omitted, and that H accordingly omitted the final speeches. In the case of Play 5, we would go further, arguing that the Group-version was designed for a production in which only the Old Testament plays were produced on the first day, as indicated in lines 448–55, while the H-version was intended for a different distribution of pageants since that passage is missing; here we believe that there were two versions of a complete play within the Exemplar since the differences between versions were too great to accommodate alternatives within a single text.

Some of the Exemplar choices concern points of belief,
and the choice may be regarded as one of censorship

So far we have not considered the possible reasons for choice, partly because such reasons were at best idiosyncratic and at worst arbitrary. Sometimes the reasons are clearly those of decorum. In 16/98, *sore skricke* ARB, for which *sore stryke* Hm seems to be an error, gives an imperfect rhyme, and H's *him beshitt* more closely indicates the probable reading of *him beshite*; similarly, at 16A/67 H's *shyte* is to be preferred for rhyme to the Group's *skricke* and its variants. These instances suggest the replacement of an "indecorous" word by a "more acceptable" one that gives less satisfactory rhyme; the motive is clear, although it is impossible to say here whether that alteration had been made in the Exemplar or at an earlier stage, so that H either reinstated a canceled word or reconstructed the required form independently. Such instances do, however, lead to interesting, if inconclusive, speculations about the choice of alternatives, and in particular of comic alternatives such as the "Ale-wife Scene" of Play 17. A particularly interesting alternative is the end of the devil's speech in 12/157–68, where the Group indicates that Satan, though defeated, will continue to fight, summoning his servants to a parliament. H substitutes for these lines a quatrain in which the devil, having recognized his fate, bestows an indecent curse upon the audience. It is difficult to know how far the indecorous words of the devil are merely a legitimate part of a comically reductive picture to which the Group provides a more dignified alternative and how far they were themselves a source of objection and choice, but the H-version, despite a modification to 156, does not give good rhyme.

But occasionally it is possible to see other objections to passages that some scribes omit. After 13/270 BH contain a quatrain necessary for stanza-structure but omitted in HmAR. The key to the omission may well be the lines addressed to Christ, "thou, that art man as well as I, makes thieself God here openly," which at once challenges the deity of Christ and the legitimacy of the actor's impersonation. That BH include the quatrain suggests that it was in the Exemplar but could be omitted, despite its metrical necessity. A second example is 16A/256, after which H has two stanzas not found in the Group. Here lines 5–8 emphasize the elect position of the Virgin Mary and constitute a plea for special favor:

> Sith thou me to thy moder chose
> and of my body borne thou was,
> as I conceived thee wemlesse,
> thou graunt me some legiaunce.

which could well have been unacceptable to Protestant critics.

This possibility of choice based upon censorship seems to underlie the problems of Peter's denial and the material in Appendix ID. Chester is unusual in not dramatizing Peter's denial, except in the incomplete and misplaced fragment. The event is anticipated in Jesus' prophecy at 15/189–92, and Peter remorsefully recalls it at 18/405–6. This second passage also expresses hope of mercy, taken up in John's reply at 18/413–16; and this hope seems fulfilled by Jesus' forgiveness at ID/73–95. But the latter also perhaps suggests why the Denial was omitted, for it strongly suggests Peter's role as the first pope:

> of this deed thou have in sight
> when thou hast soveraity.
> Therfore I suffered thee to fall
> that to thy subjects hereafter all
> that to thee shall cry and call
> then may have minning.   [82–83, 88–91]

The "Denial" forms part of the divine purpose in preparing Peter for the preeminent role that he must take, and it has the dramatic effect of drawing attention to the apostle. Such an overtly expressed view might prove controversial in post-Reformation England, and it may have been felt best to remove the interpretation of the Denial in ID and also the Denial itself, leaving only its prophecy and perhaps (depending on the position of the ending to HmAB's Play 18) a retrospective reference.

Finally, from 16A/359+SH–*Finis* HmARB and H present different, but textually related, versions of the ending of the play. These endings, despite their similarities, are different in effect. H shows a sharp division between believers and nonbelievers. On the one hand, the centurion knows "by the prophesy," IC/3, that Jesus is God's Son; Longeus, overcome by remorse, takes consolation in the prospect of Jesus' resurrection, IC/41–44; Joseph and Nichodemus attest Jesus' divinity, pray to Him as His body hangs on the cross, IC/103–8, and say that they will *ask his body of our fone*, IC/71. On the other side, Caiaphas rebukes the centurion before turning to the practical business of insuring that Jesus is dispatched, IC/9–14, and Pilate, apparently knowing of the prophecies, warns Joseph against raising him by magic, IC/93–96—an image perhaps consistent with the response of Pilate in Play 18. In the HmARB version, however, the emphasis is much more upon conviction. The centurion knows *by manner of his crye*, 16A/364, that the prophecy is fulfilled, and Caiaphas orders the piercing of Jesus' side to convince the centurion of his error, 16A/370–71, ironically producing a further sign. The miracle of the healing of *Longeus* thus becomes the means of convincing *Longeus* that this is *Christ verey*, 16A/396, and leads him to take up Christ's prayer from 16A/297–300 in his reaction:

> Of mercye, lord, I thee nowe praye,
> for I wyste not what I did   [16A/398–99]

There is no sense that Pilate is included among the enemies of the believers—*Nycodemus* seems to distinguish his response from that of *Caiaphas* at 16A/416–23, and Pilate makes no conditions in granting Joseph the body. This picture is perhaps more consistent than H's with the rational Pilate of 16–16A. Joseph's prayer at IC/103–8 is replaced by a profession of faith.

There are numerous verbal parallels between the two versions. At 16A/392–407, sts. 51–2, and IC/33–44, sts. 5–6, an interesting discrepancy occurs. IC, st. 5, consists of the first quatrain of 16A/st. 51

with the b-rhyme changed from *stead* to *affray*, followed by the first quatrain of st. 52, whose b-rhyme now rhymes with *affray*; IC, st. 6, consists of the remaining quatrain of st. 52. It is tempting to assume that H represents a revision of HmARB since the latter has two complete Chester stanzas. But it should also be noted that 16A/396–97 is somewhat similar in content and phrasing to 16A/400–402 and it is even possible that sts. 51 and 52 are alternatives. Certainly H, while destroying stanza-form, also removes a redundancy.

Admitting the difference in effect between the two versions, one may also suspect that H may represent a form that could have given offense to some reformers. The impropriety may arise partly in the use of the image of the crucified Christ as an object of prayer, suggesting the idea of the crucifix rather than the cross and of praying to images. It may also lie in the idea of praying to a mimetic Christ, which could have seemed blasphemous. But it is difficult to separate the religious from the artistic considerations in evaluating the two possibilities.

Such examples do not indicate that the Chester Exemplar was subjected to a clear and thoroughgoing censorship in the manner of, for example, the York Exemplar. A number of important points, of which the Catholic concept of Purgatory that dominates Play 24 and Jesus' reference to intercession by the saints and the Virgin Mary at 613–20 in the same play may be instanced, remain in all manuscripts (A is deficient from 24/613). But they do indicate that theological considerations could influence the choice of material. It would be unwise to place too much weight upon the presence or absence of such passages in discussing the relationships of the extant manuscripts.

The Character and Date of the Exemplar

The foregoing comments suggest that the Exemplar text was derived from an earlier form of the cycle, the Pre-exemplar; that its errors attest a number of corruptions indicative not merely of scribal error but of major textual deficiency; that it incorporates a number of margin notes which suggest that the text was a working production text; that some inconsistencies in the text suggest alternatives, so that the text constitutes a "cycle of cycles," a compendium of a number of different forms of the Chester cycle. It may be that the Exemplar was not a "civic master-copy" but simply a compilation of guild texts. It may indeed have represented a collection of "foul papers." The fragmentary episode of "Peter's Denial" may suggest that these papers were bundles in guild files in which odd fragments of other versions of the plays remained. Such a thesis might account for the address to the Magi by the infant Christ at 9/183 AR.

That the Exemplar was a working text, subject to further revisions, may be inferred from the "Peter's Denial" note. The reference to the "leaves following" clearly envisages a situation in which Plays 16 and 16A form part of a single text and are not held by independent companies. It seems possible also that some of the corrections made in the Exemplar were made by a scribe working through the full text, and one strongly suspects a single hand at work in the excision of "Peter's Denial" from its appropriate place in Play 16 and the corresponding cancellation of the end of Play 18, ignored by RH. Even as a compendium, the text continued to change.

Two important points follow from these proposals. First, "the Chester cycle" is a convenient abstraction; there is no reconstructable definitive form of the cycle, but a text that perhaps from the outset incorporated a number of different possibilities and that in any case was subject to frequent revision. Choice and change were built into the cycle-form, so that the civic authorities may have had an extensive range of decisions before them in deciding what form of the cycle should be played, and the guilds may have needed to consult the Regenal regularly.

Second, the Exemplar may have been in a poor condition. As a working text it had been subjected to all kinds of annotations and cancellations. As a collection of pages, odd pages had been lost. And as a working text it was probably a very rough copy, with misplaced sections corrected in a fashion clear primarily only to the producer using the text. The obscurities of the text presented difficulties to the scribes of the extant manuscripts. Moreover, with choice "built into" the text and with ample evidence of ongoing revisions, the scribes may well have felt justified in treating the text with some freedom.

The possible character of the Exemplar affects our view of its date. If it was a compilation of texts, it is difficult to know what one is dating; there is no set form for the cycle. Dating evidence is not extensive and can be of only marginal value, suggesting a date for a particular part of a play only. But such evidence falls into two categories—the evidence of vocabulary and the evidence provided by references to external and datable events.

Vocabulary

Any attempt to date the text by its words founders to a large extent on the lack of clear background information. OED's dates for the first and last examples of words are often suspect in themselves and do not necessarily provide an accurate indicator because later studies have often produced more and earlier examples of the forms. Moreover, dates based on the occurrence of words in written texts may give no indication of the currency of those words outside the texts, particularly for a play-text composed for performance before the people of Chester. Here we might expect to find colloquial usages and dialect-forms unrecorded until a very late date in OED or EDD. It is with these important caveats in mind that we list the following examples:

PLAY 1

exelencie 1/31 AR - required for rhyme, but replaced by *excellence* BH: recorded in required sense from 1526.

solation 1/37 BH - preferred for meaning to *solatacion* AR: recorded from 1483.

laudacion 1/49 - recorded from 1470.

comforture 1/123 - recorded once as coinage for rhyme by MED, 1500.

revisible 1/124 - the only example in OED.

repleth 1/195 - first recorded as "perfect" in 1601.

Ruffyn 1/260 - last example as 'name of fiend' in OED.

PLAY 2

thestearnes 2/12 - last example in OED, the previous example being 1377.

rayde 2/107 BH - replaced by *ryse* HmAR: last recorded c. 1525.

wyninge 2/404 Hm - replaced by *woninge* ARB, *wominge* H: last recorded c. 1575.

thee 2/702 H - replaced by *three* HmARB: listed as archaic in the sixteenth century.

PLAY 3

No examples.

PLAY 4

vowe 4/367 - recorded from 1563 in the sense of "prayer."

underfo 4/475 - replaced by *underfonge* H, *confounded* HmARB, but required for rhyme: last recorded 1513. *underfonge* H is last recorded in 1579.

PLAY 5
boone 5/75 - last recorded in 1513 as "prayer to God" (but in use long after in less specific applications).

PLAY 6
nece 6/49 - last recorded in 1508 as "female relative" (but in use long after in other senses).

PLAY 7
tyldes 7/6 - replaced by *hilles* B: last example cited by OED.
miting 7/159 - replaced by *meetinge* Hm: recorded from 1440 to 1585.
drownes 7/264 - recorded as a figurative sense of "drones" from 1529.
lendes 7/266, 272 - replaced in all MSS by *loynes* but required for rhyme: last recorded in 1550.
quiver 7/632 ARB - replaced by *quaver* Hm: recorded from 1490, but possibly a late scribal substitution here.

PLAY 8
gie 8/206 - replaced by *give* in all MSS but required for rhyme: recorded as a form of *guide* up to 1600, but *guide* has the required sense of "command" only to 1548 and nonfiguratively.
parentage 8/287 - replaced by *parage* ARBH: recorded in hereditary sense from 1490.
godlinge 8/307 - the first example cited; the second is 1570–76. But H substitutes *gedling*—the form it also uses at 10/237 for *geldinge* HmARB—which may suggest the original reading.
congion 8/328 AH - replaced by *coninge* Hm, *connyon* R, *conge* B: not recorded after the fifteenth century. Compare *congeon* 10/145 R, replaced by *commen* Hm, *connion* A, *conine* B, *conioyne* H.

PLAY 9
No examples.

PLAY 10
blaunner 10/2 - read as *blamner* HmRH, *balmer* A, *baunner* B—last

recorded in 1460 OED, from 1450 to 1509 MED.

grace 10/91 HmAR - replaced by *worship* BH: recorded as courtesy title from 1500. It is not clear which reading is earlier.

daystard 10/298 Hm - replaced by *daster* AR, *deighter* B, *drister* H: recorded from 1440.

stallon 10/314 - recorded in sense of "man of lascivious life" from 1553.

P L A Y   I I

deareworth 11/315 - the required adjectival form, replaced by *deare-worthy* HmH, *worthy* ARB: last recorded in 1557.

P L A Y   12

though [it] nye 12/140 Hm - different versions in AR, B, and H: last recorded in 1573.

sybble 12/261 - recorded as "witch" from 1589.

P L A Y   13

tabret 13/300 - replaced by *taberte* AR: last recorded as "garment" in 1568.

thester 13/355 H - last example in OED: previous example in 1400.

P L A Y   14

come 14/220 H - required for rhyme, but replaced by *commen* Hm, *commaundmente* A, *commaundementes* R, *coming* B: last recorded as sb., "arrival, coming," c. 1470.

P L A Y   15

armere 15/352 R - replaced by *armerye* Hm, *armerer* A, *armyre* H: -er forms recorded only to fifteenth century.

P L A Y   16

spurn at 16/4 - replaced by *spurn* H: recorded in sense of "kick against," etc., from 1526.

steake 16/90 HmR - replaced by *stecke* A, *seeke* B, *streake* H: last recorded, in sense of "enclose," in 1450 (but the form continues later in other senses).

stalwarde 16/181 RB - replaced by *scalward* HmA, *stanold* H: recorded from 1450.

present 16/237 - last recorded in sense of "presence" in 1470.

sues 16/340 C - replaced by *shewes* HmRB, *rewes* A, *shrewes* H: last recorded in sense "to follow as attendant" in 1522: "to follow as disciple" in 1509.

PLAY 16A

wonne 16A/158 - last recorded in 1570.

unpeace 16A/286 H - replaced by *a case* HmARB: last recorded in 1470.

horne-wood 16A/422 HmARB - recorded in 1500: H, IC/67, reads *wood*.

PLAY 17

followed 17/58 H - replaced by *baptysed* HmARB: last recorded in 1483 (in de Word printed text, 1515). Compare 20/102 RBH.

remynge 17/83 HmARB - replaced by *wepinge* H: last example in OED: previous example in 1400. But compare *reeme* 13/427.

nome 17/268 HmBH - replaced by *anon* AR: last recorded in intransitive use c. 1430 (H makes it transitive).

combes 17/314 - first example (dated ?a1400): second example in 1559. In section omitted by H.

PLAY 18

tatch 18/105 - if it is "touch" OED III.18, recorded from 1539.

swow 18/264 - required for rhyme but replaced by *swoone* HmRB, *soune* A, *sowne* H: a variant of *swoon* last recorded in sense 1 c. 1460, and sense 2, in 1513.

PLAY 19

No examples.

PLAY 20

fulloght 20/76 - replaced by *fullye* in all MSS, but required for meaning: last recorded c. 1450.

PLAY 21

No examples.

PLAY 22

No examples.

PLAY 23

wiserde 23/371 BHP - replaced by *roysard* Hm, *rasarde* A: recorded in
  sense of "a man skilled in occult arts" in 1550, but as "philosopher,
  sage" in 1440. In section omitted by R.
feard 23/597 - replaced by *fere* AR: as form of *fard* v2; recorded in
  1549.

PLAY 24

beames 24/33 - last recorded in 1500. ARB read *beanes*. Compare
  1/249.
sendal 24/150 H - replaced by *sandalles* HmARB: last recorded in 1606.
  sendalles is recorded in 1485.
laches 24/200 H - replaced by *lawes* HmARB: last recorded in sense of
  "lack of zeal" in 1494; in technical legal sense from 1574.
yonge 24/234 - replaced by *thonge* H: if a form of *yong*, "to go," last
  recorded in 1450.
sound 24/305 - replaced by *founde* A, and misunderstood by R; fifteenth-
  century form of *sand* OED sb.1, last recorded in appropriate sense
  c. 1525.
rayvinge 24/346 - replaced by *ravening* B: last recorded in 1567.

Two kinds of word on the lists inspire some confidence as evidence. The
first occurs when the scribes of the extant manuscripts evidently felt uncertain and offered alternative forms of words. These would include *solation, rayde, thee, underfo* and *underfonge, lendes, gie, congion, blaunner,
deareworth, though it nye, come, steake, swow.* Of these, *steake* is the
least secure, since it continues in use but with a slightly different sense,
and *come* at c. 1470 seems to offer less certain grounds for speculation.
But the general pattern suggests early sixteenth century overall: excluding
steake, come is last recorded c. 1470 and *solation* from 1483, while
MED indicates *blaunner* from 1450 to 1509. It is difficult to know what
weight to put upon *gie*, since OED *guide* 3 is not figurative, and other
senses might be acceptable.

More uncertain evidence seems provided by the second kind of word,
unusual or technical terminology. One word is particularly significant.
combes, a technical brewing term, is recorded only from 1559 apart from
here. It occurs in the "Ale-wife Scene" of Play 17 and may have particular
relevance in dating that part of the play; see further below. It would not

challenge a date in the early sixteenth century, but it would make dates within the fifteenth century improbable.

External References

The external evidence for the dating of the text is generally tenuous. The main possibilities are:

Play 10/217–24. The knights, boasting of the exploits against the King of Scots, may suggest memories of the Battle of Flodden Field in 1513.

Play 14/421–24. Judas's reference to the King of France and the loyalty of his subjects may suggest a time when England had possessions in France, terminating in the loss of Calais in 1558.

Play 17/276+SH–Finis. The "Ale-wife Scene" may allude to the liquor laws of Mayor Henry Gee in 1533.

Play 17/294–96. The reference to hops may limit the date to the early sixteenth century or later, since it was at that time only that hops were used in brewing in northern Europe.

Play 23/241–44. If the kingdoms distributed by Antichrist have any contemporary connotations, they might suggest the Franco-Spanish War of 1527, 1535, 1540; the Hungarian wars of 1526–49 and later; the fall of Patmos in 1537; the Danish civil wars in 1533–36.

Such scanty evidence might strengthen the case for a sixteenth-century date, and more specifically for a date in the period after the early 1530s. The following theologically significant material is found in the cycle:

1. A possible hint of the cult of the Sacred Heart of Jesus 16A/370; and at 24/421–28+SD.
2. Continuing references to Purgatory in Play 24—a doctrine rejected by Elizabeth after 1562.
3. The original inclusion of material relating to Peter, later canceled or omitted because of its implications of papal authority—Peter's betrayal, 16/379–94, and his meeting with Jesus, Appendix ID. A reference to the pope as holding "the highest office under thee," 24/55, is deleted by R.
4. Reference to the belief in intercession by the saints and the Virgin Mary, 24/609–18; prohibited in 1562.

5. References to the elect position of the Virgin Mary, including the
   Marian stanzas after 16A/256 in H, omitted in the other MSS, the
   allusion at 19/268–75, and at 24/609–18.

Such references do suggest a confident inclusion of Roman Catholic belief
in the cycle, and it is difficult to see how it could have been theologically
acceptable in its fullest form after 1562 and at certain periods before
that time.

On the other hand, a further significant piece of evidence is supplied by
the psalm specified in H at 3/252+SD. On the reasons for dating this
text after 1538, and very probably after 1562, see chapter 3, "Music in
the Cycle." Unfortunately, the text is specified only in H and may be an
independent proposal or a producer's MD that H has incorporated into
the text.

It will be seen that no positive conclusions can be reached about the
date of any form of the cycle, but it may be useful to assert that there is
no evidence to suggest that the cycle as we have it relates to the fourteenth or the first half of the fifteenth century. Even a date in the second
half of the fifteenth century must be regarded with some considerable
caution. The bulk of evidence suggests a date in the general period c.
1500–1550 when the Exemplar took material shape, although stylistic
modifications may have continued beyond that time.

Evidence for earlier stages of the cycle is best supplied by the material
in the documents that we present in this volume. It may, however, be
relevant to note here that some traces of the possible insertion of Play 23
may survive in the manuscript itself. It may be significant that HmARB
omit the play heading to 22, while H supplies a full title, perhaps based
on a reading of the play. Possibly the original title, relating to the signs of
doomsday, was no longer acceptable when the play of Antichrist was
inserted. The rather tortuous introduction of Enoch and Elias into the
exposition of Zechariah, 81–124, diverges from Jerome and seems to be
an attempt to forge a link where none logically exists. The final stanza of
Play 22, 332–40, suggests an attempt to pull together the "Signs before Doomsday" and the "Coming of Antichrist," with some confusion.
Finally, it may be noted that B omits the guild-ascription to 23 and continues directly without the customary shift to a recto page, perhaps indicating some sort of insertion within the Exemplar that the scribe did
not understand.

The Extant Manuscripts

In characterizing the Exemplar above, it was noted that there was some evidence to suggest that all the scribes were dealing with the same Exemplar but approaching it with different preconceptions and at times choosing differently among the alternatives. It may be useful at the start of this section to add some further examples that, while attesting the often obscure state of an Exemplar-reading, may further strengthen the argument for dependence upon the common Exemplar.

At 1/67 God urges the orders of angels *to walke aboute the Trenitie*, "to move around the figure of the Trinity," and urges them to keep their position. BH insert *with* before *the Trenitie*, thereby weakening meter and destroying sense. The tendency to read *aboute* as adverb rather than preposition seems to have troubled B, which substitutes *above*. ARH therefore have a line with *aboute*, and BH a line with *with* additionally; it seems probable that the variants result from some confusion about the status of *with*, perhaps an insertion.

At 1/153+SH the speaker should be *Ceraphine* B, not *Cherubyn* R or *Cherub*:H. The error probably arises in the Exemplar-reading, which A seems to reflect, *Cheraphin*.

1/174–7, st. 24. AR are correct in retaining this quatrain, but it is a stanzaic irregularity, of a kind found elsewhere in the play. B wrote the preceding SH but then omitted the quatrain and also 177+SH, moving directly to 178. H omitted 173+SH and the quatrain. That B has the SH argues strongly for the presence of the quatrain in the scribe's Exemplar; its omission suggests a cancellation, taken up by H, but not by AR. An effect of the cancellation may be the erroneous incorporation of *goe hense*, 177, additionally in 178 in ARB; H rightly omits it.

The required form, *name* H, and erroneous *man* HmAR, *men* B 2/31, would seem to derive from an Exemplar *nam*, misread or misunderstood by the Group.

The variants *supremus* 208+SD HmB, *superius* AR, *spinx* H in Play 2 suggest an underlying contracted form *spūs* in the Exemplar.

At 2/377 HmAR read *cannot este more*, B *covett anie more*, H *covet elswheare* instead of *covetteste more*. All attest an inability to decipher the second "word"; H's reading leads to a substitution for the third word, which HmARB read as *more*. The confusion extends to the verb-form, where the confusion of *n* and *v* suggests some difficulty with *u*, leading to the HmAR error. H destroys rhyme, but gives sense; B gives sense, but seems to have substituted *anie* without regard to the Exemplar-form. HmAR fail to yield sense. All derive from the same obscure Exemplar-form.

At 3/27 no manuscript has the correct height for the ark, thirty cubits. The confusion of *sixtye* HmRB and *fiftie* A, *50* H suggests that the Exemplar contained arabic numerals, *30*, which the scribes could not read. H's use of arabic numerals may confirm this suggestion.

The a-rhymes of 4/25–32 do not rhyme in Hm. They should be *wond-lond-hond* or *wand-land-hand*. The readings at 25, *worne* Hm, *wonne* AR, *woone* B suggest that the Group-scribes all read the final letter as *e* and found the third letter obscure; only H has *wond*, the required form. Evidently the Exemplar read *wonnd*, leading to an easy confusion of *e* and *d*, and with the *n*(1) too unclear to be read. The resulting breakdown of rhyme perhaps led to HmB's *landes*, 26, for the required *lande* ARH.

graweth 5/118 HmB is an error for *gnaweth*, but AR's *draweth* suggests that *r* was clear on the Exemplar and that the scribes were confused. H reads *gnawes*, IB/111.

All manuscripts show difficulties with the rhyme-word of 6/626, which should be *wemlessly*; *wemmostlye* Hm, *womanlye* AR, *woman slye* B, *wemmouslie* H. *l*(1) was evidently not clear in the Exemplar, leading to Hm's introduction of *t* to suggest a superlative, and to AR and B's substitution in the first element of the word. No manuscript has *e*(2). All clearly derive from the same reading.

HmRB lack the necessary 6/690+SH; H has it. But A has it also, misplaced after 694. Since A's error cannot be the result of an independent emendation, it may be assumed that the SH represented a margin correction, ignored as marginalia by HmB; included by A in approximately the place in the text against which it appeared; rejected by R—perhaps seeing A's error or perhaps as marginalia; but correctly adopted by H.

At 7/352 the Exemplar seems to have had the AR reading *wyste I*, erroneously transcribed by B as *wies I*. This reading would give sense if the verb in 353 was past tense: "By my faith, I thought it was almost daylight." But since this reading is not possible, Hm and H seem to have substituted fill-in phrases. At 8/72+SH, HmA omit the SH; but the line space after 72 in Hm indicates an awareness of the omission and suggests that the status of the SH was not clear to the scribe.

At 10/378 *all* is inserted with a caret in B, probably reflecting the emendation in the Exemplar. H includes the word, but HmAR omit it. The nine-line stanza, 10/417–25, contains a superfluous line, 417; H has an eight-line stanza, but achieves it by improbably omitting 420 and reversing the order of 423 and 424.

It is difficult to see the exact nature of the obscurity at 12/28, which led to four different versions of the line. The devil claims never to have known a man like Jesus, born of earthly woman "and hee yet wembles" Hm. The Hm line gives good sense if *wembles* is accepted as an error for *wemles* BH; but AR similarly have a form in *-b-*, suggesting some confusion in the *-ml-* combination of the Exemplar. ARB, however, all read *howe* for *hee*, perhaps combining a confusion of *e* and *o* with an inspired guess at the obscured ending of the word; and although BH confirm *yet*, AR read *yt*—perhaps because the word was compressed and *e* obscured, or as a substitution because the "verb" *wembles* had no subject. H, in independent dissatisfaction, changes word-order, inserts a copula, and, unconvincingly, changes the reference to the Virgin Mary, to read "and yet she is wemlesse."

A more explicable error underlies 12/47, which in Hm is "save only honge he hasse iwis"; ARBH read *hongarye* for *honge*. The latter in turn requires *is* for *hasse*; but although ARH read *is*, B confirms Hm's *hasse*. The Exemplar may well have read *hunger he hasse*, but this has subsequently been altered to *hongarye he is*, with obscurity in the ending of *hunger/hungarye* that contributed to Hm's uncertainty, and an alteration in the verb-form that was misunderstood by HmB.

At 13/174 Hm has erroneously substituted the first person for the second person plural pronoun in "and tell us truely or ere wee goe." But *or ere* looks tautologous and weakens the meter. A omits *ere*; R reads *ever*; BH read *that*. HmAR seem to derive from the same basis, with A omitting a syllable for meter and R expanding *ere* to the detriment of meter. *that* BH is syntactically preferable, but leaves the line metrically rough. But it is possible that the difficulty lies in the two possibilities— "tell us the truth before (*ere*) you go" and "tell us the truth so that (*that*) you may go." Perhaps the latter was the first reading entered, with the second inserted above as an alternative, "or ere"; the scribes generally made the choice between *that* and *ere*, but all mistakenly incorporated *or* also.

At 14/357 RBH have the appropriate past tense *came* for *comes* Hm.

The source of Hm's error is suggested by A's *come*, a past tense form capable of interpretation as present.

It seems probable that HmAR contain the Exemplar-version of 15/163, which lacks a subject in the subordinate clause. B and H independently respond to this lack, in different ways—*I* B, *it* H—each acceptable, though H seems better.

Hm's 15/183, "come syckerlye thou ney maye," is acceptable, if a little rough metrically. H's *come nye* gives a smoother meter. But the Exemplar reading is probably reflected in ARB's *come ney*; H correctly interpreted the second form, while Hm, regarding it as an erroneous duplication of the later negative, omitted it. An Exemplar-form *neye* would abet the confusion.

The two versions of 16/18, HmARB's "that one man dye witterlye" and H's "that one must dye verely," derive from an Exemplar-form that had *mon* for *man*. This was misconstrued as a verb by H, although the biblical text confirms it as a noun.

Despite the confirmation of text and biblical account that the color of Jesus' robe at this point is purple, 16/324 HmA claim "whyte his clothinge ys." Possibly the confusion arises because Jesus had been wearing the white robe given to him by Herod up to this point. But the SD at 322 is omitted in AR, and since it is that SD that calls for Jesus to be robed in purple before the speech, the inconsistency may have been removed in A. Instead of *whyte*, H reads *quoynt*, "curious, peculiar," which gives good sense. R and B seem to blend the two readings, giving *whante* and *whainte* respectively, and C also reads *whaynte*. The evidence suggests that an alteration from *quoynt* H to *whyte* HmA confused the other scribes into writing a nonce-word.

HmB probably reflect an erroneous Exemplar-form in 16A/262: "slayes ye mee and lett my sonne goe"; the metrical unwieldiness of the line is remedied by reading *him* for *my sonne*. Attempts to "improve" the line are A's omission of *ye* and *and*; H's omission of *ye*; R's omission of *and*. All respond to the same problem. At 16A/283 an Exemplar *wonndes* underlies *wondes* Hm, *wonnes* A, *wones* R, and the inappropriate *woundes* BH (suffer wounds?). At 16A/377 only A emends the erroneous Exemplar *bade* HmB, *badd* H IC/18 to *bede*; R wrongly substitutes *byde*.

It is easy to regard Hm's erroneous *yere* 17/8 as the result of confusion between *o* and *e*, and hence to regard *yore* H as the appropriate form.

ever AR, however, may suggest that the Exemplar contained an alteration from/to *yore* to/from *ere*, "ever"; this would appropriately suggest
not merely that the Harrowing was the fulfilment of a past promise
(*yore*), but that it is a sign that the promise of redemption will be fulfilled
at all times. *earst* B is evidently an independent substitution attesting the
obscurity of the Exemplar-form and thus strengthening the argument for
Exemplar alteration underlying the variants.

We have been unable to find a meaning for *nyf* 17/83, 85 Hm appropriate to the context, but Hm seems partially confirmed by *nys* B, the
confusion of *f* and long *s*. The variety of readings at 85—*ner* A, *nor* R,
nay H—may suggest that the scribes independently emended and may
therefore have acted similarly in agreeing on *nor* ARH at 83. It is possible that the Hm and B forms are influenced by the presence of cancella-
tion-strokes in the Exemplar. At 17/148 *home* HmRB, *whom* A suggest
a confusion of *o* and *e* in an Exemplar *henne* deficient by one minim in
-nn-; H's rephrasing of the line to remove the phrase suggests merely
stylistic dissatisfaction. A form unusual in the cycle, *seghe* 17/162 Hm,
may well be that of the Exemplar, since it provides a suitable base for
the derivation of *seinge* AR (to incorporate *-g-*), *sith* B (to incorporate
-h-), and *see* H (an acceptable alternative form of the verb); only H
understood the form. Similarly, the Exemplar would probably read *sines*
17/261 B to account for the correct *signes* ARH and the erroneous
synnys Hm.

makes me both 19/6 HmB lacks predicate. *me half dead* H seems to be
a substitution; *mone* AR for *me both* weakens the meter and gives incomplete sense, though *me mone* would be acceptable. AR and H are
wrestling with the same problem, while HmB must reflect the Exemplar.
In view of the use of *makes* at 4, it seems probable that the verb is an
erroneous repetition, perhaps replacing *marres*. It is just possible that
Hm's omission of *us* at 19/226 suggests an insertion to be taken in
conjunction with *and* in the following line, and the Exemplar was altered
from:

> then Jewes should have in there dangere
> all our fraternitie.

At 20/73–80, st. 10 ABH read, appropriately, *saved shall be* (76).
Since this is the A-reading, it is perhaps surprising that R does not follow
it but reads *save shall yee*. Hm confirms *save* but omits the rhyme-word.

R is only plausible if *save* was the Exemplar-form, but if so, it was a variant of *safe*; all manuscripts identify it as a form of the verb *save*—ARH emending to *saved*, R changing the construction to preserve *save*, and Hm giving up in bewilderment at the apparently ungrammatical construction. All readings originate in the Exemplar, as the AR variation suggests, but it is not possible to assess the degree of possible alteration on the Exemplar text.

At 20/166 ARH are probably correct in reading *with hart so free*. Hm omits *so*. B reads *ech hart to free*, thereby changing the construction. B appears to be an independent emendation, but perhaps based upon confusion about the third word, *so*; Hm may reflect a similar uncertainty.

At 21/127 the hymn *Veni Creator Spiritus* provides a text against which to check the reading: *spiritalis unctio*. The closest reading to this is H's *leach of langore*, but this leaves the relative clause of the following line, "that prayen here in this place," without reference. HmAR read *lenght or langore*, which gives no sense because *lenght* is a nonce-word. B, however, reads *lyght in langore*, which is open to the same objection as H, but does offer sense and a clue to the Exemplar-readings. The error of BH, and probably of HmAR, is to assume that *or* is a conjunction and the whole a noun-phrase, whereas *or* is a form of the possessive pronoun *our* and the preceding word is a verb. It is this misunderstanding that leads B and H to substitute prepositions. But in both B and H the preceding word can be taken as a verb if *or* (= our) is accepted. B confirms the *l-ght* form of HmAR, H the *le-* form, and one may suspect that the confusion in HmAR arose in an alteration involving the readings attested by B and H. Whatever the Exemplar verb-form, it is clear that all manuscripts must have had the form *or* in front of them to produce the extant readings.

In st. 38 of Play 21 only AR have the required form, *dighte*, at 301. HmB read *drest*, and the probability that this reading represents an Exemplar alteration is suggested by H's erroneous *dreight*, where the *dight*-form of AR has been combined with the *dre-t* form of HmB, perhaps because of a superscript alteration. The alteration is the more understandable in view of the confusion in rhymes and line-length throughout the rest of the stanza, attested by all manuscripts. At 21/351–58, st. 45, only H has the required rhyme-word *bowne* 353; B reads, meaninglessly, *boone*, and HmA *borne*. R, apparently troubled by the meaning of the line, rephrases it, but retains *borne* as rhyme-word. B's reading strongly suggests that the third letter of the rhyme-word was doubtful. The probability is that the Exemplar contained the form *boune* and that the final minim of *u* was indistinct, if not the whole letter. To three scribes the apparent combination of minim with ascender suggested *r*, but B was less confident, and H either saw more keenly or speculated more intelligently.

At 22/200 one immediately assumes that H is correct in reading *through their might* as rhyme-phrase, although the result is a little rough metrically, and one might then assume that this reading attests an independent H Exemplar. No Group manuscript gives rhyme here—indeed HmR merely read *through*, apparently unable to decipher the rhyme-word; and A reads *through their power*, apparently confirming H's *their* but yielding no rhyme. Again, the interesting reading is in B, *throuly*. In itself, the word is meaningless. But the line refers to Apocalypse 11/5: "Ignis exiet de ore eorum"—they slew their enemies by fire. It might be expected that the Exemplar would mention fire, and it is possible that B's *-ly* could represent *lyght*, MED 6(d) "lightning." The omission of *their* metrically improves the line. The possibility must be that *light* was changed, perhaps because of the wide range of possible meanings and the loss of the sense "lightning." A's reading may indeed represent the substitution, which was rejected by HmR because it did not rhyme and because it impaired meter; alternatively, A contains a speculation that HmR did not choose to make. But it seems more probable that H read the altered form, attested by A, and supplied a more suitable alternative to *power*, though retaining the intrusive possessive pronoun. It is difficult to envisage any circumstances in which *power* would be substituted for *might* in rhyme-position, but if they can be envisaged, then A would have had before it the H-alteration and one would have to ask why R did not follow A in a reading that was ostensibly appropriate.

Perhaps the Exemplar's obscurity at 22/288 was the cause of AR's omission of the line. Hm also omitted the line, but left the space for it, and the line was inserted in a different hand. Since Hm's reading is unique in having *manye a* rather than *main(?)/man and* BH, it seems to be based on an independent reading of the Exemplar and may suggest that a form such as that in B, where the number of minims is obscure, may have been the Exemplar-form, being read variously as *mani, main,* and *man. and* is confirmed by BH, and it may be that, reading *manye,* the Hm-corrector was compelled to replace the conjunction by the indefinite article. There is no doubt that HmAR were all at first uncertain enough of the line to omit it, whereas BH included it; yet the line was available to the later corrector of Hm, suggesting that, although its status or reading in the Exemplar may have been in doubt, it was nevertheless available.

Only Hm rhymes at 22/313, *that hydd bee*; AB read *have bene* for the verb form, and RH *hath bene*. Hm may well be an independent emendation, but the weight of ARBH suggests that a form *have/hath be* was the original and had been rejected as ungrammatical. It is, however, not clear if this rejection was made by the Exemplar-scribe, or if the Exemplar reading had subsequently been changed.

At 23/675–78, st. 90 HmH's *in hell be the hydd* 678, "they are hidden in hell," seems to have caused difficulties for the other scribes. *be*, verb, is taken as preposition, *by*, in ARB; *the*, plural pronoun, is taken as definite article, *the*, by AR, and apparently as possessive, *thie*, by B, and also by P; *hydd*, past participle, is regarded as noun, *head*, by AR, and is omitted— perhaps in bewilderment—by B (P reads *hyd*). These confusions are only possible given the HmH-form in the Exemplar.

Some obscurity surrounded the rhyme-word at 24/419. *rente* AR seems correct, but HmB read *lent* and H *hent*. AR may be an independent emendation of Exemplar *lent*, the latter a simple error in view of the preceding alliterating *lymme*. There is more pronounced confusion about the rhyme-phrase at 24/580, with BH reading, correctly, *by the rode*; AR *nowe heare*; and Hm omitting the phrase completely. BH have the correct phrase for the rhyme with *good* 576; but something has happened also at 576, for HmAR read

to put the evyll from the good

and B

to part the evyll from the good

The line should be a three-stress line, but it has four stresses, and H remedies this, independently, by reading *for good*, "for good reason," for *from the good*. It is clear that either *put* or *part* is possible in HmARB, but not in H, since H lacks the necessary prepositional phrase of separation for *put*. If indeed the additional syllable resulted from the inclusion of this phrase, then it is possible that *part* was the original verb, replaced by *put* when the line was expanded in the Exemplar. What then was the original rhyme-phrase of 576? Since 580 BH provides a rhyme for the existing 576, possibly 580 AR retains the rhyme for the original 576;

part the evyll in fere or *in sere* would give good sense and restore the three-stress line. The temptation to claim that the oath at 580 was censored by AR independently of the Exemplar seems denied by Hm's omission of any rhyming-phrase, which strongly suggests that Hm could not decide what to do at this point.

At 24/581 it is possible to state confidently that the Exemplar read "delyver these men henne." *henne* caused problems to all the scribes. Two manuscripts indicate that the scribes could not read or make sense of the form—*heine* A, *hime* B; R's *home* indicates a wild guess; H's *hence* is obviously a substitution, but whether a modernization or an independent guess is impossible to say. Hm is sufficiently unhappy to omit the word altogether, allowing *men* to carry the rhyme, and makes good the syllabic loss by inserting a monosyllabic dative: "delyver mee these men." All are coping with the same unfamiliar and probably obscure Exemplar-form.

This selection of examples serves to supplement the earlier discussion and to reinforce the claim that all the extant cyclic manuscripts were direct copies of a single manuscript, the Exemplar (R additionally using A—see below). The majority of these readings seems to derive from a common obscurity, unlikely to be repeated in any intermediate manuscript. At the same time, such readings provide additional evidence of the alterations and difficulties presented by the Exemplar. We accordingly believe that, in examining the manuscripts, one should bear in mind the state of the Exemplar and the corresponding importance of scribal choice and practice in determining the text. The discussion of the extant manuscripts that follows, therefore, is both a discussion of their place in the transmission of the text and also an assessment of the practices of their scribes.

The Huntington Manuscript: Hm2

The Huntington manuscript is the earliest of the extant cyclic manuscripts. That it was not itself the Exemplar for the later manuscripts may be inferred from the large-scale omissions unique to Hm; in such instances, the other scribes clearly had access to another text of the cycle. Salter's suggestion that in Play 16 at least A was a copy of Hm will be considered in the later discussion of Bellin's manuscripts.

Our statistical survey indicated that Hm contained 800 unique readings, fewer than any other manuscript, and that half of these were at points where the extant manuscripts present three different possibilities or more. It seems that many Hm readings were occasioned by difficulties in the Exemplar that caused problems to other scribes also. We found only 447 instances of ARBH]Hm, the lowest number in the 4]1 configuration. We also found that Hm was involved in no subgroups. Its scribe, Edward Gregorie, reached the same decision as George Bellin in AR against BH in 175 instances, but shares the H reading in 109 instances against ARB and the B reading in 101 instances against ARH. This statistical evidence confirmed our decision to choose Hm as base manuscript on the basis of convenience, since it has fewer unsupported readings than any other manuscript, but such evidence may also suggest a high degree of conservatism on the part of its scribe.

It is particularly regrettable that Hm lacks Play 1. The scribe clearly attempted to be inclusive, and there are otherwise few large-scale omissions. Such demonstrable errors as there are in Hm are, moreover, of a minor kind and readily detected. From Play 2 we may instance *enlesse* 3, *ondly* 6, *fiveth* 70, the omissions of *up* 141 and *owne* 286, *osprynge* for *ofsprynge* 204, etc. Such minor slips artificially inflate the total of unique readings, being quite different from major rearrangements of word-order or word-substitutions such as are found in other manuscripts. Other unique readings are often in the nature of intermediate forms or merely unique spellings—from Play 2, *excice* 131, *welle* 237.

It is not possible to claim that Gregorie was wholly conservative; sometimes he must be suspected of changing the text, as in 22/313 discussed above. Many of the unique readings that are not minor errors are semantically and metrically possible. *take*] *eate* ARBH 2/240 or *mee disceaved alsoe*] *deceved me thoo* AH, *deceived thoe* RB 2/295, or *above*] *over* ARBH 2/370 are all quite acceptable alternatives but cannot be derived from any form that would yield the other readings. Even allowing for alternatives within the Exemplar, Hm's reading must be regarded with some caution on such occasions. A fairly clear example of the Hm's scribe's intelligent "improvement" is at 2/254:

the fruite is sweete and passinge feare

where Bellin initially was worried by the Exemplar jingle, attested in RBH, *fayer in fere* to the extent of reversing *sweete* and *fayer* in A; Hm's reading seems to drive from the same stylistic concern as Bellin.

But Gregorie only changes his text when he feels that minor improvement is not only possible but desirable. Most of his "spelling-errors" may well derive from an honest attempt to write what he saw, and he was certainly willing to write a nonce-form at an obscure point rather than attempt a substitution. One may instance 2/274, where *thes* AR was evidently the Exemplar-reading, expanded to *these* RB, but transcribed as *this* by Hm despite the following plural *figge-leaves*; *wrauge* 3/290 for *ronge* A, *wronge* RH, *wrang* B; *kedyll* 6/36 HmAR for *bedill* BH. Gregorie's action at, for example, 22/200, in refusing to speculate about the reading is characteristic of his practice when confronted with a major crux. We would wholly accept Salter's opinion: "For the linguistic and mechanical basis of his text, an editor will do well, as Greg advises, to follow [Hm], not only because [Hm] is by a year the oldest manuscript, but also because the scribe of [Hm] shows little tendency to emend on his own" (*Chester Play Studies*, p. 45).

Bellin's Three Manuscripts: A, R, and C

George Bellin was the scribe of the next three extant manuscripts—A of 1592, C of 1599 (Play 16), and R of 1600. It is convenient first to consider briefly the two cyclic manuscripts, A and R.

Our statistical survey indicated that A contained 1,120 unique readings, of which 718 occurred in the configuration HmRBH]A, and R contained 789, of which 467 occurred in the configuration HmABH]R. But AR together shared 1,003 readings found in no other manuscript, of which 767 were in the grouping HmBH]AR. These figures for AR clearly demonstrate the close relationship between the two manuscripts that was noted by Deimling. The figures for unique readings, however, indicate that R is not merely a copy of A, for they differ in 1,909 readings. It should be remembered that the statistics did not include four-manuscript variations such as occur in Play 1, although they do include the variants resulting from the deterioration and damage to A in Plays 2 and 24.

The large-scale variants listed on pp. xxx–xxxi of our edition conclusively demonstrate that R cannot be a copy of A. A lacks the following lines which are present in R: 1/46–51, 78–81, 122–23, 258; 2/40, 537–40; 6/289–92; 7/137–40, 189–90; 8/419; 13/256, 258; 16/four lines after 16+*Annas*, four lines before 98, four lines before 102; 17/66–69; 18/77–80 and appendix ID; 21/149–52, 155–58, 215–18; 22/247;

23/460; 24/585–88, 593–96, 613–708. (Allowance must be made for manuscript damage in Plays 1, 2, and 24.) Yet if R does repair omissions in A, it also shares a number of A's omissions—1/one line after 17; 4/333–36; 6/277–88; 7/37–40, 310, 570; 8/345; 9/one line after 127; 10/197–208, 217–24, 313–20, 369–72; 14/421–24; 16A/142; 17/42 (and the one line after 254); 22/90–93, 288; 23/217–20, 225–36. Sometimes one can see Bellin wrestling with his own artistic judgment. He does not seem to have liked the banter between Octavian and his messenger in 6/277–92 and simply omitted it in A, but in R he recognized the disruptive effect of this total omission and restored the quatrain 289–92, Octavian's commission to the boy to go to Judea. In Play 10 he removes in AR the boasting speech of the knight at 197–208, but at first he retained a quatrain of the second soldier's boast, 225–28, which he decided to omit in R along with A's omitted 217–24, 229–32. He omitted the insults of the second woman at 313–20 in A and then omitted further the insults of the first woman in 309–12 in R. A further quatrain of indecent insult is omitted at 369–72 in A and the omission is then extended to the whole stanza in 369–76 R. In Play 23 Bellin cuts out 217–36 in R, but in A had kept a quatrain at 221–24; similarly, A retains 691–94 in the devils' speeches of 679–98, but Bellin omits even that in R. The changes in Play 23 may perhaps be a result of Bellin's sense of decorum.

The same procedures can be observed in small-scale variants. AR share a number of erroneous readings—e.g., 4/179, where A and R erroneously repeat the rhyme-phrase from the preceding line; 8/345, which is omitted in both manuscripts; 12/44, where AR's *fayleth* for *fayles* destroys the rhyme; 16A/395, where AR's *the streete* for HmBH's *this stead* (Exemplar error for *stidd*) destroys the rhyme; 20/148, where AR read *ever* for the required *aye*—a common "Bellinism"; 24/146, where AR's *power* for *powder* gives no sense. But on other occasions an error in A is not repeated in R—e.g., 2/83, where R restores A's omission of *beast*; 6/94, where R replaces A's *did pitiouslye* by the required *dispytuusly*; 10/140, where A's *mighte* is corrected by R to the required rhyme-form *mayne*; 17/184, where A replaces *aye* by *ever* in rhyme-position and R reads *aye*; 20/179, where R corrects A's erroneous repetition of *handlinge* from the preceding line; 23/64, where R correctly reads *alonne* against A's *above*. Unfortunately, R itself contains independent errors—e.g., 5/39, *you* for *yee* in rhyme-position; 7/309, where R, perhaps misunderstanding the stanza-form, reads *light* for *nowe*; 13/226, where R substitutes *excusse* for *discusse*; 16/198, where R destroys rhyme by reading *madd* for *wood*; 19/213, where R reads *mynes* for *mynne* (*myne* A), recognizing the lack of rhyme with *synnes*, 212, but failing to see that the error lies in 212 (cf. *sinne* H). A contains errors and idiosyncracies, but R does not represent the result of any systematic attempt to correct them, although it clearly had an Exemplar text available for cross reference.

Just occasionally, Bellin can be seen wrestling with a difficult Exemplar-form and reaching different conclusions in A and R—note A, *not* RH for the required *nought* HmB at 3/244, and *remewes* A, *renewes* R for the required *remeeves* HmBH at 3/249; 4/95, where some confusion arose from the Exemplar about the speaker, and R replaces A's *taketh of me* (appropriate to Abraham, the required speaker) by *I take of thee* (appropriate to the stated speaker, Melchizedek); 5/93, where the obscurity of the first letter of *byse* led HmA to read *kyse*, but R perhaps attempted to transcribe what he thought he saw, *gkyse*; at 7/689–92, st. 127, where Bellin at first accepted that *you* was the a-rhyme word at 689 and 691, but then in R substituted a b-rhyme, *wee*, at 691, giving a pattern abbb for the abab prevalent in the quatrains at this point.

Earlier scholars seem agreed that for R Bellin used A and another manuscript, and that AR therefore constitute a genetic group. It is in our view difficult to go beyond this statement. The main obstacle to understanding the situation more clearly is Bellin's own scribal habits. The shared readings of AR are, where not common errors, usually common substitutions that rarely seem as probable as the readings in the other manuscripts but that often have a local and limited rationale of their own. Examples are: 2/314 Hm, *thy much payne I shall multiplye*, where A decides to treat *much* as an adverb rather than an adjective and places it after *shall*; R agrees, but unlike A neglects to omit it before *payne* at the same time: 6/25 Hm, *thow beast so bright*, where Bellin evidently regarded the noun as a variant of *be-est*, second singular present of *be*, and substituted *arte*: 6/524, where the two adjectival phrases [*shall lye*] *with lee*, // *and lapped about with haye* confused Bellin into believing that the second was an incomplete main clause, thus leading to *and be lapped* AR: 7/565 Hm, *the feynd shalt thow fell*, becomes reversed in significance when Bellin, suspecting accusative after *shalt*, reads *thee* for *thow*: at 16/159 the nominative third person singular pronoun used by

Primus Judeus to refer to Herod in his response to Pilate is seen as an error for the pronoun of address by Bellin, who substitutes *you* for *he* in *him shall he have full hastelye*. But additionally, Bellin constantly substitutes words for those attested by the other manuscripts; e.g., 2/190 ylke] same AR; 2/243 much] full AR; 5/145 cruell] fell R; 5/206 warryed] cursed R [worryed B]; 9/45 cleane] fayer AR; 13/58 reforme] restore R; 17/59 prophecyed] preached AR; 19/181 soothe] truth AR; 22/118 forth] parte AR; 23/444 full] right R, syckerlye] witterlye AR. The Bellin words have no formal relationship to those attested by HmBH and seem generally to be words preferred by Bellin for stylistic or semantic reasons. As an extreme case, one may instance 22/43–44:

> the dampned thester shall be in sight,
> their doome to underfoe

where Bellin, not understanding two of the words, substitutes *sorte* for *thester* and *understande* for *underfoe* in AR, careless of formal relationships, meaning, or rhyme. Bellin's somewhat cavalier treatment of his text has the double effect of diminishing the value of A and R as evidence of the Exemplar and also of making it impossible to establish the thinking and practice behind Bellin's use of A and another manuscript in the writing of R.

It would, however, seem a simple and not implausible postulate to us that Bellin used the same manuscript as base for A and as joint base for R. It would also seem possible that this base manuscript was the cyclic Exemplar, for reasons cited earlier in discussing the existence and character of the Exemplar. It may be noted that R includes the material that concludes Play 18 and is found also in H (our appendix ID). This constitutes the main evidence for the availability of that ending to the "Group" manuscripts and the major divergence from A.

Although the derivation of R from A and the Exemplar is that of Deimling, a slightly different view was advanced by Greg, who felt that an intermediate manuscript other than the Exemplar was the source of A and R; and of Salter, who advanced the more extreme argument that, on the evidence of Play 16, A was copied from Hm, itself a copy of the Exemplar, while R was derived, like C, from a lost copy of the Exemplar and that Bellin had compared R and C with A in making these later transcripts. We shall briefly consider Salter's views here.

Salter's grounds for regarding A as a copy of Hm are three shared omissions and a shared erroneous reading. These omissions, found only in HmA, are four lines and SH after 16+SH; four lines and SH before 98; four lines and SH before 102; and the shared reading *whyte* at 324. The arguments for regarding the last as a result of alterations in the Exemplar have already been advanced; it is the weak point in the evidence, since R, B, and H have different readings at this point, all clearly textually related, whereas RBH share the lines missing in HmA.

There are two principal objections to Salter's thesis. The first is that it requires us to accept that Bellin went to different manuscripts to establish the text of different plays. Despite having Hm available to him, he did not use it consistently but turned to it only at individual points. That Bellin could not have relied solely on Hm is indicated by a comparison of the missing lines in Hm and A for the whole cycle, for A shares with other manuscripts many of the lines that Hm lacks. Granted Bellin's way with the text, it seems unlikely that he would have taken the trouble to consult a range of manuscripts that varied from play to play.

The further improbability lies in the concept of an HmA subgroup. As noted previously, there is a marginally higher agreement between Hm and AR (175 examples) than HmH (109) or HmB (101), but the difference is not statistically significant. On the other hand, agreement of Hm with A (23) and R (22) uniquely is infrequent. Even in Play 16, where we found the highest incidence of HmA agreement (4), this was still lower than the agreement of Hm with B (6) and identical with the figures for HmH; the five instances of HmAR agreement compares oddly with the ten of HmBH. Moreover, errors shared by HmA or HmAR are usually of a kind best characterized as independent errors from an obscure Exemplar:

2/410 still] freely B, sleelie H.

3/87 thither] thether B, thider H; 131 forgotte] fogetten B, foryeten H; 195 name] *om* BH; 207 thy] thou RBH.

4/241 Isaack] Isack Isack BH.

5/205 hoste] hest B(H); 379 enimyes] foes B - also 387.

8/72+SH] *om* HmA.

10/7 lyes] under me lies BH; 15 marye] mare B, mar H; 378 the] all the BH; 456 I] ever I BH.

11/117 Esaues HmA] Esayes RB; 329 Esau] Esay RBH.

12/152 lafte BH] laste HmAR.

13/21 ovibus BH] omnibus HmAR; *after* 50 BH] *om* HmAR; 236
   anoye] anie any BH; 428 gowle] a gowle BH.

14/114 wouldest] wouldest thou BH; 176 wonder] it wonder B, it great
   wonder H; 231 come] came BH; 250 preeves] thou preeves of B, thou
   preves H.

15/352 sword HmA] swordes RH.

16 (see above).

16A/241 leere] lee BH (but see note above); 357 wend] wonde BH; 446
   yf HmAR] that B.

18/106 him (2)] he BH; 114 hardlye] hardelie BH; 273 in] in a BH.

21/32+Latin non sit H] non sic HmAR, not sit B; 353 bowne RH] borne
   HmA, boone B.

22/7 where] wherin BH; 192 for] *om* BH; 266 booke] bookes BH.

23/300+SH Primus] Tertius BH; 414 hanges] heinges R, henges BH;
   710 by] *om* BH.

24/189 also] alas BH; 242 wend] now wiend BH; 347 saynte HmA]
   saintes BH; 576 put] part BH.

These errors all suggest minor difficulties arising from a common Exemplar. The marked agreement of HmA in the three omissions in Play 16 is exceptional and, given the weight of evidence against such direct derivation elsewhere in the play or the cycle as a whole, we are not disposed to accept Salter's thesis.

Greg's view—that Bellin copied from his own faulty copy of the Exemplar and was alerted to A's omission in Play 16 because he had returned to the register the previous year to copy C—seems to us possible. It is simpler to assume that Bellin returned to the Exemplar and moved between it and A in writing R. The state of the Exemplar itself would be a possible explanation for the uncertainty in Hm and A about the status of the three omitted quatrains in Play 16.

Bellin's third manuscript, C, is a copy of Play 16 made in 1599 apparently for inclusion in the records of the Coopers' Guild. Salter believed that its genesis was similar to that of R, namely that Bellin used both the Exemplar of R and also his earlier transcript in A. That Bellin did not use A alone is indicated by the presence in C of the three quatrains omitted from Play 16 in HmA. At least three further C readings suggest that Bellin was reconsidering a point of obscurity in the Exemplar that also troubled other scribes:

IIC/151 *miscarye* 16/139 *miseraye* Hm, *misserye* A, *mystarye* R, *mis arraye* BH. The word should rhyme with *saye-maye*; *mis arraye* BH may reflect scribal uncertainty about the letter following *s*, or an attempt to create a nonce-form equivalent to *disarray*, but the confusion about the letter following *s* in the other manuscripts seems to support the former possibility. A seems lexically appropriate and could readily derive from the form attested by Hm; the *-a-* in Hm may well be a scribal device to point the rhyme in *aye*, and if the Hm-form represents the Exemplar-form, the confusion is understandable; *c* in C and *t* in R would then represent other attempts to give meaning to an obscure form. But whatever the readings, they do seem to suggest a confusion in the Exemplar of which the C-form provides added evidence. It is unlikely, though not impossible, that C could derive directly from A.

IIC/163 *sayen* 16/151 *steyne* HmA, *sayen* R, *seene* B, *sayn* H. C agrees with R formally, and lexically with RH; and it might seem that RHC are correct. The difficulty is that no one has told Pilate where Jesus was born. The Exemplar-form seems to have ended in *-yne* on the evidence of HmAH and to have begun in *s*. Probably *steyne* HmA is an Exemplar-form—compare *stay* v[1], OED 2b "to cease speaking," recorded from 1551, which would fit the context. Hearing of Galilee, 147, Pilate is reminded that he already knows where Jesus was born. An Exemplar reading *stayne* in which *t* had been canceled would account for the RHC forms and for B's confusion. Again, however, the point is that C diverges from A at a place where the Exemplar was evidently obscure.

IIC/228 *hase seene ys* 16/216 *as seemes* Hm, *has seene* AR, *as seene is* BH. The readings suggest two confusions: *has* ARC and *as* HmBH; and *seene is* BHC, which Hm—by a misdivision and a confusion of minims—reads as *seemes* while AR, because of their earlier reading of *has*, omit *is*. C seems to contain the same lexical items as BH, but its form *hase* suggests a source for AR's reading and a cause of AR's subsequent omission. *has seene* does not give good sense, and an Exemplar-form resembling C would explain Bellin's imperceptive confusion. Hm's reading perhaps suggests not so much error as dissatisfaction with the Exemplar-form.

A fourth example, already discussed, is C's *whaynte*, IIC/336. C here resembles B's *whainte* and R's *whante* against HmA's *whyte* and H's *quoynt*, but it seems to represent the recurring difficulties that the various scribes had with what was evidently an altered Exemplar reading.

C does share some AR readings—65 *on*, 69 *us this harmed*, 77 *elles*, 107 *hym*, 123 *folkes*, 131 *if*, 134 *vous*, 159 *you*, 181 *never*]om, 217 *it is*, 242+SD *manibus*, 314 *will*, 367 *Barrabam*, 380 *saies*, 381 *syckerlye*]om. These strongly suggest the use of A beside the Exemplar. But C, despite some agreements with A (33 *nye*, 41 *not on worde speakes*, 178+SD *nichill* C/*nichell* A, 213 *forgetten* C/*forgotten* A, 376 *behynde* C/*be hynd* A [but cf. *behind* HmR]), rarely follows A into its unique forms and more often shows signs of reconsideration that may be found also in R (cf. *fyle* 81 HmRC, *sayen* 151 RC, *seemed* 200 RC, *soe* 262 RHC, etc.) but that may align it with other manuscripts (e.g., *the devill* 41 HC, *herken* 54 HC, *herden* 78 HmBC, 86 *thee* HC, etc.). The only simple explanation here is that Bellin was using the Exemplar and reaching conclusions at particular points reached also by other scribes.

Bellin's 1599 transcription of Play 16 is somewhat more conservative than his 1592 transcript. It might be easier to understand the differences if we knew more about the reasons for Bellin's 1592 transcript, for we may reasonably infer that in producing a guild text, Bellin might take particular pains to insure accuracy, at least to the extent of systematically comparing A with the Exemplar. Could his awareness of the deficiencies of A have led him to make a second and fuller transcript of the cycle for himself the following year? Or, following our speculation on p. xx of our edition, perhaps R may have been commissioned by a patron and Bellin felt obliged to take greater care with his cyclic manuscript in 1600? One thing does seem probable: if Bellin had access to A in 1599 and 1600, it may well have been his own copy of the cycle. This does not, of course, rule out the possibility for Bellin, or any other scribe, that the extant manuscript may be a "polished" transcript of rough notes from the Exemplar—the intermediate transcripts of Salter and Greg—but this seems an unnecessary and unhelpful supposition. Suffice it to say that Bellin had difficulties with his Exemplar and treated it freely in 1592 but that in 1599 he must have recognized at least three major errors in A, and certainly more minor errors, which he corrected in C; and in R he seems to have embarked on a second attempt at the cycle to arrive at a form more satisfactory to him (though not necessarily closer to the Exemplar). He then used A and the Exemplar; we cannot conclusively demonstrate that he did not also use C, although if he did he rejected a number of the readings.

MS Bodley 175: MS B

William Bedford's transcript of 1604 was not a copy of any of the earlier manuscripts that have survived. A glance at the list of omitted lines on pp. xxx–xxxi of our edition indicates that B has only four of its omissions in common with one or more of the earlier manuscripts, namely:

7/570, omitted in AR but found in HmH
9/ four lines after 183, omitted in HmH but found in AR
18/ 95 lines of appendix ID, omitted in HmA but found in RH
21/158, omitted in A but found in HmRH

Of these, the examples at Plays 9, 18, and 21 have been discussed previously as evidence of obscurity in the Exemplar. There is no obvious reason for the obscurity at 7/570, but it may be reasonably postulated. It would seem that B is yet another copy of the common Exemplar.

Yet B is in many ways the most interesting manuscript because Bedford seems to have been preparing a copy of the cycle for his own personal use. The manuscript is not ruled out and neatly spaced. The handwriting is hurried, often degenerating into a scrawl whose readings must be inferred. We have listed in the "Textual Notes" to our edition upward of 516 alterations, insertions, cancellations, and erasures. Bedford seems to have had no interest to serve but his own and to have been intent on hurrying the task through. His cancellations seem to suggest a mind hurrying ahead of the hand, e.g., 2/28, where Bedford canceled *shall* after *sone*, having picked it up from the following line; 12/44, where Bedford, reading *my crafte then fullye fayles*, began by adding the verb-ending to the noun, *craftes*, and then continued with the verb *fayles*, which he canceled; 16A/75, where, again misled by expectations of word-order, he wrote *ther* after *seame* because the line ends with *therin* and again had to cancel; 24/418, where he placed *fervent* after *othes*, omitting the intervening *alwayes*, and canceled. Often his hand seems to falter as he automatically writes a common, but erroneous, sequence of letters or words and then checks himself—2/253 *withouten feare* for *withouten were* (probably aided by *feare* in the following line); 3/69 a canceled *hach* for the start of *hackestocke*; 7/4 *to say* for *to save*; 17/19 *thee* for *thy*, perhaps influenced by *thee* in the preceding line, with *e*(1) altered to *y*; 23/247, a canceled *rig* for *rych*: 24/450, where he seems to have had the saved queen call to God as *thy owne sister—sist* is canceled before *thisten* (= *christen*). On one occasion we hear Bedford muttering to himself; 21/39, in the Hm sequence *dyinge rysinge*, Bedford canceled *g* after *dying*, suggesting oral elision of the two words.

The idiosyncracies of B lead us to suspect its readings. As we noted, Bedford is more conservative than Bellin in the matter of omitted lines, but he has many unique readings. We found 930 instances of the pattern HmARH]B, to which we may add a further 477 unique readings in Plays 2–24, and 48 in Play 1. But many of the readings are characteristic of the material canceled. Typical are 21/27 *hathe* for *hasse*; 21/28 *hisself* for *himselfe* and *see* for *hee*; 21/36 *youth* for *yearth*; 21/39 *drying* for *dying*. Many are simply formal variants, often errors, and easily detectable. But for this reason they are significant in suggesting a basis in the Exemplar for the error and hence, by comparison with the other manuscripts, establishing an Exemplar-form.

Bedford, in fact, seems to have no real desire to improve his text or treat it in a consciously cavalier fashion, like Bellin; nor do we suspect him of the scholarly antiquarianism of Miller. His variants fit certain well-defined patterns. As we have seen, he may unconsciously improve his text by reverting to expected sentence patterns or inflections: 12/113 Hm *say thou nowe that syttes so high*. Like AR, B places the adverb after the verb, *that sittes now*, but like HmH it retains the expected verb inflection against AR's erroneous *siteth*; it does not follow H into the "improvement" of *there* for *now*. But in the following line, where HmA read *by sleight* (indicating that 113 must have read *once on hight* for *so high*—cf. *sight* 115), B follows R and H in reading *sleigh* (*slye* H); R retains *by*, giving a meaningless phrase, but H reads *be*, suggesting an "improvement" to rhyme with the substituted *high* and making the phrase an imperative: "Be cunning"; B reads *the*, which turns the phrase into a title, "the Son of the cunning God." Given B's usual practices, we may assume that *sleigh* was an Exemplar-form, and that the preceding word probably did contain *e*; *the* is less likely to be an improvement than an oral corruption of *be*, a preposition originally, in collocation with *sleigh*. A very clear example of B's value as evidence of the Exemplar is 20/145–46:

> and that the wycked may eychone
> knowe and see all one

where B omits *may* while H reads *men* at 145 and BH read *maye knowe* at 146. B in fact also wrote *maye* after *wycked* 145, and then canceled it.

The cancellation is a deliberate act—*maye* should not be there, but the syllable seems desirable for smoother meter. The BH reading at 146 suggests that *maye* was in fact in the margin to the left of 146 but should have been inserted after *wycked* in 145 or had been excised from 145. B gives us an indication of the probable state of the Exemplar at this point and suggests that *men* H is a substitution to make good the syllabic deficiency resulting from the transference of *maye* from 145 to 146. Without B, we might conclude that H derived from a manuscript independent of the Group Exemplar.

Bedford's willingness to reveal his thought processes in his manuscript makes B a key to our understanding of the cyclic Exemplar. In Play 4, for example, B makes a continuing distinction between the English MDs and the Latin SDs, which explains the practice in the other manuscripts and almost certainly reflects the situation in the Exemplar. It is B that carries the odd margin notes, such as *restored* 13/229 or the direction about the knights to the left of 18/212–15. Possibly even the changes of hand noted on p. xxii of our edition imitate changes in the handwriting in the Exemplar.

In this respect, B's larger omissions are particularly interesting, because apart from occasional quatrains they are concentrated in large blocks. These are:

2/681–704, the return of Cain to his parents, where Bedford leaves the rest of 19v and the whole of 20r blank, to begin Play 3 unusually on a verso page. The omission was clearly deliberate, because of the gap, and suggests that Bedford was uncertain about the status of this section in his Exemplar.

15/347–66, the exchange of Jesus and Primus Judeus after the healing of Malchus at the end of the play. There is no obvious reason for the omission.

16A/181–212, much of the stretching of Christ on the Cross. Here the jump occurs at the end of fol. 119^r, suggesting that Bedford confused the identical SHs of 180+SH and 212+SH; the error is aided by the fact that the a-rhymes of sts. 23 and 27 are the same, and by the similarity of the first lines of the stanzas by Quartus Judeus: "Fellowes, will yee see," 177—"Fellowes, will you see," 209. Bedford is guilty of error here, but the error suggests that 180+SH and 212+SH were on the same Exemplar page.

18/425–*Finis*, the material of appendix ID. Bedford's omission is slightly more extensive than that of HmA, including 425–32, and he again leaves a recto-page blank to begin the next play on a verso, suggesting a consciousness of omission. The additional stanza omitted suggests that Bedford felt this also to be involved in a cancellation, strengthening our view that ID was in the B-exemplar and that it had been canceled.

Bedford's characteristic errors and his general lack of innovatory intent toward his text may be reflected in the patterns of manuscript-agreements in which B participates. It agrees with HmH against AR most frequently, of course. But its next most frequent correspondence is with H against HmAR (175) as a group or against subdivisions within that group, such as HmA]R (85). This does not suggest that BH is a subgroup analogous to AR; we found almost as many instances of disagreement between B and H as of agreement—HmAR]B/H 143, AR]Hm/B/H 68, etc. The explanation seems rather to be that BH often agree in including an altered reading not accepted by the other manuscripts. Thus at 13/30 Hm:

recorde them and keepe them in memorye

the line is metrically improved by the inclusion of an extra syllable. AR read *them ofte*; significantly, A then omits *and*, destroying the metrical improvement but suggesting some obscure cancellation or insertion in the *them and* phrase. BH read *and ofte. ofte* was evidently in the Exemplar, but the whole phrase had been altered, so that Hm omitted *ofte*, A omitted *and*, and R and BH placed *ofte* at different points in the line. A similar confusion may therefore be assumed to underlie other transpositions where such evidence is not available, e.g., 13/99 *therfore to us* HmAR] *to us therefore* BH; 13/369 *we goe*] *goe wee* BH. Like H, B tends to include lines evidently canceled in the Exemplar, as at 13/after 50 or 13/after 270, where HmAR have omissions. Occasional words, presumably inserted or canceled in the Exemplar, are included in BH and omitted in HmAR—13/212 *me*] *hath me* BH, 13/236 *anoye*] *anie any* (where the formal similarity of noun and adjective perhaps suggested independent omissions in HmAR), 13/428 *gowle*] *a gowle* BH, etc. Occasionally, a more thoroughgoing change seems suggested, as, for example, at 13/77, "when I had donne as God me badde," where HmA read *God* and BH *Christ*. It is easy to see the source of the unease—*Caecus* does not at this point recognize Christ as God (cf. 13/230), and the reading seems to be a result of confusion from *God* 73, 76. *he* R seems to acknowledge the problem but to be an independent substitution. Is *Christ* also an independent substitution in BH, or the inclusion of an

Exemplar alteration? Do such infrequent major discrepancies point to a different Exemplar for B from HmAR?

On the other hand, the divergencies from H in B are also marked, and they often seem to suggest the greater willingness of H to supply new readings. For example, 4/136 Hm: "and soe were both too," where B erroneously reads *wee* for *were*, perhaps troubled by the lack of pronoun, whereas H boldly supplies the pronoun additionally, *were they*; 4/205, where B mistranscribes Hm's *for to bye* as *for to be*, misled by *bee* in the preceding line, whereas Bellin characteristically improves as *oughte to be* AR, and H more intelligently reads *to forby*; 4/448, where B understandably changes the verb-tense in *that pleased me* HmAR from *pleased* to *pleaseth* while H substitutes *thou art worthy*. Sometimes, however, the divergence reflects different resolutions of Exemplar alternatives by the scribes, for example, 4/374 HmAR "for all that ever I have trespased to thee," where the line is metrically unwieldy and seems to incorporate two possibilities:

for all that I have trespased to thee
that ever I have trespased to thee

Of these B reflects the former, omitting *ever*; H reads: "Of that I have trespased to thee," improving upon the former. Because B's readings have some basis in the Exemplar, they allow us to check H's readings and envisage the Exemplar from which some may have arisen.

Harley 2124: MS H

James Miller evidently had overall responsibility for H, for he not only wrote the bulk of the manuscript but also went back over the section of scribe B to insert rubrics; the manuscript bears only his name. The text had clearly been studied with some care before transcript. Decisions had been taken in advance about the ruling of pages and the use of rubrication, leading to occasional miscalculations (e.g., 10/426–33). We sustain our view (our edition, p. xxvii) that "the manuscript seems to have been a presentation copy for someone of antiquarian taste."

Deimling argued that H was "not based on the common source of [ARB]," and hence he distinguished "the Group" from H as representing different textual traditions. In support of this view, he cited (a) the additions and omissions in H compared with the Group, and (b) a number of passages in which H is allegedly superior to HmARB, or where H's readings "cannot be based on the common source" of HmARB. Greg somewhat more accurately characterizes H: "We need not doubt that, given the opportunity, the scribe of H would have been ready enough to conflate his text, for he is the only one who shows any real solicitude for the form of what he transmits or indulges to a marked extent in editorial emendations" (*Antichrist*, p. lxxvii). This practice leads Greg to commend Hm rather than H as the base manuscript of an edition, despite H's general superiority in readings. But he regards H as deriving from a lost manuscript intervening between our Exemplar and H, which was also the source of a further lost manuscript on which B was based.

Salter, dealing with Play 16, reached a different conclusion, "*that essentially* H *belongs to the same immediate group as* BC [Hm]R[A]; it seems to have been drawn from the same *immediate* parent as B, [Hm], and *k*. . . . Frequently H must either have emended the same reading as is supplied by the other manuscripts, or have got a reading for which these others have accepted an emendation" (*Chester Play Studies*, pp. 38, 39–40).

Our statistical examination of variants shows the unique position of H. In the configuration HmARB]H we found 1949 instances, over 1,000 more unique readings than for B, the next highest. To this should be added 654 other readings unique among the five manuscripts and 155 unique readings in Play 1. And in many important instances, H is demonstrably superior to HmARB, as in the following examples:

2/233–40, st. 30: Only H recognizes that 240 should precede 237 (although it does not supply the required rhyme-form at 239, *als* for *alsoe*).

2/673–80, st. 85: H has a different version of 676, which supplies rhyme.

4/429–35, st. 56: After 434 H supplies a line not in HmARB but required for stanzaic regularity.

11/221–22: H's transposition of these lines gives better stanza-form and sense.

16/10: H alone omits *postie*, apparently an uncanceled error for the following *powere* but retained in HmARB.

18/201+SH–209: H alone places these lines after 217, thus correcting an error present in HmARB.

18/250–57, st. 32: H has different versions of 251–52, which restore rhyme and meter to the stanza. The lines in HmARB are clearly deficient.

23/410–16, st. 55: H supplies a line after 411 necessary for stanzaic completeness.

23/417–23, st. 56: H supplies a line after 418 necessary for stanzaic completeness.

23/448–53, st. 60: H replaces 453 by two lines, giving Enock a quatrain speech.

24/149–64, sts. 20–21: H alone places 153–60 after 164, as required for stanzaic form.

These major differences stand beside numerous minor readings that restore needed rhyme-words in stanzas, e.g., 2/388 *hase*, 4/29 *can wyn*, 7/286 *wake*, 8/332–34 *beforne-were borne*, 12/124 *mooved*, 13/76 *alwayes*, 14/220 *come*, 16/98 *him beshitt*, 16A/58 *swem*, 17/224–28 *dight-fowle afright*, 18/98–100 *draw-law-awe*, 19/212 *sinne*, 21/299 *steight*, 24/304 *als*.

H's attention to stanzaic regularity in the number of lines and in the rhyme-schemes of the stanzas suggests on the face of it that Miller had access to a "better" Exemplar than that of the Group. This in turn leads one toward the conclusion that H's other readings may be "better," and in particular that H's large-scale variations from HmARB may represent a "better"—in the sense of "less corrupted"—tradition. These major variations are:

Play 3: 47 lines "added" after 260+SD - the Raven and Dove scene
Play 4: Lines 475+SD–91 "omitted" - the Doctor's epilogue
Play 5: Substantially different, including the prophet-sequence
Play 7: 8 lines "added" after 124 - an extension of the list of foods by
     Tertius Pastor
     596+SH–640 "omitted" - the Gifts of the Shepherds' Boys
Play 8: 145–52 "omitted" - the Messenger's address to Herod
Play 11: 40+SH–210 "omitted" - a leaf lost in H
Play 12: 157–68 "replaced" by four lines after 156 - the deletion of the reference to the Parliament of Devils

Play 16: 274+SH–82 "omitted" - part of dialogue of Pilate and Jesus
    379–94 "omitted" - Peter's Denial
Play 16A: A different form of the conclusion following 359
Play 17: 66–68 different, and 69–72 omitted, from the Group-version -
    John the Baptist's account of the importance of Jesus' coming on Earth
        184+SH–92 "omitted" - speech of David
        276+SH–336 "omitted" - Ale-wife scene
Play 18: 95 lines "added" after 432 as in R - appearance of Christ to
    Mary Magdalen, the women, and Peter

It is, however, rarely possible to make assessments of these large-scale variants. Clearly, H is merely deficient at 11/41–210, and its SD, *Nuntius ibit ad Herodem*, after 144 suggests that the omission of 8/145–52 is also erroneous. It is correct in omitting 16/274+SH–82. But, as noted in discussing the Exemplar, there are grounds for believing that H was exercising a right of choice at 3/258+SD, 4/475+SH–91, 7/596+SH–640, 16A/359+SH–*Finis*, 17/276+SH–336, and 18/432–*Finis*. It is in demonstrable error in its omission of 17/184+SH–92, which departs from the Gospel of Nicodemus; and although at 17/66–72 H gives sense, it destroys stanza-form and the introductory reference to *these wordes*, 71, which constitutes a formula in this section of the play. We have noted that the two versions of Play 5 seem designed for different divisions of cyclic material, and H may have copied an alternative form of the play—not necessarily earlier or better. It is impossible to be sure of the causes of the other changes, but none is clearly "better." What is clear is that H contains a different version of the cycle from HmARB at certain points.

It must be emphasized, however, that even in smaller variants, H is not invariably superior to HmARB. It is particularly ill at ease with stanzas that do not conform to the "Chester" pattern and can be seen at 3/225–36 trying to break away from the quatrains of the Gossips' Song and to integrate it into the text. It omits 233–36; it replaces *spredeth full farre*, 226, by an a-rhyme, *breadeth in hast*, thus transforming st. 29 from abab to aaab; it removes the plural pronoun at 228 and, by transposing 225–32 to follow 242, changes the effect of the speech. In large sections of Play 7, the "non-Chester" stanzas are compressed into quatrain-spaces, and rhymes are lost at 130, 150, 330 (*om*), 348, 503, 565, 680 (*om*), 683, 685–86 (line misdivision), 691. And at 23/189–96, st. 25 H can be seen emending the text; 194 Hm reads "You kinges, also to you I tell," but in H the line is "You kinges I tell withouten bost," giving the required rhyme with *ghooste*, 193, and *moste*, 195. But in H, after *kinges, also to you* is canceled, indicating that H had the HmARB line before it. And there are other unique readings in H that seem to suggest scribal interference with the text. The misunderstanding of *pigge* at 8/381+SD and its translation as *nefrens*, noted above, indicates that H tends to translate English SDs into Latin; and the absence of many MDs from Play 4 also suggests a selective approach—those retained are given Latin form. At 8/102 the steeds of the Magi are specified in all manuscripts as *dromodaryes*, but at 108 H reads *corsers* for *beasts*, and in 112+SD renders *beastes* as *eques*. The pleasingly archaic and alliterating *carpe* for *stowpe* in 16/87 Hm: "Stowpe nowe, nowe, and creake" is, unfortunately, inappropriate. At 17/197+SH its reassignment of the speech from *David Rex* to *Jhesus* is perhaps supported by M. R. James's Latin B text of the *Gospel of Nicodemus*, but David is confirmed by the Latin A text and by *Legenda Aurea, Stanzaic Life* 8029–32. The H version of 19/69 and the additional line that follows in H transforms a seven-line stanza in HmARB to eight lines, but the changes give doubtful sense. Its *weete* for *wyde* at 20/12 gives rhyme with *feete*, 16, but the biblical text and 19/249+SD suggest that it is *feete* that should be changed to *side*. Small slips of this kind cast suspicion on the authenticity of H's unique readings in many cases.

The difficulty is that Miller is an intelligent and indeed a learned man. Not only can he translate English SDs into Latin, but H alone has corresponding biblical texts in some of its margins. As a thinking scribe, he can readily spot and remedy stanzaic deficiencies in normal stanza-forms. But he can also improve meter and sense in a way that makes either reading possible. At 16/145–46 Caiaphas protests in HmARB:

Syr, the people, us to mispaye,
converted to him all hee hase.

H reads *follow his way* for *us to mispaye*, and *perverted them* for *converted to him*. The influence of Luke 23/2: "Hunc invenimus subvertentem gentem nostram" (AV "We found this fellow perverting the nation") hangs heavily and persuasively over H, but its very plausibility seems to argue in favor of HmARB; why would one change the H reading if it had priority? The pattern is repeated at 16/147–48 HmARB:

Yea, all the land of Gallilee
cleane turned to him hase hee

where H reads *them* for *him*, thus changing the sense of *turned* from
"converted" to "went"; here the dependence of H upon Luke is negative
rather than positive, rejecting the idea of conversion for the physical
concept of travel and a nomadic ministry suggested in Luke 23/5: "Com-
movet populum, docens per universam Judaeam, incipiens a Galilaea
usque huc" (AV "He stirreth up the people, teaching throughout all
Jewry, beginning from Gallilee to this place"). A scholarly mind lies
behind these readings.

We acknowledge Miller as the first editor of the Chester cycle. We
strongly suspect an idiosyncratic element in his text and doubt whether
Chester was ever performed in the words that he supplies. But we recognize also that Miller was intent on making sense of a difficult Exemplar
and was alert, as other scribes were not, to the possibilities of choice, the
existence of error, and the desirability of completeness and coherence in
his text.

The Manchester and Peniarth Manuscripts: M and P

Our discussion of M and P is hampered by two problems. The first is the
state of the extant manuscripts. M is a fragment of Play 18 and offers
very limited evidence; P is a complete version of Play 23, but its original
writing has been inked over and readings apparently changed at times.
The second is the related problem of date. It seems impossible to date M
satisfactorily. P is usually assigned to the end of the fifteenth century;
Greg said that "it might be as late as 1500." If so, it is nearly a century
earlier than the earliest cyclic manuscript. Since the Hewsters seem to
have been assigned the play of Antichrist in 1467–68 (see chapter 5,
"Documents Providing External Evidence," items 20a and 20b), such a
date for P would make it close in time to the original versions of the play,
and a comparison with the extant manuscripts of the whole cycle might
indicate the degree of change over the century.

Although M is short, it contains fifteen readings that are different
from the readings shared by HmARBH. Added to the twenty-seven variants for these lines in the versions in the five cyclic manuscripts, there

are therefore forty-two six-manuscript variants involving M, and in this short sample the pattern HmARBH]M would occur in 36.5 percent. This would suggest a proportion of unique forms comparable with that of H. Some qualification of this conclusion is, however, necessary.

Three of the fifteen variants are "omissions" in which all or part of a word have been lost through manuscript damage. It is unlikely that three others—23 *crosse*] *croyse* in rhyme position; 25 *us*] *hus*; 21 *the*] *they* (where Hm *the* is pronominal)—should be regarded as other than spelling variants, and they would not be noted usually in the variants of the cyclic manuscripts. Hence there are only nine unique forms worthy of note, just over 21 percent of variants and hence closer to B than to H.

Similar caution must be exercised in assessing M forms where variants exist for the five cyclic manuscripts. One instance only of the pattern HmARB] H/M exists, but this is at a point where M is damaged and the cyclic variant is 12 *fynde*] *fyne* H; while the intervening letters are lost, the M reading *f—de* is sufficient to suggest that the form was that of the Group. The variant 32 *could*] *were* A produces a potential A/M pattern since M has the form *cald*, but again the important point is that M does not have the A-form, and probably the M-form should be disregarded as a spelling variant only. Similarly, 25 *lest*] *lesse* B suggests a B/M pattern since M has *least*, but again one could regard M as a spelling form. The only really doubtful case is the variant 38 *wedders*] *weither* ARBH, where M reads *weddar*; syntactically agreeing with the majority reading, formally M provides a link with Hm.

M had, like other manuscripts, difficulties in the passages of French; but most of these variants also can be seen as formal confusions, easily explained. 3 *sum*] *syn* M suggests misdivision of minims and replacement of *i* by *y*; 5 *luces*] *luyes* M suggests difficulty with the form of *c*, often found in early manuscripts, a difficulty reflected in the reading 8 *estreite*] *escrete*; 8 *loer* is transposed or anglicized to *lore*, and possibly 6 *perfoyte*] *parfite* M and 6 *deliverie*] *delyvere* M should be regarded as "anglicized" forms. No manuscript supplies the form *qui le* required at 4, but arguably *quale* M is closest to it. Because these variants occur in the French section, they are perhaps not representative of M's general practice.

Perhaps, however, it is not too fanciful to see in the remainder of the variants attempts at "emendation" to correct syntax or meter. The meter is affected by the omission of a syllable in the unique M variants *them*] *om* M (23), *beleeve*] *leeve* M (26), *can*] *om* M (28); while *cryed*] *cryden*

M (21) shows the addition of a syllable that would "roughen" the meter and could be explained either as an archaic form or as the confusion in word-division whereby the following *on* was read as the *-en* verb inflection. The change of tense in the noun-clause at 27, *began*] *beegyn* M, and perhaps the form *nyfe* for *ne* at 30 should be regarded as attempts to regularize syntax, although the latter seems perhaps to repeat the "*cryden*" error by reading *ne so* as one word, misunderstanding both the *s* and *o* forms and regularizing the resulting *nefe*.

Two interesting points of "regularization" occur. The first is in 21–22, both of which begin with *the* in Hm. As noted above, the pronominal form at 21 appears in M as *they*, which could well have been in the Exemplar; but the definite article at 22 appears in M as *these*, a unique reading. This reading could be an independent M-form, but it may most readily be explained not as an unaccountable *the*] *these* variation but as an attempt by the M-scribe to distinguish syntactically between the two *the*'s that he might have found in the Exemplar, as in Hm. The second point is at 31 where M, like H at other points in the cycle, introduces an extra syllable, only to balance this elsewhere by the compensatory omission of another syllable. The variants are:

up durst looke] durst once looke up M
great] *om* M

Three variants only require special attention. At 32 M shares with A the variant *soone*] *sore*. Since there are six examples of the pattern HmRBHM] A in this section, and since M, as previously noted, does not share the A-form *were* earlier in the line, this agreement is best explained as independent misreading of some Exemplar-form such as *sone*. There are no grounds for linking M with A.

The second variation is more complex. The M version of 31 given above is unique in its addition of *once* and omission of *great*. Hm reads *up durst looke,* "dared look up"; ARB read *up loked,* to the detriment of meter, perhaps taking *durst* as an inappropriate present tense; but A reads 32 as past—*could . . . agryse* as *were . . . agased,* with loss of rhyme. This reading, *up loked,* must be regarded as an Exemplar change that led Bellin to emend the tense of 32. Bedford, in characteristic haste, reads *agrie* for *agryse.* But H at 31 changes order to read *durst look up,* the M-order. Is the similarity the result of independent change, or are H and M in some way linked?

The third, and most important, variant is at 22; *great*] *piteous* BHM. Two points may be made about the variation. *great* seems semantically more appropriate than *piteous*, and *piteous* seems metrically preferable to *great*. A change from one reading to the other in the Exemplar according to priorities may be assumed, and M either derived from an intermediary containing *piteous* or, more simply, made the same selection as BH.

M was not the exemplar for any extant version; even in this limited section it contains too many unique readings, including omissions. It seems most probably to be another copy of the cyclic Exemplar. Greg, however, argued that "the cyclic manuscripts have a common ancestor which is not an ancestor of M." His basis for this is a number of older spelling forms in M, as he considers them; the reading *well leeve* for *well beleeve*, which he regards as preferable and as forming a base for a development *welle* M, *welbe* BH, *well beleeve* HmAR; the verb-tense *beegyn* 20 M, which he rather surprisingly finds "more natural" than *begane* 27 HmARBH; and *sore* AM for *soone* 32 HmRBH, considered above. None of these considerations seems to us conclusive and certainly not strong enough for the far-reaching proposal that Greg advances.

STS. 84 AND 85 of Play 23 in HmARBH are irregular. In Hm, st. 84 rhymes aaabcccd, 85 aaab, with the same *a* and *b* rhymes in each stanza. ARBH have four lines after 636 that are not in Hm. The resulting sixteen lines rhyme *aaabcccdcccdaaab*. P alone has the correct arrangement, placing 641–44 after 634–36 to form a regular Chester stanza, and including the additional lines before 637. What seems to have happened is that a quatrain was omitted after 636, but the scribe recognized his error at 640 and wrote the quatrain beside 633–36 with the second quatrain to follow 640 written alongside 637–40. The two resulting columns were then read vertically in turn, producing the wrong sequence. What is not clear is whether the error occurred in the Exemplar, working from a corrected Pre-exemplar, or independently in the extant manuscripts, working from a corrected Exemplar. P could have corrected the error independently, but it is strange that even H did not notice the mistake if the correction was in the Exemplar. Could the Exemplar have transmitted the error? And does the P reading suggest dependence on a version earlier than the Exemplar?

P was not the immediate source of the Exemplar-version. The "errors" of the Exemplar cannot be traced to a correction in P, and P also has a number of unique forms that are not in the Exemplar and that seem to attest a misreading of a different manuscript. "when I were come in land" 44 Hm becomes "when I were comyn rowland"; P does not give good sense and seems to originate in a misdivision of *com yn* and a misreading of *land* as an incomplete present participle (cf. *flaterand* 376 P). 47 Hm, "I thinke to fast manye hould," is acceptable, though A changes the word-order to *faste manye to* and H substitutes *to force manyfould*, contrary to standard accounts of Antichrist; but P's "I thinke to faast monye folde" does not give good sense and suggests the unthinking substitution of *folde* for *hould* through common collocation, in contrast to H where the substitution is deliberate.

In a number of cases, P preserves a reading that is demonstrably better both for rhyme and, often, for meaning. Excluding sts. 84–85, examples are:

29–31. *wond-band-sond* Hm, *wende-bende-sende* P. The Exemplar seems to have rhymed in -*o*-. Its *sond*, 31, appears as *sound* ARB and *sand* H. But the unusual form of the re-inked -*e*-(1) of *sende* P suggests that -*o*- forms underlie all the -*e*- readings of the re-inker and that it had *sonde*. B reads *wound* for *wond*, and all cyclic manuscripts *band* for *bond*, giving imperfect rhyme. But if the -*e*- forms in P all conceal -*o*- forms, P alone preserves perfect rhyme.

241–52. These lines constitute two stanzas, one of eight and one of four lines. In Hm the rhyme-scheme is aaabcccb cdce; the last quatrain contains in all cyclic manuscripts the sequence *aye-lawe-todaye*, hence cdc, but P alone has perfect rhyme, reading *laye* for *lawe*, giving ccc for cdc and hence a quatrain form cccd. The b-e rhymes in the cyclic manuscripts are *thine-kynne-fynde* Hm, but P reads *hyse* for *thine*, *kynde* for *kynne*, changing the rhyme-pattern to b-d-d. Thus P reverses the stanza-arrangement of the cyclic manuscripts, giving aaab cccdcccd. That P is better is indicated by the reliance on the long-vowel rhyme of *kynde-fynde* in contrast to the mixture of long and short vowels in *thine-kynne*. Since the cyclic manuscripts agree, it seems that they may represent an Exemplar-form that contained an emendation of *hyse* to *thine* and *kynde* to *kynne*, following the loss of a quatrain, and also the further modernization of *laye* to *lawe*.

413–15, st. 55. Hm rhymes *springes-hanges-raygnes*; it is a seven-line stanza in all manuscripts except H, which supplies an additional line after 411, and rhymes aabacdb. It is tempting to assume an original rhyme-scheme of aa(a)baaab and to postulate a sequence *springes-hinges-ringes*. But no manuscript, including P, reads *ringes*, suggesting that the Exemplar did not contain the form. *heinges* R, *henges* BH may suggest an Exemplar-form in *-e-* for *hanges*, R perhaps showing how the form evolved from the Pre-exemplar; but only P has *hyngys*, the a-rhyme.

607. *greetes* HmARB was evidently the Exemplar-form, but it gives no sense in its reflexive construction as a form of *greden* or *greten*. H emends to *girts*, which is semantically acceptable. But *graythes* P is also acceptable and preserves alliteration. The Exemplar-form may be an error for *grethes*, a possible variant of *greithes*.

Such better readings are few, but obviously important. In many other instances, P differs from the cyclic forms without being demonstrably better. One may instance lines where P has a syllable—sometimes in the form of a word—that the cyclic version does not have, e.g., 10, 22, 62, 67, 103, 174, 185, 256, 310, 323, 428, 474, 539, 597, 603, 634, 655, 681, 694; or where P lacks one or more syllables—sometimes in the form of a word or words—that the cyclic version contains, as in 21, 42, 140, 147, 264, 276, 302, 347, 357, 450, 483, 491, 530, 541, 577, 580, 585, 589, 594, 647, 651, 680, 690; or where P presents the words of the cyclic form but in a different sequence, as in 235, 246, 250, 277, 315, 334, 340, 429, 442, 547, 635, 712. In addition to these differences, many of which seem to be primarily metrical in effect, there are variants that show morphological and lexical differences, as at 24 (*them*] *hand*), 25 (*ligged*] *laykyd*), 27 (*can found*] *confounde*), 55 (*hitt*] *that*), 60 (*this*] *thus*), 82 (*rootes*] *rote*), 95 (*this*] *thus*), 102 (*verey*] *every*), 140 (*in*] *at*), 158 (*my*] *oure*), 160 (*tyll*] *but*), 176 (*hath*] *as*), 195 (*mightes*] *myghtist*), 200 (*came*] *come*), 206 (*shall*] *will*), 214 (*because*] *for*, *regions*] *regnis*), 217 (*fayre*] *fere*), 219 (*yea*] *and*), 226 (*what*] *that*), 236 (*and*] *to*), 244 (*thine*] *hyse*), 245 (*giftes*] *gifte*), 260 (*for*] *to*), 272 (*anoye*] *anyes*), 276 (*destroye*] *distryes*), 287 (*devylls*] *devyle*), 317 (*here*] *redye*), 332 (*bought*] *thought*), 343 (*came*] *come*), 368 (*thy*] *the*), 369 (*myle*] *mylys*), 376 (*flatteringe*] *flaterand*), 394 (*wee*(2)] *I*), 396 (*for*] *more*), 417 (*syttes*] *settes*), 433 (*should*] *shullest*), 436 (*whom*] *that*), 437 (*whom*] *that*, *are*] *be*), 440 (*leeve*] *lerne*), 450 (*the xx devylles*] *your*), 470 (*godes*] *God*), 483 (*but*] *then*), 510 (*this*] *that*), 546 (*agaynst*] *agayn*), 558 (*come*] *and*), 559 (*worthye of*] *worthest in*), 580 (*puttes*] *puttythe*), 611 (*teache*] *leche*), 629 (*slayne*] *shente*), 659 (*not to*] *I wolde not*), 682 (*the*] *thie*), 684 (*yee*] *he*), 688 (*lawes*] *lawe*), 693 (*heeles*] *halse*), 725 (*where*] *there*).

Extensive though this list appears—and it excludes arguably formal variants such as that at 324 (*whatever*] *whatsoever*)—most of the variants are of a syntactical nature, involving differences in verb-tense, in noun-number and pronoun-number, in verb-inflection, and occasionally of relative pronoun (*whom*] *that*), conjunction (*tyll*] *but*), or complete construction (*not to*] *I wolde not*). These changes are comparable with syllable variations and differences of word-order in that they are simple and limited changes that could readily arise from independent alteration rather than transmission. Some are errors in P; in 287 the re-inking in P suggests that the original may have been *devyls*. It must be remembered that we are dependent upon the re-inker for a number of these readings.

Excluding these forms, and the demonstrably better readings quoted, we find very few major lexical variants in P—25, 102, 244, 317, 332, 440, 450, 611, 629, and 693, ten in all. Here too the variation can often be explained palaeographically since the words are sufficiently similar in form to suggest scribal confusion, as at 102, 332, 440, 611, and 693 (although one would here assume some form such as *heales/healse*). At 25 the cyclic *ligged*, a weak variant of *lie*, "stay, dwell," has produced confusion by its collocation with *him*, which AR change to *me* and B omits; P reads *laykyd*, but *lyggedd* has been written above in a contemporary hand, which may perhaps indicate that the P-Exemplar contained *lyggedd*. The reading at 244 has already been considered. There seems, however, no way of explaining the variants at 317, 450, and 629 other than as direct substitution by one scribe or the other.

It is useful to remember the character of the P-variants when considering the relationship of P to the cyclic manuscripts. The introduction of P into the manuscript-series defines the cyclic manuscripts as a group against it. In Play 23 there is little difference between the cyclic manuscripts in the number of unique variants, though Hm is noticeably, and characteristically, lower (28 Hm, 46 A and H, 47 B, 49 R; 45 AR); P usually agrees with the majority form if not unique itself. But it is notable that P agrees with H in 16 readings against the other manuscripts, the highest correspondence of P and a cyclic manuscript.

There is, of course, no question of H looking to a manuscript like P to supplement the Exemplar. P has 129 unique readings, H 46—too many to admit any close relationship. Rather, the link is to be explained by H's emendations that may result occasionally in the restoration of an original reading, although they may equally lead in another direction. Support for this possibility comes from a comparison of the B forms in a number of these cases, for B, although basically conservative, does change to improve meter. For example:

To buyld this temple wyll I not blynne,
as God honored be therein   [37–38]

Both B and H find 38 metrically defective and attempt to remedy the deficiency by adding a syllable. B reads *so as*, H *and as*; H's solution corresponds to the P reading. But occasionally the effect can be different, as in 448 Hm, "My cursse I gyve you, to amend your meeles," where B alone decides to reduce the number of syllables by reading *mende* for *amend*, conforming with P, while H leaves the line unchanged. And just as H at 47, in recasting the line, reaches one point of agreement with P, so at 415, "so thy joye; nowe yt raygnes," B by chance agrees with P. In P this line, which, as we have seen, contains an error, reads "so do thy joye nowe ragnes," syntactically impossible but preserving the number of syllables in Hm; both AR and B, from an Exemplar-form probably like Hm, make the line a complete sentence, as seems to have been the intention in P. AR omit *nowe*, and B omits *yt*. Hence BP share the variant *yt*] *om*, but P has an extra syllable earlier in the line that B lacks. Finally, at 315, "nowe wee be readye—leeve you this," H omits *be*, while B inverts to read *bene wee*, which is also the P-reading.

This similarity of practice explains the instances of HmAR] BHP configuration in the play, of which there are five in spoken variants. A clear example is 112 where Hm reads "Crist our naue ys commen." No other manuscript has *naue*, all reading *name*. Both B and H regard the line as metrically deficient and add an extra syllable, reading *Christ that* and thus agreeing with P. In this they were almost certainly not following the Exemplar and were faced with the apparently meaningless *ys commen* as the verb of the new relative clause. B destroys the rhyme by reading *named*; H retains it by reading *nummen*. But neither corrects *ys* to give P's *has nomen*. Thus, in this line we have an example of each of the following: ARBHP] Hm, HmARBH] P, HmAR] BHP, HmAR] HP/B. One can see similar independent "emendations" producing the same variety of agreements at other points. In *lordes of lordshipp* 217 HmAR, *lordes* may have suggested *lordshipes* independently to BHP; Hm's *well yt fall*, 218, seems to have suggested the substitution of present for subjunctive, *falles*, to BHP. At 371, not in R, BHP agree on *wiserde* against *roysard* Hm, *rasarde* A, the latter evidently misreadings of the Exemplar. BHP "improve" the meter at 411 by reading *to* for *unto*, and at 710 by omitting *by*. At 625 BHP read *thie* for *this*, but H alone reads *commen is* for *ys common* Hm.

Such agreements are explicable by reference to the usual practices of the scribes, and since H reveals a greater willingness to change the Exemplar than the other manuscripts, it is not surprising that there are more agreements between H and P than between any other cyclic manuscript and P. H alone of the cyclic manuscripts corrects the Latin of 2 by reading *vobis* for *vos*; improves the meter of 15 by omitting *to*(1); changes word-order at 334 to read *doe I* for *I doe*, and at 340 to read *him light* for *light him*. Here and elsewhere it accords with P. Some of the correspondences may seem striking, but set in context and given the emending tendencies of Miller, they seem less significant. HP read *such joy* against *joye* HmARB at 23; but once it is admitted that 23 is metrically deficient, the line limits the choice of an additional syllable: "and joye right as have I." H and P reverse 193 and 194, but the significance of the agreement is perhaps minimized by the facts that the last four lines of st. 25 in Hm rhyme abab; that, although the two quatrains are separated by a SD and therefore an action, so that the second quatrain is a new address, the words of the address, "you kinges, also to you I tell," occur only in the second line in HmARB; and that H, unlike P, has also recast the transposed 194 to give an a-rhyme and thus a "regular" second quatrain. It may be merely chance that led H to read *goles*, like P's *golys*, at 513; the Exemplar confused the scribes at this point and each provides a different form in each manuscript—*gulles* Hm, *glowes* A, *gowles* R, *goioles* B. What does seem clear from HmARB is that the Exemplar form contained two letters at least between *g* and *l*, suggesting that H's form is a scribal idiosyncrasy. Such examples are not revealing as evidence that H or any other manuscript was dependent upon P or a similar version of Play 23. But they do show that scribal practice can occasionally produce identical results.

If the P-scribe was like Miller, it might be argued that P could derive from the cyclic Exemplar. If so, the unique forms discussed would be scribal idiosyncrasies, and stanzas 84 and 85 represent a particularly intelligent solution to a problem. In this connection, two agreements of BHP need special comment. At 23/143 HmAR read *burye*, BHP *laye*. The latter is metrically preferable, and alliterates. It seems probable that *burye* was an Exemplar reading, introduced in collocation with *bodye*, 142, and that it was later corrected in the margin to *laye*, surely the Pre-exemplar reading. BH accept *laye*; did P also accept it, or did its scribe have before him a form with *laye* only, or did he substitute independently? And at 300+SH BHP read *Tertius Rex* against *Primus Rex* HmAR. The sequence of speakers confirms *Tertius*. Although this looks like an error of transmission, it may well result from a confusion in which a notation such as *Ius, IIus, IIIus, IIIIus* was used and sometimes reduced as *Is, IIs*, etc. The confusion of the three-minim forms *Ius* and *IIIs* would readily explain the error of HmAR: but the agreement of BHP, while indicating that BH correctly interpreted the form, leaves the P reading open to the same speculation as before. Finally, one should note the agreement of HP at 196+SH in reading *Quartus Rex* for *Severalis Rex* HmARB. In strict speaking sequence *Quartus* is correct, but it is dramatically effective that each king in turn should acknowledge the power of the spirit sent by Antichrist. The Exemplar may have had a changed SH, or it may have read *Severalis*, for the change in SH is well within the competence of H and is to be expected because in H the SHs were entered after the text was written out and a break in sequence would be the more obvious. P may have acted independently, like H, or again worked from a different Exemplar.

Our view of the position of P in the transmission of Chester finally depends on date and on the weight that we give to different readings, especially sts. 84–85. If we accept a date c. 1500, P could not be a copy of the cyclic Exemplar (assuming a date in the 1530s), but it was also not part of the Pre-exemplar. It would then be an independent copy of the Pre-exemplar at best, and hence collateral with the cyclic Exemplar.

OUR ASSUMPTIONS AND EXAMINATIONS of the extant manuscripts therefore lead us to a simple view of Chester's descent. A set of production-texts or guild copies, themselves copies of the Pre-exemplar, were collected to form an Exemplar, which was then copied by the four scribes of the extant cyclic manuscripts—Bellin using his earlier manuscript(s) in preparing R. M also may be a copy of the Exemplar. But P may, if dated c. 1500, be an independent copy of the Pre-exemplar.

What seems to us more important than these conclusions, however, is the implication of the discussion for the concept of the "Chester cycle." There were many forms of this cycle, and some of the possibilities are incorporated into our present texts, making our edition "a cycle of cycles" rather than a definitive form. The assumption of a fixed cycle-form seems to underlie editorial discussions and also critical discussions of medieval play cycles, but it is one that, for Chester at least, we find misleading. What emerges from a study of the manuscripts is a sense of flexibility and an awareness of the responsibility that lay with both the civic authorities and the guild producers for determining the cycle-form from one performance to the next.

2.

CONCERNING

SOURCES, ANALOGUES,

AND AUTHORITIES

THE CHAPTER THAT FOLLOWS is in two sections. The first is essentially a review of the various "immediate sources and influences" that have been proposed by earlier critics for the Chester cycle, with some small additions and comments. The second deals with the wider issue of the evocation of authorities within the cycle.

Immediate Sources and Influences

We agree with the assumption that the understanding of the composition and the meaning of a text is significantly extended by comparing it with a work on which the author drew directly while writing the text. The immediate source may well provide valuable external evidence concerning the author of a text and its date of composition. We resist, however, any automatic assumption in connection with the Chester cycle that a series of immediate sources would necessarily correspond to a series of independent revisions and hence mark out different chronological "strata" in the development of the text.

In considering the sources of the Chester cycle we are conscious that much of the material was familiar, being biblical, liturgical, or legendary, and that it had been transmitted in a variety of forms over a prolonged period. There are numerous correspondences between various parts of the text and the Vulgate, *Legenda Aurea*, and standard commentaries and compendia, notably the *Historia Scholastica* of Peter Comestor and the *Glossa Ordinaria*, much of which is ascribed to Walafrid Strabo. These correspondences shed light on the familiarity of the material in the cycle and indicate points at which the cycle diverges from at least one current reading or interpretation of the material. We have not, however, attempted to establish the particular form of the material used directly by the Chester playwright(s). The substance of the Chester cycle occurs in a very wide variety of other works, for a number of which the published editions are inadequate or lacking. For example, the 1890 Graesse edition of *Legenda Aurea* has severe limitations; also, no edition of the ME *Gilt Legend* exists, making it difficult to assess Chester's possible dependence upon the *Stanzaic Life of Christ*, a work itself dependent upon some version of *Legenda Aurea*.

The discussion of "immediate sources" is complicated for a play-cycle such as Chester by a further factor. Very few English play-texts have survived from the Middle Ages. From the little evidence that is available, it would seem that material from one cycle often had counterparts in another and that cycles in different towns did on occasion draw upon a common text. We note that Chester has certain sections of text in common with plays from other towns in England, but we feel too uncertain about the processes of borrowing to propose direct influence by a play at one town on that at another; the existence at other towns or from other times of now lost versions of the same material seems to us very probable. This uncertainty persists not only for passages for which the extant English plays provide counterparts, but also for passages where critics have found correspondences only in French drama. We would be unwilling to argue that such correspondences necessarily demonstrate direct influence from French drama.

It follows from these guarded comments that we do not feel able to make a firm distinction between an ultimate source, an immediate source, and an analogue. This tendency to blur the distinction between the earliest form of the material, the form used directly by the writer, and other works, possibly unknown to the writer, which transmit the same material, has been a feature of a number of early studies of the sources for the Chester cycle, of which Hans Utesch, *Der Quellen der Chester-Plays* (Kiel, 1909) provides a good example. Later critics have attempted to establish direct sources by unique shared detail, shared sequences of material, and similarities of phrase. The following summary reviews the major proposals.

French Influence

The arguments for a French source for the Chester cycle have been judiciously reviewed by Albert C. Baugh in "The Chester Plays and French Influence," *Schelling Anniversary Papers* (New York, 1923). Baugh discusses the evidence under five headings:

1. Parallel passages in the Chester cycle and French plays, a comparison that he finds unconvincing;
2. The presence of the French language at 6/209–17, 8/65–72 and 153–60, 16/134–35, 18/1–8, which he regards as stylistic markers of class; and the presence of French derivatives in the vocabulary, which he considers insignificant;

and, more confidently, the following three features:

3. References to France at 12/259–60 and 14/421–24;
4. Features (episodes and characters) supposedly characteristic of French tradition, viz., Abraham and Melchizedek (4/1–144), Balaam and his Ass (5/96–*Finis*, IB/89–296 and 433–*Finis*), the Fifteen Signs before Judgment (22/260+Latin–332), Octavian and Sibyl (6/177–372+SD and 643+SD–98), Healing the Blind Man at Siloam (13/1–300), the Cleansing of the Temple (14/224+SD–64); also, the name of the second Midwife (*Tebell*, 6/484+SH, cf. French *Zebel*);
5. The plan of the cycle, particularly the episodes under 4 above; the structure of certain plays that combine a number of different episodes —Plays 2 (Creation, Fall of Man, Cain and Abel), 6 (Annunciation, Visit to Elizabeth, Joseph's Trouble, Nativity, together with Octavian and Sibyl), 16 with 16A (all episodes of the Passion); the management of individual episodes or plays, showing a "general parallelism with a given French text," exemplified from a comparison of Play 2 with Greban's *Passion*.

Reviewing the evidence as a whole, Baugh cautiously proposes the probability of "the influence of the French dramatic tradition."

Baugh's phraseology indicates the problems of considering "French influence" under "immediate sources." We not only agree that the material under 1 and 2 is unsatisfactory evidence, but we also feel that the two references under 3 are equally unlikely to suggest direct French influence, as Baugh himself recognizes. The only "textual" item under 4, the name of the second midwife, has been cited also in support of influence from *Stanzaic Life*, and that possibility may also be questioned (see below); it provides weak evidence for direct French influence. The other items under 4 and 5 suggest interesting general correspondences but do not isolate a specific work. Hence Baugh seems to be referring not to sources but to literary models.

Similar terminology is used by Rosemary Woolf in her *The English Mystery Plays* (London, 1972), where Chester is one example of French influence that she finds in the English cycles. She proposes the use of the *Mystère du Viel Testament* as model for a late fifteenth-century rewriting of the Old Testament plays (p. 306) and alludes to "French influences . . . in plays such as the Harrowing of Hell, Pentecost and the Last Judgment, where the *Stanzaic Life* could not provide a model" (pp. 415–16, n. 9).

Such observations are important in their suggestion of literary traditions, but we feel that closer verbal parallels would be required to establish a particular work as an immediate source. Possibly such parallels would be especially difficult to establish in comparing works written in different languages, particularly with texts that were repeatedly revised. Ruth Keane has drawn attention to some of the problems involved. In any case, the channel for such influence seems to have been lost. Rosemary Woolf herself, while believing that the influence was direct, suggests that an influential English cycle—she favors London—may have acted as intermediary and have been lost subsequently, but that is, of course, pure speculation.

English Plays

I. Chester 4/229–420 and the Brome play of "Abraham and Isaac" 105–315

The similarity of these lines in Chester and Brome was first noted by Lucy Toulmin Smith, the first editor of the Brome play. The Brome *Abraham* is extant in *The Book of Brome*, ff. 15^r–22^r, where it appears in a late fifteenth-century hand, not earlier than 1454 (see Norman Davis, ed., *Non-cycle Plays and Fragments* [London, 1970]). The text contains a number of bad rhymes, some not restorable, and it was clearly a copy of an earlier version or versions. The Chester texts were also copies of an Exemplar that had been subject to revision. If there is, as seems certain, a direct link between the two versions, then it is likely to have been at a time before the extant manuscripts were copied and it may therefore be misleading to speak simply of influence from Brome upon Chester or vice versa. As with "French influence," the origins of both versions in a lost intermediary, perhaps unconnected with either Cheshire or Suffolk, seems a probable postulate.

Debate about the direction of influence has been prolonged, but we incline to the general view expressed by J. Burke Severs in "The Relationship between the Brome and Chester Plays of 'Abraham and Isaac,'" that the Chester version represents a corruption of the Brome version, as evidenced by duplicated incidents and awkward transitions in the Chester play. Some duplicated episodes would fit a thesis of alternatives (e.g., 229–40 and 241–48) and others seem more justifiable than Severs allows (e.g., 258–80, 378), but in general it seems preferable to regard the Chester version as the "revised" form.

If indeed Chester presents a "revised" version of a text resembling Brome, then it may be that at some point a Chester writer had access to a "Brome-type" play. Why would such a version be unacceptable and require revision? In Brome, the play concerns only the sacrifice of Isaac. The bond of affection between Abraham and Isaac is stressed at the opening, in addition to the obedience of Isaac to his father and of Abraham to God. God's command to sacrifice Isaac is explained to the audience as a test of Abraham and an example to all men. When, at the end of the sacrifice, Abraham is halted by the angel, we see the release of Isaac and his naturalistic responses of delight and suspicion, followed by the exemplary exposition of the action. The Chester play, on the other hand, contains three episodes from Abraham's life—his offering to Melchizedek, his receipt of God's covenant with its associated obligation to circumcise Isaac, and the sacrifice of Isaac. After each, an Expositor offers an explanation that is at once historical in organization and figural in import—tithes and the Eucharist replace (are figured by) the offerings of Abraham and Melchizedek; baptism replaces (is figured by) circumcision; and the sacrifice of Christ the Son by God the Father is figured by (replaces) the sacrifice by Abraham of his son Isaac. The result is a play that is thematically structured, looking toward the Old Testament prefigurations of two major sacraments (the only sacraments under the Thirty-nine Articles of the Church of England) and the historical event that confirmed the transition from one "sacramental form" to the other. The unifying figure here is Abraham; the natural affection between him and his son is not developed in advance of the scene, and the play ends, not with the release of Isaac and the return of naturalism, but with the Expositor speaking against a tableau of Abraham sacrificing the lamb at the altar where Isaac apparently is still bound, the same altar used perhaps previously by Melchizedek. The Chester episode therefore serves a different function from the one dramatized in Brome.

2. Chester 11/207–Finis and similar versions in Wakefield 18 (incomplete), York 18, Coventry Weavers' Pageant 722–1192

The relationship between these plays and episodes was discussed by W. W. Greg in "Bibliographical and Textual Problems of the English Miracle Cycles. III. Christ and the Doctors: Inter-relation of the Cycles." Greg also published an edition of the episode, setting the York version, collated with Wakefield and Coventry, beside the Chester version with full manuscript variants, in "'Christ and the Doctors' and the York Play," in *The Trial and Flagellation with Other Studies in the Chester Cycle* (London, 1935).

Greg argued that the extant York text best preserves the original form of the play. Since the exact pattern of textual transmission is of only incidental relevance to the present discussion, Greg's proposals may be briefly summarized. They are:

1. The York text derives from an earlier source (perhaps a guild text), from which was also made a defective copy underlying both the Wakefield and Coventry versions;
2. The defective version directly underlies Wakefield, but was rewritten and worked over again in at least one further version which is the immediate source of Coventry;
3. The immediate source of Coventry also underlies the Chester version.

Again, there is no suggestion of direct influence by one extant text upon another. Greg himself speculates baselessly upon the possible course of transmission:

> It might not be unreasonable to suggest that *K* [the Coventry intermediary] may have been the Beverley play. Indeed, it seems not unlikely that the manuscript reached Chester first and was passed on to Coventry after it had served the purpose of the Chester playwright. That a writer at Chester should draw material from Yorkshire need not surprise us, nor need it that a Coventry writer should seek it at Chester, the headquarters of the diocese, while on the other hand a plausible connexion between Coventry and Yorkshire would be far harder to establish.   ["Problems," 317–18]

Although the paucity of extant material prevents definitive statements and encourages such speculation, it may be noted that some link between Chester and Coventry may also be suggested by other evidence (see [3] below).

The York manuscript belongs to the second half of the fifteenth century. The Wakefield manuscript may be "not earlier than the 1480s" (A. C. Cawley and Martin Stevens, *The Towneley Cycle* [Leeds, 1976], vii). Coventry's Weavers' Pageant is preserved in the manuscript written by Robert Croo in 1534. The York version underlying the extant text was therefore available before 1430–40, but could, of course, have influenced the other cycles at any time between then and the date of the extant texts.

Like Coventry, but unlike Wakefield and York, Chester treats the episode immediately after the episode of the Purification, thereby reutilizing the "temple-set" for an episode that took place twelve years later in the life of Christ. In Coventry, a dialogue of Joseph and Mary makes the change in time and occasion clear, but the Chester text lacks this clarification and shows marked signs of textual corruption in this "bridge passage," 11/206+SH–26. Other signs of textual corruption in the Chester version suggest an "edited" form of the play, while the awkwardly contrived link may have significance for the composition of the play, suggesting that the "Doctors" episode was not part of the original conception of Play 11, or at least not in the present form of the episode. Although the twelve-line stanzas of York have been easily changed to the eight-line stanzas of the Chester version, the rhyme-scheme and metrical structure are distinct from those of the Chester stanza in the "Purification" episode, and the transition would be apparent to the audience in form as well as structure.

Rosemary Woolf (*English Mystery Plays*, 212–13) has pointed out that the communal version of the play has little dramatic merit to explain its currency. In Chester, however, the play serves to mark the boyhood of Christ, from the Purification to His twelfth year, and to indicate a relationship to the Church. In the "Purification" Joseph and Mary carefully observe the customs of the Church in their offering but extend them by Joseph's offering of the candle, anticipating the service of Candlemas. Simeon, in the "book-miracle," is taught to trust the authority of the biblical prophecy, and he sees the prophecy fulfilled. In the "Doctors" episode, Jesus listens to the doctors and proves Himself versed in the law of Moses. At the same time, He extends that law by proclaiming Himself to be at one with the Godhead (231–38, 251–54), and in so doing divides the doctors but finally convinces them (255–70, 299–302). Christ's relationship with the leaders of the Church and the extent of His orthodoxy become recurring themes in the remainder of the cycle. See also J. J. McGavin, "Sign and Transition: The *Purification* Play in Chester."

The use of the Decalogue in the play recalls the previous recital in Play 5. Wakefield also has a previous recital, 7/31–90. In Chester, however, the recapitulation affirms Christ's conformity to an already established law, provides a structural link, and also rehearses the Decalogue afresh for the potentially new audience, since Play 5 took place on the first day of a three-day production and Play 11 on the second.

3. Chester 9/240–7 and Coventry Shearmen 750–53, 764–67

The correspondence between the Chester stanza and the lines from the Coventry Shearmen and Taylors' Pageant, preserved in the 1825 edition by Thomas Sharp, is clearly demonstrated by juxtaposing the two passages:

Chester Farewell, syr Jasper, brother, to you,
     Kinge of Tharsis most worthye.
     Farewell, syr Balthasar; to you I bowe.
     I thanke you of your companye.
     Hee that made us to meete on playne
     and offered to Marye in her jesayne,

send us saffe and sound agayne
to the land we came froo.

Coventry   Now farewell, Sir Jaspar, brothur, to yoeu,
Kyng of Tawrus the most worthe;
Sir Balthasar, also to you I bow;
And I thanke you bothe of youre good cumpanye

. . . .

Now he thatt made vs to mete on playne
And offur to Mare in hir jeseyne,
He geve vs grace in heyvin a-gayne
All to-geyder to mete!

Only H among the Chester manuscripts corrects the Exemplar error of *offered* for *offer*, an error resulting from the mistaken parallel of the verb with the past tense *made* rather than the infinitive *meete*.

One can only assume that the stanza has been substituted for a regular Chester stanza, perhaps because the manuscript underlying the cyclic Exemplar was obscure or damaged at this point. But this stanza would suggest that some version resembling the Coventry stanza was available to the scribe. The correspondence has added interest in view of the possible textual link between Chester and Coventry discussed under (2) above.

These three instances of correspondence between Chester and other English plays suggest that Chester may have owed a debt to the tradition of Corpus Christi plays in England that can no longer be established because of the loss of texts. But they also indicate that Chester could, as with Brome, change the significance and effect of what it borrowed. They also suggest that Chester may have altered the received texts by excisions and insertions, so that the scribe of the cyclic Exemplar had difficulty in understanding what was intended. Each case raises problems of continuity and consistency that attest textual corruption. It is, of course, possible that the corruptions were present in the received text, but in (2) and (3), and probably also in (1), there are grounds for believing that the Chester redactor had to change the received texts to produce an eight-line stanza-form, and it seems plausible to suggest that other changes, including corruptions, may have been introduced at the same time.

A *Stanzaic Life of Christ* and *Legenda Aurea*

In her edition of *A Stanzaic Life of Christ* (London, 1926), Frances A. Foster proposed influence from the *Life* on Chester Plays 6, 8, 9, 11, 12, 18, 21, and possible influence on Plays 4, 5, 10, 14. These views were refined by Robert H. Wilson in "The *Stanzaic Life of Christ* and the Chester Plays," where he considers influence on Plays 6, 8, 9, 11, 12, and 20 under three categories:

1. Random, scattered, short parallels to the *Life*, suggesting revision of an older play with remembered passages from the *Life*: 6/1–440, and 657–712, 8/113–260 and 338–413, 9/125–264, 11/121–208, 12/1–160, 20/1–4, 57–104, 153–92.
2. Extended and systematic parallels to the *Life* suggesting work directly from a text, where scenes are dramatized from the *Life*: 6/441–576, 8/1–112, 9/1–124, 11/1–120, 20/5–57, 105–52.
3. Extended and systematic parallels to the *Life* suggesting work directly from a text, where material is put into the mouth of Expositor: 6/577–656 and 713–36, 12/161–208.

To Frances Foster's examples of possible influence, Wilson also adds ID/40–*Finis (Life* 7581–612) and 24/385–436 (*Life* 9021–40).

Stanzaic Life survives in three manuscripts, all of the fifteenth century; the earliest is mid-fifteenth century. The date of composition is unknown. Foster misleadingly claims that it must have been composed in the fourteenth century because "it was known to the Chester playwright" (xiv), but this dating is based upon untenable assumptions about the date of the cycle. We can say only that the work was available from the middle of the fifteenth century at the latest. Foster affirms that the work is a compilation made in Chester from Ranulf Higden's *Polychronicon* and the *Legenda Aurea*. It would therefore have strong local associations and incorporate work by the most famous monk of Chester Abbey whose reputed association with the composition of the cycle is discussed in chapter 4, "Development of the Cycle."

Initially, the most difficult problem in evaluating the influence of *Stanzaic Life* lies in distinguishing "immediate" from "ultimate" sources. The problem is complicated by the textual history of the two works that serve as source for the *Life*. Foster points out that the version of the *Polychronicon* used was not that of the Rolls Series text but a Latin version containing a more expanded life of Christ. The *Legenda Aurea* of Jacobus da Voragine also existed in a variety of forms and translations. From some version of the *Legenda* the author of the *Life* took sections relating to the life of Christ and added a number of other sections; "the result is a nearly complete *Temporale*, which, however, lacks an Advent" (p. xxii). This was standard material, familiar and readily available. Since the establishment of the *Life* as an immediate source for parts of the cycle depends upon the details and/or phraseology shared by the *Life* and the cycle against those current in the sources of the *Life*, modern definitive editions of Latin and vernacular versions of both sources are urgently required.

In many cases, the closeness of the *Life* and *Legenda Aurea* in the Graesse edition (3d ed., 1890) makes derivation from either equally possible, while in other places the cycle seems to oscillate between the two. A case in point is Play 17, the Harrowing of Hell. The play seems not to draw all its material directly from the ultimate source in the Acts of Pilate, but from an abridgment of the account that can be compared with that in *Legenda Aurea*, followed by *Stanzaic Life*. In some respects it resembles the *Life* more closely than *Legenda Aurea*. Yet on other occasions the play seems closer to the apocryphal gospel than to *Legenda* or *Life*. We would find it difficult to establish a source on the evidence of extant texts.

In other instances, there is some evidence to show that what were once felt to be unique features in the *Life* may have been part of a wider tradition. In her note to *Tebel* 454, Foster notes that the only other English instances of this name for the second midwife are in *Geburt Jesu* (*South English Nativity*) and Chester Play 6. But *Tebel* is the form in *six* manuscripts of the *South English Nativity*, and since that work draws upon *Legenda Aurea* it is possible that a group of manuscripts of the *Legenda* transmitted the form. Similarly, the confusion in the number of birds offered by Mary in the temple has been held to show Chester's dependence upon the similarly confused *Stanzaic Life*, but if the confusion is not the effect of scribal error, it would have counterpart in the confusions in later medieval art. Such details in no way invalidate the arguments for the influence of *Stanzaic Life*, but they do indicate how much remains to be revealed about the evolution and currency of material seemingly unique to the *Life* and Chester.

A final problem of evaluation lies in the very different functions of the two works. Insofar as it may draw upon the *Life* Chester would still have to select appropriate material and would have to present that material in the form of speeches within the structure of play and cycle. Probably the playwright would have to invent and/or supplement from other sources. There seems for example a strong possibility that the playwright was familiar with the Octavian episode in *Stanzaic Life*, but there are details that may also suggest familiarity with a version closer to the source of the legend, in *Mirabilia Urbis Romae*. One may perhaps compare:

all this world has bine yore
tributarye unto Rome   [6/207–8]

Octouian þe emperour
hade made þe world suget to Rome   [*Life* 593–94]

totum mundum sibi tributarium fecerat   [*Mirabilia*]

Syth I was soverayne, warre cleare can cease,
And through this world now is peace   [6/237–38]

Of alle kyndoms conquerour   [*Life* 597]

tante prosperitatis et pacis   [*Mirabilia*]

PRIMUS / SECUNDUS SENATOUR   [6/296+SH, 304+SH]

þai thoȝt   [*Life* 599, reference unspecified]

senatores . . . dicunt   [*Mirabilia*]

We would suggest a more direct reliance upon the *Mirabilia* than upon the *Life*. Significantly, critics have also seen in this section evidence of influence from the *Mystère du Viel Testament*, similarly dependent upon the *Mirabilia* legend. Yet Wilson draws attention appropriately to Octavian's denial of deity as one point of direct dependence of the cycle upon the *Life*:

syth I must dye I wotte not what day   [6/319]

And thoȝt wel that he was dedly   [*Life* 602]

(cf. se mortalem intelligens—*Legenda Aurea*)

It is probable that the Chester speech by Octavian is either itself eclectic from a number of works, or based upon a comparably eclectic account of the legend. Although the latter is more in accord with the usual medieval practice, allowance must be made for the particular difficulties confronting a playwright who wished to create an authenticated but dramatically effective figure, realized through the spoken word. Here also the concern throughout Chester with an authority underlying the text perhaps suggests that unusual care may have been taken to adhere to accepted accounts and to minimize individual invention.

If this were the case, then the *Stanzaic Life* served to supplement or supersede *Legenda Aurea* at a number of points without removing its influence entirely. Such a theory does not also remove the possibility of influence from other versions of the *Legenda* material. Ruth M. Keane has compared the different accounts of the *Ara Caeli* legend, indicating the range of sources for individual details, including *Stanzaic Life*, and suggesting that even where critics have agreed on influence from the *Life*, the playwright may have been familiar with other versions and incorporated them. Similar possibilities exist for the miracles at the Nativity at 6/564–643. Unlike the adaptations of existing plays discussed above, the playwright seems to have treated the *Life* with critical intelligence and an awareness of the need to integrate it and the material from *Legenda Aurea* into a unified play.

The Evocation of Authority

Up to this point this chapter has been concerned with reviewing the major sources proposed by critics for the Chester cycle. It is not remarkable that none of the proposed sources is acknowledged in the cycle. What is remarkable, however, is that the cycle is proclaimed by its Late Banns to have been written by Ranulf Higden, a famous and respected monk of Chester, for the express purpose of bringing the Scriptures to the people in English at a time when only the Vulgate was permitted. And where the cycle material is not biblical, the Late Banns defend it—in such matters as the Fall of the Angels or the Harrowing of Hell, as being supported by accepted authorities; or else, as with the midwives of the Nativity, as mere comic relief.

The concern that the text can be defended for its biblical fidelity and general doctrinal soundness is carried over into the cycle itself. It seems significant that the cycle should end with the speeches of the four evangelists assuring the audience that the truth of the events that they have just seen performed is attested by their writings. Whatever the form in which the playwright received his material, the Bible is finally evoked as the explicit source of the cycle. Moreover, the Bible is quoted in Latin on a large number of occasions in the cycle:

1/1–2	Apocalypse 22/13
2/*Before* 1	id
5/131	Deuteronomy 32/37–38
5/319	Numbers 24/17–18
5/435	Psalms 105/30–31 (AV 106)
6/64	Luke 1/46
6/72	Luke 1/47
7/357	Luke 2/14
8/212	Matthew 2/2
8/268	Genesis 49/10
8/310	Matthew 2/6
8/317	Isaiah 60/3
8/324	Jeremiah 6/11, 9/20–21
8/338	Psalms 71/10 (AV 72)
10/288	Isaiah 19/1
10/497	Hoseah 11/1; Matthew 2/15
11/24	Isaiah 7/14
11/166	Luke 2/29
13/*Before* 1	John 8/12
13/8	John 10/30
13/21	John 10/11
13/35	John 8/31–32
13/356	John 9/4–5
14/208	Mark 11/9–10
16A/345–46	Mark 15/34
16A/359	John 19/30
17/32	Isaiah 9/2
17/48	Luke 2/29
17/64	Matthew 3/2
17/72	John 1/29
17/152	Psalms 23/7, 9 (AV 24)
17/192	Psalms 106/15–16 (AV 107)
19/95	Isaiah 66/13

20/*Before* 1	Luke 24/36
20/16	Luke 24/39
20/104 a–g	John 20/17; Isaiah 63/1–3
20/152	Psalms 20/14 (AV 21/13)
	Acts 1/11
21/32	Acts 1/20; Psalms 68/26 (AV 69/25), 108/8
	(AV 109/8)
21/96	Acts 1/5
21/104	Acts 1/7
21/112	Acts 1/8
21/238	John 20/23
22/*Before* 1	Ezechiel 37/1–2
22/48	Zechariah 6/1
22/124	Daniel 7/2–3
22/172	Apocalypse 11/3
23/24	Ezechiel 36/24
23/40	Psalms 5/8
23/56	Daniel 11/39
23/120	Sophonia 3/8
23/196	Ezechiel 36/26
23/722	Psalms 32/1 (AV 33)
24/*Before* 1	Apocalypse 22/13
24/508	Psalms 31/11 (AV 32)
24/540	John 3/18
24/564	Matthew 16/27
24/580	Matthew 13/49–50
IB/288	Numbers 24/17
IB/312	Ezechiel 44/1–2
IB/328	Jeremiah 14/17
IB/344	Jonah 2/3–4
IB/360	Psalms 18/7 (AV 19/6)
IB/376	Joel 2/28
IB/392	Matthew 2/6

These may be supplemented by occasional instances in which the quotation is not readily identifiable with a biblical text, as in 8/289.

We cannot demonstrate that all these texts were cited orally in performance. Indeed, many of them appear to be scribal incorporations into the Exemplar of MDs, since there is no indication in the stanzaic text that the Latin is to be uttered; examples are 2/*Before* 1, 5/131, 8/212, 268, 310, 317, 324, 338, 11/24, 13/*Before* 1, 35, 356, 17/64, 192, 19/95, 20/16, 21/96, 104, 112, 22/*Before* 1, 48, 124, 172, 23/24, 40, 56, 24/*Before* 1, 540, IB/288, 312, 328, 344, 360, 376, 392. Often the evidence for oral recital is contained in the preamble of a SD, usually indicating that the text is to be sung and is hence liturgical in connotation rather than biblical; examples are 5/319, 6/64, 7/357, 10/288, 11/166, 14/208, 17/152, 20/*Before* 1, 152, 21/238, 23/24, 40, 196, 722, 24/508. The exchange during Christ's ascension, 20/104 a–g, was sung. But on occasion the biblical text forms part of the stanza-structure, as at 1/1–2, 13/8 and 21, 16A/345–46; and sometimes there is an indication by a speaker that he is about to cite a text, as at 10/497, 17/32, 48, 72, 21/32, 23/120, 24/561–64, 579–80. These last instances are interesting because they often suggest a self-conscious learnedness, as Antichrist's:

> And as the prophett Sophonye
> speakes of mee full wytterlye
> I shall rehearse here readelye
> that clarkes shall understand   [23/116–20]

or the Devil's:

> And, lest thou forgett, good man,
> I shall mynne thee upon,
> for to speake Latten well I can,
> and that thou shall soone see   [24/561–64]

The audience, anyway, would not have been left to translate the text, for in all cases the vernacular text conveys the reference and meaning. Such examples merely indicate that the author(s) remained faithful to the biblical text and conscious of its controlling force; further, the author(s) wished the audience to be aware of that control also.

It is notable that in many instances the text includes the reference to the location of the quoted passage in the Bible. This is found occasionally even where the text is clearly to be declaimed, as at 23/24, 120. And indeed Chester tends to allude to prophets and to events with a sense of the wider context from which the few events have been selected. Understandably, prophecies are cited in anticipation of the events that they foretell, or retrospectively on their fulfillment, as in 5/319+SD–27, 8/1–40, 221–24, 233–349, 9/140–43, 11/21–36, 117–18, 13/4–7, 17/25–

88, 19/80–95, 204–13, 20/45–52, 22/1–260, 23/17–24+Latin, 40+Latin–44, 207–10, IB/249–56, 288+Latin–432. But this functional use of prophecy, found to a remarkable degree in Chester, is allied to an awareness of other prophecies and prophets not included. When the Expositor in IB/409–10 states:

> Moe prophetes, lordinges, we might play,
> but yt wold tary much the daye

this is clearly not an empty statement. Herod, in Play 8, reels off lists of prophets on two occasions (8/234–35, 261–68) and can accurately characterize those cited as he contemptuously dismisses them (8/284, 304, 354). Herod, a man of Jewish faith, though not of Jewish birth (8/276–82—another prophecy fulfilled) can justify his intention to kill Jesus by referring to the example of Athalia (8/333); the Magi allude to prophets (9/141–42, 156–58); and Christ names them (13/5, 19/80–95). It is difficult to know what such allusions conveyed to an audience beyond the sense of authority, although the use of prophecy and example by Herod (8/333) and Antichrist (23/18), for example, carries an irony if the wider context of the allusion is recognized.

But the biblical text alone can be confusing and lead to misunderstanding. Inspiration, faith, and intelligence are required to bring out the required meaning, as Simeon discovers in the "book miracle" of 11/1–103, where his disbelief of Isaiah's words is corrected. The Old Testament prophecies establish criteria for the assessment of the Messiah as the Decalogue establishes rules for the virtuous life that must also be met. Hence Jesus must conform to the Old Law while fulfilling His Messianic purpose in establishing a New. Play 12 seems to link two unrelated episodes, but both the "Temptation" and "The Woman Taken in Adultery" constitute debates about the criteria laid down in the Old Testament that Jesus should fulfil. The debate about His claims continues in later plays (cf. 13/201–54, 14/241–60, 16/1–53, etc.), until the cycle encompasses a debate on the meanings of words and their relationship to deeds. Finally, even Jesus is bound by His own words to condemn the sinful or deny His deity (24/549–72); the mercy shown to the sinner in life by his fellow sinners (Play 12) cannot be extended at Doomsday (24/605–20).

Christ may appropriately act as His own interpreter of the Bible, but Chester also emphasizes on occasion that the cycle is interpreting the text on good authority. Thus the Expositor justifies his account of the midwives from the apocryphal gospels of James and Pseudo-Matthew by alluding to *freere Bartholemewe* (6/565), although the ascription is taken directly from *Legenda Aurea* and *Stanzaic Life*. *Gregorye* is the authority for the interpretation of the Temptation (12/170), and *Augustine . . . in his homely upon St. Johns Evangelye* (12/285–87) for the interpretation of the "Woman Taken in Adultery"; in both cases, the interpretations accord with the claimed sources. The traditional ascription of the fifteen signs of Judgment is to *saynt Jerome* (22/263), although no such account is known; Chester probably takes the ascription over from its source, the *Legenda Aurea*. It is very unlikely that such references are intended to do more than evoke an aura of authority to the audience. But at the same time, two passages carry the justification of details from accepted authorities further, perhaps for the benefit of a censor. At 22/260+Latin the allusion to Jerome is qualified in more scholarly fashion:

> Signa quindecim magna quae, secundum opiniones doctorum, extremum precedunt judicium, ab antiquis Hebroeorum codicibus selecta a doctore huius paginae reticenda.

The implication seems to be that Jerome selected the details from ancient works in Hebrew, and other learned men have accepted them as signs of Judgment to come. And at 24/356+SD, the staging of Christ's descent is specified to conform to an accepted learned opinion:

> [Descendet] Jesus quasi in nube, si fieri poterit, quia, secundum doctoris opiniones, in aere prope terram judicabit Filius Dei.

Despite the fact that Chester relies upon standard compendia as immediate sources of authoritative interpretation, the material in those compendia, deriving usually from commentaries on the Bible by the Church Fathers, suggests a symbolic interpretation that gives the material in the cycle an importance beyond its literal reference. Thus, Play 1 associates the creation of the angels with the creation of light and the separation of the bad from good angels with the separation of darkness from light on the first day, an interpretation to be paralleled from Augustine. Play 7 connects literal and spiritual pastoralism through the change in the shepherds' vocation, an interpretation found in Bede. *Legenda Aurea* and *Stanzaic Life* provide possible immediate sources for the interpretation of the Magi's gifts in Play 9, but the interpretation has earlier precedent. Such commentaries thus provide the basis for a reconception of cyclic material in a manner unparalleled in the other extant English cycles.

Moreover, such large-scale reconceptions of material, whose authoritative basis is unacknowledged, are paralleled by the numerous symbolic interpretations of specific prophecies—for Chester rarely cites a prophecy without interpretation. Such passages attest a determination to provide a continuing, authoritative, and widely acceptable interpretation of dramatized events in order to demonstrate that God acts purposively. In so doing, they also impart a purposive movement to the cycle as a whole.

The concern with authority, explicit and implicit, affects the overall structure of the cycle and its dramatic devices. Three features may here be briefly noted. The first is the recurring concern with the nature and definition of Godhead, originating in the opening speech of God (1/1–35), which, like similar speeches at the beginning of other English cycles, looks to the normal arrangement and—to some extent—content of theological treatises. In Chester, this definition is recalled in various aspects throughout the cycle—one may instance particularly Octavian's distinction of Man and God at 6/313–36, Jesus' account of His nature and mission at 13/1–35, Antichrist's debate on the Trinity at 23/482–520. But the opening idea of the timeless God in whose essence lies the origin of all things underlies the general thesis of the cycle and its interpretations of material, which is that events and texts are forms that, properly understood, will lead to the recognition of the Godhead of Play 1.

The sense of God as the author of all and hence the ultimate "authority" has its counterpart in the "God-surrogate," the Expositor of Plays 4, 5, 6, 12, and 22, who may, as in Plays 6, 12, and 22, acknowledge the source of his interpretation, but who anyway speaks with the force of authority as one with the special knowledge and privilege to interpret events for the people. This second feature of the cycle can be overstressed. The Expositor does not fulfil a function different from that of, say, the Magi in Play 9. But he differs in standing outside the action, in being a self-proclaimed observer and commentator in the manner of the theologians to whom he refers. To this extent he is God-like but also Christ-like, for in the central plays of the Ministry-Ascension, Christ serves also as interpreter and authority.

But there is also an implicit authority in the playwright himself. We have already noted his debt to earlier commentators in the treatment of certain episodes. It may, however, be added that the multi-episode structures of many Chester plays involve a significant relationship between the parts of each play and that the overall structure of the cycle is also suggestive of such links. Since thematic patterns are properly the concern of literary critics, we would not wish to develop this thesis at length here. But we have already drawn attention to the significant association of episodes in Plays 4, 11, and 12. We might add, as an indication of the kind of exemplification possible, the combination of the Fall of Man and Cain and Abel in Play 2, allowing the playwright to propose a causative link between the two (2/689–96); and the link of the Decalogue and Balaam and Balak in Play 5, allowing a telling contrast (Group) or association (H) of the two recipients of God's word, the obedient Moses and the disobedient Balaam. The selection and disposition of material here leads directly to a particular thematic bias. A prior interpretation underlies the plays.

It will be clear that many of the examples cited are those for which immediate sources have been proposed, as discussed above. The effect of this discussion is not to deny the validity of those proposals. It serves instead to draw attention to function rather than origin and to emphasize the importance to the playwright of an authoritative basis for his material and also of an aura of authority in the cycle. That there is a deliberate and thematic selection of material is unquestionable. One may instance on a large scale the choice of sources for extended plays such as 6, 15, 16, 16A, and 18, where the various gospel accounts are capable of different harmonization. Or one may point to the repeated concern with images of kingship, culminating in the political bias given to the accusations against Christ in Plays 14–16.

To the audience's consciousness that their cycle was based upon biblical and theological authorities may have been added the awareness that behind the cycle also lay the authority of the Church. The spectators may not have recognized a compatibility between parts of the cycle and a work, the *Life*, composed in Chester and based partly upon the *Polychronicon* of the Chester monk Higden. But the Late Banns ascribed authorship of the cycle to Higden, and the first station on each day was outside the Abbey Gates before the clergy. The sense that the material within the cycle had the authority of the Church behind it must have been further reinforced by the use of liturgical music, sung by cathedral choristers, in the cycle. From time to time the cycle expressly directs attention toward aspects of the Christian life—to the offerings made to win God's love (2/473–74), to tithes (4/133–36) and alms-giving (24/135 et passim); to the Eucharist, its replacement of the Jewish sacrifice (4/121–28), its establishment (15/65–104), and the state in which it should be received to be efficacious (18/154–85); to the sacrament of baptism replacing circumcision (4/193–208); to the institution and continuing importance of the Decalogue (5/41–64); to Purgatory (Play 24); to Candlemas (11/143–50). And in Play 21 there is an account of Pentecost that has particular relevance because the performance was in Whit-week. There, in the legendary account of the origins of the Apostles' Creed, the audience would hear an exposition of the central tenets of their belief, most of which can be seen also as allusions to the events dramatized in the cycle.

As with references to the Bible and to authorities, however, the cycle contains allusions to specifics of Christian belief that suggest a consciousness on the part of the author of the minutiae of theological discussion. The concern with the Trinity in the definitions of God mentioned above find some point in the proximity of the performance to Trinity Sunday. Lucifer vows initial allegiance to God—created of God, he is initially good and only later becomes evil (1/94–101), so that God is not responsible for the creation of evil. The reward of the redeemed is the Beatific Vision (1/116–19). Adam and Eve figure the institution of marriage (2/157–60). There may be allusions to the Sacred Heart of Jesus (16A/370) and to the crucifix (IC/101–8). The words of the angel to Mary are those of the Angelic Salutation, not the biblical text (6/1–4). Further examples could be cited.

It is difficult to know how far the Chester cycle is additionally indebted to traditions of the liturgical plays and hence to drama deriving from the liturgy. In common with other cycles, it includes the dialogue of the Angel and Maries at the Tomb based on the *Quem Quaeritis* (18/345–60), the laments of the Maries at the Cross (16A/241–88) and on the way to the Tomb (18/309–32), and the awkward transition from the enlightened to the mourning Mary Magdalen in Play 18. The possible origins of these features are, however, diverse and we would not wish to argue for direct liturgical influence in the cycle in such matters.

It is, however, against this background of authority that the legendary, apocryphal, and historical material in the cycle should be assessed. And it is here that Utesch's discussions of sources may be reconsidered. It is true that many of the works he cites cannot be regarded as "sources" in an immediate sense. But it does seem to be true that the Chester playwright sought to develop his themes by drawing upon authoritative works to extend the material in his immediate *authorities*. He did not need to know Josephus directly to include many of the details of Cain and Abel, or particularly of Herod, which form part of the cycle. But it is true that he seeks motivation for action not in innate evil but in misplaced pride—in the succession by age for Cain (2/529–30, 589–90, 597–604) and in the Zionism of Herod, whose concern with scriptural precedent, desire to dominate the priesthood, national aspirations, and ruthlessness all accord with the picture emerging from Josephus. For Joseph, he draws on material deriving ultimately from the *History of Joseph the Carpenter* concerning age, previous marriage, etc. For Octavian, it is material from, ultimately, the *Mirabilia Romae* to realize him as a rational pagan and an exemplary figure, convinced by experience and reason while Herod, with the evidence of Scriptures, resists the truth. The playwright(s) was/were evidently familiar with both traditions of Balaam—the evil Balaam underlying the Group and supported from the biblical account, but also the elect Balaam underlying H and supported by some Jewish traditions. Octavian may similarly represent a shift from the ranting tyrant (apparently envisaged in the Late Banns and realized in Wakefield) to the more favorable picture of the *Mirabilia*. Pilate in Play 18 at times seems to resemble the evil and conniving tyrant of Wakefield, but care seems to have been taken in the Passion Plays, 16–16A, to present him as a figure of reason to stand against the prejudice of the High Priests who cannot reconcile Christ's coming with the revelation of Scripture. Here the weighting leads to an interesting harmonizing of the gospel accounts as Pilate duplicates offers of Barabbas or leads Jesus away for private dialogue. The dialogue between Pilate and Jesus (16/251–90) allows the playwright(s) to define the distinction between Roman and Jew and between earthly and spiritual kingship, present in the biblical account; but he/they also allow(s) Pilate to receive Jesus' definition of truth, drawing on the *Acts of Pilate* rather than the biblical account. The movements away from biblical authorities enable the dramatist(s) to create a fuller picture of the figures and their motives and also to introduce more exemplary material. It is to this end that he/they draw(s) upon the apocryphal gospels for the midwife episode—the first healing miracle of Christ—and on the legendaries for the Longinus episode—the last healing miracle.

In so doing, the playwright(s) give(s) the cycle an overall shape, strengthening parallels. The opening speech of God defining Godhead prefaces the historical action, preceding Creation; it is complemented by the final speeches of the evangelists, affirming that the opening purpose is now revealed in their writings, following the Judgment. In H, the prophets of Christ precede His coming as the prophets of Antichrist precede his. Antichrist is the most extensive legendary section of the cycle, the longest play, and serves as a reminder of and counterbalance to the life of Christ. The wonders attendant on the birth of Christ, from legendary sources via *Stanzaic Life*, balance the biblical wonders attendant upon His death. Herod, the tyrant, based partly upon the Bible, partly upon historical accounts, balances the legendary Octavian as the biblical priests balance the "historical" Pilate, both being part of a continuing concern with kingship.

It is unnecessary to labor this pattern of links and parallels here since the point is not to trace the structure and theme of Chester but to indicate the importance of legendary, historical, and apocryphal material to the playwright in creating a balanced structure. But it should be noted that such parallels and the overall concern with authority and meaning exist in a cycle that was performed in three days. The same audience would not necessarily be present on each day, nor would it necessarily carry clearly in its mind the events of one day into the next. But the Chester cycle is, in a sense, its own authority. The acceptance of one detail may well lead to the acceptance of a later one. Events look backward or forward to other events in the cycle. There is no need here to give a complete list of such cross-references, but it may be helpful to note just those that refer to events of previous or following days:

1. Adam's ecstasy (2/441–72, day 1) - the Incarnation and the New Law (compare 2/455 and 15/73) and Redemption (Plays 15–17, days 2–3), and Doomsday (Play 24, day 3).

2. Play 4, Abraham and Melchizedek (122–24) - the Last Supper (Play 15, day 2); Abraham and Isaac (468–75) - the Passion and Resurrection (Plays 16–18, days 2–3).

3. Play 5, the Decalogue (1–24) - repeated by the boy Jesus (11/271–98, day 2). The Group version also indicates that Balaam's prophecy (444–47) is fulfilled on the following day in that arrangement by the Magi (8/1–48).

4. By the Group arrangement, Play 6 is the first play of day 2. Octavian's definition of Godhead (329–36) - God's definitions (1/5–6, 2/1–4, day 1) and also 24/1–2 (day 3).

5. Play 12 (day 2), the Temptation (169–216) - the Fall of Man (Play 2, day 1).

6. Play 15, Christ's promise of the Holy Spirit (241–48) - Pentecost

(Play 21, day 3); the Resurrection and post-Resurrection appearances (249–56) - Resurrection, Emmaus, and other appearances (Plays 18–20, day 3).

7. Play 17, the words of Adam (9–16) - the Fall of Man (Play 2, day 1); Enoch and Elias (245–52) - Antichrist (Play 23, day 3).

8. Play 19 (day 3) - the Nativity (256–57 - Play 6, day 1); the Crucifixion (258–59 - Play 16A, day 2).

9. Play 21, the Creed, which alludes to events already dramatized in the Creation (311–14 - Plays 1–2, day 1), the Nativity (319–22 - Play 6, day 1/2), the Crucifixion (323–26 - Play 16–16A, day 2), the Harrowing of Hell (327–30 - Play 17, day 2).

10. Play 22, the Vision of St. John - the occasion (173–76) the Last Supper (15/80+SD, day 2).

11. Play 23, Antichrist's parody of Christ's miracles - raising the dead (89–92, 97–112) - the raising of Lazarus (13/301–*Finis*, day 2); death and resurrection (121–68) - the Passion (Plays 16–16A, day 2). The debate on the nature of the Trinity (482–520) takes up aspects of the definitions in 1/1–35 (day 1) and 6/329–36 (day 1/2 - see 4 above).

In considering the sources of Chester, therefore, we feel that due credit should be given to the playwright for integrating material from various sources into a coherent whole. We note the fact that this tight structure exists in a cycle whose production was somewhat disjointed, being spread across a three-day period and with each episode being staged on a wagon so that there was a sharp division between sections (cf. 4/1–8, 484–91). Perhaps in these circumstances there was added impulse to create a textual coherence that would give some unity to the total production while allowing visitors for one day the opportunity of understanding the place of what they witnessed in the pattern of the whole. But we also note that Chester, in its Banns and cycle-text, is concerned to stress its reliance on authorities, and it may be that there was a conscious attempt also to insure that anything in the cycle could be justified as orthodox and acceptable if necessary. Possibly the series of texts in the margins of H indicates just such an attempt at justification by Miller and his fellow-scribes.

3.

MUSIC IN
THE CYCLE

Introduction

ANY STUDY OF THE MUSIC in a mystery cycle must be based on
secondary material, for the actual musical remains are negligible. There
is a fragmentary Gloria in one of the Chester manuscripts, six settings of
Latin texts in the York cycle, and the two famous "carols" in the true
Coventry plays, but not a note of music survives in the N-Town and
Towneley cycles, nor in the various plays that seem to belong to cycles
now lost. If the musical remains are small, however, there is plenty of
evidence to show that music made a significant contribution in performance of the plays, for the cycles contain SDs for music and a number of
musical references in the text. The Chester and N-Town cycles are com-
paratively rich in this sort of evidence, and the Chester plays have in the
past attracted much more attention than the other cycles when musical
use has been discussed. Indeed, Chester is the only one of the English
cycles to be the subject of a separate musical study.[1]

Because of this paucity of notated remains, the study of music in the
cycles has been undertaken by specialists in literature and drama rather
than by musicians. Much of the early work, indeed, underestimated the
role of music in the play-cycles and treated the music as essentially emotive, underlining the dramatic effect of the play at certain points in the

---

1. Carpenter, "Chester Plays."

drama.[2] The first study to take the role of music seriously was Carpenter's work on the Towneley *Secunda Pastorum* (1951), a work that seemed to open up several exciting possibilities for future research. It was a long time before the leads were followed up, however, and Carpenter's own later work was disappointing.

Perhaps the most obvious disappointment in the work of the 1950s and earlier was its failure to provide an acceptable rationale for the use of music in the plays. This was eventually supplied by John Stevens in a classic paper to the Royal Musical Association (1958), in which he was able to show that the plays used music largely symbolically to represent certain types of character in the drama. Of all the scholars to study the role of music in the plays, Stevens alone has combined literary scholarship with knowledge of the history of music-making and considerable experience as a music editor. His conclusions were vital to the subject, and his work is likely to remain a standard authority.

Satisfying as Stevens's work was, it did not touch on certain matters that clearly demanded investigation. For instance, he did not discuss the possible structural and practical functions of music. More importantly, neither he nor Carpenter attempted to use the relevant guild accounts to solve the problems raised by the texts. Both of these areas were eventually treated in JoAnna Dutka's doctoral thesis (1972). As I hope to show, the consideration of structural functions may increase our understanding of the texts and is clearly an avenue to be explored further. Even more important, from all points of view, is the work currently in progress on the guild accounts, notably by the Toronto-based Records of Early English Drama (REED). It was already clear, even before the appearance of REED's first record publication (the York records), that there was far more documentary evidence on the plays than might be assumed after an examination of, say, Sharp's published work on the Coventry plays. Where matters of play-production—including music—are concerned, the main research of the next decade or so is bound to be the assimilation and interpretation of these records as they become available.

It would be wrong, however, to assume that these records will fill in all the gaps in our knowledge. Illuminating as it is to place the evidence of the play-texts side by side with that of the guild accounts, the material

2. Earlier studies are listed in Dutka, *English Mystery Plays*, p. 130 n. 1. These are largely superseded by Dutka's own work.

has too many limitations to be as useful as we would hope. Two particularly serious areas of limitation can be distinguished. First, as I hope to show in this chapter, the evidence that we have is neither comprehensive nor exclusive. We know that the evidence is incomplete, but we do not always know *where* it is incomplete, so that an absence of evidence can never be taken to signify the absence of music. In the play-texts, this can be illustrated by reference to my discussion of Play 2; in the records, it can be shown by reference to the lack of an obvious singer of the angelic Gloria. Second, the different types of evidence do not necessarily match one another. The main Chester MSS are late copies of what is apparently a medieval cycle. We can therefore assume that the construction of the plays was governed by medieval traditions, which is the assumption underlying Stevens's work on the dramatic representation of Heaven. The surviving guild accounts, on the other hand, are sixteenth century, and there is no reason to assume that the same traditions were necessarily operative in the performances to which the accounts relate. As it is, we can see that the plays being mounted in those late performances did not correspond wholly to the texts that have survived. These problems may not always be insuperable, but at present they often prevent the formation of firm conclusions.[3]

In this chapter the first section describes the representational and practical functions of music, and the second discusses the evidence for music in the Chester cycle under the headings of the text, the Banns, and the accounts. Assessment of the evidence enables us to make up a cue-list of musical items, which forms the third section. Lastly, the texts of musical items are discussed, together with their possible musical settings, and some suggestions are made about the type of instrumental music that might have been used. References to the text take the form play/line (plus, when necessary, the SD or Latin line following), as in Lumiansky and Mills, *Chester Mystery Cycle*.

3. The problems of interpreting guild accounts are discussed in Dutka, *Proceedings of the First Colloquium*, especially in the papers by Peter Meredith and Reginald W. Ingram, pp. 26–92. On the difference between text and performed play, see also Martin Stevens's comments, ibid., p. 176.

The Functions of Music

Representational Functions

Although some early work on the music in the English cycle plays tended to assume that music was used for emotive purposes, John Stevens showed in 1958 that its use was a representational one.[4] I shall illustrate Stevens's categories with reference to the Chester cycle, although I shall not follow the order of his argument precisely.

The most obvious use of music is as part of a depiction of Heaven, for medieval drama followed iconography in showing Heaven as a place where singers and instrumentalists praise God in music. More precisely, music expressed the harmony of the divinely created universe and therefore represented Divine Order. The angels sing as soon as they have been created (1/85+SD) because, as the first created beings in God's universe, they are the first expression of this Order. In Play 2 minstrelsy not only helps to represent Heaven (2/beginning) but also shows that Divine Order regulates the earthly Paradise, too: thus music is heard when Adam is placed in the Garden of Eden (2/211+SD).

Music is used for more than a merely static representation of Divine Order, for it can also show that order is restored after a period of disorder. Vocal music indicates the restoration of order when God returns to drive the rebel angels from Heaven (2/213+SD); minstrelsy shows God's ability to restore Divine Order after the Fall (2/280+SD, 384+SD) and the actual restoration of it when Adam and Eve are expelled from Eden (2/424+SD); minstrels play again when God returns to deal with Cain after the murder of Abel (2/616+SD); and Michael sings after the death of Antichrist as Enoch and Elias are taken to Heaven (23/722+SD). This last occasion leads directly to the Judgment and therefore to the ultimate restoration of Divine Order—to which the whole cycle has been progressing—as the Saved Souls, separated from the Damned, are taken to Heaven in the final working-out of God's purpose for Man (24/508+SD).

Angelic music also has its place in the representation of active intervention by God, through his messengers the angels, in the affairs of men. The angel sings the *Gloria in excelsis deo* that sends the shepherds to Bethle-

---

4. Stevens, "Mediaeval Drama."

hem and so changes their lives (7/357+SD); and there is angelic singing at the Resurrection (18/153+SD), at the Ascension (20/104+SD,
152+SD), and at the giving of the Holy Spirit (21/238+SD).

It may be thought curious that, although Heaven and Divine Order are
represented musically, God himself never sings in any of the English cycle
plays. Even Christ sings only once, in the Chester *Ascension*, where he
shares a substantial musical scene with a group of angels (20/104+SD,
and [a], [e], and [g] following), thus affirming both his divinity and his
earthly embodiment of (and submission to) the Divine Will at the moment of transition from earth to Heaven. Stevens notes this, without
offering an explanation,[5] but the reason can perhaps be inferred. Although the representation of Divine Order is the factor common to all
the examples of angelic music in the cycle, there is another factor related
to it: the element of praise. Praise of the Creator is a fundamental ingredient in Divine Order. Indeed, part of the biblical authority for this
concept forms the text of the first musical item in the Chester cycle,
Dignus es domine deus, and this and the other named piece in Play 1,
Gloria tibi trinitas, make the element of praise quite clear at the very
beginning of the cycle. But the Creator does not praise himself: therefore
he does not sing. Even when Christ sings it is not as Creator but as the
Son—"I go up to your father and my father, to your God and my God"
(20/104+SD+[a]).

The element of praise is clear, too, whenever mortals sing in the cycle,
whether in the flesh or as souls after death. In singing, they are emulating
the angels, joining in with the host praising God around the throne. This
is made explicit when Michael is ordered to "lead these men singinge /
to blys that lastethe ever" (17/211–12) and intones *Te deum laudamus*—
the greatest hymn of praise—for the released prophets to sing after the
Harrowing of Hell (17/276+SD). In the Chester cycle, then—and in any
other cycle play—the singing of mortals indicates generally that the person singing is in tune with the Divine Will. A mortal's expression of
praise or thanksgiving therefore often includes singing. Thus Mary's response to the certain knowledge that she is to be the Mother of God
(6/64+SD) is to "thanke the lord, kinge of mercye, / with joyful myrth
and melody / and laud to his likinge" (6/66–68) by singing *Magnificat*;
Simeon sings *Nunc dimittis* in praise to God ("laudes," 11/164) on see-

5. Ibid., p. 84.

ing the Christ (11/166+SD); and the citizens sing *Hosanna filio David* at Christ's entry into Jerusalem (14/208+SD). If the apostles really do sing the articles of their belief (21/310+SD and following), that is certainly consistent with the examples just cited. Even two instances that appear not to fit this pattern do so in fact. Noah and his family sing *Save me O God* at a time of danger (3/260+SD, H only), and the apostles, waiting for the gift of the Holy Spirit, sing *Veni creator spiritus* (21/120+SD). Both of these are petitions—the first for (spiritual) safety and the second for the gift of the Spirit—and they are addressed to a God known to be powerful enough to grant them if it is his Will. Submission to the Divine Will is always a form of praise, and these instances, too, show the mortals concerned to be in tune with that Will.

When mortals sing in the plays, then, their musicality is often an indication that they are the chosen instruments of God's Will, a point that hardly needs stressing in the case of Noah, Mary, Simeon, or the apostles. We must assume that both the content and the performance of the Good Gossips' Song (when it is performed as such) will place the gossips outside this category. The shepherds are certainly inside it, however, even though we do not know that they sang songs of praise to God in the Chester cycle: their wish to sing to the angel (7/436–39) and the stated intention that they shall sing "some myrth to his majestee" (7/477) are more than enough to indicate this. Moreover, their singing is characterized by joy (7/443, 447+SD [H], 477), a frequent ingredient of praise that is apparent also in the singing of Mary (6/67), Simeon (11/155), and the citizens at the entry into Jerusalem (14/205).

Consequently, mirth figures prominently in discussions of music in the cycle, for it is clear that joy can be transferred from singer to hearer, with beneficial effects on the spirits and emotions of both (6/669ff.), and even on their subsequent behavior (6/699–714, 7/651–56). So close is the connection between mirth and music that singing is a common figure of speech for joy. Thus when the Third Shepherd, wishing God's bliss on his friends, says "Amen, all singe you" (7/691), we do not assume that the shepherds actually sing an Amen, though they might sensibly say it. Both the transmission of joy and its related figure of speech have their less happy counterparts: an unmusical man is not a pleasant companion (7/202–5), and singing is used as a figure of speech giving added emphasis to sorrow, too (4/350, 17/299, 24/240).

MEDIEVAL ICONOGRAPHY would suggest that the singing of angels was often accompanied by instruments, though there is very little evidence to show that this was ever the case in the English cycle plays, and none at all in the Chester cycle. Chester Play 2 does include an unusual amount of minstrelsy, however,[6] and instrumental music also occurs elsewhere in the cycle.

According to iconographical evidence and our knowledge of the specific symbolism of certain instruments such as harp and psaltery, the proper music for Heaven must be that of the soft (*bas*) instruments—the strings and small organ.[7] These are not the only heavenly instruments, however, for the angels play on their "beames" (24/33, 46) to signal the beginning of the Judgment. These instruments, which the SD calls *tubae* (24/40+SD), are undoubtedly the ceremonial *buisine*, the long straight trumpet that is shown in medieval depictions of the Last Judgment. Trumpets were the prerogative of the nobility in the Middle Ages, but their symbolic uses associated them especially with kingship and, more particularly, with the king as judge. The use of the *buisines* in Play 24 would show the audience not merely that the all-powerful king was on the scene but also—by the sight as much as by the sound—that the king is about to sit in judgment.

So strong was the symbolism of the *buisine* that we should be wary of assuming its use elsewhere in the cycle. Carpenter's suggestion that the "Florish" of 5/111+SD is a flourish of trumpets for King Balak can fortunately be dismissed (as Dutka has done),[8] for it is only a direction to Balak to flourish his sword. The music for Herod's meeting with the Magi, however, is a more difficult matter (8/144+SD). It evidently marks Herod's entrance, so that ceremonial loud (*haut*) music would be appropriate. Carpenter, perhaps looking for an audible counterpart to the sight of the "noble kinge and worthye conqueroure, / crowned in gould" of the Messenger's salutation (8/145–46), thinks that a trumpet fanfare is required,[9] but there is much to be said against this. The Messenger's mode of address is flattery, for, despite his undoubted power, Herod is not a mighty and wise ruler. On the contrary, the music must presumably

6. In the context of this essay, "minstrelsy" denotes instrumental music.
7. Carpenter, "English Mystery Plays," pp. 28–29 and 169–70.
8. Dutka, "Mysteries, Minstrels," p. 122 n. 8.
9. Carpenter, "English Mystery Plays," p. 20.

draw attention to his temporal power and worldly pomp, helping to present it as the showy and second-rate affair that it is. In these circumstances the proper instruments for Herod are not trumpets but the standard loud consort of two or three shawms with a slide-trumpet.[10] Moreover, the use of trumpets for royalty, even at this stage of the cycle, would detract from the impact of the Last Trumpet in Play 24.

The First Shepherd's horn-blowing is certainly not a musical performance, however tempting it may be to see it as such (7/48, 164). His instrument is an ox-horn with a mouthpiece cut in the tip, commonly carried by herdsmen, huntsmen, soldiers, and others for signaling purposes. The shepherd has no aim other than that of attracting the attention of Harvey and Trowle and showing them where he is. The pipe given by the Third Boy to the Christ-child presents more difficulty (7/625–32). "Pipe" usually signifies an instrument on which tunes could be played, presumably here a simple fipple-flute (recorder). On the other hand, the accounts of the Painters' Guild show that in 1572 four whistles cost only 2d and another two "for Trowe" also cost 2d (and see the accounts for 1568 and 1575). This suggests the probability that dog-whistles are intended, presumably of simple construction and not particularly durable. In this case, there is clearly no question of musical performance. Whether the boy does blow the pipe for the baby or not is presumably a matter for the producer.

COMMENTATORS ON THE MUSIC in the cycle plays have generally tried to distinguish between the "symbolic" use of music in the dramatic representation of Heaven and its "realistic" use where it would be in real life. The distinction is not, I think, either accurate or helpful. To the medieval townsman, Heaven was a place where the host surrounding the throne praised God in music. There was scriptural evidence for this view, and all depictions of Heaven—iconographic and literary—represented Heaven in this way. No doubt a well-educated man understood the connection between the angelic music in the plays and the *musica mundana* of the Boethian universe, but most of the audience

---

10. Rastall, "Consort-Groupings," pp. 192–97, and "Royal Entry," p. 465. Herod's mention of trumpets to entertain him in the Coventry Shearmen and Taylors' play (Craig, *Coventry Plays*, p. 19) is part of a sixteenth-century attempt at realism and must be considered in isolation.

would be unaware of this connection, accepting the music simply as part of a realistic (not symbolic) stage representation of Heaven.

Nor would it be accurate to regard the loud music at Herod's court as purely realistic. Few in the audience would know how, and how often, and on what occasions, loud music was heard at a royal court. Of course most townsmen in the late Middle Ages had heard a nobleman being welcomed to a city, with loud music being played and "sights" presented along the route. Loud music, far from being strictly "real" in the plays, is representational in rather the same way as the heavenly music. Herod's loud music is as much a part of his trappings as his costume is.

There are occasions in the plays, certainly, when music might be regarded as realistic in the modern sense: some friends drinking together sing a drinking-song (3/224–36); a family, caught in a flood that has destroyed the world they knew, sing a psalm as a prayer for deliverance (3/260+SD); and a group of shepherds sing in an attempt to retrieve their sense of perspective after a very unusual event (7/447+SD). We need not doubt the essential reality of the singing of Noah's family and the shepherds, which are perhaps less obviously realistic to us than the drinking-song. Metrical psalms were much used for domestic and public devotion in the later sixteenth century (at an earlier date the family might have sung the plainsong psalm), and the context for psalm-singing is not a surprising one. Shepherds must often have used song as a pleasant means of whiling away the tedious hours. But, realistic as the songs of Noah and the shepherds may seem to us, their representational functions surely carried more weight with the audience, telling them something of the characters of the dramatis personae and their relationship with God. This being so, we must be wary of assuming that the Good Gossips' Song is a lone example in which realism is the prime function. The improbably occasional nature of the words—and the text is not a typical drinking-song, by any means—suggests otherwise, though not strongly. Realism might be better served by the use of a preexistent drinking-song, and for us this raises a problem. Would not a *real* drinking-song also delineate the character of the gossips better? Undoubtedly it would, so that realism appears not to be the dramatist's primary intention: yet he does not seem to have made full use of the opportunities for characterization, either. In this respect we must remember that much might be done with a tipsy performance (perhaps including "pub harmony"), but the Gossips' Song remains something of an anomaly.

"Symbolic" and "realistic," then, are not the simple categories that they seem at first sight, and we should be unwise to rely on them in attempting to understand the use of music in the Chester cycle. In regarding *representation* as music's primary function in the cycle, I have followed Stevens, for "representation" is a key word in his article,[11] although, strangely enough, he did not make its centrality explicit.

Structural Functions

Stevens discussed representational functions only, and there is no indication in his article that music might be a structural element in the cycle plays. The first hint of structural functions was given by Carpenter, who noted that music marks off the main structural divisions of the Towneley *Secunda Pastorum*[12] but did not explore the matter further. The subject was eventually treated in Dutka's doctoral dissertation of 1972,[13] the discussion being shortened for publication.[14] Even now, the existence of structural functions is not generally recognized.

Dutka distinguished four main structural functions; the categories discussed here do not quite coincide with hers, but the difference is one of emphasis. Eventually, no doubt, our categories must be subdivided and their definitions refined. That this is at present impossible is due entirely to our lack of knowledge of certain matters of staging in the cycle.

(a) A musical item often covers the movement of characters about the acting areas. In illustration of this[15] we may cite the shepherds' journey to Bethlehem, which is covered by a song for which there is no direction but a clear reference in the text (7/476–79); the angelic singing that covers the flight into Egypt (10/288+SD);[16] and the singing of the citizens accompanying Christ's entry into Jerusalem (14/208+SD).

11. Stevens, "Mediaeval Drama," p. 83.

12. Carpenter, "English Mystery Plays," p. 18, and "*Secunda Pastorum*," p. 213.

13. Dutka, "Use of Music," pp. 134–50.

14. Dutka, *English Mystery Plays*, pp. 7–8.

15. It is not necessary to give here a comprehensive list of examples for categories (a)–(d): these functions are indicated for all relevant items in the Cue-List, below.

16. This may be an exit, in which case it is an example of category (b): but in view of the appearance of the angel and Holy Family in the last scene of the play, I assume that they remain in sight throughout.

(b) A special case of (a) is the entrance or exit of a character. The angels sing to cover the entrance of Deus after Lucifer's rebellion (1/213+SD). Music for exits is more common: for example, the angel sings at the end of Play 10 (10/497+SD) when he, Mary, and Joseph must go off; Michael leads the singing of *Te deum* when he releases the prophets from Hell (17/276+SD), and he sings again for his exit with Enoch and Elias after the death of Antichrist (23/722+SD); and the Saved are led off with singing after the Judgment (24/508+SD).

(c) The passage of time is sometimes marked by music, and the Chester cycle includes a particularly interesting example of this. After Noah and his family have entered the ark and the water is spreading over the land, the Group MSS give a SD (marginal in A) requiring the family to sing (3/252+SD). Noah's next speech shows that time has passed and the flood is at its height; the speech itself (8 lines, 3/253–60) gives the relative time-scale for the period during which the flood covers the earth; and this is followed by a short space during which Noah shuts up the ark and is silent (3/260+SD). When he speaks again (3/261), the water has receded. In this version, then, there are three periods of time: in the first, the flood rises; in the second, Noah looks out and sees no recession of the water; and in the third, the water recedes. Of these, the first (after line 252) is probably the longest, the dramatic time being marked by the song.

The version transmitted by H has quite a different time-scale because of its inclusion of the Raven and Dove scene. Here there is no SD after line 252, the whole of lines 247–60 being a single speech during which the flood-water covers the earth. The space that follows is not a short one: indeed, it is forty days long, as Noah states immediately afterward (Appendix 1A/1). In H, then, it is here that the music comes, with a SD requiring Noah to shut up the ark, the family to sing *Save me O God*, and Noah then to open the window and look out. By means of the music here, H gives an impression of the periods of dramatic time quite different from that of the Group's version.

(d) Music is sometimes used to draw the attention of the audience to a new location. This is a difficult function to discuss, however, because it cannot always be distinguished from entrances (function b). Indeed, there is no certain example of this function in the Chester cycle, but it is probable that the loud music for Herod in the Magi play is one such, since the Messenger "must goe to the kinge" (8/144+SD), who is apparently in a different part of the playing area (probably on the wagon); and if I am right in thinking that it is Garcius who sings at 7/164+SD (discussed below), that is another possible example. It could be argued in both cases, of course, that the characters make their entrances at these moments, although it seems more likely that they are already in the audience's field of view.

(e) The last of the structural functions overlaps with all of the others and is so general that it is not included in the Cue-List, below. Whenever a musical item can be categorized as having one of the functions (a)–(d), it also marks a structural division of the play. This is hardly surprising, for it is in the nature of this type of drama that the entrance or exit of a character, the passage of time, or the change of focus from one location to another will occur at the end of a scene or important structural sub-division. On the other hand, the four functions (a)–(d) do not define the only places where music marks a subdivision, as a consideration of Play 7 shows. The first song (7/164+SD) separates the first scene, in which the three shepherds meet and share their meal, from that in which Garcius argues and wrestles with them; the angelic *Gloria in excelsis* is of course a matter of content, so its separation of the shepherds' theological discussion about the star from their discussion of the angelic message is structural at quite a different level, too (7/357+SD); but the third item, *Trolly lolly lolly lo*, almost gratuitously separates their discussion of the message from their resolve to go to Bethlehem (7/447+SD). The next song (after 7/479) follows this discussion, in which the angel joins, and marks both their journey to Bethlehem and the change to a new location for the next scene. Finally, after the adoration scene the shepherds evidently sing again during their return from Bethlehem, an intention expressed by the Second Shepherd (7/651–56). This is either at the end of the play, so that their return from Bethlehem becomes the procession out of the playing area, or perhaps after line 656, in which case the song separates the adoration scene from the shepherds' discussion of their future lives (but see below). Of these, the song after 7/447 does not fulfil any of the functions (a)–(d), while that after 7/164 is an arguable case, as we shall see.

The Overlapping of Functions

One of the problems in defining the various functions of the musical items is that there is much overlapping of functions. An item may have a representational function and also two or more structural functions, and in that case it is difficult to speak of any of them as a clearly defined function of that piece of music; different commentators will propose different functions as the primary one.

An example is the music that accompanies Adam and Eve's dismissal from the Garden of Eden (2/424+SD), for which several functions can be distinguished. It represents the restoration of Divine Order in Eden; covers the departure of the four angels from the playing-place (back to the wagon, probably); denotes the passage of the four or five decades during which Cain and Abel are born and grow up; helps to define the location of earth, now being used for the first time; and prepares the audience for a new scene. It is not easy to see how these functions can be arranged in order of importance, for we do not have the evidence that would allow us to do so with any certainty, but two suggestions can be made. First, the representational functions presumably come before the structural ones; that is, music is not used for a structural purpose unless a representational purpose has first required it. Second, we can probably assume that the purely practical considerations of covering exits, clearing the playing-area at the end of a play, and covering journeys from one location to another take precedence over academic matters of scene-division. Although music is clearly a help in staging a play with several scenes in different locations, there is no doubt that the actors had to solve the problem often enough without it.

The implications of these suggestions are far-reaching but at present largely conjectural. It is obvious, however, that the question of music was carefully weighed, and it is perhaps reasonable to assume that where there is a possibility of music being used in a play, there is a relationship between the number and type of functions to be served and the likelihood of music actually being called for.

The Evidence for Music in the Chester Cycle

The Play Text

Most of our evidence for music in the Chester cycle comes from the play-text itself, mainly in the form of stage directions. Of the twenty-five SDs that refer to vocal music, all but three name the item concerned. In some cases the SD gives the complete text to be sung; in others that is probably the case, although one cannot be certain. Most of the named items can be identified with some certainty from the texts given.

The eight SDs calling for instrumental music do not name the pieces, but that is to be expected.

Some directions, best described as "marginal," are clearly not of the same status as the majority of SDs. They are written to one side, often in the margin and sometimes beside a speech or SH. Except where they quote a Latin title, the margin directions (MDs) are in English, even when associated with a Latin SD, and in Hm they are often separated from an associated SD by brackets. The situation is apparently that seen in the MS of the York cycle, where MDs also occur. The editor of the York cycle refers to these as "in a later hand"; she also treats them as revisions,[17] which is not entirely accurate since they are additions to the text. Although much work remains to be done on the York directions, it seems most likely that the marginal ones are producer's notes added for specific performances, or at least for projected performances.*

In the Chester cycle, as in the York cycle, the MDs tend to be of a slightly different type from the SDs proper. The latter generally further the dramatic action in some way; they are integral to the drama and concern matters that we should expect to be prescribed by the dramatist. In general they are purely factual, although there are interesting exceptions in Play 4 (4/264+SD, 268+SD). The MDs, on the other hand, may either amplify a SD (e.g., by giving the title of otherwise unspecified music) or, if there is no SD present, may refer to "business" not prescribed by the dramatist.[18] In either case a MD often gives the impression

---

*After this chapter was written, work became available that has an important bearing on MDs. Peter Meredith, "John Clerke's Hand in the York Register," *Leeds Studies in English*, n.s. 12 (1981): 245–71, shows that the MDs in the York MS, British Library, Add. MS 35290, were written by the Common Clerk to the city of York. Meredith's conclusion that the MDs are a result of the city's monitoring of performances in the sixteenth century makes particularly good sense of the MDs concerning music (see especially p. 259 of his article). Although we may not assume at this stage that the Chester MDs are also the result of the city's monitoring of the plays, this is clearly a possibility that must be investigated.

17. Smith, *York Plays*, p. 53 n. 2, p. 98 n. 2, p. 101 n. 2, etc.
18. 4/48+SD, a nonmusical example, shows a marginal direction translating a SD proper.

of a mnemonic and is presumably the producer's reminder to himself or others of what is supposed to occur at a particular moment in the play. Thus "Dignus dei" ($1/85$+SD) is simply a reminder—and as such need not be particularly accurate—that the music sung by the angels is *Dignus es domine deus*. The dramatist did not need to write a SD here, because the singing has already been mentioned in the text ($1/85$).

This is not to say that any of the surviving Chester MSS was a producer's copy. The main Chester MSS are late copies, and in any case the MDs are always in the hand of surrounding text. What I suggest is that where a Chester play has MDs we can assume that a copy once existed on which a producer wrote marginal notes and that these notes have been transmitted by later copyists, often in the marginal position, though sometimes removed to the position of a SD proper.

The implications for the use of music are important. First, if a MD is added to a SD proper, we cannot assume that it follows any dramatic tradition; rather, it may reflect a purely personal choice made by a producer for a particular performance. The direction "Here singe troly loly loly loo," written to the left of $7/448-50$ in Hm, certainly amplifies the SD *Tunc cantabunt et postea dicat Tertius Pastor*, but its authority is limited in time, perhaps even to a single performance. Even if the MD dates from the early sixteenth century and was followed in all subsequent performances, we do not know what music was sung during the fifteenth century, nor what relation "Trolly lolly lolly lo" bore to that earlier music.

Second, when there is only a MD calling for music, and no SD proper, we cannot assume that the use of music there follows any tradition at all. Thus, while it is possible to show that music at a place such as $2/424$+SD is appropriate for various reasons, we cannot be certain that the dramatist expected music there. In Play 2, indeed, there is enough inconsistency among the MSS to suggest that even the precise number of places at which minstrelsy was heard might vary from one production to another.

Third, the existence of MDs cannot be taken as exclusive evidence. MS H notes no music in Play 2, only B has music at the start of that play, and no music is noted after $2/616$ in either A or R. Thus the loss of MS B would have given us incomplete directions for this play, the loss of Hm would have increased the incompleteness, and if H had survived alone Play 2 would include no musical directions at all. Our knowledge of minstrelsy in Play 2, then, may well be due to a particular producer, whose MDs have come to us by an accident of transmission. The question must arise, then, how many more musical directions have failed to be transmitted in the same way. Music would be suitable at a place such as 4/420+SD, and it would have been no surprise to us to find a MD there saying "minstrels play," or naming a piece of plainsong. Similarly, we might expect music at various places in Play 11, and here there is indeed some positive evidence for it in the surviving accounts of the Smiths' Guild.

I HAVE MENTIONED that a SD is sometimes unnecessary because relevant information is given in the text. The clear indication of a song in 1/85 is confirmed by the MD for *Dignus es domine deus*. Sometimes a clear textual reference of this sort is followed by a text, as happens in the last five lines of Play 10; here there can hardly be any doubt that the angel sings the Latin text starting *Ex Egipto*. However, not all instances of a textual reference are as simple as this. Garcius recommends singing a song to the Christ-child (7/476–79), but there is no direction for it. Do they follow his suggestion, and when? It is simplest to assume that the song follows immediately (after 7/479), before the reference is forgotten, and this would cover the shepherds' journey to Bethlehem; but if they are to sing it to the Christ-child in person, rather than simply in his honor, they must arrive at the stable before the song is finished. There is no difficulty about this, of course, but the initial assumption has begun to prescribe other details of production.

A similar question confronts us in the suggestion of the Second Shepherd (7/651–56) that they should sing as they return home. If they sing immediately, the music covers their journey back from the stable, the final scene taking place in a new location. However, this does not quite fit the text, for the Second Shepherd's speech is itself the first speech of the final scene, so that a song after it would be dramatically disruptive. If they do not sing there, there is no place for a song until the end of the play, where it would be useful in covering their exits; but in that case the shepherds do not walk home together but go their separate ways, when singing would be more difficult. The problem is not insoluble, and the song at the end of the play seems most likely. However, the reference at 7/651–56 does not tell us the dramatist's intention as clearly as we should wish.

A reference earlier in the same play is apparently contradicted by a SD.

The First Shepherd states his intention of blowing his horn for Garcius (7/161–64, although the passage suggests at first, 151–60, that the Second Shepherd blows it), but the SD seems to require him to sing instead (7/164+SD). MS H, with the reading "cantant," presumably intends all three shepherds to sing here. Garcius then speaks for thirty lines before he addresses the three shepherds directly (7/195), and in the ensuing dialogue he pours scorn on—among other things—their "sittinge with-owt any songes" (7/205). Clearly, this remark is pointless if the shepherds have just been singing.

Two factors are required to make sense of this episode. First, whoever eventually blows the horn, it is not sounded until immediately before 7/195, when Garcius, having presumably seen the other three beckoning to him, refuses to join them. Second, it should surely be Garcius himself singing at 7/164+SD: he, the most musical of the four, who can rebuke the others for "sittinge withowt any songes," would sing as the obvious way of amusing himself. Apart from its function in characterization, too, the song would fulfil the important practical function of directing the audience's attention to the new location for his soliloquy if Garcius were himself the singer.

If this is correct, we must suppose at least two mistaken revisions of the SD. The later of these is easily disposed of: in MS H, a scribe has assumed that "cantabit" refers to the First Shepherd, has decided to let all three shepherds sing (as being dramatically more interesting, perhaps), and has taken the opportunity to effect the entry of Garcius during the song.[19] The result is the SD "Tunc cantant et venit Garcius." The earlier revision is a matter of more difficult conjecture. I shall not attempt a reconstruction of an "original" SD and SH to follow 7/164, although certain guesses could reasonably be made on the evidence of the various readings. It is perhaps only necessary to point out that the general use of the present tense for the SDs in this play might suggest that "cantabit" is not part of the earliest SD, despite the use of mixed tenses in 7/299+SD and 447+SD.

CERTAIN IMPORTANT LATIN TEXTS are quoted in the Chester cycle, the Latin being followed by a paraphrase in English. In general,

---

19. This may be Scribe A, who wrote that part of H, or it may be the scribe of an earlier copy from which H is taken.

these quotations give the appearance of references, and it is possible that some of them were not intended to be spoken. Most of them certainly should be spoken, however, and some (e.g., 24/564+Latin, 580+Latin) are an integral part of the text, being referred to in the speech immediately preceding.

It is clear that in a few cases a text is first sung in Latin and then spoken in English. The dialogue sung by Christ and the angels after 20/104 is very loosely paraphrased from line 105 onward, the SH [h] emphasizing that the spoken dialogue is "in materna lingua"; the SD after 21/120 shows that the apostles sing *Veni creator spiritus* and then speak the translation that follows (". . . cantent 'Veni, creator Spiritus.' Postea dicat . . ."); and we know from the Banns (discussed below) that *Venite benedicti* was sung in Play 24, presumably immediately before the speech that paraphrases that text (24/453–56). It is important to recognize the pattern of spoken Latin + English, or sung Latin + spoken English, because several examples are not as clear as those just cited. Four important instances must be discussed individually.

The passage in which Mary apparently both sings and speaks the *Magnificat* does not say unequivocally that she sings at all (6/64+SD to 112). However, singing is implied by the SD "Maria gaudiens incipiet canticum 'Magnificat' etc.": first, by the use of the word "canticum," which is not normally used of speech; and second, by the use of "incipiet," which generally means the intoning of a liturgical piece. This meaning is seen also in 17/276+SD, ". . . incipiat Michaell 'Te Deum laudamus,' " as 17/275 shows ("I read we singe"). The use of "incipiet" and "canticum" are not conclusive proof of singing, but they are persuasive evidence; moreover, the reading in A, which adds "et dicat Maria" after "canticum 'Magnificat,' " gives extra weight to the interpretation of "incipiet" as musical. If we accept that Mary sings the first verse of *Magnificat* here, we should note that lines 65–72 paraphrase that verse only very roughly, a situation that is seen also in *Viri Galilei* and the subsequent speech (20/152+SD2, 153–56). The Latin is necessary for complete sense.

Following 6/72+Latin (" 'Et exultavit spiritus meus in Deo' etc.," which H makes into the complete second verse by adding "salutari meo etc."), Mary speaks the whole of the rest of *Magnificat* in English. The stanzas do not coincide precisely with the verses of the Latin canticle; thus there is no question of Mary singing each Latin verse before the relevant part of the paraphrase. Assuming—as seems reasonable—that this second Latin line, too, is sung, we have to ask whether Mary sings only the second verse or the whole of the rest of the canticle. Despite the "etc." of the reading in H, my own preference is for the second verse only; but that is of course open to question, and we must hope for more evidence on this point.

Simeon's singing of *Nunc dimittis* focuses the problem slightly differently. The direction "Tunc cantabit 'Nunc dimittis servum tuum, domine,' etc." (to which B adds "in pace") is unambiguous up to a point (11/166+SD). The eight lines that follow (167–74) are a close paraphrase of *Nunc dimittis*, so there is a small possibility that the English text is itself the "Nunc dimittis" sung by Simeon; but I discount this, for the English text is not a translation known from other sources, much less a metrical version associated with a musical setting. Accepting once more that the Latin is sung and the English spoken, we have to ask the same question as before: Does Simeon sing the first verse only (as B's reading suggests), or the whole canticle? As in the case of *Magnificat*, my preference is for the one verse.

As already stated, the SD for the singing of *Veni creator spiritus* shows that the Latin is sung (21/120+SD). MS H copies the first verse of the hymn complete, and again it is likely that only the one verse is to be sung, even though the complete hymn is afterward paraphrased.

The passage in which the apostles recite the Creed (21/310+SD to 358) raises no new questions. The answers are important, however, for the evidence of the method of performance is slight, and the different methods would significantly affect the dramatic impact of the scene. The whole Apostles' Creed is divided among the Twelve, each reciting a single verse in English. The division is a traditional one, found also in Wilkinson's setting of the Apostles' Creed in the Eton Choir Book, c. 1500.[20] In all of the Chester MSS the Latin verse precedes its paraphrase. The version transmitted in A places the SH after the Latin line in each case, thus apparently showing that the Latin is an unspoken reference, but the other MSS place each SH before the Latin. Assuming that in all versions except A's the Latin is intended to be sounded, our only evidence for

20. Harrison, *Eton Choir Book*, no. 50 and commentary, and *Music in Medieval Britain*, p. 414 (where Simon's name is omitted, however). Mezey, "Creed," shows that the Chester distribution of text is that most commonly found.

singing is the use of "incipiat" in the SD. Probably the producer exercised a choice in any case, choosing speech or singing according to the ability of his players to chant convincingly. There is no plainsong tune for the Apostles' Creed, which is chanted on a monotone.

The Banns

The Early Banns (no. 20a in the documents forming chapter 5 of this volume), copied in 1540, contain no mention of music or musicians. The Late Banns (20b) refer to music or musicians in three plays.

Play 7

The Painters and Glaziers are to deck out the angel, star, and shepherds "with all myrthe / and see that 'Gloria in Excelsus' be songe merely" (lines 98–99). This whole stanza makes much of the angel's appearance to the shepherds and his message to them, and, despite the shepherds' long discussion of the song (7/361–435), the emphasis on it here is perhaps surprising, for it seems from the text only a small part of the play. On the other hand, the Painters' charter of 1534 (chapter 5, document 12) also emphasizes the song, describing the play as "the shepp-herds wach with the angells hyme." Moreover, the title *Gloria in Excelsis* is written in red ink in R, which shows it to have been considered impor-tant in the cycle as a whole. To some extent this is explained by lines 101–2 of the Late Banns, which identify the Gloria as the text on which the whole play is based, but that also supports the view that the angel's song was a dramatic event of prime importance. This is in any case further supported by the emphasis on mirth in three adjacent lines of the Banns (98–100), for this indicates both musical style and resources calculated to make a considerable impression on an audience.

We may note that, as the Painters' charter antedates the Early Banns, the omission of any reference to music in the Early Banns is not signifi-cant, for this play or for any other.

Play 11

In putting on their pageant the Blacksmiths are urged to "gett mynstrelles to that shewe: pype, tabrett, and flute" (line 118). The only direction for music in the Blacksmiths' play is for Simeon's singing of *Nunc dimittis* (11/166+SD), for which instrumental accompaniment would be inappropriate.[21] There are places where heavenly minstrelsy would be appropriate in this play, however, and it is therefore possible that the three minstrels played *bas* music together. At 11/40+SD, and again at 11/71+SD, the angel actively intervenes by reversing Simeon's "correction" of the text; after 11/103 the angel again intervenes, but only to give Simeon information; and the angel returns after 11/326 to speak to the audience. From the point of view of representing Heaven, the first two of these seem very likely places for music, the third much less so, and the last most unlikely: at the first two places, too, music would cover the angel's actions. In all, music at 11/40+SD and 71+SD is a distinct possibility, but perhaps not elsewhere. In this case we should expect the "pype" to be a recorder, as opposed to the transverse "flute," and the tabor would be a small and relatively quiet instrument such as was used for marking the beat during dancing indoors.

A flute is a *bas* instrument in any case, but both pipe and tabor could be *haut* music. "Pipe" may refer to a shawm or to a bagpipe, and it is also possible that the pipe and tabor were played by one man, which would again be loud dance music. The accounts of the Smiths' Guild (see below) suggest very strongly that minstrels were employed to accompany the wagon: this would certainly be loud music.

These minstrels are discussed further in connection with the accounts.

Play 24

The Banns say that the Websters are to show Christ separating the Saved Souls, and that they are "to have that sweete worde in melodye: / 'Come hither, come hither, venite benedicitie'" (lines 184–85). The title of *Venite benedicti* is given correctly in RB, and probably refers to the Benedictus antiphon for the first Monday in Lent. The text is part of Christ's own description of the Last Judgment (St. Matthew 25/34). The piece would most appropriately be sung by Christ himself, then, although angelic performance might also be possible. Elsewhere in the cycle the pattern of a Latin text followed by an English paraphrase has the same character delivering both, which argues that Christ should sing *Venite*

21. Inappropriate because instruments would imply Heaven or royalty in the context of the plays.

benedicti; the singing must take place immediately before st. 58, the beginning of the speech starting "Come hither," in which Christ paraphrases the text of the antiphon (24/453–56). Moreover, the rest of this speech continues the paraphrase of the text from St. Matthew, just as other speeches in this part of the play follow Christ's story very closely.

Guild Accounts

Payments concerning music are found in the accounts of four guilds: the Painters (Play 7), the (Black)Smiths (Play 11), the Shoemakers (Play 14), and the Coopers (Play 16). Relevant items are printed in chapter 5 of this volume, section 17, to which the reader is referred throughout the discussion that follows.

The Painters

The surviving accounts of the Painters' Guild are for the years 1568, 1572, and 1575. In each year both singers and minstrels were hired.

In 1568 the guild spoke to "master Chaunter" (i.e., cantor) "for Sheperdes Boyes." Dutka has identified the cantor as Sir John Genson, precentor of the cathedral.[22] This payment does not necessarily mean that the shepherds' boys sang, for trained choristers would in any case make suitable child-actors, and it is not certain that the shepherds' boys are the "helpers" who sang with the shepherds at 7/447+SD (H only). On the other hand, the wages paid to the boys in various years—2/8d to four of them in 1568, 4/- in 1572, and 3/- to three of them in 1575—are too generous unless the boys were hired for a specialist skill such as singing. Moreover, we know that more than one singer was hired, for the guild spent 2d on "the iiij syngares" at an audition or rehearsal in 1572, and 1d "for synges" and 6d "for pouder [? pudding] for the sengers" in 1575. The first of these payments may be an exact parallel to the payment of 2d spent "upon the Shepherdes Boyes" during rehearsal in 1568, but in any case we may reasonably conclude that the choristers playing the

---

22. Dutka, "Use of Music," p. 4. Dutka refers to him as Johnson, a spelling that does not appear in the records.

parts of the shepherds' boys were required to sing and therefore that they are indeed the "helpers" who sing with the shepherds at 7/447+SD.

The vocal music in this play presents a problem, in that the text and the surviving accounts do not seem to agree in one important respect. As we have already noted, the angelic Gloria is an important part of the play, the high quality of the angel's singing being emphasized by the Second Shepherd's remark that the angel had a fine voice (7/406). Clearly, the play seems to require a trained singer for this part. It is therefore a surprise to find that in all three years the angel's wage was a mere 6d, the usual wage for an actor with a very small part. This was the wage given also to Mary, who, like the angel, has only a single eight-line speech in this play. It is hardly conceivable that the Gloria did not merit extra payment in these years, and the only possible explanation is that it received a professional performance from behind the wagon, the angel acting his part but not singing. A group of choristers could not sing here, for the shepherds' discussion of the Gloria (7/361–435) shows that it was a solo. Probably, therefore, the Gloria was performed by a professional singing-man standing behind the wagon, and although we do not at present recognize his name in the accounts, his identity may one day be discovered.

The payments to minstrels do not form any discernible pattern. In 1568 minstrels were paid 3/4d on the day of the play and 6d for their performance on Midsummer Eve, and the guild also paid for bread and ale provided for them by Richard Halewood's wife. In 1572 minstrels cost the guild 2/- (although they were probably given food and drink as well, recorded in an item of general expenditure), and in 1575 minstrels received only 14d. In this last year, a payment to "the mynstrelle to the plase" presumably refers to a minstrel entertaining the audience at one of the stations and does not imply music during the play; the payment of 2d to him does not show him to be a performer of high status.

The only place for minstrelsy in Play 7 is at the angelic Gloria (7/357+SD), which could be accompanied by *bas* instruments. The lack of consistency in the payments to minstrels argues against such a specific use of minstrelsy, however; rather, it suggests that minstrels were hired, to no regular plan, for a much less precisely defined purpose. The most likely purpose is the provision of loud music in the procession from one station to another (excepting the "minstrel to the place" of 1575, of course, who would be stationary). This purpose is hinted at in the payment "for bred and ale in the morning to the puteres and the mynstrelles" in the accounts for 1575, the implication being that the minstrels are part of the team responsible for moving the wagon. This use of minstrels is seen also in the accounts of the Smiths' Guild.

The Smiths

Records survive for the years 1554, 1561, 1567, 1568, 1572, and 1575. They appear to be for Play 11 as we have it, although there are some unexpected references to singers.

The Smiths' accounts show the various stages in which payments were made for singers. The guild went first to someone who could procure singers: in 1561 this was Sir Randle Barnes, a minor canon of the cathedral, and in 1567 Sir John Genson, the precentor.[23] There are then payments concerning singers at auditions and rehearsal. Finally, the guild made direct payments to the performers, one sum to the singers and another apparently to the musical director.

In 1554 "Barnes and the syngers" were paid 3/4d for performing, and the accounts for 1561 show a payment "to the 5 boyes for singing" (2/6d) and another to Thomas Ellam, a singing-man of the cathedral who presumably directed the music (12d). Probably Barnes had himself directed the music in 1554, the 3/4d being 2/4d + 12d, or perhaps 2/6d + 10d. In the next two sets of accounts the guild has evidently made different arrangements, however. In 1567 Mr. White, a singing-man at the cathedral,[24] was paid 4/-, "Mr. Chanter" (Genson) taking 12d; and in 1568 White again took 4/- ("for singinge"), while Barnes was paid 3/4d. In the last two sets of accounts there is again a change: a payment of 4/2d "for the Clergy for the songes" in 1572 is uninformative, but the 14d given "to 3 of the synngares" shows that a larger number of singers was again being hired.

23. The men whose names appear in the accounts are identified in Dutka, "Use of Music," pp. 2–5 and 222–32.

24. The accounts of the Dean and Chapter for 1567 refer to White as *magister choristarum* (Dutka, "Use of Music," pp. 231–32). It is now generally accepted that Mr. White was the composer Robert White (c. 1538–74), who could have been at Chester from 1566 or 1567 until 1570, between appointments at Ely and Westminster.

These changes coincide with other alterations in the guild's arrangements for the play. In 1554 and 1561, the actor playing the part of
Simeon was paid 3/4d, a wage that reflects not only the size of the role
but also the fact that Simeon must sing. No doubt part of the musical
director's work each year was to coach this actor in his performance of
Nunc dimittis. Simeon's name is missing, however, from the accounts for
1567 and 1568. The payment "at the . . . consell of Simion" in 1568
suggests that there was difficulty in filling this role, and it may not be
coincidence that the payment immediately following this relates to the
hiring of White and Barnes; 1567 and 1568 are the years in which White
was paid 4/-, and the obvious inference is that he played the part of
Simeon. He and Genson both appear amongst "the Players" in the accounts for 1567, but in the following year White was joined by Barnes,
the latter being paid the large sum of 3/4d. The accounts for 1572 and
1575 again include payments to Simeon but at a reduced wage. Other
payments show that "the clergy" were still involved in the music in 1572
and that in 1575 at least one of the singers, who was paid 16d "for his
panes and gloffes," was a costumed actor.

It is possible, I think, to make some sense out of these rather diverse
items. In 1554 Barnes was in charge of the music, tutoring Simeon,
perhaps, and directing the performance of professional singers. As we
have already seen, 11/40+SD and 11/71+SD are suitable places for
"heavenly" music, and it was no doubt at those places that the professionals, probably boys, sang. In 1561 the singers were five boys, apparently under the direction of Ellam. Their music was supplied by Genson
(who was paid 12d "for songes"), although we cannot know whether he
composed the music or simply provided copies from which the boys
could sing. As already stated, 1567 and 1568 are the years in which
White may have played the part of Simeon. No boys were hired to sing
angelic music in 1567, and one wonders if perhaps the Painters (who are
known to have hired boys in 1568) made an offer first and hired the
available choristers before the Smiths could do so. A payment "for carringe of the regalls" can only mean that someone—presumably Genson,
who was paid 12d—played "heavenly" music on an organ,[25] or at least
accompanied angelic singing. Since Genson appears amongst the players
that year, it is possible that he was costumed as an angel and played in

25. A regal would normally be a small organ with a rank of reeds.

full view of the audience. The following year, 1568, White presumably played the part of Simeon again. Barnes was paid 3/4d and so must have produced more lavish "heavenly" music than Genson had done the previous year. It is possible, of course, that Barnes brought some boys for this purpose and that he therefore kept 12d for himself and distributed the rest, but the supply of boys would be limited, and we know that Genson provided boys for the Painters' play that year. In 1572 and 1575 the part of Simeon was again played by an amateur; thus the singers could have been concerned only with angelic music. We cannot deduce any details from the payment of 4/2d "for the Clergy for the songes" in the accounts of 1572, but we know that in 1575 there were more than three singers and that at least one of them was costumed, presumably as an angel.

The minstrels are no easier to deal with than the singers, but a certain pattern can be seen. In general, the minstrels paid for performing "with our pagan" appear in connection with those who pushed the wagon quite as much as with the players:

1554: "To the mynstrells in mane ij s" is immediately followed by payment "to the porters of the caryegs."

1561: "To the minstrells iij s vj d Payd for drinke for ther breckfast before they play and after they had done when the were unbowninge them iij s" is followed by a payment to "the porters of the carriage."

1567: Payment of 2/- to the minstrels is several items later than payment to the porters of the carriage and immediately before those to the players.

1568: Payment of 2/- to the minstrels is several items later than that to the porters of the carriage and among those to the players.

1572: The main payment of 3/4d "To the minstrells for our pagent" is among miscellaneous expenses, but the last item in the list records a payment of 4d "For bringinge of the carriag home and spent on mynstrells and porters."

1575: The main payment of 5/- "To the menstreles at our generall rehers and Midsamer and with our pagan" is followed by the payments to players, with the porters of the carriage several items later still.

Certainly this evidence is not conclusive, but the item for 1561 reads as if the minstrels had performed independently of the players, and the second item for 1572 seems to cite both minstrels and porters as those responsible for "bringinge the carriag home." As I have already suggested, it seems most likely that these were *haut* minstrels sent out with the wagon to play in the procession between stations. This would certainly be the minstrels' function at Midsummer, and the item for 1575 therefore supports the suggestion.

There are also payments to minstrels that indicate a different use of minstrelsy:

1554: "To Randle Crane in mane ij s." This item follows immediately after that to Barnes and the singers. Crane was a minstrel: both the use of his full name and the sum paid indicate that he was a respected and skillful player.

1561: William Lutter, a minstrel, was paid $4\frac{1}{2}$d at the general rehearsal. He is later referred to as "Wm Luker" and paid an unspecified amount "for plleyinge": this item immediately follows the payment to the five choristers.

William Luter, of course, was a *bas* minstrel, the player of a lute; Crane, too, is almost certain to have been a *bas* minstrel, for a lone minstrel given the responsibility indicated by a fee of 2/- was rarely a loud minstrel. It is significant that the main payments to Crane and Luter follow those to the singers. The overwhelming probability is that they were hired to play "heavenly" music, either as virtuoso solos or as an accompaniment to the choristers, or perhaps both.

Dutka has found items of payment to Crane and Luter, dating from the 1550s, in other parts of the Smiths' accounts,[26] but from no date later than those concerned here. Perhaps Crane had died by 1561, or was working for another guild; and perhaps Luter, brought in to replace him, was himself replaced by 1567. In that year the regals seem to have been used by the Smiths, and possibly the *bas* minstrel was permanently replaced by an organist from the cathedral.

The Shoemakers

These accounts, probably for 1550, are not for Play 14 as we have it, but the differences will not affect our consideration of the music.

The only music shown in the text is the singing of *Hosanna filio David*

26. Dutka, "Use of Music," pp. 2–3.

(14/208+SD). Since this is entrusted to citizens and boys, we might expect to find a group of choristers in the accounts, but there is none. Moreover, the "vj chelder of Esaraell" who were paid 3/- between them accord better with the six *cives* of the text than with the boys.

The accounts are no more informative on the subject of minstrelsy. The single payment of 2/4d for the minstrels' wages suggests that there were two of them. There are two possible uses for minstrelsy: it might be *haut* minstrelsy played in procession between stations, or *bas* minstrelsy played at supper in the house of Lazarus (Simon the Leper in the text), for which the cue would be 14/40+SD. Of these, the *haut* minstrels playing in procession seem more likely.

The Coopers

The accounts of the Coopers' guild for 1571–1611 make no mention of either singers or minstrels. Dutka notes that Hugh Gillam, who was paid 3/4d in 1572, was a morris dancer, and she suggests that Gillam danced in the role of one of the executioners.[27] Her supporting evidence for this conjecture includes a SD in the *Ludus Coventriae* that directs the executioners to dance around the Cross, and the point is certainly worth pursuing if more evidence can be found.

The Cue-List

All musical items in the Chester cycle are listed here. Those items that are conjectured on the evidence of guild accounts are placed in square brackets.

Following the cue-line, the type of evidence is shown: SD = stage direction (including margin directions); SH = speech heading; T = textual reference; B = Banns; R = records.

The type of the item is then shown: AI = angelic music, instrumental; AV = angelic music, vocal; C = Christ; S = souls; M = mortals; L = loud music (mortal).

The next column shows the function of the music, referring to the structural functions (a)–(d) discussed above.

27. Ibid., p. 6.

The remarks in the last column give the title of the piece, if known, any necessary additional information referring to the other columns, and references to discussions of the problems arising for individual cues.

Play/ Cue-line	Evidence	Type	Function	Remarks
1/85	SD	AV	—	*Dignus es domine deus,* marginal.
125	SD	AV	(b)	In H only.
213	SD	AV	(b)	*Gloria tibi trinitas: om* H.
2/start	SD	AI	—	In B only, marginal.
112	SD	AI	(a)	"Minstrelles playe" is marginal: *om* H.
280	SD	AI	(b)	"Minstrelles playe" is marginal: *om* H.
384	SD	AI	(a)	"Minstrelles playe" is marginal: *om* H.
424	SD	AI	(a)(b)(c)(d)	Marginal: *om* H.
616	SD	AI	(b)	"Minstrelles playe" is marginal: *om* ARH. (H has the main SD after line 612.)
3/224	SH	M	(a)	*Songe* A only; *Gossip* H: see below.
252	SD	M	(c)	*Om* H. A has only the MD "Then the singe." Alternative to the following: see above.
260	SD	M	(c)	Musical direction in H only, for *Save me O God.* Alternative to preceding.
4/				No reference to music.
5/				No reference to music.
6/64	SD	M	—	*Magnificat,* first verse.
72	SD*	M	—	*Magnificat,* second verse: see above. *SD written as speech, though obviously comparable to 64+SD.

Play/ Cue-line	Evi- dence	Type	Function	Remarks
666	SD	AV	(a)*	*Haec est ara dei caeli*: "Let the music be according to the judgment of the performer." *The music covers Octavian's offering of the incense.[28]
7/164	SD/T	M	(b)/(c)/(d)*	*SD to singing, but textual reference is to blowing a horn. The Group MSS have *dicat Garcius* (function d), but H has *venit Garcius* (function b). However, function (c) is most likely: see above.
357	SD	AV	—	*Gloria in excelsis deo*: see below.
447	SD	M	—	The Group MSS give a Latin SD for singing, with a MD specifying *Trolly lolly lolly lo*; in H, the shepherds are joined by their helpers in singing a *hilare carmen* (see also 443).
479	T	M	(a)	The text seems to require a song here.
656	T	M	(a)	Here, too, the text seems to require a song: but it may be at the end of the play, rather than here. See above.
8/144	SD	L	(a)(b)(d)*	"Minstrelles here must playe" is marginal. *See above.
9/				No reference to music.
10/288	SD	AV	(a)	*Ecce dominus ascendet*: om A, misplaced after 264 R.
497	T	AV	(b)	*Ex Egipto*. Text in Latin line: singing inferred from 494–95.

28. Discussed in Dutka, *English Mystery Plays*, p. 70.

Play/ *Cue-line*	*Evi-* *dence*	*Type*	*Function*	*Remarks*
11/40	[R	AI	(a)	See above.]
71	[R	AI	(a)	See above.]
166	SD	M	—	*Nunc dimittis.* SD in B shows that Simeon sings only the first verse. See above.
12/				No reference to music.
13/				No reference to music.
14/40	[R	M	(a)(b)	Music at supper: see above.]
208	SD	M	(a)	*Hosanna filio David*: all MSS but H give "Hosanna" separately for the boys, but it seems certain that all sing the same music.
15/				No reference to music.
16/				No reference to music.
16A/				No reference to music.
17/276	SD	AV/S	(b)	*Te deum*, intoned by Michael.
18/153	SD	AV	(a)	*Christus resurgens.*
19/				No reference to music.
20/104	SD/SH	C/AV	(a)	*Ascendo ad patrem meum; Quis est iste*, etc. In B, the English is marginal.
152	SD/SH	AV	(a)(b)	*Exaltare domine.*
	SD	AV	(a)	*Viri Galilei.*
21/120	SD	M	—	*Veni creator spiritus.* First verse given complete in H: see above.
238	SD	AV	(a)	*Accipite spiritum sanctum.* No musical direction in R.
310	SDs	M	—	*Credo in deum*: see above.
22/				No reference to music.

Play/ Cue-line	Evi- dence	Type	Function	Remarks
23/722*	SD	AV	(b)	*Gaudete justi in domino.* *726 in P.
24/40	SD	AI	(a)	Two angels play Last Trumpet on their "beames."
452	B	C	—	*Venite benedicti*: see above.
508	SD	AV	(b)	Either *Letamini in domino* or *Salvator mundi domine.*

Texts and Music

Vocal Liturgical Items

Most of the liturgical pieces named in the Chester cycle can be identified without difficulty. The SDs appear to give the complete text in some cases, and in others to give at least enough to make the piece identifiable. For example, the SD after 24/508 gives "Salvator mundi domine," sufficient to distinguish the hymn from *Salvator mundi salva nos*, the antiphon. However, the given incipit belongs in some cases to more than one liturgical piece, and I give the likely alternatives in the list that follows. Where one of the alternatives seems more likely to have been intended, the probable preference is stated. It is of course quite possible that a choice of alternatives was sometimes intended for the director of a performance, the selection to be made according to the length of piece required and the ability of the singer. For example, alternative (c) for *Dignus es domine* might be used if, in a particular production, (b) was found to be too long; and the choice of piece for *Christus resurgens* might be made according to whether the singer was a professional or an amateur. That these considerations were taken into account can be seen elsewhere: *Salvator mundi domine* is prescribed as an alternative to *Letamini in domino* (24/508+SD), presumably in case the latter should prove too short to cover the movements of the players about the acting-area; and the SD for *Haec est ara dei caeli* (6/666+SD) directs the performer to use his judgment (over his own ability?) in providing music.

It may be, too, that whoever chose the music did not know of all the possibilities or, for various reasons, did not consider them all. In searching through either his memory or a service-book for the setting of a suitable text, he might well make use of the first suitable text he found, without looking further. In fact, many of the choices are clearly very obvious ones: the canticles *Magnificat* and *Nunc dimittis*, for instance, appear regularly in the Latin services and are settings of part of the Gospel account of events being dramatized; *Gloria in excelsis, Hosanna filio David*, and *Viri Galilei*, also with texts from the Gospel accounts, could easily be found by reference to the liturgy for the appropriate day; and a similar reference to liturgical books would quickly suggest such items as *Christus resurgens, Ascendo ad patrem meum, Exaltare domine, Veni creator spiritus*, and *Accipite spiritum sanctum*. Certain pieces, too, would be suggested by traditions of usage: the special performance of the respond-verse *Gloria in excelsis* by a group of boys; the singing of *Te deum laudamus* at times of rejoicing; and the traditional ascriptions of the phrases of the Apostles' Creed to individual apostles.

On the other hand, there are indications that liturgical items were chosen with some knowledge of the liturgy and with considerable care. *Dignus es domine*, the song with which the newly created angels praise the Creator (1/85), is actually the text used for that purpose by the twenty-four elders (Revelation 4/11), and it must have been well known to the man who chose it for its dramatic purpose at Chester. Two texts— those of *Haec est ara dei caeli* (6/666+SD) and *Ecce dominus ascendet* (10/288+SD)—cannot be identified as liturgical texts, and they were presumably thought so suitable for the dramatic purpose that they had to be included even though music would have to be provided for them.[29] In the case of the antiphons following *Ascendo ad patrem meum* (20/104), the texts cannot be found in the Sarum Rite, although two versions of the text, with different musical settings, are known elsewhere. The dramatist presumably looked for the version that would suit his needs, but he must also have known that the musical settings of *Ascendo ad patrem* and the following antiphons would fit together. Musical considerations must also have affected the choice of setting for *Exaltare domine*, since the setting of *Viri Galilei* (which follows immediately) has to be musically com-patible with it. The dramatist of Play 20 either had assistance from a musician or he himself had musical knowledge.

In all, it seems that those who selected the liturgical items for the

29. The sources and other known occurrences of these texts are discussed in Dutka, *English Mystery Plays*, p. 70.

Chester cycle had a good knowledge of the Bible and of the Latin services. This could hardly be said, however, of the audience. Few of the townspeople before the Reformation, or even in Mary's reign (1553–58), are likely to have had such knowledge of Latin, or to have known many of the liturgical items presented to them in the plays. Thereafter, when Latin services were no longer used in England, even fewer would have recognized the liturgical items. As the services of Divine Office were compressed into Morning and Evening Prayer, most of the texts disappeared completely, leaving no English version in the new services. It is true that there are factors tending to offset any general ignorance of Latin—the use of English paraphrase after *Magnificat, Nunc dimittis, Credo,* and *Venite benedicti,* and the actions that would visibly explain at least the gist of *Dignus es domine, Hosanna filio David, Christus resurgens,* and perhaps some other pieces. But we are left with a residue of items that almost certainly would not have been understood by many in the audience. This is not to say that such music was ever pointless, of course. Even to someone who understood no Latin, the music would still fulfil the representational and structural functions already discussed and would in addition serve to draw attention to the spectacle of the plays.

THE MAJORITY of the liturgical items specified in the Chester cycle can be found in the Roman service-books currently available. In the late Middle Ages, however, the Roman Rite was not used in England—much of the country used the rite of Salisbury, with variants at Worcester, York, and elsewhere. The variants were suppressed by the Act of Uniformity in 1549, after which only the Sarum Rite was used in England. In searching for the items to be performed in the Chester cycle, therefore, it is necessary to deal with the Sarum Rite rather than the Roman. The Sarum processional, gradual, and antiphoner are all easily available, with their music,[30] and they are cited here as PS, GS, and AS, respectively. Where a piece is not available in these three works I have cited the most easily accessible of the Roman service-books, the *Liber Usualis* (LU). Where I have been able to identify a piece in the Sarum books its liturgical position is that of the Sarum Rite, which is not necessarily the same as its position in the Roman Rite.

30. Pynson, *Processionale;* Frere, *Graduale Sarisburiense* and *Antiphonale Sarisburiense.*

Plainsong pieces vary between the simplest music for congregational singing and extremely difficult virtuoso pieces for trained soloists; thus some basic information about the music is included in the catalog of pieces that follows.

(a) The chant is shown as either syllabic, neumatic, or melismatic. Roughly, syllabic chant has one note per syllable, though a few syllables may have short groups of notes; neumatic chant usually has short melismas—perhaps on average three or four notes per syllable, though it is not closely defined; and melismatic chant has longer melismas. Although these categories are very rough, I have thought it worth while to give a slightly more detailed description in certain cases: "neumatic/melismatic" has on average fewer notes per syllable than "melismatic/neumatic" chant.

(b) The musical range is given, using the Helmholtz notation (c'–b' is the octave from middle C upward). In the Middle Ages there was no standard pitch, so these ranges do not indicate absolute pitch-ranges: nevertheless, the range indicates relatively the pitch at which a chant would be sung, so that a congregational piece is usually notated at a lower pitch than one for a choir, and a soloist's music is notated highest of all.

(c) To help in the matter of pitch, I have shown the clef used. Clefs were movable (and indeed frequently changed their positions on the staff in the middle of a piece), so that the value of this is limited. An f-clef, however, always indicates a lower general pitch than a c-clef, which may help to distinguish between music for untrained singers and music for professionals.

This information is not given for canticles (which use psalm-tones) or hymns, since these pieces are liturgically congregational in any case.

PLAY 1/85+SD   *Dignus es domine*

Dignus es Dei	A
dignus es Domine	B
Dignus Dei	R

In the Sarum Rite there seem to be three possible items:

(a) Responsory for the first Sunday after Easter (AS 251):

Dignus es domine accipere librum et aperire signacula eius quoniam occisus es et redemisti nos deo. In sanguine tuo. Alleluia.

This is a neumatic/melismatic chant, range f–f', c-clef.
(b) The Benedictus antiphon for the second Sunday after Easter (AS 256):

Dignus es domine deus noster accipere gloriam et honorem et virtutem quia tu creasti omnia et propter voluntatem tuam erant et creata sunt salus deo nostro qui sedes super thronum et agno. Alleluia.

Largely syllabic chant, range c–c', f-clef.
(c) Antiphon for the sixth Sunday in Lent (Palm Sunday) (GS 82, PS 45r):

Dignus es domine deus accipere gloriam et honorem.

Largely syllabic chant, range c–g, f-clef.
Of these three items, we can dismiss (a): first, because its text is less suitable to the occasion (the newly created angels praising the Creator); second, because its omission of "deus" as the fourth word makes it less likely than (b) or (c) to give rise to the readings of AR. Of (b) and (c), the former is more appropriate, since it refers specifically to the creation.

PLAY 1/213+SD *Gloria tibi trinitas*
Vespers antiphon for Trinity Sunday (AS 286).
Largely syllabic chant, range c–d', c-clef.

PLAY 6/64+SD, 72+SD *Magnificat*
Vespers canticle: for the purpose of performance in a play the solemn tones would perhaps be suitable (LU 213–18), but the choice might depend partly on the musical ability of the actor.

PLAY 6/666+SD *Haec est ara dei caeli*
I am unable to identify this text as a liturgical piece, although there are several parallel texts (on which this could have been modeled) in the services for the consecration of a church. The first verse of *Salve festa dies* on this occasion begins "Hec est aula dei pacis" (PS 129r). However, the direction "Let the music be according to the judgment of the performer" may show that music must be found or composed for this text

and hence that none existed for it. Dutka suggests that the "judgment of the performer" is needed to make the music the right length for the dramatic purpose,[31] which would certainly be a major consideration.

PLAY 7/357+SD   *Gloria in excelsis*
This is not the Gloria of the Mass: as the SD and the shepherds' discussion both show, it is the incipit Gloria with text up to "voluntatis." The text appears twice in the services of Christmas day:
(a) As the verse of the first responsory at Matins, *Hodie nobis celorum rex* (AS 47).
    Syllabic/neumatic chant, range f–d', c-clef.
(b) Benedictus antiphon at Lauds (AS 53). The text has two alleluias added.
    Syllabic chant, range d–c', c-clef.

The lack of alleluias in the SD points toward (a) rather than (b). Both versions are known in liturgical dramas, but in England there was a tradition of special performance of the responsory verse, which was sung by a group of boys placed above the high altar.[32] This dramatic treatment of the responsory verse in a liturgical context suggests that the responsory verse rather than the antiphon would come to mind as a dramatic item.

The identification of the Gloria as the responsory verse is supported also by the fact that in England the responsory verse rather than the antiphon was given polyphonic treatment. All six settings of the incipit Gloria in the Pepys manuscript use the text of the responsory verse, as does the single setting in Cambridge University Library Add. MS 5943.[33] In H there is a line of music written out, with the text "Gloria in excelsis deo" underlaid. The style of this tune shows it to be from a polyphonic setting. It is possible that the setting was chant-based, but this is extremely unlikely, for neither the music of the fifth-mode responsory verse (even if transposed down a fifth) nor that of the eighth-mode Benedictus

31. Dutka, *English Mystery Plays*, p. 70. However, I cannot accept Dutka's suggestion that the music might be improvised.

32. Harrison, *Music in Medieval Britain*, p. 107.

33. Cambridge, Magdalene College, Pepys MS 1236, c. 1460–65: see Charles, *Pepys MS 1236*, nos. 7, 36, 47, 71, 76, and 82; for Add. MS 5943, c. 1400, see Rastall, *Fifteenth-Century Song Book*, ff. 166v–167r, and *Four Songs in Latin*, no. 4. Sixteenth-century settings have still to be examined, but those by Sheppard, Tallis, and Taverner are all of the responsory verse.

antiphon can easily be made to fit the D-minor Chester tune. Almost certainly the piece from which this voice was taken was a free composition, which at present remains unidentified. The line was presumably copied as an incipit showing which setting of the words was used on some particular occasion. A polyphonic performance seems to be proscribed by 7/372–432, where the Gloria is shown to have been a solo. A vocal solo accompanied instrumentally would, however, fulfil this condition. It is also possible that the line was copied for the angel to perform it as an unaccompanied monody, but this seems very unlikely.

The underlaying of the first four words is not a mistake, for the tune as it stands does not contain enough notes for the complete text. Another musical phrase is needed for "et in terra . . . voluntatis." Of the six settings of the Gloria in the Pepys MS, all but the last have structural divisions after "deo," and the last has both voices cadencing at that point. Thus it is reasonable to assume that the line given in H represents the first section, musically complete, of the whole composition.

PLAY 10/288+SD   *Ecce dominus ascendet*
Unidentified as a liturgical text.

PLAY 10/497+Latin   *Ex Egipto*
This occurs as a Magnificat antiphon and also, with the same music, as the Vespers antiphon on Friday in the first week in Advent (AS 20, 21). The Sarum text is the same as the Roman (LU 1081):

Ex Egipto vocavi filium meum: veniet ut salvet populum suum.

This is not the same as the Chester version, but no doubt the same piece is intended.
Syllabic chant, range f–e', c-clef.

PLAY 11/166+SD   *Nunc dimittis*
(a) Compline canticle: several tunes are available (LU 271, 784, 1744).
(b) Antiphon at Matins, Feast of the Purification (AS 404):

Nunc dimittis domine servum tuum in pace quia viderunt oculi mei salutare tuum.

Syllabic chant, range g–e', c-clef.

FIGURE I.   *(British Library, MS Harley 2124, f. 42r)*

^{a} The underlay has been emended slightly: for the original, see Lumiansky and Mills, *Chester Mystery Cycle*, 1:605.

^{b} This note is written as a minim, but the stem is canceled in the usual way.

PLAY 14/208+SD   *Hosanna filio David*

Antiphon for the sixth Sunday in Lent (Palm Sunday) (AS 206). This is the only piece that begins "Osanna filio David," but it adds the words "rex Israel" after "in nomine domini": that is, it follows St. John's version of the entry to Jerusalem rather than St. Matthew's, which omits these two words.

Syllabic/neumatic chant, range f–e', c-clef.

The antiphon *Pueri hebreorum vestimenta* (AS 206–207, PS 40r) uses St. Matthew's version in a musically complete section, but it does not include the final "Hosanna in excelsis" of the SD. It seems probable that the antiphon *Hosanna filio David* is intended, despite the omission of "rex Israel."

PLAY 17/276+SD   *Te deum laudamus*

Prose hymn: there is a choice of solemn or simple tone (LU 1832, 1834). *Te deum* was the hymn sung at Matins, but it had a long tradition of performance at times of rejoicing or thanksgiving.

PLAY 18/153+SD   *Christus resurgens*

(a) Alleluia verse, Easter Day (GS 127).
    Melismatic chant, range g–g', c-clef.
(b) Antiphon for Easter Day (AS 241, PS 83v).
    Neumatic/melismatic chant, range c–b$^\flat$, f-clef.

There seems little to choose between these two. The antiphon ends with "Alleluia, alleluia," which may be thought appropriate, and it is not as difficult to sing as (a).

PLAY 20/104+SD   *Ascendo ad patrem meum*

The verses [a]–[g] are identifiable as follows ([b] being a SD and [h] a SH):

[a] is the Benedictus antiphon at Lauds on Ascension Day (AS 270); the scribe of H may have confused it with the short responsory at None (LU 850), which places two alleluias in the middle of the text. Syllabic chant, range g–g', c-clef.

The remaining texts of this scene are drawn from Isaiah 63:1–3. As these verses are long, they are given here with numbered subsections.

  1 (i)   Quis est iste, qui venit de Edom, tinctis vestibus de Bosra?

     (ii)   iste formosus in stola sua,

    (iii)   gradiens in multitudine fortitudinis suae?

    (iv)   Ego qui loquor justitiam, et propugnator sum ad salvandum.

  2 (i)   Quare ergo rubrum est indumentum tuum,

     (ii)   et vestimenta tua sicut calcantium in torculari?

  3 (i)   Torcular calcavi solus, et de gentibus non est vir mecum;

     (ii)   . . .

In the Roman Rite these verses form part of the Old Testament reading at Mass on Wednesday in Holy Week, and as such they could be sung to a reading tone.[34] If the Chester speeches are performed in this way there is of course no musical problem in singing them after [a].

The Chester speeches are also found as Vespers antiphons for the Feast of the Blood of Jesus (1 July) in the Roman Rite (LU 1536–37), although they have not yet been identified in the Sarum books. Antiphon 1 is Isaiah 63:1 (i) and (ii); antiphon 2 is v. 1 (iv); antiphon 3 is from Revelation 19:13; antiphon 4 is Isaiah 63:2; and antiphon 5 is v. 3 (i). As will be seen below, the Chester verses do not distribute the original text quite as these antiphons do, and this suggests that a normal reading of the text to a Tonus Lectionis may have been intended. So too does Chester's omission of the Revelation text and its inclusion of Isaiah 63:1 (iii), omitted from the antiphons.

---

34. *Missale Romanum*, p. 170. The opening of this lection is also given as the example of the Tonus Prophetiae in the *Graduale Romanum*, p. 102*.

The antiphons cannot be dismissed easily, however, and the search for these speeches in Sarum books must be continued in case the Sarum Rite contains antiphons based on the same passage from Isaiah but with the text differently distributed. One reason for this possibility is that the Roman antiphons are musically compatible with the Sarum *Ascendo ad patrem meum* (see below); another is that, as Dutka has pointed out, three of the Chester speeches are found also in the Fleury *Peregrinus* play, with different music.[35] It may be, therefore, that French uses also included antiphons based on this Isaiah text. The Fleury play does however distribute parts of this text among lines from elsewhere (see under [g], below, for instance), but it seems sensible to consider the Fleury version, as well as the antiphons, in the discussion that follows.

[c] is the first two-thirds of the Roman antiphon 1 (Isaiah 63:1 [i]).
> Syllabic chant, range g–e', c-clef.
> In the Fleury version, the text corresponds precisely.
> Syllabic/neumatic chant, range f–c', c-clef.

[d] completes antiphon 1 (v. 1 [ii]) and adds text not in the Roman version (v. 1 [iii], "gradiens . . . suae?").
> Syllabic chant, range g–d', c-clef.
> In the Fleury version, the text again corresponds precisely.
> Neumatic/syllabic chant, range e–c', c-clef.

[e] is antiphon 2 (v. 1 [iv]).
> Syllabic chant, range f–d', c-clef.
> This text does not appear in the Fleury play.

[f] is the second half of antiphon 4 (v. 2 [ii]: the antiphon starts with v. 2 [i], which Chester omits).
> Syllabic chant, range e–d', c-clef.
> This text does not appear in the Fleury play.

[g] is antiphon 5 (v. 3 [i]).
> Syllabic chant, range c–a, f-clef.
> In the Fleury play this text appears as the second half of a speech, with the changed word-order "Solus calcavi torcular": the first part of the speech begins "Quid turbati estis" (Luke 24:38).
> Syllabic/neumatic chant, range c–a, c-clef.

The readings from the Fleury play are perhaps slightly closer to the

---

35. Dutka, *English Mystery Plays*, p. 69: for the music, see Coussemaker, *Drames liturgiques*, pp. 198–99.

Chester version than are the Roman antiphons. The sections from Isaiah 63 are not contiguous in the Fleury manuscript, however, and more information is needed about the exemplar of the Fleury version before we can come to any conclusion about the Chester dramatist's source for this scene.

The music for the Roman antiphons is compatible with the Sarum version of *Ascendo ad patrem meum* (identical with the Roman version), which is in mode 7. The music of [c] is also in mode 7, that for [e] and [f] is in mode 8, and that for [g] is in mode 2, so that the whole scene works well musically if the Roman antiphons are used. The Fleury settings of [c], [d], and [g], on the other hand, are all in mode 4, which would not follow well from the mode 7 of *Ascendo*: and although it would not be impossible to put the Sarum *Ascendo* with the Fleury settings of the antiphons, that is not an ideal solution. Perhaps it should not be assumed that the Sarum setting of *Ascendo ad patrem meum* was intended.

PLAY 20/152+SD 1   *Exaltare domine*
(a) Antiphon 6, Ascension Day (AS 271):

> Exaltare domine in virtute tua: cantabimus et psallemus.
> Alleluia.

Syllabic chant, range f–e′, c-clef. Mode 2, transposed up a fifth.
(b) Responsory, Ascension Day (AS 274):

> Exaltare domine, Alleluia: in virtute tua, Alleluia.
> ℣ Cantabimus et psallemus.
> ℟ In virtute [tua, Alleluia].

Neumatic/melismatic chant, range f–f′, c-clef. Mode 7.
MS H gives "Alleluia" only after "psallemus virtutes tuas," which suggests (a), but no other Chester MS gives an Alleluia there or elsewhere. The inclusion of "virtutes tuas" ("virtute" in B) after "psallemus" points to (b), but in any case the text is corrupt.

Since *Viri Galilei* follows immediately, however, we must take into account the musical factors that would allow (or hinder) a smooth transition from one to the other. *Viri Galilei* is in mode 7, which follows well from (b) but would not follow easily from the transposed second mode of (a). It therefore appears that (b) is the correct item here.

PLAY 20/152+SD 2   *Viri Galilei quid aspicitis*
Antiphon on Ascension Day (AS 269).
Syllabic chant, range f–e', c-clef. Mode 7.

PLAY 21/120+SD   *Veni creator spiritus*
Verse hymn on Whit Sunday (LU 885). The SD in H suggests that only
the first verse is sung, the whole verse being written out.

PLAY 21/238+SD   *Accipite spiritum sanctum*
Benedictus antiphon on Whit Sunday (AS 280).
Syllabic chant, range c'–c'', g- and c-clefs.

PLAY 21/310+SD   *Credo in deum*
The Apostles' Creed is chanted on a monotone; thus there would be no
difficulty in singing the Latin verses in this scene. Further on this item,
see above.

PLAY 23/722+SD   *Gaudete justi in domino*
There are two possibilities:
(a) Alleluia verse for the Mass of St. Thomas the Apostle (21 December)
    in the Roman Rite (LU 1327):

> Gaudete justi in domino: rectos decet collaudatio.

Melismatic/neumatic chant, range c–c', c-clef.
(b) Communion, Mass of Two or More Martyrs (GS 218):

> Gaudete justi in domino, Alleluia: rectos decet collaudatio,
> Alleluia.

Neumatic/melismatic chant, range c–c', f- and c-clefs.
Of these, (b) is the more likely: it is found in the Sarum Rite; it is a
common item, which is more likely to be used than an item from a specific
saint's day, unless that saint is himself involved; and the item is sung in
the play as the martyred Elias and Enoch are led to glory, so that music
from the Common of Martyrs is an obvious choice.

PLAY 24/452   *Venite benedicti*
(a) Introit for Wednesday in Easter Week (GS 120):

Venite benedicti patris mei; percipite regnum: Alleluia.
Quod vobis paratum est ab origine mundi: Alleluia, alleluia,
alleluia.

[Then follows the psalm-verse *Confitemini*, which is unnecessary
here.]

Neumatic chant, range f–f', c-clef.

(b) Benedictus antiphon, Monday following the first Sunday in Lent (AS
158):

Venite benedicti patris mei percipite regnum quod vobis
paratum est ab origine mundi.

Syllabic chant, range g–e', c-clef.

Perhaps (b) is more likely here, being a simpler presentation of the text
about to be paraphrased.

PLAY 24/508+SD   *Letamini in domino*
Offertory for the Common of Martyrs (GS 218). A non-Sarum version is
given (GS 217) as the alleluia verse for the Common of Martyrs, but
without music.

Neumatic chant, range c–c', f- and c-clefs.

(Alternative to the following)

Salvator mundi domine

Verse hymn (AS 46).

(Alternative to the above)

As the foregoing shows, the nineteen identifiable items include antiphons, antiphonal Mass-chants, a responsory, a responsory verse, canticles, hymns, and the Apostles' Creed. Music from the Divine Office is
predominant, with only two Mass-chants among the items likely to have
been intended in performances of the cycle. Moreover, of the remaining
three possible items of Mass-music, one (the Introit *Venite benedicti*) is
also an antiphonal chant. The only soloist liturgical music in the cycle,
then, is one responsory and one responsory verse. Even if my identifica-
tions of *Christus resurgens* and *Gaudete justi in domino* are wrong, thus
doubling the amount of soloist music by the addition of two alleluia
verses, antiphonal and congregational chants would still predominate.

FOR THE PURPOSES of the above discussion, I have assumed that all of the liturgical pieces were sung to their plainsong tunes, in unison. The question does arise, however, whether any of these pieces might have been performed in polyphonic settings. Carpenter believed that polyphony might be indicated in cases where angelic music was sung by a specified small number of angels, and she cited the two angels singing *Christus resurgens* in Play 18 as an example.[36] The possibility is supported by the existence of written polyphony for the angels in York Play 46 and also by the suggestion of John Stevens that the *Ave regina caelorum* at the end of York Play 45 was sung by four angels "Cum uno diabolo" because the angels were too few to perform a five-part setting.[37]

This argument is unconvincing as a general case for polyphony. York 45 and 46 are Marian plays, where we should expect special musical resources, if anywhere. The written polyphony of York 46 is all in two parts, however—quite special enough for York in the late fifteenth century—and a five-part setting of *Ave regina caelorum* is most unlikely to have been performed at that time. In the later sixteenth century, perhaps, with simpler notational and musical styles, it would be possible. But it would be a special case, even then.

Nor is the number of angels of any real significance in this respect. The two who sing *Christus resurgens* (18/153+SD) are specified by one of the Gospel accounts (Luke 24:4–7, although Matthew 28:2–7 and Mark 16:5–7 specify a single angel); the four angels at the Ascension (20/152+ SD) are required for dramatic reasons in the scene after 20/104 (the account in Acts 1:10–11 specifies only two); the two angels at the giving of the Holy Spirit (21/238+SD) are unlikely to perform polyphony while they "throw fire over the apostles," for such actions are not conducive to the precise ensemble necessary; and the singing by two angels at the Judgment (24/508+SD) is unlikely to be polyphony for a similar reason, for they separate the Saved from the Damned and lead the procession to Paradise as they sing. There are, on the other hand, a number of liturgical occasions when a select group of singers would perform plainsong,[38] so that we need not regard this circumstance as in any way indicative of polyphonic performance.

36. Carpenter, "English Mystery Plays," pp. 7–8.
37. Stevens, "Mediaeval Drama," p. 85.
38. Harrison, *Music in Medieval Britain*, pp. 107–8.

For fifteenth-century performances, then, there is no evidence that polyphony was sung in the Chester cycle, and the balance of probability is surely against it. We should demand very strong evidence before we modify a general supposition that the plainsong settings were always used. For the later sixteenth century, however, we need not be so certain of the absence of polyphony—not because there is incontestable evidence of it but because of a general change of musical climate. The Coventry "carols," dating from 1591 or earlier,[39] show that by then three-part polyphony might be heard in a cycle-play (which does not mean that it was then normal, although a payment in the Coventry Drapers' accounts for 1558 "to Ihon to synge the basse"[40] suggests that it was). We have already noted that the fragmentary Gloria in H is apparently the incipit of a polyphonic setting: and although we do not know that it was sung polyphonically, or indeed sung at all, in any performance of the cycle, polyphonic performance must be admitted as a possibility.

Vocal Nonliturgical Items

PLAY 3/225–36   *The Good Gossips' Song*

The passage concerned is comprised of sts. 29, 30, and 31. It is variously headed "The Good Gossips" (HmRB), "The Good Gossip" (H), and "The Good Gossipes Songe" (A): this heading is a SH in HmARH, but it is marginal in B. The absence of the word "song" in HmRBH does not, of course, positively preclude singing, but as A is the only version to mention a song we may confine ourselves to it for our present purpose.

Despite the SH in A, some commentators have treated only st. 31 as the song, preferring to see the two previous stanzas as introductory speech.[41] Perhaps, like Dutka,[42] they follow F. M. Salter in regarding sts. 29 and 30 as a late revision, only st. 31 being part of the original song. This seems

39. Sharp, *Dissertation*, pp. 92, 112, and 113.
40. Ingram, "Pleyng geire," p. 77.
41. Deimling and Matthews, *Chester Plays*, 1:57n; Kolve, *Corpus Christi*, p. 262; Carpenter, "English Mystery Plays," p. 16.
42. Dutka, *English Mystery Plays*, pp. 78–79. The only real distinctions to be made are the different rhyme-scheme of stanzas 29 and 30, and the omission of stanza 31 from H.

too speculative—to treat the passage thus is to claim that we can distinguish speech (sts. 29 and 30) from song (st. 31), and there is no internal or external evidence to support such a claim. If it is possible to see the whole passage as a song as it is transmitted in A, then we should need good evidence that sts. 29 and 30 ought to be spoken before we can regard the SH as untrustworthy.

There is, however, some reason for thinking that st. 29, at least, belongs to the second half of the sixteenth century and is therefore a late addition. This stanza should be compared with the beginning of *Save me O God*, quoted below. It expresses an anxiety that parallels the spiritual anguish of the psalm; and the phrases "The flood comes fleeting in full fast" (225) and "For fear of drowning I am agast" (227) awaken such pre-echoes of the psalm to follow—subconscious on the writer's part, perhaps, but surely not coincidental—that one may well see the same hand at work in st. 29 and the choice of "Save me, O God" a few lines later. St. 29 is not a parody, however, and the meter of sts. 29 and 30 does not allow the tune of "Save me, O God" to be used for them.

Producers of the play may prefer to use one of the readings in HmRBH, and to treat these stanzas as speech. If A is used, a tune might be composed for this passage. In the Chester performances a preexistent tune probably was used, well known to players and audience, and although there is nothing now to show which tune was used it is possible that a suitable one could be found.

PLAY 3/260+SD *Save me, O God*
This title is given only in H. Some version of Psalm 69 is presumably indicated, the first two verses being (in the Authorized Version):

1. Save me, O God; for the waters are come in unto my soul.
2. I sink in deep mire, where there is no standing: I am come into deep waters, where the floods overflow me.

Subsequent verses would not be relevant in the dramatic context. Granted that this is the obvious source for whatever is sung, two questions arise. First, what sort of psalm-setting would be sung domestically and could be performed by Chester citizens in the late sixteenth century? Second, what pieces in that category were then available to them?

On the first question, we can presumably dismiss any method of singing the Latin text of a psalm. The SD is itself in Latin, so that the use of English for the title must indicate a vernacular version of the psalm. The possibilities remaining are:

(i)   The chanting of the prose psalm to a plainsong psalm-tone.
(ii) A polyphonic setting of either a prose or a metrical version of the psalm.
(iii) A metrical version, sung in unison.

Of these, I dismiss both (i) and (ii) as unsuitable to almost any but trained singers, the only possible exceptions being such members of a gentleman's household as had a musical education enabling them to sing madrigals, etc. On the other hand, (iii) is eminently suitable, for metrical psalms were originally written to be sung in unison and their use was widespread at the relevant time.

As to the metrical versions available, it is hardly necessary to look very far. Following the *Goostly Psalmes* of Coverdale (? 1539) and the psalters of Crowley (1549), Seager (1553), and Day (1560), the history of the metrical psalter in England is almost entirely concerned with the works of Thomas Sternhold and John Hopkins. Sternhold's earliest collections did not include Psalm 69, which was added by Hopkins for the complete psalter of 1561. In that edition the setting was a monophonic one, but from 1563 onward the tune was sometimes used as the basis for a setting in parts.[43] Hopkins's version of Psalm 69 continued to be used for the many editions of "Sternhold and Hopkins." To say that the Sternhold and Hopkins psalter was a success would be a gross understatement— Steele lists no fewer than eighty surviving editions in the period 1562– 1600, with another seventeen "ghost" editions now lost.[44] In view of this astonishing record we can be sure, I think, that the general public was used to the tunes and at least the style of the texts by the late sixteenth century, while most people probably knew the more popular items by heart.[45] Not only did the various editions of the Sternhold and Hopkins psalter continue to use Hopkins's version of Psalm 69 and the tune asso- ciated with it—sometimes giving the text only, sometimes with a mono-

43. Frost, *Psalm and Hymn Tunes*, p. 122.
44. Steele, *Music Printing*, pp. 94–100.
45. On the much-used condition of surviving copies, see Krummel, *Music Printing*, p. 35.

phonic or polyphonic setting—but psalters by other compilers made use of them, too. Text and tune appear in the psalters of Day (1565), Daman (1579), Este (1592), Allison (1599), and Barley (1599) in the period that concerns us here.[46]

The Hopkins version of Psalm 69, then, was ubiquitous in the second half of the sixteenth century, and the SD following 3/260 almost certainly refers to it. The first stanza—the stanza always underlaid to the music—could hardly be more suitable for the purpose, for it covers the first two verses of the psalm:

Save me, O God, and that with speed,
    the waters flow full fast:
So nigh my soul do they proceed
    that I am sore aghast.

I stick full deep in filth and clay,
    whereas I feel no ground:
I fall into such floods, I say,
    that I am like be drowned.

The different editions of the Sternhold and Hopkins psalter contain a number of minor variants, both in orthography and in the rhythm of the music. In general, there is no need to regard these as printer's errors. There are also pitch-variants, however, and here we must try to distinguish errors from genuine variants, since it is desirable to approach as closely as possible to a definitive melodic version. The best opportunity for doing this is afforded by those editions that use *solfège* notation, a didactic notation in which each note on the staff follows the initial letter of the relevant sol-fa syllable. Where the note's position on the staff varies from that of the majority of editions, the *solfège* letter may confirm the majority reading, thus showing the note itself to be a printer's error. My transcription is made from the edition of 1579: the rhythm differs slightly from the version given by Frost,[47] but no pitch-variants remain after correction by reference to the *solfège* letters.

46. Steele, *Music Printing*, pp. 94–100; Frost, *Psalm and Hymn Tunes*, p. 122; Allison, *Psalmes of David*, sig. [I3]v–[I4]r.
47. Frost, *Psalm and Hymn Tunes*, p. 122.

FIGURE 2.

ª The note is F, but the *solfège* gives S[ol].

ᵇ The note is A, but G is shown by the direct on the previous line and by the *solfège* letter S.

ᶜ All the sharps are editorial suggestions. In each case the note F has the *solfège* letter F[a], indicating F natural, but sol-fa syllables invariably follow the written notes, without taking account of accidentals to be added by the singer in performance.

ᵈ The note is A, but B♭ is shown by the direct on the previous line and by the *solfège* letter F.

ᵉ The note is F, but G is shown by the direct on the previous line and by the *solfège* letter S.

PLAY 7/411 *Pax Merry Maud*

This sounds as if it should be a popular song, but I have not been able to identify it. The line is only a reference, however, and there is no question of performance here.

PLAY 7/447+SD *Troly loly loly loo*

"Trolly lolly lo" was a not uncommon refrain in the sixteenth century, but there is only one song that seems to fit the title as it is given in the Chester MSS: a three-part piece by William Cornish, dating from about 1515:[48]

Trolly lolly lolly lo,
Sing trolly lolly lo:
My love is to the greenwood gone,
Now after will I go.
Sing trolly lolly lo.

The song is unique to the British Library, Add. MS 31922. As it stands the text is perfectly suitable for the shepherds to sing, but if it is fragmentary, as seems likely despite John Stevens's remark that it is "probably complete, even though short,"[49] subsequent verses may well have been less innocent than this one. If this setting was used for the Chester shepherds, they probably sang in unison, taking the top line of Cornish's setting as the tune.

Unspecified Vocal Items

Having discussed the vocal items of which the titles are known, we turn to those for which no title is transmitted to us. By reference to other cycles we may suggest pieces to be performed at these places in the Chester cycle, or at least discover the type of text that will be suitable.

PLAY 1/125+SD

This SD occurs only in H. There are probably many possible pieces giving praise to the Creator, which is what is necessary here. In the York cycle God's bestowal of authority on Lucifer is followed by the singing of the Sanctus section of *Te deum*, the opening of which has already been sung.[50] The antiphon *Tua est potentia* (AS 323) is only one of many relating to the Creator's power, but it also has a prayer for peace, which

48. Stevens, *Court of Henry VIII*, no. 39 and p. xix. This and other lyrics using the "Trolly lolly lo" refrain are discussed in Stevens, *Music and Poetry*, pp. 243 and 401.

49. Stevens, *Music and Poetry*, p. 401.

50. This is not, as stated by Carpenter, "English Mystery Plays," p. 5, the (complete) *Te deum* followed by the Sanctus of the Mass.

is of immediate relevance in this Chester play. Alternatively one might look for a piece that treats the subject of light, since God has just referred to the brightness of his face and Lucifer is about to boast of his own brightness.

PLAY 3/252+SD

This SD is the Group MSS's equivalent of 260+SD, where H names "Save mee O God." On the matter of comparability of the two SDs, see above. The most obvious piece to perform here, then, is *Save me, O God* itself, the identity of which has already been discussed. Of other Noah plays needing music, York's does not name a piece, but the N-Town play names *Mare vidit* and *Non nobis domine* as music sung by Noah and his family.[51] These are both psalm-verses (Psalm 114/3 and 115/1, respectively) and could presumably have been chanted to a psalm-tone. They occur at the end of the play, however, when the danger is over, and they are unsuitable as alternatives to *Save me, O God*.

PLAY 7/164+SD

If Garcius sings here, a cheerful song of the "Trolly lolly" type would be suitable. Other cycles do not name a piece sung by the shepherds before the angelic Gloria. A nativity song would be inappropriate here, though a secular Christmas song such as the carol *Make we merry, both more and less*[52] would be acceptable.

PLAY 7/479, 656

On the analogy of the Coventry Shearmen's play, in which the shepherds sing the two verses of *As I out-rode* on the way to and from Bethlehem, respectively, the Chester shepherds might even sing *Troly loly loly loo* again here, especially if a version with more than one verse can be found. But they are in serious mood, and it would be better to have them sing in unison something with a suitable religious content. Probably it should be in English—an old carol like *As I lay upon a night* or a lyric such as *Sweet Jesus is come to us* (which is to be sung to the tune of *And I were a maid*):[53] or they might sing a well-known Latin piece such as the anti-

---

51. Block, *Ludus Coventriae*, 4/253+SD.
52. Greene, *Carols*, p. 6. No music survives for this carol.
53. Stevens, *Mediaeval Carols*, no. 1A, p. 110, seems to be a version of the first verse of the carol printed in Greene, *Carols*, pp. 92–94: the whole carol could be

phon *Hodie Christus natus est* (AS 54), though this must not sound like a poor performance of "angelic" music.

PLAY II/40+SD, 71+SD
If there is angelic singing at these two places it presumably needs to be on a text affirming the virginity of the Mother of God. There are several possible pieces, but in view of the action taking place it should perhaps be a relatively simple item musically, such as the antiphon *Benedicta es tu, Virgo Maria* (LU 1381).

Instrumental Music

It is hard to say anything about the instrumental music of minstrels without relying heavily on conjecture. For the Middle Ages, it would be fair to say that since minstrels did not read mensural notation any reconstruction of their musical style must be based on methods of improvisation over a given tune. Although most composed "instrumental" polyphony of the Middle Ages seems to follow the styles of vocal models, there are a few pieces from the late fifteenth century that probably approximate in style to instrumental minstrelsy. Examples of this are *Falla con misuras* (a setting of the basse dance tenor "La Spagna") and *Quene note*, both in two parts.[54]

What tunes should be used as the basis for polyphonic "improvisation" in style similar to these? A simple and convenient rule might be that a plainsong tune should be used in a "heavenly" context (as in Play 2), and a basse dance is the obvious courtly tune for use in Herod's palace.[55] Roughly, this may well represent the tradition of performance at Chester and elsewhere, at least to the end of the fifteenth century.

In the sixteenth century, however, there grew up both a simpler reper-

---

sung to this music, and it is partly set thus in Dobson and Harrison, *English Songs*, p. 275. *Sweet Jesus* is printed in Greene, *Carols*, pp. 48–50: the tune for it, *And I were a maid*, is named in the MS. The song *And I were a maiden* is in Stevens, *Court of Henry VIII*, no. 101. Stevens thinks that the third voice is the tune.

54. *Falla con misuras* is available in several editions, including Trowell, *Invitation* 4, pp. 34–35; *Quene note* is in Trowell, *Invitation* 3, pp. 31–32.

55. The main basse dance repertory is in Jackman, *Basse Dances*.

tory of instrumental music and, to some extent, a generation of instrumentalists who could play it from the written or printed page. This repertory is largely secular and its distributors continental—Susato, Phalèse,
and others. Nevertheless, it is possible that in sixteenth-century performances of the Chester cycle composed polyphony was played, even in
"heavenly" contexts such as that of Play 2.

4.

DEVELOPMENT

OF THE CYCLE

OUR PURPOSE IN THIS CHAPTER is to evaluate the external evidence for the cycle in order to suggest a context for the extant texts of the cycle.[1] That context has two aspects. One is the historical context: the tradition of dramatic production of religious drama by the Chester guilds, with such changes and modifications therein as can possibly be established. The other is the dramatic context: the way in which the plays were prepared for production and presented in Chester.

The evidence for these contexts is often selective in character, ambiguous in expression, and sporadic in occurrence; it often reaches us in late, and possibly corrupt, copies. Chronology is often difficult to establish except within very broad limits. In approaching the evidence, we have assumed that the account given in a document is accurate unless other evidence expressly calls it into question and that each document has textual integrity rather than several strata of revision unless there is good reason for believing otherwise. Our conclusions are obviously tentative, and other scholars examining the same evidence may prefer different conclusions.[2]

1. Numbers in parentheses refer to item-numbers in chapter 5, "Documents Providing External Evidence."
2. The scholars who have paid greatest attention to the documents are W. W. Greg, F. M. Salter, and—most recently and thoroughly—L. M. Clopper. See especially Greg's *Trial and Flagellation*, Salter's *Mediaeval Drama*, and Clopper's "History and Development" and *Records*. We are particularly indebted to Clopper's work.

It should be emphasized finally that none of the documents concerning the cycle describes it exactly as it is evidenced by the extant texts. References in the documents to a particular guild or play-subject should therefore not be thought of as necessarily referring to the version of the play assigned to the guild in the extant versions of the cycle. The reader is invited to compare the discussion of the external evidence here with the discussion of the internal evidence for the cycle in chapter 1, "The Texts of the Chester Cycle."

The Traditions of Origins and Authorship

By the sixteenth century a number of traditions about the origin and authorship of the Chester cycle had grown up and / or been deliberately fostered by the city authorities. The traditions suggest a partnership between the ecclesiastical and the civic authorities in Chester, the former providing the text and the latter producing the cycle. These traditions are of doubtful historical value, but they served to suggest that the cycle was of considerable antiquity—indeed, the oldest in England. In the latter years of the plays the traditions were invoked to support a view of the cycle as an established civic event and a part of the city's heritage, a matter that attracted antiquarians.

Four names are associated with the cycle's origin—those of Pope Clement, in whose papacy the cycle is said to have been composed; Sir John Arneway, during whose mayoralty in Chester the cycle is said to have been first performed; Henry Francis, a monk at St. Werburgh's Abbey, Chester, who is said in some accounts to have first written the cycle; and Ranulf Higden, another Chester monk, who according to other accounts was responsible for the cycle's composition. The traditions of authorship and date—set variously at 1269, 1327, 1328, 1332, and 1339—are attested by Lists of Mayors and Sheriffs (16), the Proclamation (10), the Late Banns (20b), and Rogers' *Breviary* (19).

POPE CLEMENT
Clement V, pope in 1305–14, was responsible for the institution of the Feast of Corpus Christi with which the Chester play was associated; this link may have suggested the reference in the Proclamation (10). Coincidentally, Clement VII, pope in 1523–34, was pope at the time when Newhall drew up the first version of the Proclamation, and the coinci-

dence may have aided the allusion. But from a historical standpoint, Clement VI, pope in 1342–52, is the probable referend. Clement VI had a particular connection with Chester, since in 1346 Abbot Bebington of St. Werburgh's had the Abbey exempted from the see of Lichfield and placed under the pope's direct control; this exemption continued under Bebington's successor and was not revoked until 1363. The exemption caused serious division within the abbey chapter and also between the abbey and the crown. Clement VI's dates would correspond to the period of residence of Higden and perhaps also of the young Henry Francis.

SIR JOHN ARNEWAY

Arneway was traditionally Chester's first mayor, an error transmitted in successive mayoral lists and corrected only in 1594 by Mayor William Aldersley. He showed that Sir Walter Lynett had been first mayor in 1257–58, 1258–59, and 1259–60. Arneway historically was mayor in consecutive terms between 1268 and 1276. He cannot be assimilated into any plausible chronology for the cycle's development; his mayoral terms antedate the establishment of the Feast of Corpus Christi with which the Chester play was associated. But William Smith's uncorrected list of mayors, which established the erroneous tradition, would correspond to Higden's residence at Chester; hence the association of the two men in the tradition.

HENRY FRANCIS

This name appears on three lists of monks of St. Werburgh's: (1) 5 May 1377 (Catalogue of Adlington Deeds, Bundle 5-5); (2) 4 June 1379 (Second Register of Bishop Robert de Stretton, 1360–85, and copy by Randle Holme); and (3) 17 April 1382 (Catalogue of Adlington Deeds, Bundle 16-2). His position in the abbey is not stated,[3] but he is the third signatory, following the subprior William de Merton, and he may therefore be assumed to be senior. Salter confused the Benedictine Francis with a Carmelite monk of the same name who in 1389 was recorded as chaplain to Pope Urban VI, a "pseudo-appointment" that Salter speculated might have been a reward for writing the Chester cycle.[4] Since nothing else is known of Francis, Salter further speculated that the ascription of author-

---

3. Salter erroneously calls him "abbot," but the abbot at the time was Thomas of Newport (*Mediaeval Drama*, p. 41).

4. Ibid.

ship to him must be authentic, particularly since he is recorded in the
1370s when mystery cycles from other English towns are beginning to be
recorded. Stemmler has suggested that if Francis was old in 1382, he
could have been a young monk at the time of Clement VI's papacy and
hence author of the cycle in the mid-fourteenth century. These arguments
are, however, entirely speculative.

RANULF HIGDEN

DNB notes that "his name is variously given as Higden, Hydon, Hygden,
Hikeden etc., and his Christian name as Ranulphus or Radulphus, Ranulf, Ralph, or Randle. The first is his own spelling." He took monastic
vows at St. Werburgh's in 1299 and died in March 1364. He was famous
as author of *Polychronicon*, completed in 1327 but subject to revision up
to 1340. This Latin work was translated into English in 1387 and was
printed in English in 1482, 1495, and 1527. It may have exerted an indirect influence on the Chester cycle through its influence upon *A Stanzaic Life of Christ*. Higden's dates correspond to those of Clement VI
and perhaps of the young Henry Francis. He is, however, associated with
the composition of the cycle in documents somewhat later than the Proclamation (10), notably in the Late Banns (20b) where his name is linked
unhistorically with that of Arneway.

An attempt to reconcile some of the conflicts in the traditions of origin
and authorship may be seen in the antiquarian notes by Randle Holme
that preface manuscript H of the cycle's text and are presented in chapter
5 as item 10d.

The Corpus Christi Play in Chester

In 1264 Pope Urban IV created by means of the bull *Transiturus* a feast
to be called Corpus Christi and to be held on Thursday after Trinity
Sunday, the first Sunday after Pentecost (Whitsunday). The date specified
for the occasion then varied from 23 May to 24 June, depending on the
date for Easter. But Urban died in the same year and the feast was not
instituted until 1311, at the Council of Vienne by Pope Clement V. A
dramatic performance was not called for as a part of the celebration of
this feast by either pope. They called for a joyful flocking to church by

the faithful.[5] We do not know how or when in Chester or in other English towns a dramatic performance became a part of the celebration on Corpus Christi Day.

The traditional reasons for the creation of the Chester cycle, as stated in the Proclamation (10), are probably accurate: "not only for the augmentation and increase of the holy catholick faith[6] of our Savior Jesu Christe and to exorte the mindes of comon people to good devotion and holsome doctrine therof, but also for the comon welth and prosperity of this citty." Such a combination of financial betterment from the money spent in Chester—by the people coming to see the cycle—with the spiritual betterment of those people could not fail to interest all parties.

That a Corpus Christi play existed in Chester in 1422 is evident from the controversy between the Ironmongers and the Carpenters (1). The Weavers' agreement of 1429–30 with other guilds (2), the Bakers' Charter of 1462 (3), and the Fletchers' and Bowyers' Charter of 1468 (4) all indicate those guilds' participation in a play and "light" of Corpus Christi. The "light" was a "yerely" (annual) procession (6) on foot by representatives of the guilds, carrying torches, with the Host borne at the head of the procession. Lines 156–71 of the Early Banns (20a) describe this procession.

The route for the Procession of Lights is also indicated in the Bowyers' and Fletchers' agreement of 1474 with the Coopers (6): "from Saint-Maire-kirk-opon-the-hill . . . unto the Colage [college] of Seint Johns." All of the documents cited above describe the Corpus Christi dramatic performance as *a play* rather than as *plays*. The individual divisions of this *play*—for which the various guilds were responsible—are at times called "pageants" (1, 18c) to distinguish them from the Play. We can develop some idea of the contents of and the arrangements for this *play* from the documents mentioned above, from records of rent paid to the city by guilds for places to store their carriages (17a), from the Saddlers' Charter (5), and from the List of Guilds in Harley 2104 (18b).

In 1422 the Fletchers, Bowyers, Stringers, Coopers, and Turners are instructed to continue with responsibility for the *Flagellation*, the Iron-

5. Browe, *Textus*, p. 32.
6. The "holy catholick faith" is the "sanctam ecclesiam catholicam" of the Apostles' Creed. It was used in both Roman Catholic and Anglican churches.

mongers for the *Crucifixion,* and the Carpenters "for their pageant" (1). No other document mentions the Carpenters as having responsibility for a part of the dramatic performance. In the Banns (20) and in the cyclic texts, however, the *Nativity* is assigned to the Wrights. Since a primary meaning for *wright* was *carpenter* (*OED* wright sb.[1] 3), we shall here make two assumptions: (a) that the Carpenters of 1422 are the Wrights of the later documents, and (b) that the *Nativity,* assigned to the Wrights in the later documents, was in some form the assignment for the Carpenters in 1422.

We should also note here that this document from 1422 indicates the existence of an "Original." That this word refers to the master-copy for the Play kept in the Pentice or City Hall under the supervision of the civic authorities can be inferred from payments made by guilds in later years for copying their parts of the cycle (17b).

The Weavers, Walkers, Chaloners, and Shermen agreed in 1429–30 to contribute to costs of the light and Play (2) and, although their pageant is not there specified, the Weavers are later responsible for the *Last Judgment* (20a, 20b). This pageant is assigned to the Weavers and Walkers in Rogers' *Breviary* (19), and to the Websters in the cyclic texts; also, Weavers and Walkers appear together in the Harley List of Guilds (18b). For these reasons we shall consider the *Last Judgment* as part of the agreement in 1429–30.

In the Early Banns (20a) and in lists of rents paid by the guilds to the city (17a) we find mention of carriages used in connection with the Play; but we are not furnished sufficient grounds for speculation about the exact function of the carriages or the manner of performance at St. John's. The rentals do indicate, however, that certain guilds were involved in the Play, and we shall consider the episodes assigned to those guilds by later documents. The rentals indicate that carriages were owned by the Mercers (before 1437–38), the Fishmongers (1438–42), the Tailors (1439–42), the Drapers (before 1467–68), the Shermen (1467–68), and the Saddlers (1480–83). The later documents give these guilds responsibility respectively for the *Presentation* (of the Magi's Gifts), *Pentecost,* the *Ascension, Adam and Eve,* the *Prophets Before Doomsday* (or *Antichrist's Prophets*), and *Emmaus.*

The Bakers' Charter of 1462 (3) mentions the Play without indicating the particular pageant, but later documents assign the *Last Supper* to the Bakers. For the Saddlers a comparable situation exists: their Charter of

1472 (5) refers to the Play but does not specify the pageant; as indicated above, later documents assign *Emmaus* to the Saddlers.

One seeming anomaly appears in the foregoing discussion: the Shermen are involved with both the *Last Judgment* and the *Prophets Before Doomsday*. In 1429–30 (2) the Shermen agreed to contribute jointly to the costs of the Play—presumably for the *Last Judgment*—with the Weavers, Walkers, and Chaloners; but in 1467–68 (17a) they seem to be bearing the costs singly for storing a carriage. In the list of companies in Harley 2150 (18c) they are singly assigned the *Prophets Before Dooms-day*. Possibly by 1500 the Hewsters (Diers) were producing *Antichrist* (18b), immediately before the Weavers' and Walkers' *Last Judgment* and immediately after the Shermen's pageant, which in the Early Banns (20a) is called *Antichrist's Prophets*. The Shermen's play in the cyclic texts prophesies both Antichrist and Doomsday. These circumstances point to the probability that (a) the Shermen were originally jointly involved with the *Last Judgment*, (b) by 1467–68 the Hewsters were assigned *Antichrist*, and (c) at the time (b) occurred the Shermen were separated from the Weavers' and Walkers' *Last Judgment* in order singly to produce a pageant prophesying both Antichrist and Doomsday.

We have some evidence for three other episodes, two probably sixteenth-century additions, which formed part of the Chester Corpus Christi Play. Lines 128–31 of the Early Banns (20a) state that the "worshipful wives of this town" will present a pageant concerning the Assumption of the Virgin. The Lists of Mayors and Sheriffs (16b and c) indicate that the Wives performed this pageant as a separate play in 1487–88 and 1498–99. Also, the Harley List of Guilds (18b) includes the Wives, plus a notation associating the performance of the *Assumption* with them. In addition, the *Assumption* was performed separately in 1515–16 (16d). The Wives were not a craft guild comparable with the companies responsible for the presentation of the other episodes in the Play. Probably they were a religious guild, although they could have been an association of the free women of Chester, since women over the age of forty could engage in trade. The *Assumption of the Virgin* may not have been a regular feature of the cycle.

The petition in 1523–24 by the Cappers to Mayor David Middleton (9) states that this guild was first charged with producing "Kynge Balak and Balam the proffet" during the mayoralty of Thomas Smith. The Cappers and their pageant appear in lines 37–40 of the Early Banns (by

1521). Thomas Smith senior served five terms as mayor: 1504–5, 1511–12, 1515–16, 1520–21, and 1521–22. We shall take it that the Cappers had their pageant by 1521.

The 1534 Charter (12) for the Painters and the occupations associated with them to become a guild states that for "tyme out of minde" they have been responsible for presenting "the shepherds' watch and the angel's hymn." The Painters are not included in the Harley List of Guilds (18b), but they do appear in the Early Banns (lines 49–52). Also, from Thomas Smith's mayoralty of 1515–16 we have a statement that the *Shepherds* was performed in that year. Presumably, the mayor would not have called upon a guild to present an untried play; the Painters, we assume, had borne responsibility for the *Shepherds* in some form for some time before 1515–16.

We cannot be certain of either the date or the function of the Harley List of Guilds (18b). On the basis of the handwriting, Greg and Salter dated it to 1500; we shall accept that date.[7] Because of the order in which the guilds are listed and the inclusion of the Wives, with assignment of the *Assumption* to them, these scholars considered the document a list of the guilds producing pageants. Clopper, however, considers it a list of guilds participating in the Corpus Christi Procession of Lights. He noted that succession for a part of the list is Ironmongers, Cooks, Tapsters and Hostlers, and Skinners—a circumstance that would call for four separate pageants. Since the Ironmongers are regularly responsible for the *Crucifixion* and the Skinners for the *Resurrection*, and since the basic narrative provides only one possible episode—the *Harrowing*—between those two events, Clopper concluded that the list could not be a record of guilds responsible for pageants in the cycle.[8] Further, because the Cooks and the Tapsters and Hostlers—separated in the Harley List of Guilds—are collectively responsible for the *Harrowing* in some of the documents, and because in 1474 Mayor John Sotheworth ruled that the Bowyers-Fletchers and Coopers—groups collectively associated by later documents in responsibility for the *Trial and Flagellation*—could be separately placed in the procession, the latter just ahead of the former, Clopper maintained that the Harley List—which places Cooks one line above Tapsters and Hostlers—records the guilds, and their order, for participation in the procession.

7. Salter, "Banns" (1940), pp. 9–10.
8. Clopper, "History and Development," pp. 224–25.

That representatives of the guilds participated in the Chester Corpus Christi Procession of Lights is clear from documents cited above. But we have no evidence that their order in the procession generally matched the order of their presentation of pageants in the cycle. Also, guild assignment for the *Harrowing* includes variation: in the Early Banns (20a) it is Cooks and Hostlers, in the Late Banns Cooks alone; in the cyclic texts it is Cooks, except for manuscript H, which has Cooks and Innkeepers. In addition, the ever-present possibility exists that the scribe in preparing the list erroneously moved down one line for the separation of Tapsters and Hostlers from Cooks; or that he felt the space insufficient for all three on one line.[9] We shall side with Greg and Salter in this difference of opinion: the list in Harley 2104 (18b) we take to be an ordered list of the guilds presenting pageants. Thus we need not assume that the order of guilds participating in the Procession of Lights matched the order for presentation of pageants.

The Harley List of Guilds (18b) includes eleven groups not yet mentioned here, which may have had pageants by 1500: Drahers of Dee; Barburs; Vyntenors; Goldsmythus and Masons; Smythus; Butcherus; Glovers; Corvisors and Barkers; Cokus, Tapsters, and Hostlers; Skynners; and Heusters (Diers). In the later documents these guilds are associated respectively with *Noah's Flood*, *Abraham and Isaac*, the *Three Kings*, the *Slaughter of the Innocents*, the *Purification*, the *Temptation*, the *Raising of Lazarus*, the *Entry into Jerusalem*, the *Harrowing of Hell*, the *Resurrection*, and *Antichrist*. Earlier we speculated that the Carpenters mentioned in the controversy with the Ironmongers (1) were the Wrights and that the pageant associated with them by 1422 was the *Nativity*, assigned to the Wrights in later documents. The fact that the Harley List of Guilds includes the Wrights in appropriate order for that assignment perhaps permits more confidence that the *Nativity* may have been an earlier part of the Play.

The only major segment of the cycle as we know it from the cyclic texts, which has not so far appeared in some fashion in this discussion, is the Tanners' *Creation and Fall of Lucifer*. In the Harley listing of 1500 (18b) the Tanners (Barkers) appear jointly with the Corvisors (Shoe-

---

9. Assistant Keeper of Manuscripts Schofield in the British Library has written, "The writer could have added 'Tapsters and Hostlers' on the right side of the paper, alongside 'Cooks', but in my opinion he would have had to reduce the scale of his writing very slightly" (letter of 31 July 1978).

makers), immediately after the Glovers and immediately before the Bakers. In other documents the Corvisors regularly have responsibility for dramatic action that includes Christ's entry into Jerusalem; the Glovers' episode regularly includes the raising of Lazarus, and the Bakers' the Last Supper. By 1521, however, we find in the Early Banns (20a) that the Corvisors have single responsibility for *Jerusalem* and that the Tanners now have responsibility for the opening pageant presenting the creation of the angels and the fall of Lucifer. As Newhall's Proclamation of 1531–32 and later documents—including the cyclic texts—indicate, that assignment continued.

If we assume that the guilds in the Harley List (18b) presented pageants, then possibly by 1500 all segments of the cycle as we know it from the cyclic texts—plus the Wives' *Assumption*—might have been present in some form except the Cappers' *Balaam and Balack*, the Painters' *Shepherds*, and the Tanners' *Creation and Fall of Lucifer*. As stated above, the Painters had their pageant by 1515–16, the Cappers and the Tanners theirs by 1521. Thus by a combination of fact and inference we have derived a full structure—admittedly debatable—for the Play presented by 1521 at St. John's on Corpus Christi Day.

It may be helpful in concluding this section to list the pageants that we surmise constituted the Chester Corpus Christi Play, together with the dates of their first record, or of the producing guild's first record, as part of the Corpus Christi celebration. The dates do not in general indicate anything about the growth of the Play, and the list represents the fullest version of the Play that we can reasonably postulate. It does not follow that all of these pageants were presented on any one occasion, or that the content of episodes was necessarily comparable with that in the cyclic texts, or that each episode was mounted on a separate carriage.

1. Tanners—*Creation and Fall of Lucifer*—by 1521
2. Drapers—*Adam and Eve*—by 1467–68
3. Waterleaders and Drawers of Dee—*Noah's Flood*—by 1500
4. Barbers—*Abraham and Isaac*—by 1500
5. Cappers—*Balack and Balaam*—by 1521
6. Wrights—*Nativity*—before 1422
7. Painters—*Shepherds*—by 1515–16
8. Vintners—*Three Kings*—by 1500
9. Mercers—*Gifts of the Magi*—by 1437–38
10. Goldsmiths and Masons—*Slaughter of the Innocents*—by 1500

11. Smiths—*Purification*—by 1500
12. Butchers—*Temptation of Christ*—by 1500
13. Glovers—*Raising of Lazarus*—by 1500
14. Corvisors—*Entry into Jerusalem*—by 1500
15. Bakers—*Last Supper*—by 1462
16. Fletchers, Bowyers, Stringers, Coopers, and Turners—*Flagellation*—by 1422
17. Ironmongers—*Crucifixion*—by 1422
18. Cooks, Tapsters, and Hostlers—*Harrowing of Hell*—by 1500
19. Skinners—*Resurrection*—by 1500
20. Saddlers—*Emmaus*—by 1472
21. Tailors—*Ascension*—by 1439–42
22. Fishmongers—*Pentecost*—by 1438–42
23. Wives—*Assumption*—by 1487–88
24. Shermen—*Prophets of Antichrist* and *Doomsday*—by 1467–68
25. Hewsters—*Antichrist*—by 1467–68
26. Weavers—*Judgment Day*—by 1429–30

Except for the *Flagellation,* the *Crucifixion,* and the *Assumption,* we have little exact information about the content of the individual pageants at this time. Titles of individual pageants are probably identifying labels rather than exact descriptions; it is therefore difficult to decide what significance should be attached to their failure to include segments present in the cyclic texts. Thus "Kynge Balak and Balam the proffet" is specified for the Cappers, but no mention is made of the section on Moses and the Law—present in the five cyclic texts—and the procession of the prophets —present in manuscript H. Similarly, the Painters are responsible for "the sheppards wach with the angels hyme," but no mention is made of the shepherds' visit to Bethlehem and their presentation of gifts—present in the five cyclic texts.

Concerning the frequency of performance of the Corpus Christi Play we know little. Newhall's Proclamation of 1531–32 (10) speaks of performance "from tyme to tyme" in the past. The same phrase occurs in the Vintners', Diers', and Goldsmiths'-Masons' agreement of 1531–32 (11). In the Bakers' Charter of 1462 (3) that guild is required to pay expenses for "the Play and Light of Corpus Christi as oft tymes as it shall be asseset." It is possible that the Play was not necessarily always performed at regular intervals.

The Whitson Playe

The first indication of a change in date for the guilds' dramatic performance is found in the agreement between the Founders-Pewterers and the Smiths of 4 February 1521 (7). In that document the two groups, although they remain separate guilds, agree to share the expenses for "Whitson Playe and Corpus Christi Light." Whitsun (White Sunday, Pentecost), the celebration of the coming of the Holy Ghost, is the seventh Sunday after Easter and occurs eleven days before Corpus Christi Day. The use of "Whitson Playe" here rather than "the Whitson Plays"—the customary usage in all later documents—reflects the same usage as "Corpus Christi Play" and perhaps indicates that the Whitsun Play reflects the simple transference of the Corpus Christi one-day "Play," with its structure and production methods, to a new date. We know from the Early Banns (lines 156–63) that when the guilds shifted the date of their Play, the Procession of Lights continued on Corpus Christi Day and that a play of some sort was put on then at St. John's by the clergy. We also know from the Early Banns (line 12) that "Whitsonday-tide" was the time of performance for the cycle. We have no evidence as to why the shift in date for the guilds' dramatic performance occurred.

The shift of performance from Corpus Christi Day to Whitsunday may have been the reason for the original composition of the Early Banns (20a). One passage in the Banns possibly resulted from a need to inform the public of the new time for performance of the Play:

> Our wurshipfull mair of this citie,
> with all this royal cominaltie,
> solem pagens ordent hath he
> *at the fest of Whitsonday-tide.*   [9–12, italics added]

Surely the phrase *the fest of Whitsonday-tide* means the same day—Pentecost itself—as *Wytsonday* in line 127 of the Banns and is not synonymous with *Whitsuntide* or *Whitsun Weeke*, used in connection with the later three-day performances. Presumably, the Banns for subsequent performances of the cycle on Whitsunday—if any occurred—would not have needed so specific a reference to the appointed day. There seems no reason to doubt that *tyde* was intended as the rhyme-word in line 12. Although the b-rhyme in line 16 is *while*—"yf ye will abyde a while"— that line must originally have read "yf ye will a while byde" or "yf ye will a while abyde."

The later passage in the Banns (156–71), which has the effect of assuring the public at some length that the shift to Whitsunday will not deprive them of the Procession of Lights and a play on Corpus Christi Day, may also suggest that the shift in date of performance, evident by 1521, motivated the original composition of the Early Banns. The Banns were later revised to suit the three-day pattern (lines 148–87), and were further altered by erasures as a result of the separation from Rome (20, Textual Notes for E).

The heading for the List of Companies (18c) preceding the Early Banns in Harley 2150 does include the statement that the guilds in the list presented the "pagyns in the pley of Corpus Christi." This list, however, like the heading, gives information about the cycle different from that furnished in the Early Banns, and the heading may well have nothing to do with the Banns. The Newhall Proclamation, probably of 1539–40 and revised because of anti-Catholic feeling, which also precedes the Early Banns in Harley 2150, certainly differs in tone from the Banns and has no connection with their dating. In sum, one may think—without being able to prove the point—that the original composition of the Early Banns might have occurred as a result of the decision taken by 1521 to shift the performance of the Play from Corpus Christi Day to Whitsunday.

We need to examine further this matter of original composition of the Early Banns for a performance of the cycle on Whitsunday by 1521. The dominant stanzaic pattern in the Banns, as in the cyclic texts, is *rime couée*: an eight-line stanza most frequently rhyming aaabaaab, the a-lines normally having four stresses and the b-lines three. For the most part the Banns assign four lines—a half-stanza, aaab—within an eight-line stanza to each pageant. But eight sections of the Banns do not match this pattern: *Creation and Fall of Lucifer* (Tanners), *Nativity* (Wrights and Slaters), *Shepherds* (Painters, Glaziers, and Broderers), *Three Kings* (Vintners), *Presentation* (Mercers), *Slaughter* (Goldsmiths and Masons), *Assumption* (Wives), and *Prophets of Antichrist* (Shermen). Earlier commentators[10] have taken these irregularities in stanzaic form as evidence that the content of the cycle was augmented or otherwise altered after the original composition of the Banns, and that the pertinent sections of the Banns as we have them were therefore added or revised to match the additions or other alterations in the content of the cycle.

10. See the discussion by Salter, "Banns," and Clopper, "History and Development."

The earlier scholars may be right, but it is at least possible that their basic assumption is unwarranted. The original author of the Banns—writing, in our view, by 1521 at the time the Play was shifted to Whitsunday—may never have intended to produce a completely regular assignment of four lines for each pageant—aaab—within eight-line Chester stanzas. Certainly, the writers of the cyclic texts did not feel that absolute conformity with the Chester stanza was mandatory. In those texts we find stanzas intentionally in rhyme royal—ababbcc—at Play 8, 290–345, and Play 13, 1–35; and six-line stanzas—aabaab—at Play 7, 275–79, 300–375, and Play 21, 153–58. One can say, of course, that dramatic and thematic considerations, not present in the Banns, dictated these shifts from the normal Chester stanza. But the cyclic texts also contain the kind of stanzaic variety that matches "irregularities" in the Banns, in circumstances where such considerations seem not to be pertinent.

Two of the eight irregular stanzas in the Banns—Painters, Glaziers, and Broderers (*Shepherds*); Wives (*Assumption*)—stand alone as independent quatrains rhyming aaab, rather than serving as half-stanzas in eight-line arrangements. The cyclic texts also present instances of such independent quatrains where we have no evidence that they are corruptions, late additions, or revisions: for example Play 1 (*Creation and Fall of Lucifer*), 56–59; Play 3 (*Noah's Flood*), 233–36; Play 4 (*Abraham and Isaac*), 401–4; Play 5 (*Balaam and Balack*—HmARB), 336–39; Play 7 (*Shepherds*), 324–27 and 584–87; Play 8 (*Magi*), 177–80; and Play 23 (*Antichrist*), 377–80. Perhaps no more examples are needed to show that an independent quatrain—aaab—such as occurs in the sections of the Early Banns devoted (a) to Painters, Glaziers, and Broderers, and (b) to Wives, is not necessarily evidence there for addition or alteration after original composition. It may also be noteworthy here that these two quatrains in the Banns are used for the two plays that were upon occasion abstracted from the cycle for individual presentation, as was pointed out above.

Five sections of the Banns are irregular in that they include eight lines rather than the usual four for each pageant, and one section is irregular in that it includes eleven lines. Whatever the content in the cyclic texts of the plays assigned to the pertinent guilds, three of these six sections clearly describe double-actions for the performance announced by the Banns: the Tanners have the creation of the angels *and* the fall of Lucifer; the Wrights and Slaters have the Annunciation *and* Octavian-Sybil; the Vintners have the assembly of the three kings *and* their audience with

Herod. Perhaps the original author of the Banns decided that pageants with double-actions should have eight lines rather than four. Each of the sections with four lines for a pageant describes a single action, so far as we can determine from the lines of the Banns, with one possible exception, the Drapers:

> You wurshipffull men of the Draperye
> loke that paradyce be all redye;
> prepare also the Mappa Mundi,
> Adam and eke Eve. [25–28]

Whether "Mappa Mundi" means that a part of this pageant was devoted to God's creation of the world, as in the cyclic texts (lines 1–80), and that then another part was devoted to the expulsion of Adam and Eve from Paradise, is not clear. Certainly we have no indication that a part concerning Cain and Abel was included, as in the cyclic texts. Possibly "prepare also the Mappa Mundi" means only that just as the set on the carriage-stage should have Paradise as the locale for the expulsion of Adam and Eve, so also should that set have the map of the universe—as God may have created it in the Tanners' preceding pageant—as background for the expulsion. If so, we have no exception to the observation that the four-line sections of the Banns describe single dramatic actions, while these three eight-line sections describe two dramatic actions.

Another consideration in connection with these three eight-line sections has to do with "selling points." As the opening passage indicates, the fundamental purpose of the exercise was to create high expectations for the coming performance among the people gathered to hear the Banns. Thus in the main body of the document (lines 17–147) the reciter emphasizes what the author considered the most attractive and appealing aspects of each guild's coming performance. These emphases include the importance of the narrative to be enacted, the devotion with which the particular guild will carry out preparations for and enactment of the performances, and the visual appeal of the pageant. In the three eight-line cases under consideration, however, particular stress is given to the impressive spectacle that the sets on the carriages and the actors themselves will present, and it may be that desire for such stress accounts for the eight—rather than the four—lines.

The Tanners will present "the heavenly manshon," the angels "made so clear," and the presumably spectacular fall of Lucifer. The Wrights' and Slaters' carriage—"that royall thing"—will impressively include two sets, one for Mary and the other for Octavian and Sybil. Further, this pageant will include the entertaining spectacle in which the page (Preco) impudently condemns the master (Octavian) to the gallows (Play 6, 277–88). The Vintners will present "3 kings royall" spectacularly appearing before Herod "proude in paulle."

This emphasis on spectacle is especially marked for the one eleven-line stanza in the Banns: the Mercer's *Presentation*. Other than this title the lines do not specify the content of the pageant, and such a title usually refers to the Presentation of Christ in the Temple. But in the lists of companies in Harley 2150 (18c) and Rogers' *Breviary* (19) the Mercers are assigned the *Three Kings of Cologne*, immediately following the pageant presenting the assembly of the three kings at Mount Victorial and the audience with Herod. Since the immediately preceding Vintners' pageant in the Banns also includes the kings' audience with Herod, we take it that the Mercers' *Presentation* enacted the kings' giving of gifts to Christ. Also, the heading for Play 9 in MS H reads "De Presentatione sive Oblatione Trium Regum." The stress that the author of the Banns placed upon color and richness is certainly appropriate for such a "royal" episode, which serves as the spectacular highpoint for the cycle—a function that possibly accounts for the use of eleven lines.

One point stands out in the fourth eight-line section, Goldsmiths and Masons (*Slaughter of the Innocents*): the author chooses to specify that "2 crafts" are involved in the production of this pageant. Eight other sections of the Banns include more than a single designation for the workers involved:

1. Waterleaders and Drawers of Dee
2. Barbers and Wax-chandlers
3. Cappers and Pinners
4. Wrights and Slaters
5. Painters, Glaziers, and Broderers
6. Fletchers, Bowyers, and Coopers,
7. Cooks and Hostlers
8. Saddlers and Foysters

In seven of these instances (1, 3, 4, 5, 6, 7, and 8) the skills designated are closely related; thus we may speculate that the workers named in each of those instances were associated in a single guild. That the work of Barbers (hair-cutting, surgery, and dentistry) and of Wax-chandlers (making candles) is similarly closely related is not apparent, but certainly the author of the Banns did not specify that they are two separate guilds. He did so specify in the case of the Goldsmiths and Masons, using a whole quatrain to address these guilds; in most other instances he used only one line for that purpose. He may have felt eight lines appropriate here because two separate guilds shared responsibility for the *Slaughter*.

The fifth eight-line section of the Banns—the Shermen's *Prophets of Antichrist*—is less easily accounted for. But two considerations are perhaps pertinent. Earlier we saw the possibility that before 1467–68 the Shermen's pageant prophesied both *Antichrist* and the *Last Judgment*. Although lines 132–39 of the Banns do not mention the second, for this performance the Shermen may have continued to prophesy both and the author may have felt that such double prophesying called for eight lines. A less questionable explanation has to do with the stress placed on the fact that the Shermen will actually perform: "That carriage I warrand shall not myst [i.e., be omitted], but [shall] sett forth full dewly"; and "The Shermen will not [be left] behynd, but [will] bring theire cariage with good mynde." It is true that in line 84 the audience is told that the Butchers' pageant "shall not be myst" and that that guild has only the usual four lines. But here the emphasis is much stronger. The impression is that for some previous performance or performances the Shermen had not been allowed to take part and consequently had become incensed. Now the author wants not only to make clear to the audience in general that the Shermen will participate but also to assure the Shermen that this time they will have no occasion to feel offended—"with good mynde."

We have set forth above the considerations that lead us to believe that (a) the original composition of the Early Banns occurred by 1521 with the shift of performance to Whitsunday, and (b) the eight irregular sections of the Banns may represent parts of that original composition. In conclusion, we should point out that earlier scholars have based much of their claim—that the eight irregular sections of the Banns are present because of revision resulting from additions or other alterations in the structure of the cycle—on the fact that five of the irregular sections, including the Mercers' eleven lines, are contiguous. The contiguous sections cover the dramatic action from the *Annunciation* through the *Slaughter*. We offer no explanation for this circumstance, except to observe that it may be the coincidental result of the considerations we have set forth.

The Whitsun Plays

In 1531–32—ten years after the evidence cited above for "Whitson Playe"—William Newhall, Clerk of the Pentice (City Hall), wrote a Proclamation (10b) for "Whitsone Plays" to be performed in the "Whitsonne weeke." Later documents—revised Early Banns, Late Banns, and the list of guilds and plays in Rogers' *Breviary*—indicate that in later years the cycle was performed on Monday, Tuesday, and Wednesday in Whitsun week: nine plays on the first day, nine on the second day, and seven on the third day. Although we have no direct evidence that Newhall's "in the Whitsonne weeke" means that those three days were used in 1531–32, certainly the phrase admits performance at times in Whitsun week other than Whitsunday itself. The likelihood is that sometime between 1521 and 1531 the decision was made to adopt the three-day schedule.

Perhaps the change in terminology from "Playe" to "Plays" was the result of the change from a single performance at St. John's on Whitsunday to performances on Monday, Tuesday, and Wednesday in Whitsun week.[11] Items in Rogers' *Breviary* (19), in the guilds' expenses (17), and in the Lists of Mayors and Sheriffs (16) point to performances at four locations with moveable stages: first at St. Werburgh's, second at the High Cross, third in Watergate Street, and fourth in Bridgestreet.[12] We have no evidence to show why the decision to perform in several locations with moveable stages, rather than at one location, was made.

The first two locations for performances were clearly dictated by "official" concerns: first at the Abbey Gates of St. Werburgh's (later the Cathedral) in Northgate Street for the clergy, then at the High Cross before the Pentice at St. Peter's Church, where the four main Roman

11. We stated above that the Early Banns may well have been prepared for a single performance of the Play on Whitsunday at St. John's. The use of *playes* rather than *play* in line 14 of the Early Banns would seem to contradict such a statement. But *pagens*—the expected term for line 14—occurs in line 11; repetition may have seemed undesirable. Also, *play* does not fit the meaning of the line. The occurrence of *play* rather than *playes* in line 150 comes in a section added to the Early Banns after the shift to a three-day performance. This occurrence would thus seem to contradict the distinction in terminology, but "these godely plays" would have disrupted the rhyme-scheme.

12. The evidence does not suggest that the Plays were performed every year, or that every performance involved all four locations, or that the content of individual plays remained constant.

"streets" met, for the Mayor and the Council. The third and fourth locations—Watergate Street and Bridgestreet—may have been regarded as a proper balancing, for the benefit of the guilds and the people at large, of the two "official" performances. Newhall's Proclamation (10b and c) clearly shows such balance between the Mayor and "his bretheren" (the Common Council), on the one hand, and the "whole cominalty" of the city, on the other. The latter term—"whole cominalty"—seems to mean "the people of the community" (*OED* commonalty 1). We know from Harley 2125, folio 40v, that many citizens were distressed by the performance in 1575 because the Plays were performed in only one part of the city.

The route followed is downhill all the way from the Abbey to the River Dee. As described, the Plays were performed in three of the four Roman "streets," the journey between Watergate Street and Bridgestreet being made through the lanes to avoid passing the location at the Pentice again. To go from Bridgestreet to Eastgate Street would have meant moving uphill.

One extant legal document (14) in connection with the performance for 1568 deserves comment here. On 5 June of that year—several weeks before the scheduled performance of the Plays—a "varyaunce" [dispute] between John Whitmore and Anne Webster was heard before Mayor Richard Dutton and Recorder William Gerrard. The dispute concerned the "claime, right, and title of a mansion, rowme, or place" for the Whitsun Plays in Bridgestreet. It seems that Mistress Webster and other "tenuntes" paid rent to one George Ireland for locations in premises of some sort from which they could watch the performance of the plays in Bridgestreet and that Whitmore was arguing that he, not Ireland, owned those premises and was entitled to receive the rent. The two officials ruled that (a) since Mistress Webster and Ireland's other tenants had occupied their places without dispute "for ii tymes past whan the said plaies were plaied"—that is, in 1561 and 1567—Mistress Webster should again occupy her place without dispute for the whole of the 1568 performances, with the understanding that her doing so would not prejudice the claim of either Ireland or Whitmore to ownership of the premises; (b) at a convenient time after Pentecost-Sunday an objective inquest would be held concerning ownership; and (c) if such an inquest should determine that Whitmore has better claim to the premises than Ireland and his tenants, Mistress Webster must pay Whitmore for her place at the rate for 1568.

This document not only informs us of the practice whereby citizens rented covenient places from which to watch the performances of the Plays, but it also gives evidence that on at least three occasions—which, on the basis of the recorded performances of the cycle, would be 1561, 1567, and 1568—Bridgestreet was one of the locations for performance.

From the Vintners', Diers', and Goldsmiths'-Masons' Agreement (11) of 1531 or 1532 we are able to observe one of the practical effects of the change to the three-day performances on moveable stages. That document shows that (a) the Vintners and Diers had been sharing the costs and use of a carriage in the past, and (b) agreement is now reached for the Goldsmiths-Masons to share the costs and use of that carriage with the Vintners and Diers. The Vintners were responsible for the *Three Kings*, the Diers for *Antichrist*, and the Goldsmiths-Masons for the *Slaughter of the Innocents*. Both the *Three Kings* and *Antichrist* present a tyrant-figure, and the sets for both require a throne. It was thus logical for the Vintners and Diers to share a carriage when the Play was presented on one day in one location, and such sharing could continue when the shift to the presentation of the Plays over three days at several locations occurred: the Vintners played on Monday and the Diers played on Wednesday. We do not know the Goldsmiths'-Masons' earlier arrangement for a carriage. If they owned one separately, they have here decided to give it up, probably to save money; if they earlier shared a carriage, the sharing must have been with a guild that later performed—as did the Goldsmiths-Masons—on Tuesday. Obviously, guilds performing on the same day could not share a carriage after the shift by 1531 to the pattern of three days and more than one location. But the same carriage could serve the Vintners' *Three Kings* on Monday, the Goldsmiths'-Masons' *Slaughter* on Tuesday, and the Diers' *Antichrist* on Wednesday. Further, the Goldsmiths-Masons—like the Vintners and Diers—needed a set with a throne for a tyrant-figure (Play 10, 73).

That control of the Corpus Christi Play and the Whitson Playe resided with the Mayor and the City Council was clear in the documents cited earlier (1–9). The same situation continues for the Plays in Whitsun week. The Harley list of companies and plays (18c), organized to match the three-day performance, concludes with the following note: "Provided alwais that it is at the libertie and pleasure of the mair, with the counsell of his bretheryn [the members of the City Council], to alter or assigne any of the occupacons above-writen to any play or pageant as they shall think necessary or convenyent." Certainly the clergy must have approved of and cooperated in the Playe, and that situation also continued during the time of the Plays; indeed, in 1568 and 1572 St. Werburgh's generously bought a barrel of ale for the players (17c). But the final responsibility, like the acting itself, was not clerical.

When the Mayor and his Council decided that the Plays were to be performed in a given year, that fact seems to have been made public by the riding of the Banns perhaps a month before the performance. We find the following statement in Rogers' *Breviary* (19): "And before these playes weare played there was a man which did ride—as I take it upon Saint Georges Daye [23 April]—throughe the cittie, and there published the tyme and matter of the playes in breeife." The man who rode was the Town Crier (17b. ii), and apparently he was accompanied by representatives of the guilds in their play-costumes (17b. ii). His method of "publishing" was to read the Banns aloud. We do not know where such reading took place. Perhaps the group first rode through the city streets and then the Crier read the Banns to the citizens assembled at the Cathedral or the Pentice.

Between the time of the decision that the Plays would be performed in a given year and the time of the riding of the Banns, the Mayor and his Council would need to assign the individual plays to the specific guilds and approve the content of those plays. Expenditures noted in the Smiths' accounts for 1567 and 1568—"For our bill [petition] we put up to mr. meare iid"—suggest that at times a guild might be required, as a part of this preliminary process, to submit a formal request to the Mayor for permission to present a play. Possibly such a requirement applied only when the content of the play was being altered. As we have seen earlier and as we shall see below, the documents furnish considerable evidence that shifting in both assignment and content occurred. Just who did the consequently necessary revising of the Banns and the play-texts, we do not know; certainly the Mayor and the Council bore the final responsibility. One record of expenditure in 1561 by the Shoemakers (17b. i) suggests a necessity for the guilds' payment as a result of revision: "more over the shote at the makynge op of the playe iid ob[olus]." Probably "over the shote" means spending more than was in hand; the occasion— "making up of the play"—perhaps was necessary because the guild may have been assigned in that year a segment of biblical history somewhat different from its previous assignment and thus had to pay for copying out the new text. The Smiths' accounts for 1568 also show expenditure for "making up our booke."

The approved text of the Plays, with their assignment to the individual guilds, was to be found in a document called the "Regenall" (Original). This document was kept at the Pentice, presumably in the care of the Clerk. That the extant cyclic texts have episodes not in the Late Banns may suggest that the Regenall included more approved segments within individual plays than were presented in any particular performance and that a selection among segments was made for each performance. Further, the form of the Regenall clearly changed on a number of occasions. Records of the guilds' expenses (17b) show the guilds needing to copy their plays afresh from the Regenall, presumably because of changes in the texts. The Shoemakers spent three shillings four pence in 1564 "for the copynge out of the oregenall," and the Smiths' accounts for 1556 show two pence spent "for the Reggenall." Other guilds, for which records of expenses are not extant, must have needed to do similar copying of the Regenall. Perhaps such activity explains the disappearance of the Regenall in 1568 (13). In April of that year the Mayor called Randall Trever before him and demanded the return of "the originall book of the Whydson Playes." Trever stated that he had borrowed the book, and he swore that he had later returned it when told to do so. "But where the same is now, or to whom he then delivered the same book . . . he knoweth not."

After the Mayor and Council decided in a given year on performance and approved the assignment and content of the individual plays, and after any necessary fresh copying of individual plays from the Regenall, the guilds turned to preparation of their carriages, sets, costumes, and properties for the performance, and to rehearsal of their plays. The extant records of expenses (17b) include payments in connection with both of these activities. For example, the Shoemakers in 1550 had expenditures for a dozen boards, two planks, three guy-ropes, a rafter, and nails to repair their carriage after its being in the storage area since the last performance; the carriage-wheels also needed attention. Payment was additionally made for a coat for Mary Magdalene, "glaves" for the players, the gilding of God's mask ("fase"), and the painting and gilding of "the pleyeng gere." Three shillings three pence were spent for beef at "our severall reyherse." The extant accounts of the Smiths, of the Painters, and of the Coopers give even fuller illustration for these two preliminary activities.

Two items of expenditure—one in the Smiths' accounts for 1567 and one in the Coopers' accounts for 1572—suggest that the guilds held "tryouts" for parts in the plays: Smiths—"Spent after the chosinge of the litle God xd"; Coopers—"In primis, the herryng of the players and leverynge [delivering] of persells [parts] to the holle [to all the players] ys ixd." The "percells" seems to mean the lines that each actor will speak in the play. The process would appear to have been that the guild secured a copy of its play from the Regenall and then made or had made individual "persells" [parts] for each of the actors' lines. Another item in the Smiths' accounts for 1567—"At rehersinge before mr. meare   iis, vid"—shows the Mayor requiring a preliminary viewing before he finally approved the Smiths' possibly altered play.

We have little evidence as to just when and how in the activities preliminary to actual performance the Proclamation (10) was made public. The main purpose of that document is to warn the people to behave peaceably during the performance of the Plays and not to bring weapons with them. The second part of this warning would have little point for the audiences on that day if the Proclamation had been delivered as a prologue to the first day's performances on Monday of Whitsun week. The document calls Henry Francis "monk of *this* monastery"—St. Werburgh's. Whoever delivered the Proclamation—presumably the Town Crier—seems to have been standing in the Cathedral or in the large square outside it. We guess that the Proclamation was delivered at one or the other place on Sunday, the day before the Plays began on Monday in Whitsun week.[13]

As L. M. Clopper has shown,[14] the idea of yearly performances of the Whitsun Plays first appeared in David Rogers' initial revision of the *Breviary*, and is thus without support in the earlier documents. In William Snead's mayoralty, 1531–32, Newhall's Proclamation (10a and b) was written, presumably for a performance in 1532. Probably the Goldsmiths'-Masons', Vintners', and Diers' agreement (11) was made for the same performance. The Proclamation was revised (10c) in 1539–40, presumably for a performance in 1540, but we have no supporting evidence for

13. The Proclamation for the York Cycle is similarly concerned with preserving the peace. It was delivered on the evening before Corpus Christi Day. See York Memorandum Book: Purvis, *From Minster to Market Place.*

14. Clopper, "Frequency of Performance."

performance in that year. The Shoemakers' accounts (17b. i) indicate performance in 1550 (?), but again we have no confirmation elsewhere. Notes in the Lists of Mayors and Sheriffs (16) point to performances in 1546, 1554 (?), 1561, 1567, 1568, and 1572. The Smiths' accounts (17b. ii) furnish supporting evidence for performance in these years. The Painters' accounts (17b. iii) confirm performance for 1568 and 1572, as do the Coopers' accounts (17b. iv) for 1572. The Trever and Webster cases (13, 14) give added proof for performance in 1567 and 1568. Such is the extent of available evidence for performances of the Plays in Whitsun week.

Certain entries in the extant guild accounts suggest that the Mayor and the Council exercised careful scrutiny to be sure that the guilds' performance of the plays did not vary from the approved texts. The Shoemakers' accounts (17b. i) include an item "To the Reygenall beyrer [bearer]   xiid"; the Smiths' accounts (17b. ii) include for 1561 "For redyng [reading] the Aurygnall [Original]   iid," and for 1572 "For redinge the orrignall book iid"; the Painters' accounts include for 1568 "Item to him that rydeth [readeth] the Orrygynall   xiid," and for 1575 "Item for the rydenge [reading] of the Regenall   xiid"; and the Coopers' accounts include "Item paied Houghe Sparke for redinge the Regynall iis." These items seem to mean that for the series of performances each of these guilds had to pay for a person, representing the Mayor and the Council, to be present with the text of the play from the Regenall, to follow the lines as the play was performed, and to prevent any deviation from the approved text. The records of expenditure (17b) also regularly show payments to the actors who took part in the performances.

The term *carriage*, used in the earlier documents, appears regularly in the guild accounts during the time of the Plays. Numerous items in those records of payment show that the carriages were stored between performances, that they needed considerable repair when taken from storage, that the stage sets were built upon the carriages, that the carriages had wheels, and that porters were hired presumably to push or pull the wheeled carriages from location to location. The Late Banns (20b) also uses the term "carriage" for the moveable stage (lines 60, 108, 128, 151, 161). Variation in terminology first occurs in Rogers' *Breviary* (19). There (19a) we find "And everye companye broughte forthe theire *pagiant*, which was the *cariage* or place the [i.e., they] played in," and "These *pagiantes* or *carige* was a high place made like a howse." A bit further along, however, *pageant* is dropped: "And when they had donne with one *cariage* in one place, theie [i.e., they] wheled the same from one streete to another"; "for before thei [i.e., the] first *carige* was gone from one place, the second came." The version of the *Breviary* in Harley 1944 (19b) matches the situation for 19a. In 19c, however, we find that *cariage* has disappeared and only *pageant / pagiant* remains as designation for the moveable stages. In 19d, 19e, and 19f *cariage* is similarly not used. It would seem that for Rogers *pageant* was interchangeable with *carriage*, but that in Chester *carriage* was the term traditionally applied to the wheeled vehicles on which the sets were transported. No document gives evidence for contemporary use of the modern term *pageant-wagon*.

Additional information about the carriages—beyond that available from the rentals (17a), the Early Banns (20a), the Goldsmiths'-Masons' agreement (11), the Late Banns (20b), and the guild accounts (17b)—does come from Rogers' *Breviary* (19), and it may well be accurate for some of the carriages. Certainly the various requirements for stage sets and action must have resulted in variety among structures for the carriages. Rogers says that the carriages had four wheels and two rooms, "being open on the tope," which may mean that the upper room was open so that the audiences could see the plays. In 19a and 19b we are told that the lower room was used for dressing and the upper as the stage; 19c has the lower room "hanged aboute richly and closse"; 19d restates the same functions for the two rooms, but 19e specifies only "with a lower and a higher rowme." Although such a two-tiered structure would seem extremely awkward to wheel through the streets, and even more difficult to wheel through the lanes, we have no way of knowing whether Rogers' description is correct or not.[15]

In 1534 the Act of Supremacy made Henry VIII head of the Church of England. To bring Protestant doctrine to England was not Henry's goal; the *Ten Articles* (1536) present a creed that generally conforms to the older order, and the *Six Articles* (1539) reaffirmed Catholic views. Also, during Henry's reign persons refusing to accept Catholic doctrine were executed alongside those who refused to accept Henry's authority over the Church of England. These circumstances no doubt explain the lack of evidence for revision of the Plays before the reign of Edward VI (1547–53). Newhall's Proclamation (10c) was revised in 1539–40 to remove Catholic references, but no anti-Catholic statements were added.

Both Edward VI and his Lord Protector, Edward Seymour, were

15. Clopper, "Rogers' Description."

strongly Protestant. The *Six Articles* were repealed, and the *First Prayer Book* was put into general use in the Church of England. We now begin to see signs of alteration in the Plays. The Corpus Christi celebration was suppressed in 1548; probably at that time the lines in the Early Banns promising the Procession of Lights and the play by the clergy were erased (20a, textual notes for E). Perhaps at the same time the Wives' *Assumption* was also suppressed. We have no note in the Early Banns erasing the pertinent lines for that play, but there is such a note for line 185: "and his blessed mother marie"; the Wives' *Assumption* does not appear in the Late Banns (20b), in the lists of companies and plays in Harley 2150 (18c) and Rogers' *Breviary* (19), or in the cyclic texts.

The Early Banns (20a) may have been written for the shift of the Play from Corpus Christi Day to Whitsunday by 1521, then revised by 1531 for the shift to three-day performance of the Plays in Whitsun week at several locations, and then in part "erased" to match the suppression of the Corpus Christi celebration. Obviously, the Protestant Late Banns (20a) were written to replace the revised Catholic Early Banns, but just when the original Late Banns were composed is not clear because of the scarcity of evidence.

We have some evidence for alteration of the cycle in connection with the *Last Supper*. The Early Banns assign "the Maunday" to the Bakers, who in 1462 were issued a charter in which they agreed to pay for costs of the Corpus Christi Play (3). The Late Banns also assign the *Last Supper* to the Bakers, and the list in Harley 2150 gives them "Cristes Monday [Maundy], where he sat with his Disciples" (18c). All five cyclic texts assign to the Bakers "De Caena Domini et de eius Proditione" (Concerning the Supper of the Lord and Concerning his Betrayal), and the texts match that title. In 1552–53, however, the Bakers received a second charter that contains no reference to their involvement in the Plays (3, later note). Further, items of expenditure in the Shoemakers' (Corvisors') accounts for 1550 suggest that the Bakers' play may have been omitted from the cycle and that necessary connecting events were put into the immediately preceding Corvisors' play, using John 12:1–8 rather than Mark 14:3–9. The List of Companies (18c) assigns the Corvisors "the comyng of Christ to Jerusalem"; the two versions of the Banns give them the "Jerusalem-carriage." In the cyclic texts their play is headed "De Jesu Intrante Domum Simonis Leprosi et de Aliis Rebus" (Concerning Jesus Entering the House of Simon the Leper and Concerning Other Matters); the "other matters" are the entry into Jerusalem, the cleansing of the

Temple, and Judas's plot. The Shoemakers' accounts for 1550 show payments to God, Mary Magdalene, Martha, Judas, the six children of Israel, Caiaphas, Annas, two knights, the jailer, and the jailer's man. There is also payment for an ass and a boy to lead it. Simon is absent and Martha is present; the scene must be Lazarus's house (John 12:1–2) not Simon's (Mark 14:3). We note, however, large payments of ten shillings three pence for three "stryke of wyete" (bundles of wheat) and four shillings eight pence "for bakyng of Godes brede." Further, after the Bakers with the *Last Supper* reentered the cycle, they are instructed in the Late Banns to "caste Godes loves abroade with accustomed cherefull harte," a dole that seems to have become the Shoemakers' responsibility in 1550. For other action, the list of actors paid seems to indicate that the 1550 Shoemakers' play included not only the scene at Lazarus's house and the entry into Jerusalem, but also Judas's betrayal, the capturing of Jesus by the two knights, and his delivery to Caiaphas, Annas, the jailer, and his man. As earlier noted, we have record (17b. i) of the Shoemakers' paying two pence in 1561 "at the making up of the play." Perhaps from that record we may infer that in 1561 the Bakers returned to the cycle with the *Last Supper* as we know it in the cyclic texts and that the Corvisors then were assigned their play as it appears in the cyclic texts.

The circumstances concerning the Smiths' play also point to Protestant influence. In the Harley 2150 listing of companies and plays the Smiths are assigned the *Purification*, and in the Early Banns they have "Candilmasday." Both entries would seem to reflect primary attention to the Virgin Mary. But in the Late Banns the Smiths have *Christ Among the Doctors*. Their play in all five cyclic texts is headed "De Purificatione Beatae Virginis," but only lines 119–50 are related to the *Purification*. The play additionally includes (a) Simeon, Anna, and the Presentation of Christ in the Temple; (b) Christ and the Doctors (lines 207–326); and (c) a return to Simeon in the final eight lines, spoken by the angel. The cast-lists in the Smiths' accounts (17b. ii), which begin in 1554, point to a play similar to that in the cyclic texts. Perhaps the material concerning *Purification* was suppressed in 1548, along with the Corpus Christi celebration[16] and the Wives' *Assumption*.

The documents concerning the cycle after 1560 show increasing Protes-

---

16. Harley 2054, ff. 15r–16r and Harley 2177, ff. 21v–27r indicate that the Corpus Christi celebration was resumed during Mary's reign and continued through 1560.

tant antagonism toward it. The tone of the Late Banns (20b) is markedly
defensive, with specific statements aimed at rebutting antagonism to the
performance of the Plays. Clopper speculated that the Banns as we have
them were read to the Mayor and the Council in 1572 at the Pentice to
help insure a vote *for* performance in that year.[17] Given the ways of Tudor
censorship, however, the Banns may represent an official legal application
for a license to perform the Plays, which would be publicly declared.[18]

Clopper also considered it possible that we can see in the Late Banns
original composition (1548–61) and two revisions (1561–72). For him,
the original version presented the descriptions of the individual plays, in
quatrains rhyming abab, much as in MS B; the first revision added the
defensive introductory stanzas in rhyme royal (ababbcc) and similarly
altered seven of the descriptive stanzas, much as in MS R; and the second
revision added the conclusion, also in rhyme royal. In large part, Clopper's view is based on the occurrence of the two different stanzaic forms.
Here, as we did with the Early Banns, we should note the possibility that
the writer of the original version may not have intended absolute conformity to a single stanzaic form.

The increasing Protestant antagonism to the Plays is apparent from
notes in the Lists of Mayors for 1571–72 (16k). In that year Mayor John
Hankey and his Council decided that the Plays would be performed.
Apparently some citizens opposed to the performance informed the Archbishop of York of this decision: "and an inhibition came from the Archbishop to stay them, but it came too late"; the plays were performed "to
the dislike of many." Another note suggests that opposition was to some
individual plays rather than to the performance as a whole: "In this year
the whole Playes were played, though manye of the cittie were sore against
the settinge forthe therof." The clergy at Chester Cathedral, however,
seems to have favored the performance; they built a "mansion" for the
occasion over the Abbey gates and gave beer to the players (17c).

The Final Performance, Midsummer 1575

Sufficient support to warrant performance of the cycle, motivated by
pride in the city's ancient customs, continued into 1575. On 30 May of

17. Clopper, "History and Development."
18. Keane, "Kingship."

that year Mayor John Savage and his Council voted 33 to 12 in favor of performance (15a). As the City Certificate Concerning Mayor Savage (15e) puts it, this decision resulted "only accordinge to an order concluded and agreed upon for dyvers good and great considerations redoundinge to the comen wealthe, benefite, and profitte of the saide citie in assemblie there holden, acording to the auncyente and lawdable usages and customs there hadd and used for above remembraunce . . ." (15e).[19] But a number of alterations were stipulated in an effort to offset Protestant antagonism. The time of performance was shifted from the religious festival of Whitsuntide to Midsummer, a secular occasion during which the Midsummer Show was customarily held. The plays began on Sunday after Midsummer Day (24 June) rather than on Monday as usual,[20] they continued on Monday, Tuesday, and Wednesday (16l), and they were not performed before the Abbey gates. Further, some of the plays were omitted "for the superstition that was in them" (16l). The Council's decision to hold the performance specified "with such reformation as master Maior with his advice shall think meet and convenient" (15a).

Despite these conciliatory efforts, the Archbishop of York and the Earl of Huntingdon, Lord President of the North, reacted vigorously (16l). A summons arrived for Savage to appear before the Privy Council in London. From London Sir John requested the Chester City Council to send him a statement that the Council had authorized the performance (15c). The City Council sent a certificate indicating that neither Savage in 1575 nor Hankey in 1572 had acted without authority (15d and e). No record exists of the Privy Council's taking up this matter; perhaps the charge was dropped upon receipt of the certificate from the City Council. Savage returned to Chester, apparently unpunished.[21] But we have no evidence to suggest any later performance of the cycle. The case of Andrew Tailer (15f), the Painters' accounts (17b. iii, 1575), and the Smiths' accounts (17b. ii, 1576) indicate Protestant antagonism so strong as to move seven guildsmen to refuse to pay their charges for the 1575 performance. Nevertheless, despite such antagonism, interest in the Plays remained suffi-

19. "Used for above remembraunce" means "practised for time beyond memory."

20. In the cyclic texts HmARB we find a statement near the end of Play 5 (lines 450–51) indicating the close of the first day's performance, which may reflect this change from the usual nine plays on the first day.

21. *State Papers: Domestic,* 1:565, shows Savage discharging civic responsibilities in November 1577.

ciently strong to motivate the preparation of the five cyclic texts over the period 1591–1607. But no doubt David Rogers' statement of 1609 represents the view at that time of the large majority in Chester: "And we have all cause to pour out our prayers before God that neither we nor our posterities after us may never see the like abomination of desolation [as the Plays], with such a cloud of ignorance to defile with so high a hand the most sacred Scriptures of God. But, oh, the mercy of God: for the time of our ignorance, He regards it not" (19a).

The Cyclic Texts

In the preceding sections of this chapter we have at times pointed to the relationship between guild-ascription, play heading, or general content of certain plays as provided by the cyclic texts, on the one hand, and such information as is furnished by various documents, on the other. Perhaps it will now be helpful to summarize and augment the earlier comments in systematic fashion.

The five cyclic texts are not acting texts to serve performance. They are versions prepared for historical purposes from sixteen to thirty-two years after the last performance of the cycle: Hm (1591), A (1592), R (1600), B (1604), and H (1607). The five versions do differ; see the Introduction to our edition and to chapter 1 of this volume, "The Texts of the Cycle." But it seems likely that all five were prepared from the Regenall remaining in the Pentice after the final performance in 1575. That Regenall may have reflected some of the shifts of the cycle's final years, and it may also have retained at some points evidence of the cycle's previous states. Thus perhaps the scribes for the cyclic texts at times made choices between alternative materials present in the Regenall. Some of the differences between the five texts must, however, have resulted from scribal error rather than from alternative possibilities in the Regenall. Others may have originated in scribal initiative. For R, Bellin clearly copied from A, but presumably he also had the Regenall before him.

An examination of guild-ascriptions, play headings, and general content of plays follows; we regularly use the item-numbers from chapter 5 to refer to Early Banns (20a), Late Banns (20b), and the Harley List of companies and plays (18c).

PLAY 1 (lost from Hm).

The four cyclic texts ascribe the play to the Tanners, as do 20a and b; 18c has Barkers or Tanners. A omits the play heading; RB have a Latin play heading that indicates the content as creation of the heavens, the angels, and the infernal species; H has the *Fall of Lucifer*. 20a calls for creation of the orders of angels and the falling of Lucifer, 18c and 20b for only the falling / fall of Lucifer. The Proclamation (10) specifies both creation and fall of Lucifer. The play itself presents the creation of heaven (39), of the orders of angels (42), and of the earth and hell (73–74). Then comes the fall of Lucifer (86–283) and the creation of day and night (292–93), ending with God's statement that the first day of creation is completed.

PLAY 2

All five cyclic texts ascribe the play to the Drapers, as do 20a and b; 18c lists Drapers and Hosiers. HmARB have a Latin play heading limited to God's creation of the world; H's Latin play heading calls for the creation of the world and of Adam and Eve, and for their temptation. 18c has only the creation of the world. 20a specifies Adam and Eve, possibly preceded by creation of the world (Mappa Mundi). 20b includes creation of the world, Adam and Eve, and Cain and Abel. In the play God recreates day and night on the first day (9–16) and proceeds with the additional acts of creation, including Adam and Eve (17–160); next comes the Fall and the expulsion from Paradise (161–424), followed by Cain and Abel. B's omission of 681–Finis probably has nothing to do with the text he was working from; it seems to result from his stopping work after 680 and then beginning with Play 3 on the verso of a fresh folio when he returned.

PLAY 3

All five texts assign the play to the Waterleaders and Drawers of Dee, as do 20a, 20b, and 18c. The play headings in HmB and H specify Noah's Flood, as do 20a and b and 18c. The play matches this description. The heading is omitted in AR. In H, but not in the Group-texts, a 47-line passage concerning Noah's sending out the Raven and the Dove occurs after 260+SD (our edition, Appendix IA). Perhaps H prepared the passage in order to match the biblical narrative; or perhaps the Regenall included indication that this passage had been "cut" in production—like the indications of omission in the Early Banns—and HmARB honored the "cut."

PLAY 4

HmBH assign the play to the Barbers; AR to Barbers and Waxe-chaund-
lers; 18c has Barbers, Wax-chandlers, and Leches or Surgions; 20a and b
have Barbers and Wax-chandlers. The Latin play heading in HmARB
indicates that the play begins with Abraham's return from defeating the
four kings and that Lot and Melchizedek are involved; H's Latin play
heading states the same information more clearly; neither heading mentions Isaac. 20a calls only for the Abraham-Isaac narrative; 18c has
Abraham and Isaac; and 20b describes both Abraham-Isaac and the presumably preceding Melchizedek-segment. The play has the two episodes
—Abraham-Lot-Melchizedek and Abraham-Isaac.

PLAY 5

HmBH ascribe the play to the Cappers, AR to Cappers and Linen-drapers. 20a has Cappers and Pinners, 20b Cappers and Linen-drapers, and
18c Cappers, Wiredrawers, and Pinners. B has no play heading; HmAR
indicate only Moses and the Law; H calls for that episode plus Balack
and Balaam. The five texts present two versions of the play: HmARB and
H (our edition, Appendix IB). The former includes Moses and the Law,
Balack and Balaam, and the Moabite women; the latter has the first two
of these episodes but substitutes a procession of prophets for the third.
Presumably the Regenall included both versions of the play.

PLAY 6

HmRH attribute the play to the Wrights, AB to Wrights and Slaters. 20a
and b have Wrights and Slaters, 18c has Wrights, Slaters, Tilers, Daubers,
and Thatchers. The play heading in all five texts calls for Salutation and
Nativity. 18c has only Nativity. 20a mentions Mary, Octavian, Sybil,
and possibly Preco ("page"); "that royall thing" seems to mean the
highly ornamented carriage. 20b specifies Octavian and Sybil, the birth
of Christ, the apocryphal Midwives, and the Expositor's "historical"
passages (564–643, 699–722). The play presents the Salutation—Angel,
Mary, Elizabeth, Joseph; Octavian-Sybil; Nativity, with midwives; Octavian-Sybil; and the Expositor's two comments on miracles. The characterization of Octavian in 20a as "cruell and kene" does not match the
Emperor's behavior in the play, although 185–272 may derive from his
having been presented earlier as a Herod-like raging tyrant. The comment
in 20b that Octavian could not easily accept Sybil's prophecy does not fit
with the action of the play.

PLAY 7

18c and 20a assign the play to Painters, Glaziers, Broiderers; 20b to Painters and Glaziers. HmRB have only Painters; AH have Painters and Glaziers. The charter for the Painters, Glaziers, Broiderers, and Stationers (12) specifies "the plae of the sheppherds wach with the angells hyme." 18c calls the play the Shepherds' Offering, 20a the Shepherds' Play; 20b mentions the Angel's hymn and points to the nonbiblical nature of most of the other material. The play presents the shepherds' gathering, eating, and wrestling with Trowle; the appearance of the star, the Angel's song, and the Shepherds' puzzlement and song; the journey to Bethlehem, the visit with gifts for Christ, and their leave-taking. In HmARB, but not in H, the gift-giving by four Boys follows that by the Shepherds. The Latin stage direction after 447 suggests that H first intended to include the Boys but later decided to omit them, perhaps feeling that the play should not present additional nonbiblical material. Expenditures in the Painters' accounts (17b. iii) are for the play as we have it, including the four Boys.

PLAY 8

The five cyclic texts and 20a ascribe the play to the Vintners. 18c has Vintners and Merchants, 20b Merchant-Vintners. In the five texts the play heading specifies Three Kings of the Orient. 20a and b call for three kings to come before Herod; in 20a they are "of Cologne." 18c has King Herod and the Mount Victorial. The play shows the kings assembling, then praying on the Mount Victorial, before the interview with Herod.

PLAY 9

The five cyclic texts, 20a and 20b ascribe the play to the Mercers; 18c has Mercers and Spicers. The heading in HmARB calls for the Offering of the Three Kings, H for the Presentation or Offering of the Three Kings. 18c names the play Three Kings of Cologne, and 20a simply has the Presentation; 20b does not name the play, but points out that the biblical scene is much more humble than the Mercers' expensively decorated carriage. The play presents the journey to the stable, the kings' offerings, the Angel's warning, and the kings' departure. After 183 AR include a speech by the infant Christ, seemingly requested at 149 and 183. Perhaps the other scribes omitted this speech as nonbiblical and as a possibly sacrilegious representation of Christ.

PLAY 10

HmRBH ascribe the play to the Goldsmiths; A, 18c, 20a, and 20b have Goldsmiths and Masons. The heading of the five texts calls for Herod's Slaughter of the Innocents, as do 18c, 20a, and 20b. The last also specifies Herod's rage at the three kings' escaping him (1–40). The flight into Egypt (256–88) and the return to Judea (458–97) are nowhere specified.

PLAY 11

All five cyclic texts assign the play to the Blacksmiths; 18c has Smiths, Furberers, and Pewterers; 20a and b have only Smiths. All five texts and 18c call the play the Purification; 20a calls the carriage "Candlemas-day." 20b calls for Christ among the Doctors. The play includes Simeon and Anna, a hint of the Purification (136–38), the Presentation of Christ in the Temple, and Christ among the Doctors. Expenditures in the Smiths' accounts (17b. ii) are for the play as we have it.

PLAY 12

The five cyclic texts, 18c, 20a, and 20b assign the play to the Butchers. 20a, 20b, and the play headings in the five texts call for Christ's temptation in the desert. 18c has the Pinnacle and the Woman of Canaa. The play presents the three temptations by Satan; the Doctor's comment as to how Christ's refusing the temptations atones for Adam's succumbing to them; and the woman taken in adultery, with a further analysis by the Doctor.

PLAY 13

The five cyclic texts, 20a, and 20b ascribe the play to the Glovers; 18c has Glovers and Parchment-makers. The play heading in all five texts calls for the Blind Chelidonius and the Raising of Lazarus. 18c, 20a, and 20b specify only the second of these two episodes. The play presents both.

PLAY 14

All five cyclic texts, 20a, and 20b assign the play to the Corvisors; 18c has Corvisors or Shoemakers. 20a, 20b, and 18c specify the entry into Jerusalem; all the play headings call for Jesus' entry into the home of Simon the Leper and other matters. The play includes the scene at Simon's house, the fetching of the ass and foal by Peter and Phillip, the entry into Jerusalem, the cleansing of the Temple, and Judas's plot. The Shoemakers' accounts of 1550 (17b. i) point to a different play: since Simon is not included in the cast-list, the opening scene must be at Lazarus's house; also the presence of knights and jailers indicates inclusion of events through Jesus' captivity.

PLAY 15

The five cyclic texts, 20a, and 20b assign the play to the Bakers; 18c to Bakers and Millners. The play heading in the five texts announces the supper of the Lord and his betrayal; 20a and 18c specify Christ's Maundy, 20b the Last Supper. The play presents the Last Supper, Judas's betrayal of Christ, and the capture of Christ.

PLAYS 16 AND 16A

H and 20b present the two as a single play; H ascribes it to Bowyers, Fletchers, and Ironmongers; 20b to Fletchers, Bowyers, Coopers, Stringers, and Ironmongers. H's heading calls it the Passion of Christ; 20b specifies Christ's scourging, whipping, bloodshed, and passion. The controversy of 1422 (1), HmARB, MS C, 18c, and 20a indicate division into two parts. For the first part, HmAR and C assign the Fletchers, Bowyers, Coopers, and Stringers; B erroneously adds Ironmongers; 20a assigns only Coopers; 18c has Bowyers, Fletchers, Stringers, and Turners; and the controversy has Fletchers, Bowyers, Stringers, Coopers, and Turners. The controversy calls the two parts Flagellation and Passion; the same division is indicated in 18c and 20a; but HmARB call both 16 and 16A Passion. In HmARB and 20a the second part is attributed to Ironmongers; 18c has Ironmongers and Ropers. At the end of 16, HmARB have "This storye is finished in the leaves followinge," with minor variation in wording.

The evidence suggests that the two guilds—Fletchers et al., on the one hand, and Ironmongers, on the other—remained separate but jointly participated in one long play called the *Passion*, which included the *Flagellation*. The Coopers' accounts (17b. iv) show payments to actors, but the number of actors paid is insufficient to fill all the roles demanded by the *Scourging*. Perhaps the two guilds furnished actors who performed in both 16 and 16A. The variation between lines 359+SH–*Finis* in H and HmARB (our edition, Appendix IC) presents no real difference in narrative content.

PLAY 17

HmARB assign the play to the Cooks, H to Cooks and Innkeepers; 20a has Cooks and Hostlers, 20b Cooks, and 18c Cooks, Tapsters, Hostlers, and Innkeepers. The play headings in the cyclic texts specify *Christ's Descent into Hell*; 18c, 20a, and 20b call for the Harrowing of Hell. H omits the final scene, which presents the ale-wife who remains in Hell, perhaps considering it indecorous.

PLAY 18

The cyclic texts, 20a, and 20b ascribe the play to the Skinners; 18c has Skinners, Cardmakers, Hatters, Poynters, and Girdlers. All eight documents and MS M specify the *Resurrection*. A possible reason for the omission in HmA and in B of narrative material found in RH is advanced in the comment on Play 19 below.

PLAY 19

HmARB ascribe the play to the Saddlers; H omits ascription; 18c and 19a have Saddlers and Foysters; 19b has Saddlers and Frysers. 19a calls only for Christ's appearance to Cleophas at the castle of Emmaus; the cyclic texts specify Emmaus and the disciples; 18c has Castle of Emmaus and the Apostles. 19b additionally calls for Christ's "often speeche to the woman [women] and his desiples deere," which seems to describe the material present in RH for Play 18 but omitted there by HmA and B. Perhaps alternative distribution for the material was indicated in the Regenall.

PLAY 20

Ascription is to the Tailors in all eight instances. All eight call for the *Assention*, and no variation in narrative content occurs in the five texts.

PLAY 21

Ascription is to the Fishmongers in all eight instances. The play heading in the cyclic texts specifies the election of Matthew and the coming of the Holy Ghost as the apostles recite the Creed. 18c has Whitsunday, the making of the Creed; 20a has only Whitsunday; and 20b has Holy Ghost. No variation in narrative content occurs in the five texts.

WIVES' ASSUMPTION

We have no text for this play and it is not included in 18c or 20b. It is a part of 20a and of the Harley List of Guilds (18b). Perhaps the play was suppressed in 1548, along with the Corpus Christi celebration, and was never restored.

PLAY 22

HmARB assign the play to Clothworkers; H to Clothiers or Shermen; 18c, 20a, and 20b to Shermen. Hm has no play heading, but has the quotation from Ezechiel; AR call the play Ezechiel; B does not name it; H specifies prophets prophesying concerning the Last Judgment, Antichrist, and Enoch and Elias. 20a and 20b call for the prophets of Antichrist. 18c has Prophets afore the Day of Doom. The prophecies in the play put greater stress upon the coming of Doomsday than upon the coming of Antichrist.

In 1429–30 (2) we see the Shermen agreeing to share the costs of the Play, presumably for the *Last Judgment*; but in 1467–68 (17a) they seem to be bearing the full costs for storing a carriage. By 1500 the Hewsters are probably presenting *Antichrist* immediately before the Weavers' and Walkers' *Last Judgment*, and immediately after the Shermen's pageant. It would seem that by 1467–68 the Shermen were separated from the Weavers' and Walkers' *Last Judgment* and singly presented the pageant prophesying both Antichrist and Doomsday.

PLAY 23

HmARH attribute the play to the Diers; B omits the guild-ascription. 18c has Hewsters and Bell-founders; 20a has Hewsters; and 20b has Diers and Hewsters. The five cyclic texts, MS P, 18c, and 20a call for the coming of Antichrist. 20b puzzlingly speaks of Antichrist's "Doctor" first expounding "whoe be Antechristes the worlde rownde aboute." No such exposition occurs in the texts; perhaps some revision, indicated in the Regenall, is lost. 20b also stresses the role of Enoch and Elias, much as they appear in the play.

PLAY 24

HmARH ascribe the play to the Websters; B omits the ascription. 20a and 20b have Weavers; 18c has Weavers and Walkers. The cyclic texts are headed the Last Judgment; 20a, 20b, and 18c specify Doomsday. No variation in narrative content occurs other than A's loss of the final two folios.

5.

DOCUMENTS

PROVIDING EXTERNAL

EVIDENCE

THE FOLLOWING DOCUMENTS[1] are reproduced in this chapter:

1. Controversy between Ironmongers and Carpenters concerning Fletchers et al.
2. Weavers', Walkers', Chaloners', and Shermen's Agreement
3. Excerpt from the Bakers' Charter
4. Excerpt from the Fletchers' and Bowyers' Charter
5. Saddlers' Charter
6. Bowyers'-Fletchers' and Coopers' Agreement
7. Founders'-Pewterers' and Smiths' Agreement
8. Excerpt from an Abstract of the Smiths' Charter
9. The Cappers' Petition
10. The Proclamation: Four Documents
11. Vintners', Diers', and Goldsmiths'-Masons' Agreement
12. Excerpt from Charter for Painters et al.
13. The Trever Case
14. Anne Webster's "Mansion"
15. The Last Performance: Six Documents

---

1. The manuscripts denominated *Harley* and *Additional* (Add.) are in the British Library, London. Locations of other manuscripts are indicated in the text.

1. Controversy Between Ironmongers and Carpenters Concerning Fletchers et al.

This document is among loose papers in the Coopers' Records, Chester. It is dated 1422 and is in Latin. The bracketed words in the translation below represent guesses because holes occur at those places in the manuscript. As the document indicates, the Ironmongers were responsible at this time for the *Passion*, and the Fletchers et al. for the *Flagellation*; the Carpenters may be the Wrights, with responsibility for the *Nativity*.

Memorandum concerning the discord and legal controversy which arose between the Ironmongers of the City of Chester as one party, and the Carpenters of the same city as the other party:
Whether one party or the other should have all the Fletchers, Bowers, Stringers, Coopers, and Turners of the same city as helpers in putting on the Play of Corpus Christi of the same city. Held at length in full Portmote with the assent of both parties at Chester the Monday next after Easter, in the tenth year of the reign of King Henry, the fifth since the Conquest, before John Hope, mayor of the foresaid city.

The enquiry was conducted to determine the truth concerning the foresaid matter—whether they should or should not [help] one party or the other—of course under oath, by John de Hatton, Senior, William Hope, Richard Weston, Alexander Hennebury, Adam de Wotton, John de Hatton, Junior, Robert Wolley, Richard Lynakre, William de Pykton, Thomas de Hellesby, John William, and Richard Thomworth—the Inquirers.

They said under oath that the foresaid [Flet]chers, Bowers, Stringers, Coopers, and Turners should not either undertake to perform or be participants with one party or the other—the foresaid Ironmongers or Carpenters—in their pageants for the foresaid Corpus Christi Play. But they (the Inquirers) said that they (the Fletchers et al.) should themselves

continue to be responsible for their assigned pageant in this Play—
namely, the *Flagellation of the Body of Christ*, with its accompanying
material according to the "Original," up to the *Crucifixion of Jesus
Christ*, just as it occurs in the said "Original"—and that the foresaid
Ironmongers should be responsible for the pageant of the *Crucifixion* in
the foresaid [Corups Christi Play], and the foresaid Carpenters for their
pageant according to the foresaid "Original."

To the testimony of this present Enquiry into this case, the foresaid
mayor has caused to be affixed the seal of his foresaid mayor's office;
done on the day and year foresaid.

2. Weavers', Walkers',[2] Chaloners',[3] and Shermen's Agreement

This document is in the Chester Archives, Mayor's Roll MR/485, and
is dated 1429–30. It is in Latin through the word "Conquest" and in
French thereafter. The bracketed periods in the translation below indicate illegible words. It is likely that the pageant produced at this time by
the occupations here mentioned was the *Last Judgment*.

Record of the Portmote of the City of Chester held in Chester before
John Walssh, mayor of the said city, the Monday next after the Feast of
St. Dunstan,[4] in the eighth year of the reign of Henry the sixth after the
Conquest. Let it be remembered that on the Monday next after the feast
of St. Dunstan, in the seventh year of the reign of our most sovereign
lord, King Henry the sixth after the Conquest, before John le Walssh,
mayor of the city of Chester, the sheriffs, and the twenty-four aldermen
of the said city: by the consent, agreement, and good will of Richard
de Hawardyn and Richard de Brogheford, stewards of the occupations of
the Weavers, Walkers, Chaloners, and Shermen of the said City, upon a
petition in full Portmote by the said mayor, sheriffs [. . .] twenty-four
aldermen [. . .], it was ordained, established, and agreed that it shall be
in perpetuity that each person of whatever estate or condition who

2. *Walkers*: fullers of cloth.
3. *Chaloners*: makers of blankets.
4. May 19.

practices or sets up in any of the said occupations within the said city be contributory [. . .] or compelled to pay all [. . .] of which he is or will be assessed by the stewards of the said occupations for the time being towards the costs and expenses [. . .] light of our Lady St. Mary and of Corpus Christi, and for the Play of Corpus Christi, both for the one and the other, and for each and every time that it will happen that the said light is carried or the said Play is performed; and that each one who does not send the sum which he is assessed by the said stewards shall pay within the month the said assessment, or he shall incur the forfeit [. . .] pain of 13s 4d, that is to say, 6s 8d to the sheriffs of the said city for the time being, and 6s 8d to the stewards of the same occupations for the time being; and the same sum shall be levied as a distraint; and that it is allowed as well to the said sheriffs for the 6s 8d which is allotted to them [. . .] said stewards for the 6s 8d which is allotted to them, and [. . .] for the said sums thus assessed, to distrain any person on whom the said sum has thus been assessed [. . .] refuses to send or pay the said distraint, to anyone unless the said case of non-payment be agreed to be given and held impossible [. . .] always.

In testimony of which [. . .] ordinance, decision, and agreement indented and enrolled as well, the said mayor for himself, the said sheriffs, and twenty-four aldermen [. . .] the seal of office of the mayoralty, [. . .] the said [. . .] stewards for themselves and all the craftsmen of the occupations mentioned foresaid have set their seals.

Given at Chester on the day and year mentioned above.

3. Excerpt from the Bakers' Charter

This document is in Harley 2054, f. 36v, and is dated 1462. The Bakers produced the *Last Supper*.

. . . and to be redy to pay for the costs and expenses of the Play and light of Corpus Christi, as oft times as it shall be asseset by the same stuards for the tyme being. . . .

A later note in this same manuscript (f. 38v) probably concerns suppression of the Bakers' Play for doctrinal reasons.

vide post 60: a grant from the Citty in tyme of William Glasior, Mayor,

7 E 6 [1553], wherin the words about Whitson Pleas are put out [i.e., excised].

A second Bakers' Charter, issued in 1552–53, contains no references to the Plays (Harley 2054, ff. 39v–40r).

4. Excerpt from the Fletchers' and Bowyers' Charter

This document, which incorporates the Fletchers and Bowyers, is in the Records of the Coopers' Guild, Chester. It is dated 1468. These workers, together with the Coopers, were responsible for the *Flagellation*.

The script and composicion made by all the maisters and brederin of the craft of Fletchers and Bowers within the cite of Chester.
. . . Also that every maistir and journeman shalbe contributorie to pay for the sustentacion and fortheraunce of the light[5] of Corpus Christi, and othir charges that shall to the Playe of Corpus Christi, and othir charges belongyng therto, opon payn of xiiis iiiid to be levyed by way of distresse, or enprisonment of the person that so offendys, or levy of his godys by the styward of the seid craftes atte their elleccion, and that every person that shall be made brothir in any of the seid craftz shall paye atte his entre to the sustentacion of the seid light and othir charges xxvis viid, and that noo person be receyvyd to the seid brethirhode in noon othir wyse; nor any apprentice to be take by any maistir of any of the seid craftes unto any of the same craftz but for terme of vii yeres—or above and not undir—opon payn of brekyng of the othes afore-rehersyd; and forfaiture of xls to theyr companyes box, to be kept and levyed to the performyng and upholdyng of their light and othir charges in the fourme aforeseyd. . . .

5. Saddlers' Charter

This document is in London, Public Record Office, Chester, PRO/2/144.7. It is dated 1472 and is in difficult legal Latin. The translation below attempts to simplify somewhat the constructions without damaging

5. The Procession of Lights.

the meaning. The Saddlers produced *Christ on the Road to Emmaus and Doubting Thomas.*

Letters patent of the Saddlers in the City of Chester. Edward, by the grace of God, King of England and France and Lord of Ireland: to all to whom these present letters come, salutation.

   You should know that we have been informed by our beloved servants Richard Sadiller and Henry Ellome—stewards—Richard Ellome, John Yong, Richard Yong, and Henry Yong—aldermen—and the resident masters and workers of the guild and occupation of Saddlers within our city of Chester how, because of the unwarranted entry into, practice of, and occupation with this same craft in our foresaid city by strangers and persons of incurably obstinate disposition—they not agreeing to and supporting the debts and costs of the Play and pageant with the members of this same craft and city, those expenses for the Play and light in honor of Corpus Christi assigned to the members of this craft and occupation in the foresaid city for annual support and custody, nor many other kinds of debts annually levied in honor of God and our foresaid city upon those same craftsmen within our foresaid city for support and succor—the foresaid subjects are heavily damaged and thus are not able, from lessening of their income, to continue with these same expenses or to bear them in the future, without favor and help from us in this matter.

   Therefore, having of our grace given close consideration to the matters previously stated, we grant as a special concession to our previously listed subjects—wardens, aldermen, resident masters, and workers of this craft and occupation of Saddlers—and to their successor wardens, aldermen, resident masters, and workers of this same craft and occupation of Saddlers living within our city of Chester in the future—that no person or persons of the city during the coming forty years shall enter, practice, or be occupied with the foresaid craft and occupation of the Saddlers in our said city, or within the boundaries of its freedoms, without the freely granted assent, license, and agreement of our foresaid subjects and of their successor wardens, aldermen, masters, and workers of the same guild of Saddlers, or of the major part of them living within our foresaid city.

   A fine of 100 shillings is placed upon whatever person enters, practices, and occupies himself with the foresaid craft or occupation without the freely granted license and agreement specified above; the fine is to be paid as often as he so acts without such license. Half of these hundred shillings are to be paid to us, our heirs, and our successors. The other half of these hundred shillings are to be paid to the specified wardens, aldermen, masters, and workers of the same craft and occupation of Saddlers within our foresaid city at the time, to be used for the support of the earlier mentioned pageant, light, and Play. The fine is to be levied by the Sheriffs in our foresaid city at the time.

And, in addition, of our greater grace, we have granted to the specified subjects and to their successor wardens, aldermen, masters, and workers of the said guild of Saddlers living afterward in the said city and its freedoms that it shall be permitted them in the future as often as they deem necessary to arrange, make, and prepare among themselves such ordinances and statutes to be held within and among the wardens, aldermen, masters, and workers of that craft in the foresaid city as will provide properly for the effective support of the pageant of the Play of the guild of the foresaid Saddlers within the foresaid city and its freedoms.

In testimony of these matters we have caused these letters patent to be made. Witnessed by me, myself, at Chester on 8 March in the twelfth year of our reign.

6. Bowyers'-Fletchers' and Coopers' Agreement

This document is in the Chester Archives, Mayor's Book, M/B/5, f. 216r. It is dated 1474. The brackets below indicate holes in the document. The dispute concerned the guilds' positions in the Corpus Christi Procession of Lights.

Memorandum: [   ] ther hath been on Corpus Day [   ] reign of King Edward the Fourth [   ] and contraversies betwix the Bowers and the Fletchers of the cety of Chester, on that on[6] partie, and the Cowpers of the said cety, on that other partie, and for the beryng and goyng in procession with thaire lightes on the said Day; which seidez parties have agreit thaym and ichon of thaym to abide, perfourme, and obeie such ordenaunce, dome, and awarde as John Sotheworth, squire, mayor of the cety aforesaid, shulde make theryn.

6. *on*: one.

Wheropon the said maire the iii^de day of the monyth of September, of the said Corpus Day the next ensuyng,[7] hath herde the grevaunce and compleyntes of aither of the saides parties by gode deliberacion. And the said maire by the advice of dyvers of his breder hath ordenet, demed, and awerdet the saides parties to be gode frendes, of and for all the premysses.[8] Also he hath ordenet and awardet that the saides Cowpers, and thaire successors Cowpers of the said cety, from hensforth shall bere thaire lightes yerely—iii lightez on that on[9] side the pavement, and iii on that opposite—from Saint-Maire-kirke-opon-the-hill of the cety afore-said unto the Colage of Seint Johns next before[10] the lights of the saides Fletchers and Bowers; and the said Bowers and Fletchers evenly to bere thaire lightes next to[11] the saides Cowpers by the said award in the [   ].

Yeven the thridde day of September on the yere aforesaid.

7. Founders'-Pewterers' and Smiths' Agreement

This document is in the Chester Archives, Mayor's Book, M/B/12, f. 24v, and is dated 4 February 1521. In the Early Banns and in the List of Guilds, Harley 2150, the Smiths are responsible for producing the *Purification*, the same play ascribed to that guild in the cyclic texts.

> *Memorandum: quarto die Februarii, anno xii Henrici octavi.*
> This indenture made the iiii^th daye of February in the xii^th yere of the reigne of King [Henry] the eight betwene Richard Laye and Edward Taillir, stuardes of th'occupacion of Founders[12] and Pewtrers within the citie of Chester, opon the oon partie, and Richard Taillir—smyth—and Richard Anderton, stuardes of th'occupacion of Smyths within the Citie of Chester, opon that other partie.
> Witnessith that the seides stuardes and all theire holle occupacion,

7. This phrase means "the September following the Corpus Christi Day on which the 'contraversies' between the guilds occurred."

8. This phrase means "despite all the aforesaid difficulties."

9. *on*: one.

10. *next before*: immediately preceding.

11. *next to*: immediately behind.

12. *Founders*: metal-casters.

apon asemble made and comunycacion had betwene the seides occupacons for the wele and goode hele of the same, byn fully condecendet
and agreid in manner and forme foloyng: that is to witte, from hens-
fourth the said stuardes of th'occupacions of Founders and Pewtrers for
the tyme beyng to receyve the incomes and forfetes of all such personnes
that will cum into the seid occupacion of Founders and Peutrers and be of
theire brotherhod, the stuardes of th'occupacion of Smythes in no wise to
intromedill ne have enything to do therwith. And in like wise the stuardes
of th'occupacion of Smythes to receyve the incomes and forfetes of all
such personnes as will cum into the seid occupacion of Smythes and be of
theire brotherhod, the stuardes of th'occupacion of Founders and
Pewtrers in no wise intromedelyng ne havyng enythyng to do therwith.

Also, the stuardes of th'occupacion of Founders and Pewtrers, as the
stuardes of th'occupacion of Smythes aforeseid, byn fully condecendent
and agreid to berre and drawe to[13] Whitson Playe and Corpus Christi
Light, and to bere to the fyndyng[14] of the preste of Seynt Loye Chapell
and all other costes, as they of olde tyme have donne and used.

Also, the stuardes of th'occupacion of Founders and Pewtrers in the
name of all theire holle occupacion, as the stuardes of th'occupacion of
Smythes in all the holle name of theire occupacion, byn fully condecendet
and agreid that the stuardes of aither occupacion for the tyme beyng shall
every yere in the Feste of Seynt Loye,[15] or within viii dayes the seid Feste
of Seynt Loye imediatly foloyng, yefe afore the stuardes of th'occupacion
and iiii aldermen of the seid occupacion a juste and a true accompte of
al maner incomes and forfetes by theym receyvet duryng the tyme they
stonde stuardes, so that, apon the seid accompte had, the prophetes[16]
thereof shall groo but to[17] the prophetes of Seynt Loye Chapell, opon the
payne of theym that contrarye to this agrement to forfete to the same use
fyve poundes of leyfull money of Englond.

In witnesse wherof to these indentures the stuardes of aither of the
seides craftes, in the name of theire occupacion enterchaungably, have
sette theire sealles. These beyng witnesse: Thomas Smyth, Maire of the

13. *berre and drawe to*: bear the expenses of.
14. *fyndyng*: board and lodging.
15. St. Loy's feast day is December 1. St. Loy (Elegius, Eloi) is patron saint of
metal workers.
16. *prophetes*: profits.
17. *groo but to*: be added only to.

Citie of Chester; Thomas Colburne and Cristofer Werinycham, Shireffes of the Citie aforeseid; and mony other. Yeven at the Citie of Chester aforsed, the daye and yere above rehersed.

8. Excerpt from an Abstract of the Smiths' Charter

This document is in Harley 2054, f. 25r, and is dated c. 1676. The Smiths et al. produced the *Purification*.

. . . and that the companys divers that have relation to oure and other artes have joyned themselves in on society or company may appeare from the tyme of Sir John Arnway, Knight, maior of this citty in tyme of King Henry 3, about 1266, 410 yeares since when the auntient playes used in this citty, commonly called Whitson Plays, wherin they joyned for their pagents showes. And when the use therof was layd downe, and the wach or showe on Midsomer Eve began in the tyme of Richard Dutton, maior 1498, the sayd artes, misterys, societyes, craftes, occupations—or by what other stille they were called by—did also joyne together in the sayd show as on company. And that the company of Smythes, Furbers[18] or Cutlers, and Pewterers and Founders, the rest of their associates, were a company, then by the sayd ould bookes of the Whitson Playes appereth, and what part the acted in the sayd plays, tyme out of mynd.

9. The Cappers' Petition

This document is in Harley 1996, f. 120r. It dates from 1523–24 when David Middleton was Mayor. The Cappers produced *Moses and the Law and Balaack and Balaam*.

To the right worshipffull and full discrete David Myddelton, Mayer of the Citie of Chester, and his Co-brethren and Aldermen of the same:
    Humbly shewen unto your gode maystershippes your pouer supply-auntes and besechers, the Cappers of this citie, that wheras they of late tyme by the right worshipffull Thomas Smythe, in tyme of hys mairealtie, were onerated and charged to brynge forthe a playe concernynge the

18. *Furbers*: polishers of metal.

store of Kynge Balak and Balam the proffet, and at the same tyme by the
sayd Thomas Smythe and his co-brethren it was promysed that whereas
your saydes pouer supplauntes fonde theyme grevyde and gretely hurtyd
and impoveryshed by reason that not only the Mercers of the sayde citie
but as well dyverse others occupacions of the same citie do dayly occupye
theire sayd occupacion, as well in retayllynge of cowrse wares under the
price of xvi of the dossen as above; and as yet no reformacion therof can
be had, allthaghe they therfore have made greate instance and request as
well to your maystership now in your tyme of mayreltie as to others your
predecessors as is aforesayd, it may please your gode maystershipps,
considerynge the greate and importable hurtes and hyndraunces of your
saydes pouer supplyauntes, whiche be but verrey pouer men and have no
thynge to lyve by but their sayd occupacion, other to see for due and
lauffull reformacion of the promysses, or elles to exonerate and discharge
theyme of and for the bryngynge forthe of the sayd playe—wherof they
wolde be right sorye, yf the meanes myght be fonde that they myght be
hable to brynge it forthe. And the remedye therof lyethe myche in your
maystershippes, if it wolde please you of your godenes to putte your gode
wyllez and myndes therunto. For the fulle and holle myndes and
consentes of all and every your saydes besechers is now, and at all tymes
to come shall be, to brynge forthe theire sayd playe, and that in theire
best manner, to the pleasure and god worship of mayster maire and this
citie. Wherfore they beseche you of your charite other to se for the
reformacion of the promysses, or elles to take no displeasure with theyme
if they for lakke of habilitie do not brynge forthe theire sayd play. And
this at the reverence of God, and they shall daylye praye to God for
you etc.

10. The Proclamation: Four Documents

These documents are found in (a) Chester Archives, A/F/1, f. 12r; (b)
Harley 2013, f. 1r; (c) Harley 2150, f. 86r; (d) Harley 2124, folio preceding f. 1. In the transcription of the first, brackets indicate the numerous damaged spots; the two italicized words—*somtyme* and *dissolved*
—are in the manuscript above the words following them; the scored-
through passages appear here as they do in the manuscript. In the fourth
document, only the final paragraph reproduces material in the first three.
The first two documents are versions of William Newhall's Proclama-

tion in 1531–32. The third is a revision probably in 1539–40. The fourth perhaps can be dated 1609.

(a) Chester Archives, Assembly Files, A/F/1, f. 12r

The Proclamacion for the Plaies, newly made by William Newhall,
[   ] pentice, the first year of his entre.
   For as m[   ] as of old tyme—not only for the augmentacion and
incres [   ] faith of o[   ] auyour Jhesu Crist and to exort the
myndes of the common people [   ] doctryne th [   ]f, but also
for the commen welth and prosperitie of this citie—a Play [   ]
and diverse stor [   ] of the Bible, begynnyng with the creacion and fall of
Lucifer and endy [   ] jugement of th[   ] world, to be declared and
plaied in the Witsonweke, was devised and m[   ] Henry Frauns
[   ], *somtyme* monk of this *dissolved* monastery, who obteyned and gate
of Clement then beyng [   ] daiez of par [   ], and of the Busshop
of Chester at that tyme beyng xlti daiez of pardon, [   ] thensforth
[   ] every person resortyng in pecible manner with gode devocion to
here and se the s [   ] from tyme to tyme as oft as they shalbe
plaied within this citie—~~and that every person [   ] disturbyng the~~
~~same plaiez in eny maner to be acursed by thauctoritie of the s[   ]~~
~~Pope Cleme [   ] bulles unto suche tyme as he or they be absolved~~
~~therof~~; whiche plaiez were d[   ] to the honor of God by John
Arneway, then mair of this citie of Chester, and his brethern and holl
cominal [   ] therof, to be bro[   ] forthe, declared, and plaid at
the costes and chargez of the craftesmen and occupacons of [   ] said
citi [   ], whiche hither-unto have from tyme to tyme used and performed the same accordin[   ]—
   Wherfore maister mair in the kyngez name straitly chargeth and
commaundeth that every person and [   ]—of what esta[   ],
degre, or condicion so ever he [   ] they be, resortyng to the said plaiez
—do use th[   ] pecible witho [   ] akyng eny assault, affrey, or other
disturbans wherby the same [   ] shalbe disturbed, and that no manner
person or persons, whosoever he or they be, do use or we [   ]
unlaufull wepons within the precynct of the said citie duryng the tyme of
the said p [   ], ~~not only opon payn of cursyng by thauctoritie of the~~
~~said Pope Clement bulles, but al~~so opon payn of enprisonment of their

bodiez and makyng fyne to the kyng at maister mairis pleasure. [   ]
God save the kyng and maister mair etc.

per me W. Newhall, factum tempore Willielmo Sneyde, draper, secundo
tempore sui maioralitatis.

(b) Harley 2013, f. 1r

The Proclamation for Whitsone Playes made by Wm. Newall, clarke of
the pentice, 24[   ], Wm. Snead, 2ᵈ year maior.

   For as much as ould tyme—not only for the augmentation and increase of the holy and catholick faith of our saviour Jesu Christe and to
exort the mindes of comon people to good devotion and holsome doctrine therof, but also for the comon welth and prosperity of this citty—a
play and declaration of divers storyes of the Bible, beginning with the
creation and fall of Lucifer and ending with the generall judgment of the
world, to be declared and played in the Whitsonne weeke, was devised
and made by one Sir Henry Frances, somtyme moonck of this monastrey
disolved, who obtayning and gat of Clemant, then Bushop of Rome, a
1000 dayes of pardon, and of the bushop of Chester at that tyme 40
dayes of pardon, graunted from thensforth to every person resorting in
peaceble maner with good devotion to heare and see the sayd playes from
tyme to tyme as oft as the shall be played within the sayd citty—(and that
every person or persons disturbing the sayd playes in any maner wise to
be accursed by the authority of the sayd Pope Clemants bulls untill such
tyme as he or they be absolved therof); which playes were devised to the
honor of God by John Arnway, then maior of this citty of Chester, and
his bretheren and whole commalty therof, to be brought forth, declared,
and played at the cost and charges of the craftesmen and occupations of
the sayd citty, which hither-unto have from tyme to tyme used and
performed the same acordingly—

   Wherfore maister maior in the kings name stratly chargeth and
comandeth that every person and persons—of what estate, degree, or
condition so ever he or they be, resorting to the sayd playes—do use
themselves peacible without making any assault, affray, or other dis-
turbance wherby the same playes shall be disturbed, and that no maner of
person or persons, whosoever he or they be, do use or weare any un-
lawfull weapons within the precinct of the sayd citty during the tyme of

the sayd playes (not only upon payn of cursing by authority of the sayd Pope Clemants bulls but also) upon payne of enprisonment of their bodyes and making fine to the king at maister maiors pleasure.

(c) Harley 2150, f. 86r

For as myche as of old tyme—not only for the augmentacon and incresse of the holy and catholyk faith of our savyor Cryst Jhesu and to exhort the myndes of the comen peple to gud devocon and holsom doctryne therof, but also for the comen welth and prosperitie of this citie—a play and declaracon of many and dyvers stories of the Bible, begynnyng with the creacon and fall of Lucifer and endyng with the generall jugement of the world, to be declared and playde now in this Whitson weke, whiche playes were devised to the honor of God by John Arneway, sometyme maire of this citie of Chester, and his bretheryn and holl comynaltie therof, to be brought forth, declared, and plaid at the costys of the craftysmen and occupacons of the said citie, whiche herunto have from tyme to tyme used and performed the same accordingly—

Wherfore master mair in the kinges name straitly chargith and comanndyth that every person and persons—of what astate, degree, or condicon so ever he or they be, resorting to the said playes—do use theym selff peceably without making any assault, afrey, or other disturbans wherby the same playes shalbe disturbed, and that no maner person or persons, whoever he or they be, do use or weyre any unlaufull wepons within the precinct of the said citie duryng the tyme of the said playes apon peyne of imprisonyment of there bodies and making fyne to the king at maisters maires pleasure. And God save the kyng, maister mayre etc.

(d) Harley 2124, folio preceding f. 1

The Whitsun playes first made by one Don Randle Heggenet, o monke of Chester Abbey, who was thrise at Rome before he could obtaine leave of the Pope to have them in the English tongue.

The Whitsun playes were playd openly in pageants by the cittizens of Chester in the Whitsun weeke. Nicholas the fift then was Pope, in the year of our Lord 1447.

Sir Henry Francis, sometyme a monke of the monastery of Chester, obtained of Pope Clemens a thousand daies of pardon, and of the Bishop of Chester 40 dayes pardon, for every person that resorted peaceably to see the same playes; and that every person that disturbed the same to be accursed by the said Pope, untill such tyme as they should be absolved thereof.

11. Vintners', Diers', Goldsmiths'-Masons' Agreement

This document is in the Chester Archives, A/F/1, f. 11r. It is dated 1531 or 1532. The bracketed periods below indicate damaged places in the manuscript. The Vintners produced the *Three Kings*; the Diers produced *Antichrist*; the Goldsmiths and Masons produced the *Slaughter of the Innocents*.

Memorandum that the xiiii^(th) day of August in the xxii [. . .] King Henry the eight.
It was condescended and agreed before [. . .] of the citie of Chester in the Pentice of the same citie[. . .] William Bexwik, stiwardez of the occupacion of vynteners withi[. . .] Kettell and Thomas Hasilwall, stiwardez of the occupacion of [. . .], of th'one partie, and John Trevor, goldsmith, stiward of th'occupac[. . .] Wosewall, stiward of the occupacion of mason within the citi[. . .] th'other partie, in forme folowyng; that is, to witt: The saides s[. . .] and Diers for theym and their successors be agreid and graunten by these presentes [. . .] stiwardez of Goldsmythez and Masons and their successors from hensforth shall occupie and pecible enjoy frome tyme to tyme the cariage nowe of the Vynteners and Diers to and for the plaiez of the saides Goldsmythes and Masons and [. . .] successors to be plaied at Whitsontide to serve theym for their saides [. . .] when and as oft as nede shall require, without eny lett. If the saides [. . .] of Vynteners and Diers or their successors for which cariage so in manner [. . .] abovesaid to the saides stiwardez of Goldsmythes and Masons and their su[. . .] graunted to and for their saidez plaiez from tyme to tyme as is afor [. . .] saides stiwardez of Goldsmythez and Masons for theymself and th[. . .] ben agreid, covenaunten, and graunten by these presentes to consent [. . .] cause to be paid unto the saides stiwardez of Vynteners and Diers [. . .] sterling at the makyng herof. And from hensforth yerely [. . .] fynd, kepe, and

susteyn the thrid parte of all and every reparacion [. . .] necessariez belongyng or in eny wise apperteynyng to the same [. . .] shall require, and also to consent and pay or cause to be paide yerely from [. . .] the thrid part of all the rentes due or to be due for the house wher [. . .] said cariage now standeth or herafter shall stand. . . .

12. Excerpt from Charter for Painters et al.

This document, dated 1534, appears in Harley 2054, f. 87v. A seventeenth-century copy appears on f. 88r of that manuscript. Another copy appears in London, Public Record Office, Chester, 2/323, 13–14 Charles 2 m. 4. The Painters et al. produced the *Shepherds' Play*. The transcription below is from Harley 2054, f. 87v.

. . . and for as much as the severall craftes, arts, and facultis of Painters, Glassiers, Imbrauderers, and Stationeres have by thesse hembel petecion desired that the might be incorpureted into one body by grant under the citty seale; it also appereinge to us that the have bine tyme out of minde one Brotherhood for the costs and expences of the plae of the sheppherds wach with the angells hyme,[19] and likewayes for otherr layinge out[20] conserninge the wellferr and prosperetie of the saide citty, it is therefore orderred and declarred bie jointe present of us—the mayor, aldermen, and common consell—that the saide Painters, Glassiers, Imbrauderers, and Stationers, and therre successors from henceforth and forever, shalbee taken and reputed as one speciall company of the said citty. . . .

13. The Trever Case

This document is in the Chester Archives, Mayor's Book, M/B/19, f. 45v, and is dated 1568. The "originall book of the Whydson Plaies" was the city's "master-copy" of the cycle, kept in the Pentice, the City Hall.

Memorandum that the xxx[th] *daie of Aprell in anno decimo Elizabeth etc.* Master Randall Trever, gentlemen, was called before the maior of the

19. *hyme*: hymn.
20. *layinge out*: expenses.

citie of Chester and was demaunded for the originall book of the
Whydson Plaies of the said citie, who then and ther confessed that he
have had the same booke, which book he deposeth upon the holy evan-
gelist of God that by comaundement he delivered the same booke againe.
But where the same is now, or to whom he then delivered the same
booke, deposeth likwise he knoweth not.

14. Anne Webster's "Mansion"

This document is in the Chester Archives, Mayor's Book, M/B/19, f.
52r, and is dated 5 June 1568.

Memorandum that whereas varyaunce presently dependeth betwene
John Whitmore, esquier, upon th'on partie, and Anne Webster, widow,
tenaunt to Georg Ireland, esquier, upon th'other partie, for and concerning the claime, right, and title of a mansion, rowme, or place for the
Whydson plaies in the Brudg-gate strete within the cyty of Chester,
which varyaunce hath ben here wayed and considered by Ric. Dutton,
esquier, maior of the cyty of Chester, and William Gerrard, esquier,
recorder of the same cyty, by whom it is now ordered that forasmuche as
the said mistres Webster and other the tenuntes of the said master Ireland
have had their places and mansions in the said place now in varyaunce in
quiet sort for ii tymes[21] past whan the said plaies were plaied, that the
said Anne Webster in quiet sort for this presente tyme of Whydsontide,
during all the tyme of the said plaies, shall enjoy and have her mansyon
place, and the said place and rome now in varyaunce, provided alwaies
that the having of the said possessyon of the said rowme, place, or
mansyon shall not be hurtfull nor prejudice to nether of the said parties
in whom the right of the said premisses is or hereafter shalbe found or
proved to be.

And also yt was then further ordered by the said maior that after the
Feast of Pentecost next coming at some convenient tyme an indifferent[22]
enquest shalbe charged and sworne for the triall of the right of the said
rowme or place now in varyaunce, and that in case yt be found by such
enquest that the said master Whytmore hath better right to the said

21. The performances of 1561 and 1567, according to available evidence.
22. *indifferent*: not prejudiced.

premisses thann the said master Ioreland and his tenuntes, it is ordered that then the said mistres Webster shall consent and pay unto the said master Whytmore so much money for the said rowme and place as hath ben accostomed for this one yere to be payed heretofore within the said cyty of Chester.

Richard Dutton
William Gerrard

15. The Last Performance: Six Documents

(a) Chester Archives A/F/3, f. 25r, 30 May 1575

Assembly in the commen hall, whether the accostomed plaies called the Whitson Plaies shalbe sett furth and plaied at Midsummer next or not:

Meet[23] to be plaid and to begin Sonday after Midsummer Day next—33	Not meet—[24] 12

Agreid they shall be sett furth in the best fayssion, with such reformacion as master Maior with his advice shall think meet[25] and convenient.

(b) Chester Archives, Assembly Book, f. 162v, 30 May 1575

Ad congregacionem tentam in interior Pentice communi aula placitorum civitatis Cestrie; ibidem tentam xxx^{mo} die May, anno regni Regine Elizabeth etc. xvii^{mo}.

At whiche assembly yt was ordered, concluded, and agreed upon by the said maior, aldermen, sheriffes, and comon counsaile of the said citie that the plaies comonly called the Whitson Plaies at Midsommer next comynge shalbe sett furth and plaied in such orderly manner and sorte as the same have ben accostomed, with such correction and amendement as shalbe thaught convenient by the said maior; and all charges of the said

23. *meet*: voting "aye."
24. *not meet*: voting "nay."
25. *meet*: agreeable for the audience.

Plaies to be supported and borne by th'inhabitantes of the said citie, as have ben hertofore used.

(c) Mayor Savage's Letter to the Chester City Council, Chester Archives, Corporation Lease Book, 1574–1705, CHB/3, f. 28r; also Harley 2173, f. 107v, 1575

After my right hartie comendacons:[26]
Where it hathe bene enformed to the Prevey Counsell that I caused the Plays laste at Chester to be sett forwarde onely of mysellf—which your-sellves do knowe the contrary, and that they was by comon assemblie apointed, as remayneth in recorde, for the easinge and qualefyinge all controversees growen abowte the same—I am moste hartely to desyre you to sende me a certificate under your haundes and seale of your citie to testefy that the same Plays were sett forwarde as well by the Counsell of the citie as for the comen welth of the same, whereby their honours may be the better satisfied therof, and hopinge thereby to reduce all suche matters quiett as are risen nowe againste me and master Hankye, whom you muste make mencyon of in the certificate, as well as mysellf; whiche I pray you may be sente me with as muche convenient speede as is possible.

So for this tyme I bidd yow farewell at London, the xth of November, 1575.

Your lovinge frende
John Savage

(d) Minutes of the City Council Concerning Mayor Savage, Chester Archives, A/B/1, ff. 162v–163r, 1575

Tempore prefati Henrici Hardware, maioris civitatis predicte, ad congracionem ibidem, tentam in interiore Pentice eiusdem civitatis, die lune videlicet xxi die Novembris, anno regni Regine Elizabeth etc. xviii.

Whereas informacon was geven to the saide maior and certein others

---

26. *comendacons*: compliments, respects.

his bretherne on the behallf of Sir John Savage, knighte, that he shuld be charged to have sett furthe and caused to be plaide the accostomed pageons and plays, called the Whitson Plays, in the tyme of his maioraltie at Midsomer laste of himsellf, to satisfy his owne will and pleasure and contrary to his othe and dutie, without the assente or consente of the reste of his bretherne and of the Common Counsell of the same; and where allsoe the saide Sir John Savage hath addressed his letters to the saide maior and his bretherne th'aldermen requestinge them under the cities seale to certefy the trueth therein, together with the transcripte of an order therof taken—

Wherupon this assemblie was called and the premisss hearde, wayed, and considered; and wher allsoe at this assemblie John Hanky, alderman, enformeth the same that he was burthened with the like offence— videlicet, for the settinge furthe himsellf of the Whitson Plays without any assent or consente of the aldermen and Comen Counsell in the tyme of his late maioralty of this city—that is to say, the xiiii[th] yere of the raigne of the Quenes majestie that nowe is—who allsoe made requeste that this assembly wolde allsoe certefy with him the manner howe the saide plais were sett furth in his late maioralty, whether of himsellf or by assente and consente of the aldermen and Commen Counsell of this citie, which allso beinge likewise wayed and considered; and for that ther appereth of recorde, entred in the booke of the orders of this citie, a certen conclucion, order, and constitucion made in the tyme of the maioraltie of the saide Sir John Savage, aucthorisinge him with assent of th'aldermen, sheriffes, and Comon Counsell of the saide citie to sett furthe the saide plays in the saide tyme of his maioralty; and for that allsoe it is confessed by this whole assemblie that the saide John Hanky in the tyme of his maioralty of the saide citie did sett furthe the said plays by th'assent and consente of the aldermen, sheriffes, and Commen Counsell of this citie, and so waranted and auctorised so to doe by assemblie—

It is nowe, the day and yere firste above remembred, ordered, con-cluded upon, and agried by the saide maior, the aldermen, sheriffes, sheriffes peeres, and Common Counsell of the said city that certificate shalbe made from and in the name of the corporacion of this citie, and under the commen seale of the same city, proportinge the same in-formacion; and that at suche requestes as before suche certificate is made that the saide surmyses alledged againste the saide Sir John Savage and

John Hankie are untrue, and that the saide plays set furthe in their severall maioralties was severally don by th'assent, consente, good will, and agreamente of the aldermen, sheriffes, sheriffes peeres, and Comen Counsell of the saide citie, and so determyned by severall orders agried upon in open assemblie, acording to the auncyent and lawdable custom of the saide citie whereunto and for the performance wherof the whole citizens of the citie are bounde and tyed by othe, as they are to other their orders; and that they, the saide Sir John Savage and John Hanky, nor either of them, did nothinge in their severall tymes of maioralties towchinge the saide plays but by th'assent, consent, and full agreamente of the aldermen, sheriffes, and Comen Counsell of the saide citie in the sellfsame manner and forme as the same nowe is penned and redd to this assembly.

And it is further ordered that as well the saide severall letters of the saide Sir John Savage towchinge his saide requeste, as allsoe the saide such certificate, shalbe entred verbatim in the saide booke called the Table Booke of the saide city for the inrolmentes of all the indentures, leases, and dedes concerninge the landes of the saide citie. All which was and is so donne acordynglie.

(e) The City Certificate Concerning Mayor Savage, Chester Archives, Corporation Lease Book, CHB/3, f. 28v. See also Harley 2173, ff. 107v–108r, 1575

To all true Christen people to whom this presente writinge shall come to be seen, hearde, or redd, Henrie Hardware, nowe maior of the city of Chester, and the citizens of the same citie sende gretinge in our Lord God everlastinge.

Forasmuche as it is enformed unto us, the saide maior and citizens, on the behallf of Sir John Savage, knight, that it is reported that he, the saide Sir John Savage, knight, beinge the yere laste paste maior of the saide citie, did then of his owne power and auctoritie in the saide tyme he was maior, to the great abuse of the same office, unleafullie and by indirect and synistre ways and meanes cause and procure to be plaide within the same citie certen pagions or plays, comonlie there called Witteson Playes, for the satisfying of his owne singuler will, luste, and pleasure to the great coste and charges, losse and harme of the citizens and inhabitauntes of the saide citie, and to their no little impoverishemente, and not by the orderly assente of his then bretherne, the aldermen and the Comen Counsell of the saide citie, as he should and oughte to have donne, nor to and for the wealth, benefite, and comoditie of the same citie acordinge to his dutie.

All which surmyses we well knowinge to be untrue, and that the saide Sir John Savage, knighte, did nothinge the saide laste yere duringe the tyme he was maior as is aforesaide in or abowte the settinge furth of the saide pagions or plays but only acordinge to an order concluded and agreed upon for dyvers good and great consideracons redoundinge to the comen wealthe, benefite, and profitte of the saide citie in assemblie there holden, according to the auncyente and lawdable usages and customes there hadd and used fur above remembraunce by and with the assente, consente, and agreamente of his saide then bretherne, the aldermen of the saide citie, and of the Comen Counsell of the same, did in execucion and accomplishment of the saide order. To the performance wherof both the saide Sir John Savage and we all that were then citizens and freemen of the saide citie were bounden and tyed by our othes, so as we be to all our orders taken and made in and by our assembly.

And therefore at and upon the mocion and requeste made unto us in our assembly holden the day of the date of thes presentes, on the behallf of the saide Sir John Savage we, the saide maior and citizens have caused the tenor and transcripte of the saide order to be here written as folowethe: Ad congregacionem tentam in communi aula placitorum civitatis Cestrie, xxx° die Mai, anno regni Regine Elizabeth etc. xvii°.

At which assemblie it was ordered, concluded, and agried upon by the saide maior, aldermen, sheriffes, and Common Counsell of the saide city that the plays comonlie called the Whitson Plays at Mydsommer next cominge shalbe sett furth and plaide in suche orderly manner and sorte as the same have bene accustomed, with suche correcion and amendemente as shalbe thought conveniente by the saide maior. And all charges of the saide plays to be supported and borne by th'inhabitauntes of the saide citie, as have bene heretofore used. And in wytnes that this is a true copy and transcripte of the saide order and warrante whereby and in accomplishment wherof the saide Sir John Savage did cause the saide pagions and plays to be sett furth and playde as is aforesaide; which did begyn the xxvi[th] of June laste paste, in the afternone of the same day, and there contynued untill the Wednesday at eveninge then nexte folowinge.

And that allsoe this presente day in our saide assembly, holden and kepte within the Pentice of our saide citie acordinge to the good and lawdable usages and accustomes aforesaide, John Hanky, one of the aldermen and late maior of the saide city—to wytt, in the xiiii[th] yeare of the Quenes majestes raigne that nowe is—made his humble peticion to the saide assemblie that it might please the same to publishe by theis presentes by what warrante he, the saide John Hanky, caused the saide plays to be sett furthe and plaide in the aforesaide yere that he was maior, as is aforesaide, of the same cittie; which saide peticion—consideringe the same is verey reasonable—thaught mete to grante the same. And therefore the saide maior and citizens doe publishe and declare that it was this day confessed by the saide assembly that the saide John Hanky, alderman, did in the tyme of his saide maioralty cause the saide plais to be sett furth and plaide onlie by vertue and in execucion of an order taken by assemblie of the saide citie, holden there the xxix[th] of Aprill in the saide xiiii[th] yere of the Quenes majestes raigne that nowe is, and by and with the consente and assente of his saide bretherne, the then aldermen of the saide city, and Comen Counsell of the same.

And allsoe in wytnes hereof we, the saide maior and citizens, have to this presentes sett the comon seale of the saide citty, dated at the saide citie the xxi[th] day of November in the eightenth yere of the raigne of our soveraigne ladie Elizabeth, by the grace of God of England, Fraunce, and Irelaund, Quene Defendor of the Faith, etc.

(f) Chester Archives, Mayor's Book, M/B/12, f. 187v, 1576

Apud civitatem Cestrie, xxv[to] die Octobris, anno regni Regine Elizabeth etc. xvii[mo].

Whereas Andrew Tailer, of the said citie, tailer, usinge the occupacion of Diers within the same citie, was taxed and sessed to beare with the compeny of Dyers by the same compeny for the charges in the setting furth of their parte and pagent of the plaies sett furth and plaied in this citie at Midsommer laste past—comonly called Whytson Plaies—and by the said compeny rated and appointed to paie for that entent iiis viiid—which he refused to paie; and whereas upon the complainte of the said compeny of Diers againste the said Andrew to the right worshipfull Sir John Savage, knight, late maior of the same citie, in the tyme of his mairalty—wherupon the same Andrew, beinge called before the same

then maior in that behalff, denied to paie the same. And therfore the said
Andrew Tailler was then and ther by the said then maior comytted to
warde,[27] where he hetherunto hath remayned.

And whereas John Banester and Edmunde Gamull, gentlemen, cam
before Henry Hardware, maior of the said citie, William Gerrard and
William Glaseor, esquiers, aldermen of the same citie, and others—the
justices of peace within the same citie—the daie, yere, and place firste
above remembred,[28] and willed that the said Andrew Tailer upon payment of the said iiis viiid might be of his said impresonment enlarged,
wherupon now the said John Banester and Edmund Gamull have paied
and discharged the said iiis viiid for the said Andrew. And upon such
payment the said Andrew Tailer the said daie, yere, and place was of his
said imprisoment enlarged and sett at libertie by the said now maior, the
said aldermen, and others of the justices of the peace aforesaid.

16. Excerpts from the Lists of Mayors and Sheriffs

Important information about the occurrence of performances of the cycle
comes to us from the numerous surviving lists of Mayors and Sheriffs of
Chester, which—in addition to the names of the officials and their dates
in office—include notes on special events in the city's history. The officials were elected in October of each year (Harley 2009, f. 27r).

These lists fall into two groups: those in which John Arneway is incor-
rectly listed as first Mayor, and those that reflect corrections made by
Mayor William Aldersey in 1594. In Additional 29780 (f. 93r), Aldersey
states that his corrections were made from authoritative documents.
Most of the lists were copied out by seventeenth-century antiquaries.

The incorrect lists are to be found in Harley 1046, 1944, 2105, 2125,
(Lists 1 and 3), Add. 11335, 29777, 29779, manuscript 23.5 in the Harold Cohen Library of the University of Liverpool, and Lysons' notes from
Rogers' *Breviary*. The corrected lists are to be found in Harley 2057,
2133, Add. 29780, 39925. In addition, six manuscripts include lists that
show no significant variation from the manuscripts noted in the two preceding sentences: Bodley MS Top Cheshire e-11, Cheshire Record Office

27. *warde*: jail.
28. *remembred*: noted.

MSS DCC 1, 3, 11, 19, and John Rylands MS 202. Also, five manuscripts include lists that present no information about the plays: Harley 1989, 2125 (List 2), 2133, Chester Assembly Book, Chester Archives copy of Rogers' *Breviary*.

(a) Harley 2125 (List 1), first entries

1327 Sir John Arnwaye, knight
The Whitson Playes first made by one Don Randall Heggenett, a monke of Chester Abbey, who was thrise at Rome before he could obtayn leave of the Pope to have them in the English tonge. [Heggenett and the last twenty words are later interpolations.]

1328 Sir John Arnwaye, knight
The Whitson Playes played openlye in pageantes by the cittizins of Chester in Whitson Weeke.

[In connection with these entries see Add. 29779 f. 11, where *Heggenett* is changed to *Higgden*; the flyleaf of MS H of the cycle for a comment on the origin of the cycle; and Harley 2125 for similar comment giving 1269 as the date for Arneway as Mayor and for Higden's authorship.]

(b) Add. 29777, item 163

1487–88 Rauffe Davenport
In this yeare the Assumption of our Ladye was plaid in the Bridgestrete of Chester before my Lorde Strange.

[In Harley 2125, f. 31r, the location is given as "the High Crosse."]

(c) Harley 2133, f. 36r

1498–99 Richard Goodman
Prince Arthur came to Chester the 4 of August and the Assumption of our Ladie was plaid before the Prince at the Abbey gates the 26 of August. The Prince made master Goodman Esquire. And the 9 of September he departed from Chester.

[See also Add. 11335, f. 23r; Add. 29780, ff. 62r, 124r; Add. 29777, item 173 under John Clyffe, 1498–99; Add. 39925, f. 18r; manuscript 23.5 at the University of Liverpool, and Lysons' notes (*Breviary*) under John Southworthe, 1475–76. See also Harley 2125, f. 32r; Add. 29779, f. 19r; Harley 2057, f. 26v; Harley 2054, f. 25r. The chief difference is that the play is said to have been put on at the High Cross as well, or at both places.]

(d) Harley 2125, f. 33v

1515–16 Thomas Smith Senior
The Shepards Play and the Assumption of our Lady was played in Saint Johns churchyard.
[This statement does not appear in any other MS.]

(e) Harley 2105, f. 95r

1545–46 William Holcroft
In this yere master Holcroft died and master John Walles was chosyn Mayor. And the plaies went that same yere.
[No other MS corroborates this statement, unless the Smiths' account for 1554 has been misdated and should read 1545.]

(f) Add. 29777, item 228

1553–54 Jhon Offley
Also this yere the Playes were playde.
[The 1554 Smiths' account would match this evidence, but the dating of that document may be in error.]

(g) Add. 29780, f. 130r

1560–61 William Aldersey
This year the Playes called Whison were played.

[See also Harley 2057, f. 28v; Harley 2125, f. 192r; Add. 29777, item 235; Add. 29779, f. 24v; manuscript 23.5 in the University of Liverpool, and Lysons' notes (*Breviary*); and the Smiths' accounts for this year.]

(h) Add. 29780, f. 130r

1565–66 Thomas Greene
This yeare Whitson Playes were played.
[No other evidence appears for this statement.]

(i) Add. 29779, f. 25r

1566–67 Sir William Sneade
In this yeare the Whitson Playes were played in this cittye by the cittizins of Chester.
[See also Add. 29777, item 241; Harley 2057, f. 29r; Harley 2125, f. 39r; manuscript 23.5 in the University of Liverpool, and Lysons' notes (*Breviary*); and the Smiths' accounts for 1567.]

(j) Harley 2133, f. 42v

1567–68 Richard Dutton
This yeare the Whitson Playes were plaid and divers other pastimes.
[See also Harley 2125, f. 39r; Add. 29777, item 242; Add. 39925, f. 20v; the Smiths' and Painters' accounts; and the Trever and Webster cases.]

(k) Harley 2133, f. 43r

1571–72 John Hankey
This yeare Whitson Playes were plaied. And an inhibition was sent from the Archbishop to stay them, but it came too late.
[See also Add. 29780, f. 131r; Add. 39925, f. 20v; Harley 2057, f. 29r; manuscript 23.5 in the University of Liverpool, and Lysons' notes

(*Breviary*); all reproduce this statement. Harley 1944, f. 86r, and Add. 29779, f. 25v note the performance but not the inhibition. The performance is attested by the Smiths', the Painters', and the Coopers' accounts, and by the City Certificates sent to absolve Savage and Hankey. A number of the manuscripts indicate strong opposition to this performance of the cycle: Add. 29777, item 246: "In this yeare the whole Plays were playde, thoughe manye of the cittie were sore against the settinge forthe therof"; Harley 1046, f. 163v: "This yeare the Maior would needs have the playes (commonly called Chester Playes) to goe forward, againste the willes of the Bishops of Canterbury, Yorke, and Chester"; Harley 2125, f. 39v: The plays were performed "To the dislike of many."]

(l) Harley 2133, f. 43v

1574–75 Sir John Savage
The Whitson Playes were plaid at Midsoummer, and then but some of them, leavinge others unplaid which were thought might not be justified for the superstition that was in them, allthough the Maior was enjoyned not to proceed therein.

[See also Add. 29780, f. 131r; Add. 39925, f. 20v; Harley 2057, f. 29r; manuscript 23.5 in the University of Liverpool, and Lysons' notes (*Breviary*); these MSS reproduce the statement given above. Harley 1944, f. 86v and Add. 29779, f. 26r note the performance without additional comment. Add. 29777, item 249: "The playes calld Whitson Playes were at Mydsomer sett forthe to the misliking of manye." Harley 1046, f. 164v: "This year the said Sir John Savage caused the popish plaies of Chester to bee playd the Sunday, Munday, Tuesday, and Wensday after Midsummer Day, in contempt of an inhibition and the Primates letters from Yorke and from the Earle of Huntington, for which cause hee was served by a Purseuant from Yorke the same day that the new Maior was elected, as they came out of the common hall; notwithstanding, the said Sir John Savage tooke his way towards London. But how his matter sped is not knowne. Also master Hanky was served by the same Purseuant for the like contempt when hee was Maior. Divers others of the citizens and players were troubled for the same matter." One document, Harley 2125, f. 40v, gives the dissatisfaction with this performance a different motivation: "The Whitson Playes played in pageantes in this cittye at Midsomer to the great dislike of many because the playe was in on part of the citty." The one place was probably the High Cross by the Pentice, where the city officials sat to see the performance.]

(m) Harley 2133, f. 44r

1577–78 Thomas Bellin
In Julie the Erle of Darbie, the Lord Strange, with many others, came to this citie and were honorablie receaved by the Maior and citizens. The Sheppards Play was plaied at the High Crosse and other Tryumphs on the Roods eye.

[See also Harley 1944, f. 87r; Harley 2125, f. 41r; and manuscript 23.5 in the University of Liverpool, and Lysons' notes (*Breviary*). In the margin of f. 41r, Harley 2125, Holmes III notes "the scollers of the Freescole also playd a comody before them at master Maiors howse."]

17. Expenses for the Cycle

(a) For Carriage Houses

Two lists of rentals paid by the guilds to the city for places to store their "carriages"—the Treasurer's Account Rolls, Chester Archives, TAR/6, 8–13, 16, and Harley 2158, ff. 33v–65r—include the following information:

(i) 16 Henry 6 (1437–38)
Senescallus del Mercers pro redditu de shipgate   viiid

(ii) 17–20 Henry 6 (1438–42)
Senescallus Piscatorum Cestrie pro quadam parcell terre   vid

(iii) 18–20 Henry 6 (1439–42)
Senescallis Sissor[29] Cestrie pro quadam parcell terre   vid

29. *Sissor* = *Scissorum*: of the Tailors.

(iv)   Before 7 Ed. 4 (1467–68)

Mercatoribus civitatis Cestrie pro aysiament pro cariag suo   6d
Pannariam civitatis Cestrie pro aysiament pro cariag suo   8d

(v)   7 Edward 4 (1467–68)

Senescallus de le Shermen pro aysiament carregii sui   iiiid

(vi)   1539–40

The occupacion of the Mercers for a serten place to bild a house on, in
the which the put ther caryage   vid

(vii)   19 and 20 Edward 4 (1479–80 and 1480–81)

The Drapers of the City de redditu alterne shope place terre in Grayfrere
Lane pro caragii suo 2 years   xvid
The Marchants of Chester de unius vacue place terre in Grayfrere Lane
pro carriagii suo, 2 yeares unpayd, 19.20 E4   xiid

(viii)   20–22 Edward 4 (1480–83)

Tho. Rokley and Jo. Smyth, senescallus arte Sellari infra civitatis Cestri,
quodem aysiament cariagii sui   iiiid

(ix)   26 Henry 8 (1534–35)

The occupacion of Tailliores for a cariage house.   iiiid

Several other documents give information about carriage houses:

(i)   Chester Archives, Assembly Book for 26 Henry 8 (1533–34),
excerpts from ff. 53v–56v

Northgate Street
The occupacon of Smeythys for a place to sett ther carage, adjoynyng
to the Shermen under the walles nygh unto a toure cauled the Dyllys
Towre   iiiid

The occupacon of the Shermen for a place to sett ther carage iiid
Love Lane
The occupacon of Tailliores for a cariage house iiiid
The occupacon of the Sadlers for a place called Truantes Hole, by
yere iiiid
Grayfriars
The occupacon of the Drapers for a certen place to bild a house on,
which they put ther cariage in, nyghe to the gate of the Freres Minores,
by yere viiid
The occupacon of the Mercers for a serten place to bild a house on, in
the which the put ther caryage vid

(ii)   Harley 2054, f. 17rv

Early 1560's, Smiths: to Weavers for rent of the carriage house ivs
1567, Smiths: for gettinge the cariage out of the Axeltree viiid

(iii)   Chester Archives, TAR/16, 1576–77

Mercers: pro domo cariag sua   vid

(iv)   Harley 2172, f. 17r

Rich. Dutton, maior etc., grant in fee farme to Robt. Hill, tayler: The
whole buildinge or howse called the Taylors Carriage Howse, lyinge in
the south part to a lane called Fleshmonger Lane nere to the lands called
Wolfes Gate or New Gate, now in tenure of the aldermen and stewards
cetus sutarum vestiarum infra civitatem, contayninge in length v yards, in
breeth 3 yards and halph, paying iis, vid at 2 feasts, Saint Michael and
Ladyday, provyso as before dated 10 Aug. 16 Q Eliz. [1574]
A similar grant of land "comonly called the Drapers Carriage Howse,
contayning in length xi yards, in bredth 5 yards" to Edward Martin,
draper, for twelve pence twice yearly.

(v)   Chester Archives, Mayor Dutton's Presentment Inquiry,

July 20, 1574
The caryadg howse for the Mercers now converted to a stable, which

was granted to master Moris Williamz, and now the stewardes hath it the yerely rent vid.

(vi)   Chester Archives, undated city roll copied in 1614

Watergate Street upon both sides
Item: for a stable sometymes the Mercers carridge howse, per annum iiis, iiiid
More for voyd grownd sometymes the Drapers carriadge howse, per annum   xiid

(b) For Performances

Twelve accounts of payments by the guilds survive: one from the Shoemakers, six from the Smiths, three from the Painters, and two from the Coopers.

(i) Shoemakers' Accounts, Chester Archives G 8/2, f. 16rv. Probably for 1550

The Expense to Our Play

Item peyd for reydeng the banes   xixd
Item peyd for a dosyn bordes to the carych   iis, viiid
Item peyde for ii plankes for lasses[30]   viiid
Item pay for iii gyse and haffe a sper[31]   xiid
Item peyd for neyles   viiid
Item peyd for freityng of the weyles[32]   xvid
Item peyd for wryght Notte and the beyrech[33]   iiis, iiiid
Item peyd for iii stryke of wyete   xs, iiid
Item peyd for ii yerdes and a hauffe of flaxson clauth to make Meyre
    Madelentes coute   xxiid

---

30. *lasses*: braces, *OED* lace sb. 4.
31. *gyse*: ropes, *OED* guy sb.^{1}2; *sper*: rafter, *OED* spar sb.^{1}1.
32. *freityng*: decorating; *weyles*: wheels.
33. *beyrech*: barrage, cost of drink.

Item payd for bakyng of Godes brede   iiiis, viiid
Item payd for beffe, to our generall reyherse   iiis, iiid
Spend over the shoute[34]   xviid
Item payd for glaves[35] to the pleyers   iiiis
Item payd for seteng op of oure stepoll and for tember   xviid
Item payd for the pleyers breykefaste   viiis, iiiid
Item payd for dreynke to the pleyers and poters of the carych   iis, viiid
Item paid for geyldeng of Godes fase and for peyntyng of the geylers
    fasses   xiid
Item payd for dressyng of the chauernes[36] and for the as   viiid
Item peyd for the menstrells wages   iis, iiiid
Item peyd for payntyng and gyldyng of the pleyeng
    geyre   vs
    Some   lviiis
Item payd for gryndyng the wyette   iid
Item payd for ii cordes   iid
Item payd for soupe   id
Item spend at the bryngeng up of our charych   vid
Item payd for wine to the barkers[37]   xxd
Item payd to the potters of the carych   xviiid
Item payd for drenke to the potters of the carych   iis
Item payd for the marchantes ware   iiiid
Item payd for wypcord and pake thryd and conchyse[38]   viid
Item payd floures   id
Item payd to the lade for leydeng the as   id
Item payd for beyryches   iiiid
Item to God   iis
To Mare Madeline   xd
To Martha   viiis
To Jodas   xvid
To vi chelder of Esaraell   iiis

34. *over the shoute*: more than estimated for drink. *OED* shot sb. [1]10.
35. *glaves*: arrow or small spear.
36. *chauernes*: some kind of equipment for the *as* (donkey)?
37. *barkers*: tanners, who apparently sold wine and spirits; see the item in the Smiths' account for 1561 (seventeenth entry after list of names).
38. *conchyse*: shallow vessels, conch shells?

To Keyfase   xd
To Anas   viiid
The to kneythtes   viiid
To the geyler   xvid
To the geylers man   xiiiid
To the Reygenall beyrer   xiid
Item payd for wyne that Roger Glover and Perse Toung dranke   iiiid
   Some   xxis, iiiid

   Two other pertinent entries occur elsewhere in the manuscript:
   f. 39v, 1561: more over the shote at the makynge op of the playe   iid
   ob.
   f. 52r, 1568: item payde Newton and the presonares that day that
   whe[39] rode the banes   vd

(ii) Smiths' Accounts, Harley 2054

1554, ff. 14v–15r
For ridinge the banes   xiiid; the Citty Crier ridd
Spent at potyng aute of carriges at Rich. Barkers   4d
We gave at geting aute of the carriag   4d
We gave for an axeyll tre to Rich. Belfounder   vid
For another axell tre to Ric. Hankey   iiiid
Payd for dressing of the carriage   xd
For ropes, nelles, pyns, sope, and thrid   xd
For wheate   iis, iid   for malt   iiis, 4d   for flesh   iis, xd
For flesh at the breckfast and bacon   iis, 8d
For 6 chekens   xd   for 2 cheeses   xvid
Item we gave for gelldinge of Gods fase   xiid
Item we gave botord beere to the players   4d
For bred in Northgate streat   iid
We drank in the Watergate street   vid   at Jo.a Leys   xd   at
   Ric. Anderton, founderer   xiid   at Mr. Davison tavarne   xiiid
To the mynstrells in mane   iis
We gave to the porters of the caryegs   iis
For gloves   xiiid
We gave to the Docters   iiis, 4d

   39. *whe*: we.

We gave to Joseph   viiid
We gave to letall God   xiid
We gave to Mary   xd
To Dam Ane   xd
We gave to the Angells   vid
To ould Semond   iiis, 4d
We gave to Barnes and the syngers   iiis, 4d
For more wheate   18d
Malte   iis, iid
Flesh   3s, 4d
A chese   ixd
To Randle Crane in mane   iis
Spent at Mrs. Davison tavarne   iis, id
For the charges of the Regenall   xiid
To the Skayneares   iiis
For makinge of the copes   vs
For dressinge of the stands and janddasses[40]   xiid
For gelding of the fane[41] and for carriages of the lights   xiid

In all   iiili, 4s, 7d

1561, ff. 16v–17r

The names of the company, 1561, and receved of them:
of Hugh Massy   13s, 4d
Receved of Master Moumfort, alderman   iis, 4 ob.

Rich. Skryvener	Irrian Ryder	Tho. Towers
Jo. Parsyvall	Robt. Urmeston	Wm. Jonnson
Jo. Plumer	Jo. Dooe	Hugh Massy
Jo. Robynson	Jo. Ball	Jo. Harrison wife iis, iid
Rich. Barker	Meowe Trafford	Rich. Barker wife
Roger Ledsham iis, 4d	Rich. Smyth	Robt. Hancock
Gilbert Knowes		
Robt. Crockett	Rich. Newall	
Rafe Smyth	Rich. Brasse iis	
William Loker	Rand. Latton	
Law. Gesley	William Clyffe	
Hugh Stokton iis	Jo. Huntington	

40. *janddasses*: ?
41. *gelding of the fane*: gilding of the banner.

All the rest   iis, iiiid ob. apeece

Receved of the Jurneymen   vs

Of the Jurneymen at the generall rehearse   xvid

Payd on election day in our aldermans howse   vis, vid

To mynstrells   4d

To master Tho. Massy for tymber   8s, 9d

To carter and men to gett it out   7d ob.

For wod to make welles[42]

Cost us the rydinge the banes: our horses and ourselves, of the which
   Symyon was one   iis

Payd for the first rehearse at Jo. Huntington's howse   vid

For paper to coppy out the parcells of the booke   vd

Berrage[43] of our wheles   9d ob.

Spent hyring the cartwrights in Geff. Cokes sellor   iid quarta

Spent at deliveringe forth of the parcells and gettinge pillers   4d ob.

Payd for making the welles to the cartwright   7s, 4d

To master Boydle for bords and other tymber   vs

Payd the wright for makinge the carriage and for berrag   8s, 5d

For nayls   vid

For drink in barkers after the rehearse   xviiid

Payd Jo. Byrth for beaffe agaynst the generall rehearse   6s, 8d

For three ould cheeses   4s

For frettinge the wheles and nayles   xviiid

For going to warne the occupations, spent   4d

Spent in Sir Rand. Barnes chamber to gett singers   iiid

Spent at Robt. Jones at rehearse   xixd

To William Lutter at genrall rehearse   4d ob.

For 6 crokes for alle at generall rehearse   xs

A crocke of small ale and 2 gallons   xxd

A hoppe of wheate to the genrall rehearse   iis, iiid

To James Tayler for bread and cakes for genrall rehearse   iis, viid

For wyne to the sayd rehearse   iis, viid

For another hoppe of wheat agayne the Whyttsontidde   iis, iiid

When we brought our carragge to the Wayevers howse   vid

Payd the wrights for settinge the wheles   viiid, and carriage forth of the
   water   viiid

42. *welles*: wheels.
43. *berrage*: transporting.

For a pound of gray sope for the wheles   iiid

For 2 chekens   vid

For naylles to dresse the carriage   iiid ob.

For makinge a faxe, payntinge and dressynge the pillers gere, and a
crowne for Mary [?]

For 3 curten cowerds[44]   iiid

For pynnes   iiid

For flesh for a breckfast at Whitsontyde   3s, 8d

For glowes[45]   iis, viiid

For guildinge of litle Gods face   xiid

For makinge the players to drinke in the Watergate street   vd

For drinke to the players in the Bridgstret   iiid

To Jo. Layes wife for drinke   xiid

To Jo. Dooes for drink   xiid

To the minstrells   3s, 6d Payd for drinke for ther breckfast before they
play, and after they had done when the were unbowninge them   iiis

Payd the porters of the carriage   xviiid

Payd to Symyon   3s, 4d

Payd to Sir Jo. Genson for songes   xiid

To the 5 boyes for singing   iis, vid

To the Angell   vid

To Dame Anne   xd

To Tho. Ellam   xiid

To the first Docter   xvid; to the 2^d xiid; to the 3^d docter   xiid

To the lyttel God   xvid

For redyng the Aurygynall   iid

To the Skynners   iiis; to the Wevers   4s; to Hugh Stoken   xviiid

To Wm. Loker for plleyinge   xvid

To Robt. Crockett for a lord   iiid

To Jo. Dowes for drink   xvid

Spent in the tavarne on Midsomer even in Mr. Moumforts tavarn   iis, 4d

Payd in stuards howse, same night   xiid

To the prisoners in Castell   iiid

Spent at makinge up our buke   xvid

In all   vii li, viiid ob.

44. *cowerds*: cords.
45. *glowes*: gloves.

1567, f. 18rv

The recets of the bretheren for the Plays:

Of master Founder for the plays iis, viiid William Johnson iis, viiid

Of master aldreman Screvener	Jo. Andro
Of master Knowles	Hughe Masse
Robert Croket	Tho. Hollme
Roger Ledsham	Jo. Kempe
Jo. Bradshae	Rich. Brasse iis, vid
Jo. Robenson	Gye Cormell
William Richardson	Tho. Symcocke
Robert Hancoke	Rog. Callcote
Jo. Ball	Jo. Hatton iiis
Yerreon Ryder	Dave Founder iiis
Hughe Stoken iis, vid	William Cradoche
Meehoo Trafforte	Widow Hareson o
Robert Hormeson	Widow Percevall iiis
Jo. Doo	Harry Seston xxd
Ric. Smythe	Jo. Smyth xxd
Ric. Richardson	Of 6 jurneymen xvid apeece
Rondull Lawton	All the rest above iis, viiid apeece
Tho. Towres	
All rest iis, viiid apeece	

The Moneys Layd Downe For Our Play by William Richardson and Tho. Towers, Stewards:

Inter alii—

For our bill we put up to mr. mere for the plays iid[46]

To Newton for the banes id

For bred for our horses that day we rod the banes xiid

For gloves and drinke iiiid

Spent on mr. Chanter in mr. Pooles Tavarne iiiid

For prisoners in Castell iiiid

Spent at the heringe of the payers[47] xd

At rehersinge under St. Johns xiiiid

At rehersinge before mr. maior iis, vid

---

46. *iid*: the cost of preparing the petition (*bill*) from the Smiths to the Mayor for permission to perform their play.

47. *payers*: error for *players*.

Spent after the chosinge of the litle God   xd
To 2 of the clarkes of the Menster   viiid
Spent on the Sonday morninge at the hearinge of the Docters and litle
   God   4d
For the steple and the trestle or forme   iiis, viiid
For gettinge the carriage out of the Axeltree   viiid
And settinge in of the carrige into the Wevers howse   viiid
For a whole chese   iis, vid   a bushell of malt   4s, 4d
For a barrell and quart of beare   vs, viiid   3 hoopes of wheate   4s, 8d
For gorse, salt, buter, safforn, and a spyte[48]   xd
For gildinge God's face   xiid
To x porters of the carrage   iis, viiid
To the Stewards of the jorneymen for wachinge the carrage all night   viiid
Payd one for carringe of the regalls[49]   iid
For mending the crowne and diadem   xd
For 2 parcells   iid
For mending 2 faxes[50]   viiid
To mynstrells   iis
To the Players: Robt. Rabon   xvid; to the litle God   xvid; to the 2
   Docter   xiid; to the 3 Docter   xiid; to Joseph   xiid; to Dame
   Anne   xiid; to the Angell   viiid; to master White   4s; to master
   Chanter   xiid; to William Couper   xiid
For gloves for the players   iiis
For alle, and spent at Aldermans tavarne   iis
For skynnes for play   iiis
To Hugh Stocken   iis   Rich. Brasse   iis

1568, ff. 18v–19r
   Another reseveste[51] of the bretheren for the Plays:

Reseved of master Mounfort iis, iid	Called before master Founder:
Of our allderman Scrifnor 2s, iid	William Jonson
Of master Knowlles	Jo. Andro
Of Robert Coket *ante* Crocket	Hu Masse
Rogers Ledsame	Tomas Holmes

48. *a spyte*: a spit used in cooking.
49. *regalls*: a small organ.
50. *faxes*: wigs.
51. *reseveste*: list of payments received.

Jo. Brosho *Bradshaw ante*
Ric. Newas
William Richardson
Robert Hankock
Jo. Ball
Herryen Ryder
Hu Stoken
Meo Traffort
Robert Ormson *mort*
Jo. Doo
Rich. Smythe
Rich. Robynson   o
Jo. Honteton
Ron Laton
Tho. Towers

Jo. Kemp
Gye Cromell
Tomas Simkoke
Roger Kalket
Jo. Haton
David Mounfort *ante Founder*
William Cradok
Wido Robinson
Wido Persuow   xiid
Jo. Smythe
Tho. Haswall
Ed. Borlay
Rich. Ledsham
Rich. Jonson

all   iis, iid appeece

Thes byn the somes of monaye that ware lade doune by Ric. Newhous and Wm. Jonson about our playes thys yere, which is the ix yere of our reyne.   Anno Domini 1568.

For our byll we put up to mr. meare   iid

For gloves and horsbred when we rid the banes   xviiid

Spent on the chanter and clarke of the Mynster   vd at our first reherse

At alderman Skruenors   iis, 4d

To prisoners in Castell   4d

Given to mr. Mere towards the makinge of a new booke   xiid

At the hyerynge of the menstrells and consell of Simion   iiid

Spent at Gilb. Flowers upon mr. Wite and Sir Randle Barnes   viid

For 2 bosshell malt   viis, 4d ob.

For wheate   iis, iid ob.   2 ould cheses   iis, 8d

For beefe at our generall reherse   viis, xd

For a pound of grey sope   iiid

For boled mete for them that broght the new cheses   xiid

For kakes at our generall reherse   iis   spice   viid   salt   iiid viniger   3d

For bourne[52]   4d

For bacon on Tewsday morning for players brekfast   xd

---

52. *bourne*: water carried from a well.

For vele, same time, 14d   chekens   xvid   bred   viiid
For Griff Yevans wife to pay for wessing[53] the curtens   4d
For neles, pinns, nedles, cords   ixd
To 10 men for portage of carrag   iis, 6d
To the prentis when we gat in our cariage, to drink   viiid
To the right[54] for gettinge the carriag off and on   viiid
To master Rond. Barnes   3s, 4d
To master Wyte for singinge   4s
To Mary   2s   To Joseph   xiid   To litle God   xvid
For gylding God's face on Midsomer Even   xiid
To Newton and Prisoners   vid
To the Doctors and litle God   xiid   To menstrells   iis
For gloves to litle God and Docters   ixd
Spent at master Mounfforts   iiis, iid
Receved—the Teylers, for rent—iis, vid
Payd for rent of meeting-howse   vs   making up our booke   xvid
Receded of Tho. Hasellwall for his coming in   xliiis, 4d
Of Ed. Borlaye   xxvis, viiid
Of Rich. Ledshome   xiiis

1572, f. 19v
   For the Banes: *about 1571*
For dressinge our huddes[55]   xiiiid
For gloves, same day   xd
To the Cryor   id
For horsbred, same day   xiid
Spent at our aldermans, same day   xiiiid   at May Kynnes   iid
When I went to borrowe a touyle   iiid

   For the Playes:
Layd downe about seekinge our players   xvid
For parchment to make a new orriginall booke   3s, 6d
For beefe for our genrall rehearse   7s, 8d   2 cheeses   3s
6 cart-clouts and nayles   viid
For nayles to nayle the bords of the carrage   4d

53. *wessing*: washing.
54. *right*: wright, carpenter.
55. *huddes*: hoods.

For 2 stays for carrage   iid
For tallow for wheles   iid   pinns for the axtrees   iid
Hoope wheat   iis   bred, same day   1od
At first reherse   22d   At second rehearse   iis, iid
When we went to mr. Maiors about the plays   viid
For ale to our genrall rehearse   xs   beare ixd
For spices for the meats   4d
To the waytes and our musysyens   xiid
To mynstrells   vid
For dressinge the fane and diadem   xviiid
For ynckill pynns[56] and nayles to our carriage [?]
For a rybben for our scotchen[57]   iiid
For gloves   iiis, iid
For dressinge our carriage, and after our play spent at our aldermans
    iis, 4d
To the minstrells for our pagent   3s, 4d
For sope to wash clothes   xd
For small beare in Bridgstreet   iiiid
The names of the Players:
Symion, Dame Anne, 2 Angells   xiid
Joseph, Mary   xviiid
Deus   xvid
Primus Docter   xvid, 2 Docter, 3 Docter [?]
For the Clergy for the songes   4s, 2d
For breckfast on Twesday morning   8s
Gildinge of litle God's face   viiid
Porters for carriage   xviiid
To the Clarke for lone of a cope, an alter cloth, and tunecle[58]   xd
For redinge the orrignall book   iid
To the Skinners   iiis
For bringinge of the carriag home and spent on mynstrells and
    porters   4d

1575, ff. 20v–21r
    The Recetes of hus, Tho. Towres and Davye Moumford, for the
Ockepassion for Ther Yousse; 4 July, 1574:

56. *ynckill pynns*: pins for linen tape.
57. *scotchen*: escutcheon.
58. *tunecle*: tunicle (ecclesiastical garment for sub-deacons).

Spent on the players and other things necessisary   xiis

Spent at Tyes, to heare 2 plays before the Aldermen, to take the
 best   xviiid

For drink at our generall reherse   vs

Led out att Medsamar yevan to the presnars   iid in Northgate

For thryd to sowe the bowes[59] ger that went afore hus att Mydsamar   iid

For horsse bred for the nag he red apon   4d

Our bangket when we cam from the wache   vis

For tallow for the carrage   iiid

To the menstreles at our generall rehers and Midsamar and with our
 pagan   vs

To litle God   20d

To oure Marye   xviiid

To our 2 Docter   xvid

For sope to wache our gere we borrowed   viiid

For penes and nayles   xiid

For bere at mr. Burgeses   viiid

For 9 men to carry our carryche and one tressell, and 2 that did help me
 in the morninge   3s 9d ob.

For making the bowes gowne   4d

For knetting of our bowes house[60] that rid before us at Midsamar   viiid

For the Banes and dring at the Barrs   xiid

At Medsamar Yven to presnars   4d

For the syne and faxe[61]   xiid

For the copes and clotthe   xiid

To 3 of the synngares   xiiiid

Spent at Jo. Dowes   xvid

At the Banes for glowffes, and to the plears and Aldermen at bringinge of
 our pagen forth   3s, 2d

On of the syngares had for his panes[62] and gloffes   xvid

To Jo. a Shawe for lone of a Docters gowne and a hode for our eldest
 Docter   xiid

Payd for our First Angell   vid

For dryngke at dressinge our carrge   vid

59. *bowes*: boy's.
60. *house*: hose.
61. *syne and faxe*: sign and wig.
62. *panes*: pieces of cloth for a garment.

To Seameon   iiis
To our Frest Doctor   xvid
To our Tret Doctor   xiid
To our Dame An   xd
To Gossep   xvid
To Secon Angell   vid
To the Skenars   iiis

Undated Entry, f. 21r (right after the 1575 accounts given above)
Rec. of the accounts of the pleayes   xis, iiid

1576, f. 21rv
Of our sister Hancocke for the please   xvd
Of Robert Crockett   xvd
Of Ric. Locker   xvd
Of 2 smythes in Hanbridge for the please   iis, viiid
Of Jo. Andro for please   xvd
Spent in gatharing our play mony   xviiid

(iii) Painters', Glaziers', Embroiderers', and Stationers' Accounts, Chester, the Painters' Guild

1568, ff. 35r–37v

Whitson Plays

For Whytsone Playes, the yeare of oure Lord God a thousant fyve hundreth thrye score and eyght; then mayor of the sytte of Chester, Mister Rychard Dutton

Furst payd for the reste of acounte at our firste metyng   iid
Item payd to the Sharemen for the dressyng of our skynes   viiid
Item payd to Gryffe Tayler for makyng of oure huddes   xiid
Item for our horsses at the rydynges of the Banes   xvid
Item to the prysoners   id
Item to Newton for rydying of the Banes   id
Item for ii [. . .] of [. . .]   d
Item spentt at Thomas Jonson's to speke with master Chaunter for
    Shepertes Boyes   iid
Item payd for paper to coppye the Orrygenall   iid
Item payd at oure first rehersse at our Aldermans   xvid

Item payd for the rest of acounte at a meeting anenest[63] Rychard Garralt
    for the rest of a shote   vd
Item spente at Rychard Halowodes about the hyryng of the caryge   iiiid
Item spente at Mister Hankyes abowte Master Bryd   vid
Item spente at Master Hankyes at a rehersse the same daye   vd
Item spente at oure Aldermans the same daye   xiid
Item sppente at oure Aldermans when we rehersed before Mister
    Mayre   iis, vid
Item spent at our Aldermans the furst tyme we mett in the comenhall   xxd
Item spent for boreyng of coveryng and a naked chyld   iid
Item payd for mogges[64]   iis, vid
Item payd to the beryg[65] for payntyng of oure ox and asse and our pye in
    common hall   iiiid
Item payd for a bestes baly to dener   xd
Item payd for wosshyng puddynges   id ob.
Item payd for coppyng of our Orygenall   xiid
Item spente at Johan Cockes to borrow bottelles   iid
Item payd for botter to the playe   viiid
Item for chesse   vd
Item payd for nayles   iiid
Item payd for a corde   iid
Item for whysteles   id
Item for pynnes   id
Item for poyntes   id
Item spente at Rychard Halewodes upon Wytson Sondaye in drynke   iiiid
Item spente the same daye upon the Shephertes Boyes   iid
Item payd for bryddes   iid
Item payd for crabefysshes   iid
Item for mendyng Trowes cote   iid
Item for coppyng a parsell   iiiid
Item for potes of ale at Rychard Halewodes when we dressed oure playes
    and when we made our capes and cotes   vid
Item payd for bred to the playe   iiiid

63. *anenest*: in the presence of.
64. *mogges*: mugs for drinking.
65. *beryg*: city.

Item payd for bere to them that puted[66] the caryge   vid
Item payd to viii putters of the caryge   iiis
Item payd to the mynstrelles   iiis, iiiid
Item payd to Joseph   xd
Item payd for mete for the asse   viiid
Item payd towardes the fecchyng of him   iiiid
Item payd for horsse brede to Harvey's horse   iiiid
Item payd to Johan Howtton for a qarter of vele   xvid
Item for a qarter of corsse vele   viiid
Item for a bestes bely and calves fette   viiid
Item for a myd-calffe and an ox tonge   viiid
Item for a calves hed   iiiid
Item for a grone   iiid
Item for a [. . .] of [. . .]   vid
Item to the mayde for a [. . .] hed   iiiid
Item for a tuppes hed   iid
Item for ale at Johan Cokes   iiiid
Item to Oure Ladyes wayges   viiid
Item to iiii Shephardes Boyes   iis, viiid
Item for the hyre of oure caryge   iiiid
Item for a payre of pumpes and Trowes shewes   xvid
Item to Rychard Chalewoddes wyffe for xvi hagays[67]   viid
Item to her for bacon   vid
Item to her for a calves hed   iiiid
Item to her for bred and ale in the mornyng to the puteres and the
    mynstrelles, and at our supper   iiiis
Item for parbolyng of the garbyge   xvid
Item to iiii Sheppertes Boyes   iis, viiid
Item for a quarter of a lambe to John Howton   xd
Item for v haggassys to Rammesdales wyffe   iis, iid
Item for a garnyshe[68] for the lyttell chyld   iid
Item for one pottell of bere at our Alldermans   iid
Item payd to the mynstrelles uppon Mydsomer Even   vid
Item to the prysoners the same tyme   id

66. *puted*: transported.
67. *hagays*: haggis.
68. *garnyshe*: a dish of light food.

Item to Rychard Halewoddes wyffe for brede   viiiid vppon Mydsomer
 Even
Item to her for [. . .] the drynke, the same tyme   iis, viiid
Item for a pottell of whytt wyne   vid
Item for samontt[69]   iis, iiiid
Item to the eldest sheppertt   iis
Item to the second sheppert   xxd
To the thryd sheppert   xxd
Item to Trow   iis
Item to Trowes Boye   vid
Item to two Shepperttes for goyng uppon Mydsomer Even   xd
Item to the two Sheppertes when the Banes were rydden   xd
Item to him that rydeth the Orrygynall   xiid
Item to the Angell   vid

The sum ys   iiiili, iis, vid

  The hole some of the Whytsone Playes and all the charges of oure
occupacyon, except quarteryges from Saynt Luke Daye untyll the vth of
July, ys iiiili, iis, vid, wyche ys for every brother v[s], vid, whereof Thomas
Powle ys bated in his parte iiid.
Item Memorandum: That Rychard Calye ys indetted to the occupacyon
 for Whytsone Playes   vs, vd
Item due to him for income of brydren   iis, ixd
Item he ys behind for charges uppon Saynt Luke Daye   iiid
For oure expensys sencys the vth of July when we recond for Wydsones
 Playes   [?]
Furst payd for the rest of a shott at Thomas Gylones the vth of July   iid.

1572, ff. 47r–48r
  For Whitsone Playes the yeare of our Lord God a thowssande fywe
hunderthe sevente and ii; the Mayre of the sytte of Chestar Mastar John
Hankye. [Whitson Playes went this yeare, 1572, and Mesomer Show
also, per accounts.]

Item for our horssces at the rydyng of the Banes   xvid
Item for papare   id
Item for ryddyng the Banes   id
Item for the reste of a shoute at the fyrste rehersce   vid

---

69. *samontt*: salmon.

Item spende on the iiii syngarse at Rondylle Ynces　iid
Item for xiiii yerthen moges　iiis
Item spende at Tomas Lynecarsse for the baryage of the cariage　vid
Item pede to Doosse wyfe farneste the hagoosscys　xiid
Item spentte in Wyllam Dones　iiiid
Item spentte in Tomas Lynecars　id
Item spentte in Rychart Twyssces spekynge for the asse　id
Item before the generall reherce in Robart Halewodes　vid
Item lede done[70] goinge to loke for skynnes　iid
Item lede done at the generaulle rehersce denar　vis
Item payde to Roger Colarke for ii yarne stabylles[71]　iiid
Item payde for iiii wyestlles　iid
Item payde at the hyrynge of the caryages　id
Item payde for ii chessces　vd
Item for a gambone, a bacone, and iiii fytte　vid
Item for ii gannokes from Waryntone[72]　iid
Item spente goynge to borrow bogyttes[73]　iid
Item for a besstes tonge and iiii colfes fytte　viiid
Item for bowttare　viiid
Item for a haulle[74]　iiiid
Item payde to Doosses wyffe for lethes and levarse[75]　xiid
Item payde for gettyng wedes[76]　iid
Item spend at gettynge cattes[77] an bottylse　iiiid
Item payde for a topes hede[78]　iiiid
Item for nelles, corde, pynes, pynttes, and paketryde[79]　ixd
Item for the as lede doune　xiid
Item for pentynge the houke[80] and ass, the styltes and the stare　xiid

70. *lede done*: laid down, paid.
71. *ii yarne stabylles*: two lengths of woolen yarn.
72. *gannocks from Waryntone*: oatmeal cakes from Warrington in Lancashire.
73. *bogyttes*: buckets.
74. *haulle*: awl.
75. *lethes and levarse*: lungs ("lights") and livers.
76. *wedes*: clothes.
77. *cattes*: small pieces of wood used in a children's game; *OED* cat sb. 10. To be given as gifts to the Christ-child in the play?
78. *topes hede*: head of a sheep.
79. *pynttes and paketryde*: paints and pack-thread.
80. *houke*: hook.

Item for crabes   id
Item for a lawne a velle[81]   vid
Item for a tryne platar[82]   iiid
Item to viii pottarres of the caryages   iis, xd
Item to Petar a Moston for Troues shone-makyng, and for hys penes an labore   xvid
Item for bayre[83] that Rochart Doby hade   id
Item for payntes to bone the pleares[84]   iid
Item payde to the mynstryles   iis
Item for ii wystyles for Trowe   iid
Item for the brekefast to the plears and pottares of the caryags   vs, viiid
Item for bred and bear to the plle[85]   xd
Item to master Brearwood for hortyng of skyngnes[86]   vid
Item payde to Robart Radeborne   xiid
Item payde to Dosse wyfe for hagocyes   vis, viiid
Item payd to Sheppertes Boyees   iiiis
Item to Roger Calcotte for a ierne[87] to the caryge   iid
Item a skynne to Trowes shewes   vid
Item to Trowes Boye   vid
Item to Our Lady   vid
Item to Johan Casker for a lord[88]   iiid
Item a pott of beare   id
Item payd for the caryge   vs, iiiid
Item for Harvyes wages   xxd
Item for Tuddes wages   xxd
Item for Trowes wages   iis
Item for the wages of the Angell   vid
Item for rydyng the Orygenall   xiid
Item for drynke to the players   iiiid
Item for a payer of lether garteres   vid

81. *lawne a velle*: loin of veal.
82. *tryne platar*: wooden platter.
83. *bayre*: beer.
84. *bone the pleares*: prepare the players.
85. *plle*: players.
86. *hortyng of skyngnes*: storing of skins.
87. *ierne*: piece of iron.
88. *lord*: error for *bord* (board)?

Item for a shype hoke[89]   vid
Item for goyng uppon the styltes at rydyng the Bannes   vid
Item for another payer of sewes for Trowe   xvid

                            3li, 3s, 2d

For the pley everye man hathe payde that is crafte   iiis, iiid
Item for Thomas Poolles child, bycose he pled not our God   iiiid

1575, ff. 59r–60r
For Whytson Playes in the yere of oure Lorde God 1575, and in the same
yere Soure John Savyche mayre of this syte of Chester.
Item for bred to oure horses when wye rede the Banes   viiid
Item to Rycharson at the Banes rydeng   id
Item to the presnars at the Castell   id
Item to the berynge of the caryge   vd
Item I layde downne at the [. . .] reherse by Soure Mastar Mayre   xiid
Item for bere to the pleares at the same reherse   id
Item for ii got skynes for Trow shous   iiid
Item for xii erthen moges   xxid
Item for the hayare of the ii bardes and Trowes cape   vid
Item for wystelles   iid
Item layde downe at mr. Alderman Halwods for the reste of the shot one
   Medsomers Eve   xvid
Item to the menstrelles   xiid
Item to the presnares in the Castell   iid and the presnares in the Northe
   Gate   id
Item for synges   id
Item for the brekynge of the botell   iid
Item for neles, pynes, and pakethryde   vid
Item payd to Anderasone   iiiid
Item for pouder for the sengers   vid
Item for the leg, loyne, and tonnge of vell   xvd
Item for the topas hed and the groyne   iid
Item for the calves fyte   id
Item for the boylange and dressynge the garbyche   xiid
Item for vi hagosses   iiis, vid
Item for ii chysses   iiiid

  89. *shype hoke*: sheep-hook.

Item for the copynge of a parsell   iiiid
Item for vii poutters of the caryche   iis, iiiid
Item for Peter of Mosten for makynge of Troules shoues and hys
  paynes   xiid
Item iii Shepardes Boyes   iiis
Item for Troulles Boye   vid
Item to Joseph   xiid
Item to Marye   vid
Item to oure Angell   vid
Item for a janokes   iid
Item for cakes   iiiid
Item for bouter   vid
Item for drynke to the ples[90]   xd
Item to Rychard Dobye for goynge one the styltes at the Banes
  rydenge   vid
Item for goynge one the styltes one Medsomare Eve   vid
Item for the mynstrell to the plase   iid
Item in borowenge tangkeres bages   iid
Item for wedes   iid
Item for the souper to the pleares   vs
Item bystoued one drynke to the pouters when the play was donne   vid
Item for Troulles wages and hys shoues   iiis
Item payde for the caryge   vis, iiiid
Item spend at the same tyme   iiiid
Item for Hankyns wages   iis
Item for Harveys wages   xxd
Item for Toudes wages   xxd
Item for the rydenge of the Regenall   xiid
Item for the pleares at mr. Aldermanes house   iid
Item to mr. Alderman Halwod for the makynge the bohye and pentenge
  the styltes   xd
Item for a paste balye[91]   viiid
                    The some is   lis, xid
Roger Framwall is unpaid this year, 1575.
Item for the pleayse   iiis, iiid

90. *ples*: plays.
91. *paste balye*: ball made of paste.

(iv) Coopers' Accounts, Chester, Coopers' Guild, Account Book,
1571–1611

1572, f. 3rv

The xx[th] November: Elizabethe, by the grase of God Quene of Englande, Frans, and Ierland, Defender of the Fathe, and the xiiii yerre of hyr rene; then beynge mayre John Hanke; shrevys Rychar Baman, Wyllyam Walle; stuardes Thomas Leneker, John Stynson; to make all syche contes as belonge to the Flechers, Bowyers, Coopers, and Strengers for this yere.

Resevyd of the Paynters and of the Skyners for the caryge   xs, iiiid

Lede done of expenses

In primis, the herryng of the players and leverynge of persells to the holle
    ys   ixd

Item spend of the ryddyng of the Banes and other thynges   xiid

Item spend at the forst reherse and the delyveryng of oure gerre to the
    payntter   xd

Item coste the brekynge of the caryge, the bernggyn yt up to the stuerdes
    doure   xviiid

Item too selles[92] to the caryge, the pryse   iis, viiid

More payde to John Croulay for the makyng of the caryge, and nayles
    iiiis

Item for the carynge the welles to the water and frome, and the berygh of
    the caryge   viid

More spende whan the payntars came to garne the bereghe, and at the
    second reherse in the stuardes Lenekers   ixd

Item for ieren and byndyng of a welle, and one stable, one neue welle,
    and the dresyng of one howlde welle—the wyche comes to   vs, id

More spende in gresenge of the caryghe welles and grese to yt, the ladar,
    and the settyng up of yt one the welles   xiiiid

More for frettes and for axeltre penes   viiid

Item spende at the brengeng up of yt to the Menster gate for cordes and
    penes to sette up the howsynge of the caryghe   iis

More spend at denar one the company and one players, and at nyght
    whan the undressed them and all the daye   viis, iiiid

Payde for the carynge of Pylates clothes   vid

Payde to Wyllyam Rogerson for a cope and a tenekell   vid

92. *selles*: sills.

Payde to Wyllyam Trolloke by the consant of the company   viid
Payde to vii men, putters of the caryghe   iis, iiiid
Payde to Hugh Gyllam   vis, viid
Payde to Thomas Marser   iis, iiid
Payde to John Stynson   iis, iiid
Payde to Rychard Kalle   xvid
Payde to Hugh Sparke for ryedyng of the Ryegenalle   iis
Item payde to John Proulay for the brekyng of the caryghe   viid
   The some ys in all that the playes lyes in XLIXs, Xd
More payde to John Joanson for laynge the caryghe in hys seller   xviiid
More spend at the takyng done of yt and at the laynge in of yt   viid
Item payde for the payntyng of oure gere   iiis, viiid
Item spend one Sante Edmondes daye on the companye   iiis, xd
More payde for the armes one Medsomereven   xiid
Item a perre of gloves to the chylde that caryede the armes, and a quarte
 of wyne to hys mother, and for the makynge of hys cloke   xid
More to Wyllyam Rychyrson and to the presoners   iiid
More to Rondul Thrope for the bryngyge upe of the horse   id
Spende in John Stynson one Medsomereven   xxiid
More spende at the resevynge of the Paynters and Skyners mone[93]   vid

1575, ff. 7r–8r
Item receaved of the stuardes of the Paynters for our cariadge   vs, iiiid
Item receaved of the stuardes of the Hatmakers and Skyners   vis, 8d
Item spent in our Aldermans at the rydinge of the Banes   xiid
Item spend in horsbred   vid
Item paied for wryttinge the parceles   vid
Item paied for ii peare of gloves   vid
Item spend apon Thomas Marser to get him to pleay   iid
Item geven William Rycharson   id
Item spent at the receavinge custome   iiiid
Item spent at the fyrste rehearse   vid
Item spend at the secunde rehearse   xiid
Item spend at the thred rehearse   xiid
Item paied for a peare of whelles   iiiis
Item geven the presonars when we rode the Banes   iid

93. *mone*: money.

Item paied for nealis to the cariadge   xiid
Item spend at the dressinge the cariadge   xd
Item paied for the payntinge the playars clothes   iis, viiid
Item spend on Margery Gybbon to get our regynale   iid
Item paied unto Robart Slye for helpinge at the cariadge   vd
Item spend at our generall rehearse   iis, xd
Item for a borde to the cariadge   iiiid
Item for nealis to neale the hingis   iid
Item spent at the bringinge up the cariadge   viiiid
Item spent on Rychard Doby   iid
Item spend on Edwarde Porter and for ii copes   viiid
Item nealis, pynnis, and cordes, ard drynke at the bowinge[94] our
   cariadge   vid
Item at the fyrste dresnge the cariadge for cordes   iid
Item for newe housinge to our cariadge   vid
Item for thre clapes[95] of iren to the cariadge   xvid
Item for the mendinge of Arrates[96] vysar   iiiid
Item spent at the bowninge of the players   iid
Item paied for drynke to the players   iis
Item spent at the unbowninge of the players in drynke and bred   xiid
Item paied unto Pylat and to him that caried Arrates clothes, and for
   there gloves   vis, vid
Item paied unto the Turmenters   iiiis, vid
Item paied unto Annas   xxiid
Item paied the putters of our cariadge   iis, viiid
Item paied the wright for settinge up our cariadge and takinge yt done
   and asonder   iis, xd
Item spend at the takinge downe of our cariadge on som of our
   compeny   xiid
Item spend at the receavinge of our mony for the cariadge, of the
   Paynters   iiiid
Item entringe a accion agaynste John Ashewode and for the arestment of
   him   viiid
Item more spent when we went to paye the players   vid
Item paied Houghe Sparke for redinge the Regynall   iis

94. *bowinge*: preparing.
95. *clapes*: clasps.
96. *Arrates*: Herod's.

1575–76, f. 9r
Item more receaved for a peare of the cariage whelles   iiiis, viiid

(c) By the Cathedral

The Treasurer's Accounts for the Dean and Chapter, Chester Cathedral, 1561–84, include two sets of entries which show expenses in connection with the cycle:

1568, page 52
Item paid for a brode clothe againste the Whitson Pleaes   vis, viiid
Item for a barell of bere to yeve to the pleares to make them to
   drinke   vis
Item for packe threed at Witson Daye to hange up the clothe   iid

1572, page 120
Item for the hyre of a clothe for the mansyon over the gates   vis
Item for cordes   xvid
Item for a barrell of byre to the players   viiis

18. Three Lists of Guilds

Two lists of guilds in Chester, although not directly connected with the cycle, may furnish assistance in dating probable changes in the development of the cycle. The first was compiled in 1475–76 to record apprentice fees for each guild. The list has been reordered below to match the order of guilds in the cycle. The second list is in Harley 2104, f. 4r, and has been dated 1500. It probably indicates the order of the guilds for performances of the cycle. The third list, from Harley 2150, seems to date from 1539–40.

(a) Chester Archives, Mayor's Book, M/B/6a, f. 3v

Drapers
Drawers of Dee
Barbers
Mercers

Goldsmiths
Butchers
Glovers
Barkers
Bakers
Coopers
Bowers and Fletchers
Ironmongers
Cooks
Skinners
Fishmongers
Shermen
Hewsters
Weavers and Walkers

(b) Harley 2104

Drapers
Drahers of Dee
Barburs
Wryghtus
Vynteners
Marcers
Goldsmythus and Masons
Smythus
Bucherus
Glovers
Corvisers and Barkers
Baxters[97]
Flecherus and Cowpers
Hyrunmunggers[98]
Cokus
Tapsters and Hostlers
Skynners

97. *Baxters*: Bakers.
98. *Hyrunmunggers*: Ironmongers.

Sadelers
Taylers
Fychemungers
The Wyfus of the Town: "Assumpcion Beate Marie"
Scheremen
Heusters[99]
Wevers and Walkers

(c) Harley 2150, f. 85v

These be the craftys of the citie, the whiche craftys bere the charge of the pagyns in pley of Corpus Christi; and were the auntient Whitson Playes in Chester sett out at the charges of theis occupations, yearly playd on Munday, Tewsday, and Wensday in Whitson Weeke, beinge first invented and putt into English by Rand. Higden, a monck of Chester Abby.

Barkers or Tanners	The Falling of Lucyfer
Drapers and Hosiers	The Creation of the World
Drawers of Dee and Waterleders	Noy and His Ship
Barbers, Waxchandlers, and Leches or Surgions	Abram and Isack
Cappers, Wyerdrawers, and Pynners	Kyng Balac and Balame, with Moysez
Wrights, Slaters, Tylers, Dowbers, and Thacchors	Nativitie of our Lord
Paynters, Brotheres, and Glasiours	The Sheppards Offeryng
Vynters and Marchauntes	King Herod and the Mount Victoriall
Mercers and Spycers	iii Kinges of Colyn

These ix playes and pagents above written be plaid on the fyrst day.

Goldsmythis and Masons	The Sleying of the Children of Isarell by Herod

---

99. *Heusters*: Hewsters, Dyers.

Smythes, Furbours, and Pewters	Purification of our Lady
Bochers	The Pynacle with the Woman of Canany
Glavers and Parchement-makers	The Rising of Lasare from Deth to Lyff
Corvesers or Showmakers	The Comyng of Crist to Jersalem
Bakers and Mylners	Cristes Monday, where he sat with his Apostles
Bowers, Flecchers, Stryngers, Cowpers, and Turners	Scorgyng of Cryst
Ironmongers and Ropers	Crusyfing of Christ
Cokes, Tapsters, and Hostelers, and Inkeepers	The Harowyng of Hell

Theze ix playes or pagents above writen be plaid apon the secund day.

Skynners, Cardmakers, and Hatters, Poynters, and Gyrdlers	The Resurrection
Sadlers, Fusters	Castell of Emaus and the Appostles
Tailers	Assencion of Crist
Flesshemongers[100]	Whitsonday, the Making of the Crede
Shermen	Profettys afore the Day of Dome
Hewsters and Belfounders	Antecrist
Weyvers and Walkers	Domezday

Plaid appon the third.

On Corpus Christi Day the collegis and prestys bryng forth a play at the assentement of the maire.

Provided alwais that it is at the libertie and pleasure of the mair, with the counsell of his bretheryn, to alter or assigne any of the occupacons above-writen to any play or pagent as they shall think necessary or convenyent.

19. Excerpts from Rogers' Breviary

Robert Rogers (d. 1595) was Archdeacon of St. Werburgh's Cathedral in Chester. He collected extensive material concerning the history of the

---

100. *Flesshemongers*: an error for *Fishmongers*.

city. His son David continued the collection of material and produced four editions of *A Breviary*, which contain important information—and some misinformation—concerning the cycle. These four editions, a later version, and an excerpt are now to be found in (a) Chester Archives, unnumbered manuscript, (b) Harley 1944, (c) Cheshire Record Office, DCC 19, (d) Harley 1948, (e) Harold Cohen Library, University of Liverpool, manuscript 23.5, and (f) Additional 9442.

The first five versions are probably in the hand of David Rogers; the sixth item is an excerpt prepared by Daniel and Samuel Lysons as notes for their *Magna Britannia* II. ii (London, 1810), p. 584.

The preface to the first version is dated 1609; the material concerning the cycle was probably completed in 1610, and other material was added during 1610–19. The second version is a copy, with a few changes, of the first, made in 1619. The third version is an extensive revision done in 1619. The fourth version shows further revision about 1623. The fifth version includes additional changes and is dated 1637. The sixth item seems to have been copied from the fifth version.

(a) Chester Archives, C/B/182

Title:
A Brevary or some fewe collectiones of the cittie of Chester, gathered out of some fewe writers and heare set downe and reduced into these chapters folowinge.

From the Table of Contents:
4. Of the buldinge and changeinge of some parishe churches in Chester; certayne lawdable exercises and playes of Chester.

The Preface:

TO THE READER

Gentle Reader, I am boulde to presente unto your sighte a Brevary of Chester, that anchient cittie—the which, howsoevar it be not profitable for anye that seeke devine consolation, yet it maye be delightefull to many that desire to heare of antiquitie. The which worke heare followinge was the collectiones of a lerned and reverende father within this cittie. The which worke I muste crave the readers hereof not to contemne because of the defectes herein, assuringe you that whatsoevar is wantinge either for lerninge or readinge, it is not for the wantes that weare in the author hereof; for both this cittie and these partes did fullye knowe his full abillitye and sufficiencie in those respectes. And therefore I alledge the resones that moved the author to this worke, and the reson whye it is not perfected in that perfection that he intended, craveinge pardon for any thinge herein either nakedly or improperly set downe.

The resons that moved hime heareunto, as I conseave, was because he was heare borne and his predicessors also, and some of them beinge of the beste rancke within this cittie; and also because he himselfe was a continuall resident within this place and did desire the continuall honor, wealth, and good estimation of this anchiente cittie. But the reson whye it was not prefected was the erevokeable will of God who, before he coulde finishe this or many much more excellente and devine treatises, called hime and gathered hime to his fathers in a tymely death and full of dayes. And soe he lefte this and manye more of excellente vallue unfinished, even as a bodye without a head.

Therefore againe I crave the readers hereof to impute the defectes herein to the unskillfull writer, whoe indeede is altogether unfitt to take anye such matter in hande, whoe wanteth both learninge and readinge in this kynde to finnishe up this treatise; and also, I maye bouldlye saye, wanteth tyme to combine it in that fashon which it requireth, craveinge only but acceptacion for my desyre, willinge to displease none, but desiringe that all defectes herein may be imputed to the unskyllfull writer; and if any good effecte, that it be imputed to the Author.

And thus wisheinge the honor and perpetuall good estate of this moste anchiente and righte worshipfull cittie, I ever reste a continuall wellwisher, obliged in all love as God, nature, and reason byndethe mee.

per David Rogers
July 3th, 1609

Folios 18r–23r:

Chapter 4

Now of the playes of Chester called the Whitson Playes: when they weare played, and what occupationes bringe forthe at theire charges the playes or pagiantes.

Heare note that these playes of Chester called the Whitson Playes weare the worke of one Rondoll, a moncke of the Abbaye of Sainte Warburge in Chester, whoe redused the whole historye of the Bible into Englishe storyes in metter in the Englishe tounge. And this monke in a good desire to doe good published the same. Then the firste maior of Chester—namely Sir John Arnewaye, knighte—he caused the same to be played.

The manner of which playes was thus: They weare devided into 24 pagiantes acordinge to the companyes of the Cittie. And everye companye broughte forthe theire pagiant, which was the cariage or place which the played in. And before these playes weare played there was a man which did ride—as, I take it, upon Saint Georges Daye[101]—throughe the cittie and there published the tyme and the matter of the playes in breeife.

The weare played upon Mondaye, Tuesedaye, and Wensedaye in Whitson Weeke. And thei firste beganne at the Abbaye gates. And when the firste pagiante was played at the Abbaye gates, then it was wheled from thense to Pentice at the Highe Crosse before the maior. And before that was donne, the seconde came; and the firste wente into the Watergate streete and from thense unto the Bridge streete. And so one after another, tell all the pagiantes weare played appoynted for the firste daye. And so likewise for the seconde and the thirde daye.

These pagiantes or carige was a highe place made like a howse with 2 rowmes, beinge open on the tope. The lower rowme, theie apparrelled and dressed themselves; and the higher rowme, theie played. And thei stoode upon vi wheeles.[102] And when the had donne with one cariage in one place, theie wheled the same from one streete to another: firste from the Abbaye gate to the Pentise, then to the Watergate streete, then to the Bridge streete through the lanes, and so to the Estegate streete. And thus the came from one streete to another, kepinge a directe order in everye streete, for before thei firste cariage was gone from one place, the seconde came; and so before the seconde was gone, the thirde came; and so tell the laste was donne—all in order withoute anye stayeinge in anye place. For worde beinge broughte howe everye place was neere doone, the came and made noe place to tarye tell the laste was played.

Hereafter followeth the readinge of the Banes which was reade before the begininge of the Whitson Playes, beinge the breeife of the whole Playes.

[The Late Banns follow; see item 20. After the Banns, the commentary continues.]

---

101. 23 April.
102. *vi* is an error for *iv*: see Cheshire Record Office, DCC 19 below.

And thus muche of the Banes or breife of the Whitson Playes in Chester. For if I shoulde heare resite the whole storye of the Whitson Playes, it woulde be tooe tediose for to resite in this Breavarye. As also the beinge nothinge profitable to anye use, excepte it be to showe the ignorance of oure forefathers and to make us, theire offspringe, unexcusable before God, that have the true and sincere words of the Gospell of oure Lord and savioure Jesus Christe, if we apprehende not the same in oure liffe and practise to the eternall glorie of oure God,[103] the salvation and comforte of oure owne soles.

Heare followeth all the companyes as the were played upon there severall dayes, which was Mondaye, Tuesedaye, and Wensedaye in the Whitson Weeke; and how many pagiantes weare played upon everye daye at the charge of everye companye:

The companye or trades that playe		*The storye that everye companye did acte*
1. Barkers and Tanners	bringe forthe	The Fallinge of Lucifer
2. Drapers and Hosiers		The Creation of the Worlde
3. Drawers in Dee and Waterleaders		Noah and his Shipp
4. Barbers, Waxechandlers, Leeches		Abraham and Isacke
5. Cappers, Wyerdrawers, Pynners		Kinge Balack and Balaam with Moyses
6. Wrightes, Sclaters, Tylers, Daubers, Thatchares		Nativytie of Our Lord
7. Paynters, Imbrotherers, Glasiores		The Sheperdes Offeringe
8. Vinteners, Marchantes		Kinge Herod and the Mounte Victoriall
9. Mercers, Spicers	bringe forthe	The Three Kinges of Colin

These 9 pageantes above written weare played
upon the firste daye, beinge Mondaye.

1. Gouldsmythes, Massons		The Destroyeinge of the Chilldren by Herod

103. *and* should follow *God*; see Harley 1944.

2. Smithes, Forbers, Pewterers	Purification of Our Ladye
3. Butchares	The Pinackle with the Woman of Canan
4. Glovers and Parchmente-makers	The Risinge of Lazarus from Death to Liffe
5. Corvesters or Shooemakers	The Comeinge of Christe to Jerusalem
6. Bakers, Mylners	Christes Maundy with his Desiples
7. Boyers, Fletchares, Stringers, Cowpers, Turners	The Scourginge of Christe
8. Irnemongers, Ropers	The Crusifieinge of Christe
9. Cookes, Tapsters, Hostlers, Inkeapers	The Harrowinge of Hell

These 9 pageantes above written weare played
upon the second daye, beinge Tuesedaye.

1. Skinners, Cardemakers, Hatters, Poynters, Gyrdlers	The Resurrection
2. Sadlers, Fusters	The Castell of Emaus and the Apostles
3. Taylors	The Ascension of Christe
4. Fishemongers	Whitsondaye, the Makeinge of the Creede
5. Shermen	Prophetes Before the Day of Dome
6. Hewsters, Bellfownders	Antechriste
7. Weavers, Walkers	Domesday

These vii pageantes weare played upon the
third daye, beinge Wensedaye.

And these Whitson Playes weare played in Chester, anno domini 1574, Sir John Savage, knighte, beinge Mayor of Chester, which was the laste tyme that the weare played. And we have all cause to power[104] out oure prayers before God that neither wee nor oure posterities after us maye

104. *power*: pour.

nevar see the like abomination of desolation with suche a clowde of ignorance to defile with so highe a hand the moste sacred scriptures of God. But, oh, the merscie of oure God: for the tyme of oure ignorance, he regardes it not.

And thus muche in breife of these Whitson Playes.

From Folio 105r:

In the time of the firste maior of Chester, whoe is thoughte to be Sir John Arnewaye, the Whitson Playes weare made by a monke of Chester and was by the saide maior published and sett out at the charges of every company with theire pagiantes, as is afore expressed. And the said monke Rondulph, whoe did make the saide playes, lyeth buried in the marchantes ile within the Cathedrall Church of Chester.

(b) Harley 1944

This manuscript varies only slightly from the Chester Archives manuscript in the material concerning the cycle:

The entry for Chapter 4 in the Table of Contents reads—after "lawdable exercises"—"in Chester yearelye theire used, and of the playes in Chester."

The fourth-to-last word in the Preface reads "and" for "as."

In the second paragraph of Chapter 4 read "24 pagiantes or partes" for "24 pagiantes."

In the same sentence read "the number of the companyes" for "the companyes."

In the next sentence "yerelye" occurs between "And" and "before."

In the same sentence for "man" read "man fitted for the purpose."

In the same sentence for "breeife" read "breife, which was called the readinge of the Banes."

In the next-to-last sentence before the listing of companies and plays, read "oure God and" for "oure God."

(c) Cheshire Record Office, DCC 19

Title:

A Breavary or collectiones of the moste anchant Cittie of Chester, reduced into these chapters followeinge by the reverend master Robert

Rogers, Bachlor in Divinitie, Archdeacon of Chester, and one of the prebundes of the Cathedrall Church in Chester; written anew by his sonne DR, a well-willer to that anchant cittie.

Folios 39v–42v:

Now of the Whitson Playes in Chester

The origenall of the Whitson Playes	Concerning the Whitson Playes of Chester, the origenal of them was in the time of Sir John Arneway who—by most copies—was the first maior of Chester, about anno domini 1332. Then the weare firste played and sett forthe.
The Author	The author or maker of them was one Randoll, a monke of the Abbay in Chester who made the same in partes, as it was.
The Matter	The matter of these playes weare the historie of the Bible, composed by the said author in a holy devotion, that the simple might understand the scripture, which in those times was hid from them.
The Actors	The actores or players weare the companies or tradesmen of the citti of Chester, who at theire owne costes and charges sett forth and alsoe played the same playes yerelye. The last time they weare played in Chester was anno domini 1574, Sir John Savage beinge maior of Chester, master John Allen and master William Goodman being shereffes.
The time of the yere when they were played	The time when they weare played was 3 days togeather: On Monday, Tueseday, and Wenseday in Whitson Weeke.
The places where they played	The places where they weare played were in every streete of the cittie, that all people that would mighte behoulde the same.
The manner how they plaied	The manner of these playes was: every company made a pageant on which they played theire partes, which pagiant was a scaffolde or a high foure-square buildinge with 2 rowmes, a higher and a lower, the lower hanged aboute richly and closse, into which none but the actors came. On the higher they played their partes, beinge all

open to the behoulders. This was sett on 4 wheels, and soe drawne from streete to street. They first beganne at the Abbay gates where, when the first pagiante was played, it was wheled into another streete and the second pagiant came in the place therof. And so till all the pagiantes for the day weare ended. Soe into every streete, and it was soe orderly attended that before the one pagiant was played another came in place to satisfye the beholders in everye streete at one time.

Also, every yere that these playes were played, on Saint Georges Day before was the Banes read: which was a man did ride, war-like apparaled like Saint George, throughe every streete, with drume-musicke and trumpetes. And there was published that the playes were played that yeare, and that the breife or Banes of the playe was reade what every company should playe, which was called the readinge of the Bannes, the wordes of which conclusion was this:

All those that be minded to tary,
On Monday, Tweseday, and Wensday in Whitson
Weeke begines the storye.

For the better explainge I have here sett downe the companies severall pagiantes and partes the played in those Whitson Playes.

[The list of companies and their plays follows.]

Folios 112v–113r:

In the yere when this Sir John Arneway was mayor of Chester the Whitson Playes, made by a monke of Chester Abbay named Rondoll, was by the said maior published and caused to be sett forth and played at the charges of every company within the said cittie, with theire pagiantes as in the former chapters is fully expressed; and the said Rondoll the author, in the prologue before his booke of the Whitson Playes, doth shew more fully. And the said monke Rondoll who did make the said playes lyeth buried within the marchants ile within the Cathedrall Church of Chester.

(d) Harley 1948

Title:

A Brevarye or some collectiones of the most anchant and famous cittie of Chester, collected by the reverend master Robert Rogers, Batchlor in Divinitye, Archdeacon of Chester and Prebunde in the Cathedrall Church of Chester, and Parson of Gawsworth,[105] written by his sonne David Rogers and reduced into these chapters followeinge.

Folios 64r–67r:

Now of the Playes of Chester called the Whitson Playes:

The author of them	The maker and first inventer of them was one Rondoll, a monke in the Abbaye of Chester, whoe did transelate the same into Englishe and made them into partes and pagiantes, as they then weare played.
The matter of them; the first time played	The matter of them was the historye of the Bible, mixed with some other matter. The time they weare first sett forthe and played was in anno 1339, Sir John Arneway beinge mayor of Chester.
The players and charges thereof	The actors and players weare the occupations and companies of this cittie. The charges and costes thereof, which weare greate, was theires also. The time of the yeare they weare played was on Monday, Tuesday, and Wenseday in Whitson Weeke.
The manner of them	The maner of these playes weare: every company had his pagiant or parte, which pagiants weare a high scafolde with 2 rowmes—a higher and a lower—upon 4 wheeles. In the lower they apparelled themselves; and in the higher rowme they played, beinge all open on the tope that all behoulders mighte heare and see them.
The places where the played them	The places where the played them was in every streete. They begane first at the Abay gates, and when the firste pagiante was played it was wheeled

---

105. "and Parson of Gawsworth": added in a later hand.

to the Highe Crosse before the mayor. And so to
every streete. And soe every streete had a pagiant
playinge before them at one time, tell all the
pagiantes for the daye appoynted weare played.
And when one pagiant was neere ended, worde
was broughte from streete to streete that soe the
might come in place thereof, excedinge orderlye.
And all the streetes have theire pagiantes afore
them all at one time playeinge togeather. To see
which playes was greate resorte, and also scafoldes
and stages made in the streetes in those places
where they determined to playe theire pagiantes.

[The list of the companies and their pageants is included next. The
discussion of the plays ends with the following comment.]

The laste time these playes weare played in Chester was anno domini
1574, Sir John Savage beinge mayor of Chester, John Allen and William
Goodman sheriffes. Thus in briefe of the playes of Chester.

(e) Harold Cohen Library, University of Liverpool, manuscript 23.5

Title:
Certayne collections of anchante times concerninge the anchant and
famous cittie of Chester, collected by that reverend man of God,
Mr. Robert Rogers—Bachellor of Devinitie, Archdeacon of Chester,
parsone of Gooseworth, and prebunde in the Cathedrall of Chester—
beinge but in scatered notes, and by his sonne reduced into these chapters
followinge.

Comment:
Nowe of the Playes of Chester called the Whitson Playes:
These playes were the worke of one Rondoll Higden, a monke in
Chester Abaye, whoe in a good devotion transelated the Bible into
severall partes and playes soe as the comon people mighte heare the same
by theire playinge and alsoe by action in theire sighte. And the firste time
they were acted or played was in the time of Sir John Arnewaye aboute
the firste yeare of his maroltie, aboute anno domini 1328. We muste

judge this monke had noe evill intension, but secrett devotion therein; soe also the cittizens that did acte and practize the same to their gret coste.

Here I muste showe the manner of the performinge of these anchante playes—which was, all those companyes and occupationes which weare joyned togeather to acte or performe theire severall partes had pagents, which was a buildinge of a greate heighte with a lower and higher rowme, beinge all open and sett upon fower wheeles and drawne from place to place where they played.

The firste place where they begane was at the Abaye gates where the monkes and churche mighte have the firste sight. And then it was drawne to the Highe Crosse before the mayor and aldermen. And soe from streete to streete; and when one pageant was ended another came in the place thereof, till all that weare appoynted for that daye was ended.

Thus of the maner of the playes, all beinge at the cittizens charge—yet profitable for them, for all bothe farr and neere came to see them.

Now follow what occupationes bringe forth at theire charges the Playes of Chester, and on what dayes theye are played yearely. These playes ordard sett forthe, when the are played, upon Monday, Tuesdaye, and Wensedaye in the Whitson Weke.

[The list of companies and their playes follows. The entry ends with the following comment.]

These Whitson Playes weare played in anno domini 1574, Sir John Savage, Knighte, beinge mayor of Chester—which was the laste time they weare played. And we may praise God and praye that we see not the like profanation of Holy Scripture. But, O, the mercie of God! For this time of our ignorance, God, he regardes it not, as well in everi mans particular as alsoe in generall causes.

(f) Additional 9442, f. 295r

These notes reproduce the excerpts from (e) above with only a few spelling differences.

20. An Edition of the Banns

Introduction
    The Manuscripts
    Selection and Presentation of Materials
20a. The Early Banns: Harley 2150 (E)—British Library
20b. The Late Banns: Rogers' *Breviary* in Chester City Archives (Ch)
Variant Readings for the Late Banns (R, B, L)
Textual Notes
    Manuscript E
    Manuscript R
    Manuscript B
    Manuscript Ch
    Manuscript L
Explanatory Notes
    The Early Banns
    The Late Banns

Introduction

The Manuscripts

Five versions of the Banns are known.[106] They appear in the following manuscripts, listed in chronological order:

E—Harley 2150—1540
R—Harley 2013—1600
B—Bodley 175—1604—Oxford University
Ch—copy of Rogers' *Breviary*—1609—Chester City Archives
L—Harley 1944—1609

The five versions fall into two categories: Early Banns, E, with 187 lines; and Late Banns, R, B, Ch, and L. Of the Late Banns, L and Ch—the two

---

106. The nineteenth-century version bound as part of Huntington Manuscript 2 is not listed here because as simply a copy of R it has no early authority. Concerning that version, see Textual Notes in Volume I of our edition and the second paragraph in the description of R given above. See also the fascimile of HM2, *Leeds Texts and Monographs*, 1980.

longest versions with 213 lines—are quite similar; R, with 187 lines, and B, with 126 lines, differ from L and Ch and from each other. Descriptions of the five manuscripts of the Banns appear below.

MANUSCRIPT E

This manuscript has not earlier been given a letter designation. E for Early Banns seems appropriate. Rupert H. Morris first drew attention to this version; Greg, Salter, and Clopper have more recently studied it. According to the Catalogue of 1808 of the Harley manuscripts, 2150 was bound together by Randle Holme III with the title "Deedes and Customes, with other Notes conserning the Citty of Chester," and it contains materials "written by several persons and at several times." Further, among these materials is "an old book called the White book of the Pentice (or a copie of it)." Since the cataloger, Humphrey Wanley, makes no mention of the Banns in his listing of the manuscript's contents, he presumably considered the Banns a part of "the White book."

Greg concluded, however, that the manuscript is not the White Book, or a copy of it, but a parallel "collection of documents (or a copy of it) which has been collated with the White Book." In addition, he saw evidence that the Banns were a part of the original White Book and that one leaf of E was "actually transcribed from the White Book itself." Salter pointed out the probability that Holme, in collating the version of the Banns with that in the White Book, observed discrepancies, tore out a leaf from E, and inserted a leaf matching the text of the White Book. Thus Salter says, "It is desolating to think that in so doing he probably destroyed all evidence for the reasons why this new copy was made at that time [1540]; but the net result is that we have a copy of the Banns as these were used not specifically in 1540 but earlier."

Clopper takes 1539–40, Henry Gee's mayoralty, as the *terminus ad quem* for the Early Banns as we have them. He believes, however, that 1505–21 is the *terminus a quo* for original composition and sees at least two revisions.

Harley 2150 consists of 217 paper folios, numbered in pencil in December 1880, according to a note on a back-flyleaf. A numbering in ink, from 181 through 387, was presumably done by Holme; the inked numbering begins after the first three folios, which present an index to "Thinges of most note in this booke anno 1669." The present edition follows the penciled numbering. Humphrey Wanley's description of the manuscript's contents, as he points out, is not a full listing. Just before the Banns, the manuscript includes some comment about the plays, and a dozen or so documents concerning the Chester Midsummer Show appear later.

The folios are of varying sizes; the majority measure about 8½ inches across by 12 inches down. The manuscript was last bound in January 1896. The binding is leather and board, with the Earl of Oxford's seal on front and back. On the spine occurs "R. Holme. Collections Relating to Chester. Brit. Mus. Harley 2150." On folio 1 is pasted a vellum rectangle with Holme's title for the manuscript upon it. The folios were separated from their gatherings and placed in guards, singly or doubly, when the manuscript was last bound. The paper is of several kinds. The folios containing the Banns (86r–88v) are like the majority. No watermarks are visible on these folios. There are no rulings, but blocks of lines— usually quatrains or octaves—are separated by line spaces. No catchwords appear.

MANUSCRIPT R

This manuscript is described in considerable detail in the "Introduction" and "Textual Notes" to Volume I of our edition. The manuscript of 205 paper folios includes the Proclamation, the Banns, and all of the plays. The Banns cover folios 1r–3v, and the first play begins on 4r. Folio 1r has as folio-heading "The Readinge of the Banes—1600." On folio 3v, after the Banns, occurs *Finis deo gracias/per me georgium Bellin/1600.* The appearance and characteristics of the first three folios are the same as in the remainder of the manuscript. The Heading of the Banns and the first word or words in most quatrains are in red ink.

A copy of the Banns and Play 1 in this manuscript was made in the nineteenth century to replace lost folios in Huntington Manuscript 2. The copy includes a number of minor differences in readings from R. Content of pages for the 187 lines of the Banns in HM 2 is Ir, 1–20; Iv, 21–48; IIr, 49–75; IIv, 76–102; IIIr, 103–26; IIIv, 127–56; IVr, 157–81; IVv, 182–Finis.

MANUSCRIPT B

This manuscript is described in considerable detail in the "Introduction" and "Textual Notes" to Volume I of our edition. The manuscript of 180 paper folios contains the Banns and all of the plays. The Banns cover folios 1r–2v, and the first play begins on 3r. This version of the Banns begins at line 70; whether any preceding material was lost or never present is not known. *Finis* does not occur after the final line (195), and numerals and guild names do not appear in the margins. Blocks of lines are clearly separated throughout the Banns by the fact that the first word of the first line of each block is in much larger and heavier script than the regular writing, which is like that of the remainder of the manuscript. At 96 the space for a large *The* is lost because the leaf is torn. At 190 the *The* is in usual rather than heavier script.

MANUSCRIPT CH
This manuscript is coded C/B/182. It has had no letter-designation previously; *Ch* for *Chester* seems appropriate. The manuscript is one of five known versions of *A Breviary or some fewe Collections of the Cittie of Chester*, compiled from the materials of Archdeacon Robert Rogers of St. Werburgh's Abbey in Chester, who died in 1595, by his son David. The latter seems to have started work on the book in 1609. The other versions are Harley 1944, Harley 1948, Cheshire Record Office MS, DCC 19, and manuscript 23.5 in the Harold Cohen Library of the University of Liverpool. The five differ considerably; see Chapter 5, item 19. Ch may be David's original version.

In 1962 Helen E. Boulton, former City Archivist of Chester, stated in *Chester Mystery Plays*, "The manuscript [Ch] was formerly among the Cowper papers in a collection of manuscripts belonging to Reginald Cholmondeley Esq. of Condover Hall, Salop. It was purchased by the [Chester] Corporation in 1956" (p. 33). Mrs. Elizabeth E. Berry, formerly City Archivist in Chester, had reason to consider that information erroneous. She wrote, in a letter dated 10 March 1971:

> The last list of the Corporation records, compiled by W. Fergusson Irvine in 1906, contains no reference to the *Breviary*, but recently I have discovered that it is referred to in the correspondence of Mr. Lamacraft, who repaired many of the Corporation records in the 1930s. Mr. Lamacraft rebound this volume for the Corporation in Oct. 1938.
>
> From this, one would deduce that the volume was acquired by the Corporation between 1906 and 1938, but I can find no reference to it in the Corporation minutes where other gifts and purchases are recorded. Therefore one can only conclude that either it was in the Corporation collection by 1906 and was overlooked by Mr. Irvine, or

that it was acquired by the Corporation between 1906 and 1938 and not recorded in the minutes. The Corporation minutes for the 19th century have not yet been calandered, and as the inscription on the flyleaf of the *Breviary* is of George Wilbraham of Delamere House, Cheshire, 30 July 1849, possibly a reference to this volume will be found in these minutes.

There are 123 numbered paper folios, preceded and followed by an unnumbered folio. Folios 110r–123v are blank. The Banns occupy 18v–21v. The material is very clearly written, and no damage or blurring has occurred. The pages are ruled at top, bottom, and sides. Beneath each block of lines a single ruling with a small decoration at each end appears. "Chapter 4" occurs as heading for each page of the Banns. Considerable material is written in the margins to the left of the text (see Textual Notes). Four catchwords occur: *Of* (19v), *And* (20r), *The* (20v), *To* (21r). The Banns are preceded and followed by historical comment concerning the cycle.

MANUSCRIPT L

The version of the Banns included in this manuscript was earlier designated *A* for *Archdeacon* Rogers, but that designation conflicts with our use of *A* for MS Additional 10305, one of the cyclic versions of the Plays. We therefore use *L*, for Late Banns. The manuscript is a part of the Randle Holme collection, concerning which see the description of Harley 2013 (R) in Volume I of our edition. It is also one of the five known copies of Rogers' *Breviary*; see the description of Ch above.

The manuscript contains 117 paper folios, numbered in pencil in May 1873, according to a note on a back-flyleaf, and measuring about 6 inches across by 8 inches down. An earlier numbering in ink runs to 159, with jumps from 60 to 68, 70 to 72, 113 to 115, and 125 to 128. The penciled numbering includes, as the series in ink does not, the first two folios, headed "Things of most note in this booke," presumably prepared by Holme. The Library records show that the manuscript was last bound in October 1901. The gatherings were separated and the folios attached individually to guards. Four empty guards are to be found between folios 25 and 26, but no indication of lost folios appears. The binding is leather and boards, with the Earl of Oxford's seal on front and back. On the spine "R. Holme. Chester Collections. Brit. Mus. Harley 1944" appears.

In the 1808 Catalogue of Harleian manuscripts, Wanley divided the contents of this manuscript into the *Breviary* (folios 3–100 in the penciled numbering), the "Accompts of Hugh Dod of the Citie of Chester Yeoman" (101–5), a "Discourse or Relacon (amongst other thinges) of the ancient and moderne Fees issuing out of the Courts held at the Common Law within the Citie of Chester" (106–16), and "Part of an order . . . 20 Febr. 1626, against Mr. Robert Brerewood Esquier, Clerke of the Pentice" (117). The Banns cover the lower third of 22r through the upper third of 25r, in Chapter 4 of the *Breviary*. On 21v, 22r, 25, and 26 comment concerning the plays occurs. The Banns are carefully written in a clear small hand. The pages are not ruled. Beneath each block of lines— quatrains or seven-line stanzas—a single ruling with a small decoration at each end appears. Catchwords are regularly used. "Chapter 4" heads each page. Marginal material and historical comment are present as in Ch (see Textual Notes).

Selection and Presentation of Materials

The Early and Late Banns differ so markedly that presentation of both in full is required. For the Early Banns only E has survived for presentation. Among the four versions of the Late Banns, B lacks eighty-seven lines (1–69 and 196–213), and R lacks twenty-seven lines (143–45 and 190–213). Ch and L lack only one line, that following 10, which is present in R. Thus the choice of base text for the Late Banns lay between Ch and L. The differences between the two are slight: both are wrong in 94, where *If* rather than *In* is called for; L has ten minor omissions of words present in Ch, no one of which alters the meaning (5, 22, 85, 92, 94, 104, 133, 144, 146, 160); Ch lacks no words present in L; L has two additional errors that hinder the meaning, *them* for *then* in 56 and the omission of *by* in 58; Ch has no additional errors. From this tally it would seem that Ch has a slight edge over L as choice for base text. That choice is bolstered by the fact that L was probably copied from Ch.

In presenting E and Ch we have followed the same principles that we used in the presentation of the text of the cycle (Hm) and the Appendices in Volume I of our edition. Those principles are set forth in the "Introduction" to that volume. Similarly, the principles here governing Variant Readings and Textual Notes are those we used and explained in that volume.

20a. The Early Banns: Harley 2150 (E)—British Library

86r
(lower
third)

The comen bannes, to be proclaymed and ryddon with the stewardys of every occupacon:

1   Lordinges royall and reverentt,   1
    lovely ladies that here be lentt,
    sovereigne citizins, hether am I sent
    a message for to say.   4
    I pray you all that be present
    that you will here with good intent;
    and lett your eares to be lent,
    hertffull I you pray.   8

2   Our wurshipffull mair of this citie,
    with all this royall cominaltie,
    solem pagens ordent hath he
    at the fest of Whitsonday-tyde.   12
    How every craft in his decree
    bryng forth their playes solemplye,
    I shall declare you brefely
    yf ye will abyde a while.   16

86v   3   The worshipfull Tanners of thys towne
    bryng forth the hevenly manshon,
    th'orders of angelles and there creacon
    according done to the best.   20
    And when th'angelles be made so clere,
    then folowyth the falling of Lucifere.
    To bryng forth this play with good chere
    the Tanners be full prest.   24

4   You wurshipffull men of the Draperye,
    loke that paradyce be all redye;
    prepare also the Mappa Mundi,

2. *lentt*: arrived, come.
8. *hertfful*: sympathetically.
10. *cominaltie*: city council.
11. *solem*: ceremonious.
18. *manshon*: pageant-wagon.

Adam and eke Eve. 28
The Waterleders and Drawers of Dee,
loke that Noyes shipp be sett on hie
that you lett not the storye—
and then shall you well cheve. 32

5 The Barbers and Wax-chaundlers also that day
   of the patriarche you shall play,
   Abram that putt was to assay
   to sley Isack his sonne. 36
   The Cappers and Pynners forth shall bryng
   Balack, that fears and mightie kyng,
   and Balam on an asse sytting;
   loke that this be done. 40

6 Youe Wrightys and Slaters wilbe fayne;
   bryng forth your cariage of Marie, myld quene,
   and of Octavyan so cruell and kene,
   and also of Sybell the sage. 44
   for fyndyng of that royall thing
   I graunt you all the blessing
   of the high imperiall king,
   both the maister and his page. 48

7 Paynters, Glasiars, and Broderers in fere
   have taken on theym with full good chere
   that the sheppardes play then shall appere,
   and that with right good wyll. 52

8 The Vynteners then, as doth befall,
   bringe forth the 3 kings royall
   of Colyn, or pagent memoryall
   and worthy to appere. 56
   There shall you see how thos kyngs all
   came bouldly into the hall

31. *lett*: hinder.
32. *cheve*: achieve.
35. *assay*: test.
41. *fayne*: eager.
49. *in fere*: together.

before Herald, proude in paulle,
of Crysts byrth to heare.   60

87r   9   The Mercers worshipfull of degre,
the Presentation, that have yee;
hit fallyth best for your see
by right reason and skyle.   64
Of caryage I have no doubt:
both within and also without
it shall be deckyd that all the rowte
full gladly on it shall be to loke.   68
With sondry cullors it shall shine
of velvit, satten, and damaske fyne,
taffyta, sersnett of poppyngee grene.

10   The Gouldsmyths then full soone will hye,   72
and Massons theyre craft to magnyfye.
Theis 2 crafts will them applye
theyre worshipp for to wyne:
how Herode, king of Galalye,   76
for that intent Cryst to distrye
slew the inosents most cruely
of tow yers and within.

11   Semely Smythis also in syght   80
a lovely caryage the will dyght;
"Candilmas-dey" forsoth it hyght,
the find it with good will.
The Butchers pagend shall not be myst: 84
how Satan temped our Savyour Cryst;
it is an history of the best,
as wittneseth the gospell.

59. *paulle*: rich cloth.
64. *skyle*: skill.
71. *sersnett*: fine silk; *poppyngee*: parrot.
72. *hye*: hurry.
77. *distrye*: destroy.
82. *Candilmas-dey*: the Presentation of Christ, 2 February; *hyght* : is called.
83. *the*: they; *find*: furnish.

12   Nedys must I rehers the Glover;   88
the give me gloves and gay gere.
The find the toumbe of Lazarey—
that pagend cometh next.
Also the Corvesers with all their myght,   92
the fynde a full fayre syght.
"Jerusalem" their caryage hyght,
for so sayth the text.

13   And the Bakers, also bedene,   96
the find the Maunday as I wene;
it is a carriage full well besene,
as then it shall appeare.

87v   Flechers, Bowyers, with great honors   100
the Cowpers find the tormentors
that bobbyde God with gret horrors
as he sat in his chere.

14   The Yronmongers find a caryage good;   104
how Jesu dyed on the rode
and shed for us his precyus blud—
the find it in fere.
Cryst after his Passion   108
brake hell for our redempcion;
that find the Cookes and Hostelers of this towne,
and that with full good chere.

15   Also the Skynners they be bowne   112
with great worsap and renowne;
they find the Resurection—
fayre maye them befall.
Sadlers and Foysters have the good grace: 116
the find the castell of Emawse

96. *bedene*: forthwith.
97. Maunday: Holy Thursday, Last Supper.
102. *bobbyde*: beat.
105. *rode*: Cross.
112. *bowne*: ready.

where Crist appered to Cleophas—
a faire pagend you shall see.

16 Also the Taylers with trew intent   120
have taken on them, verament,
the Assencyon by one assent,
to bringe it forth full right.
Fysshemongers, men of faith,   124
as that day will doe thair slayth
to bringe there caryage furth in grayth;
"Wytsonday" it hight.

88r 17 The wurshipffull Wyffys of this towne   128
fynd of our Lady th'Assumpcon;
it to bryng forth they be bowne,
and meytene with all theyre might.

18 The Shermen will not behynd,   132
butt bryng theire cariage with good mynde;
the pagent of prophettys they do fynd,
that prophecied full truly
off the comyng of Anticrist   136
that Goodys faith wold resist.
That cariage I warrand shall not myst,
butt sett forth full dewly.

19 The Hewsters that be men full sage   140
they bryng forth a wurthy cariage;
that is a thing of grett costage—
"Antycryst" hit hight.
They Weyvers in very dede   144
fynd the Day of Dome—well may they spede!
I graunt theym holly to theire neede
the blysse of heven bright.

121. *verament*: truly.
125. *doe thair slayth*: exercise their skill.
126. *in grayth*: in proper order.
131. *meytene*: sustain.

20 Sovereigne syrs, to you I say 148
and to all this feyre cuntre
that played shalbe this godely play
in the Whitson-weke—
that is, brefely for to sey, 152
uppon Monday, Tuysday, and Wennysday.
Whoo lust to see theym, he may,
and non of theym to seke.

21 Also, maister maire of this citie 156
with all his bretheryn accordingly,
a solempne procession ordent hath he
to be done to the best
appon the day of Corpus Christi. 160
The blessed Sacrement caried shalbe
and a play sett forth by the clergye
in honor of the fest.

88v 22 Many torches there may you see, 164
marchaunty and craftys of this citie
by order passing in theire degree—
a goodly sight that day.
They come from Saynt Maries-on-the-Hill 168
the churche of Saynt Johns untill,
and there the Sacrament leve they will,
the south as I you say.

23 Whooso comyth these playes to see 172
with good devocon merelye,
hertely welcome shall he be
and have right good chere.
Sur John Aneway was maire of this citie 176
when these playes were begon, truly.

154. *lust*: desires.
155. "and none of the plays will be difficult to find."
158. *ordent*: ordained.
171. *south*: truth.

God grunt us merely,
and see theym many a yere.

24   Now have I done that lyeth in me   180
          to procure this solempnitie
          that these playes contynued may be
          and well sett fourth alway.
          Jesu Crist that syttys on hee   184
          and his blessyd mother Marie
          save all this goodely company
          and kepe you nyght and day.   187

178. *merely*: happily.
180. *that*: that which.
184. *hee*: high.

20b. The Late Banns: Rogers' *Breviary* in Chester City Archives (Ch)

18v
(near
top)

Heareafter followeth the readinge of the banes which was reade before the begininge of the Whitson playes, beinge the breeife of the whole playes:

The Banes

1

Reverend lordes and ladyes all	1
that at this tyme here assembled be,	
by this message understande you shall	
that sometymes there was mayor of this cittie	4
Sir John Arnewaye, knighte, whoe moste worthelye	
contented himselfe to sett out in playe	
the devise of one Rondall, moncke of Chester Abbaye.	

2

This moncke—not moncke-lyke in Scriptures, well seene,	8
in stories traveled with the beste sorte—	
in pageanttes sett forthe apparante to all eyne,	
interminglinge therewithe onely to make sporte	
some thinges not warranted by anye wrytte	12
which glad the hartes—he woulde men to take hit.	

3

This matter he abreviated into playes xxiiii^{tie}.	
and everye playe of the matter gave but a taste,	
leaveinge for better learned the cercumstance to acomplishe,	16
⌐ for all his proceadinges maye appeare to be in haste.	
Yet alltogether unprofitable his labor he did not waste,	
for at this daye, an ever, he desearved the fame	
which fewe monckes deserve, proffessinge the same.	20

---

12. *anye wrytte*: any part of the Bible.

19r   4   These storyes of the testamente at this tyme, you
                 knowe,
              in a common Englishe tonge never reade nor
                 harde.
              Yet thereof in these pagiantes to make open showe,
              this moncke—and noe moncke—was nothinge   24
                 affrayde
              with feare of burninge, hangeinge, or cuttinge of
                 heade
              to sett out that all maye deserne and see,
              and parte of good belefe, beleve ye mee.

      5   As in this cittie dyvars yeares the have bine set out,   28
              so at this tyme of Pentecoste called Whitsontide—
              allthoughe to all the cittie followe labore and
                 coste—
              yet, God giveinge leave, that tyme shall you in
                 playe
              for three dayes togeather begine on Mondaye,   32
              see these pageantes played to the beste of theire
                 skill,
              wherein to supplye all wante shalbe noe wante of
                 good will.

      6   As all that shall see them shall moste welcome
                 bee,
              so all that doe heare them we moste humblye   36
                 praye
              not to compare this matter or storye
              with the age or tyme wherein we presentlye
                 staye—
              but to the tyme of ignorance whearein we doe
                 straye.
              And then dare I compare that, this lande   40
                 throughout,
              none had the like nor the like darste set out.

28. *the*: they.

7   If the same be lykeinge to the commons all,
    then oure desyre is satisfied; for that is all oure
        gayne.
    If noe matter or shewe thereof enyethinge speciall   44
    doe not please but mislycke the moste of the
        trayne,
    goe backe againe to the firste tyme, I saye.
    Then shall yow finde the fine witte, at this daye
        aboundinge,
    at that daye and that age had verye small beinge.   48

8   Condemne not oure matter where groosse
        wordes you heare
    which importe at this daye smale sence or under-
        standinge—
    as sometymes "postie," "bewtye," "in good
        manner," or "in feare"—
    with such-like wilbe uttered in theare speaches   52
        speakeinge.
    At this tyme those speches caried good lykinge;
    thoe if at this tyme you take them spoken at that
        tyme—
    as well matter as words—then all is well fyne.

19v 9   This worthie knighte Arnewaye, then mayor of   56
        this citte,
    this order tooke, as declare to yow I shall,
    that by xxiiii^tie occupationes—artes, craftes, or
        misterye—
    these pagiantes shoulde be played after brefe
        rehearesall:
    for everye pagiante a cariage provided withall.   60
    In which sorte we purpose this Whitsontyde
    oure pagiauntes into three partes to devide.

42. *lykeinge*: pleasing.
51. *postie*: power; *in feare*: together.
58. *misterye*: guild.

10   Now yow worshipfull Tanners, that of custome
      olde
      the fall of Lucifer did trulye sett out,   64
      some writers awarrante your matter; therefore be
      bolde
      lustelye to playe the same to all the route,
      and if anye therefore stande in anye dowbte
      your author his author hath; youre shewe lett   68
      bee.
      Good speeche! Fine playes! With apparell
      comlye!

11   Of the Drapers, you the welthie companye,
      the creation of the worlde, Adam and Eve;
      acordinge to your welthe sett oute wealthelye,   72
      and howe Cayne his brother Abell his life did
      bereave.

12   The good simple Waterleaders and Drawers of
      Dee,
      see that in all poyntes your arke be prepared.
      Of Noe and his chilldren the whole storie,   76
      and of the uneversall floode by you shall be
      playde.

13   The sacrefise that faithfull Abraham of his sonne
      should make,
      you Barbers and Waxe-chandlers of antiente tyme
      in the 4th pageante, with paynes ye did take,   80
      in decent sorte sett out—the storye is fyne.
      The offeringe of Melchesadecke of bread and
      wine
      and the preservation thereof sett in youre playe.
      Suffer yow not in enye poynte the storye to   84
      decaye.

14   Cappers and Lynen-drapers see that ye forthe
      bringe

73. *bereave*: take away forcibly.

in well decked order that worthie storye
of Balaam and his Asse and of Balaacke the
   kinge.
Make the Asse to speake, and sett hit out lyvelye.   88

20r   15   Of Octavyan the emperower, that coulde not well
   allowe
the prophesye of antiante Sybell the sage,
you Wrightes and Slaters with good players in
   shewe
lustely bringe forth your well decked caryage.   92
The birth of Christe shall all see in that stage.
In the Scriptures a warrunte not of the midwives
   reporte!
The author tellethe his author—then take hit in
   sporte.

16   The appearinge angell and starr upon Cristes   96
   birthe,
the shepperde poore of base and lowe degree,
you Paynters and Glaseers decke out with all
   myrthe
and see that "Gloria in Excelsus" be songe
   merelye.
Fewe wordes in the pagiante make merthe trulye, 100
for all that the author had to stande uppon
was "glorye to God on highe and peace on earthe
   to man."

17   And yow worthie Marchantes-vinteners that now
   have plentye of wine,
amplye the storye of those wise kinges three   104
that through Herodes lande and realme, by the
   starr did shine,
soughte the sighte of the Savioure that then borne
   shoulde bee.

---

90. *antiante*: ancient.
94. *a warrante not*: no evidence.

18 And you worshipfull Mercers, thoughe costelye
  and fyne
 ye tryme up your cariage as custome ever was; 108
 yet in a stable was he borne, that mightie king
  devine,
 poorelye in a stable betwixte an oxe and ane asse.

19 Yow Goldesmythes and Massons, make comlye
  shewe
 how Herode did rage at the retorne of those 112
  kinges,
 and howe he slewe the tender male babes
 beinge under twoe yeares of age.

20 Yow Smythes—honeste men, yea and of honeste
  arte—
 how Criste amonge the Doctors in the temple did 116
  dispute,
 to sett out your playe comlye hit shalbe youre
  parte;
 gett mynstrelles to that shewe: pype, tabrett, and
  flute.

20v 21 And nexte to this, yow the Butchers of this cittie
 the storye of Sathan that woulde Criste needes 120
  tempte
 set out as accustomablie used have ye:
 the devell in his feathers, all rugged and rente.

22 The death of Lazarus and his riseinge againe,
 yow of Glovers the whole occupation, 124
 in pageon with players orderlye—let hit not be
  payne—
 finelye to advance after the beste fashon.

23 The storye howe to Jerusalem our Savioure tooke
  the waye,

117. *comlye*: attractively.
118. *tabrett*: a small drum.
121. *accustomablie used*: customarily.
122. *rugged and rente*: ragged and torn.

yow Corvysers that in number full menye be,   128
with your Jerusalem-carryage shall sett oute in
    playe:
a commendable true storye and worthy of
    memorye.

24   And howe Criste our Savioure at his laste supper
gave his bodye and bloode for redemtion of us   132
    all,
yow Bakers see that with the same wordes you
    utter
as Criste himselfe spake them, to be a memorall
of that deathe and passion which in playe after
    ensue shall.
The worste of these storyes doth not fall to your   136
    parte;
therefore caste Godes loves abroade with ac-
    customed cherefull harte.

25   Yow Fletchares, Boyeres, Cowpers, Stringers, and
    Irnemongers,
see soberlye ye make oute Cristes dolefull deathe:
his scourginge, his whippinge, his bludshede and   140
    passion,
and all the paynes he suffred till the laste of his
    breathe.
Lordinges, in this storye consistethe oure chefe
    faithe.
The ignorance wherein hathe us manye yeares soe
    blinded,
as though now all see the pathe playne,   144
yet the moste parte cannot finde it.

26   As our belefe is that Christe after his passion
decended into hell—but what he did in that place
though oure author sett forthe after his opynion,   148
yet creditt yow the beste lerned; those he dothe
    not disgrase.

137. *loves*: loaves.

We wishe that of all sortes the beste you imbrace.
Yow Kookes with your cariage see that you doe well;
in pagiante sett oute the Harrowinge of Hell.   152

21r   27   The Skynners before yow after shall playe
the storye of the Resurrection—
how Criste from deathe arose the thirde daye—
not altered in menye poyntes from the olde   156
fashion.

28   The Sadlers and Frysers shoulde in theire pagiante declare
the appearance of Christe, his traveyle to Emaus,
his often speeche to the woman and his desiples deere
to make his risinge agayne to all the worlde   160
notoriouse.

29   Then se that you Taylors with cariage decente
the storye of the Assention formallye doe frame,
wherebye that gloriose bodye in clowdes moste ardente
is taken upp to the heavens with perpetuall fame.   164

30   This of the oulde and newe testamente to ende all the storye
which oure author meaneth at this tyme to have in playe,
yow Fishemongers to the pageante of the Holye Goaste well see
that in good order it be donne, as hathe bine   168
allwaye.
And after those ended, yet dothe not the author staye,
but by prophettes shewethe forthe howe Antechriste shoulde rise,

160. *notoriouse*: widely known.
163. *ardente*: shining.

which yow Sherman see sett out in moste comlye
 wise.

31 And then, yow Diers and Hewsters, Antechriste 172
 bringe oute—
firste with his Doctor that godlye maye ex-
 pownde
whoe be Antechristes the worlde rownde aboute.
And Enocke and Helye, persones walkinge on
 grownde,
in partes well sett yow out, the wicked to 176
 confownde;
which, beinge understanded Christes worde for
 to be,
confowndethe all Antechristes and sectes of that
 degree.

32 The commynge of Christe to geve eternall judg-
 mente,
yow Weavers laste of all your parte is to playe. 180
Domesedaye we call it, when the Omnipotente
shall make ende of this worlde by sentance, I
 saye.
On his righte hande to stande, God grante us that
 daye,
and to have that sweete worde in melodye: 184
"Come hither, come hither, venite benedicitie!"

21v 33 To which reste of joyes and celestiall habitation
grante us free passage, that all together wee—
acompanyed with angells and endles 188
 delectation—
maye continuallye lawde God and prayse that
 kinge of glorye.

Conclusion of the Banes

34 The sume of this storye, lordes and ladies all,

---

182. *sentance*: judgment.

I have breifelye repeated, and how the muste be
    played.
Of one thinge warne you now I shal: 192
that not possible it is those matters to be
    contryved
in such sorte and cunninge and by suche players
    of price
as at this daye good players and fine wittes coulde
    devise.

35   For then shoulde all those persones that as godes 196
    doe playe
in clowdes come downe with voyce, and not be
    seene;
for noe man can proportion that Godhead, I
    saye,
to the shape of man—face, nose, and eyne.
But sethence the face-gilte doth disfigure the man, 200
    that deme
a clowdye coveringe of the man—a voyce onlye
    to heare—
and not God in shape or person to appeare.

36   By craftesmen and meane men these pageauntes
    are playde,
and to commons and contry men accustomablye 204
    before.
If better men and finer heades now come, what
    canne be sayde?
But of common and contrye players take yow the
    storye,
and if anye disdayne, then open is the doore
that lett hime in to heare. Packe awaye at his
    pleasure!   208
Oure playeinge is not to gett fame or treasure.

191. *the*: they (the stories).
200. *face-gilte*: paint for the face; *deme*: consider.
203. *meane men*: commoners.

37   All that with quiett mynde
can be contented to tarye,
be heere on Whitson-Mondaye;   212
then begineth the storye.

        Finis

Variant Readings for the Late Banns (R, B, L)

Heading]	The Banes which are reade beefore the begininge of the
	playes of Chester 1600 4 June 1600 R, *om* B
Title]	*om* RB
1–69]	*om* B
5	knighte] *om* L
7	one] one done R
8	not] *om* R
10	apparante]apparently R
After 10]	the olde and newe testament with livelye comforth R
13	which] which to R hartes] hearers R
14	abreviated] abrevited R
15	a] *om* L
16	learned] learninge R
19	an] and R desearved] deserveth R
20	fewe] all R deserve] deserves R, deserved L
	the same] that name R
22	a] *om* L
24	noe] *om* R
25	burninge hangeinge] hanginge breninge R
27	of] *om* R belefe] be lefte R
32	begine] begyninge R
34	wherein] wher R wante (1 *and* 2)] wantes R
36	doe] *om* R humblye] humble R
39	to] in R doe] did R
40	and] *om* R dare] doe R
41	darste] dose R, durste L
43	satisfied] to satisfie R
44	enyethinge] *om* R
46	againe] I saye R I saye] againe R
50	importe at] impart as L
51	sometymes] sometyme R bewtye] lewtie R
54	if] *om* R
55	all is] is all R fyne] and fyne R
56	then] them L
58	by] *om* L
60	provided] to be provyded R
64	trulye] *om* R

67   therefore] therof R

69   playes] players R

75   in all poyntes your arke] your arke in all poyntes RB

78   of] to R

80   with] with the B   did] doe R

83   preservation] presentacion B

84   decaye] take awaye R

85   forthe] *om* L

89   the emperower] themperour B

92   well decked] *om* L

94   in] yf RB   the (1)] *om* L

95   in] *om* L

96   the appearinge] ____ppearinge B

97   the] to R   shepperde] sheapeardes RB

99   Excelsus] Excelsis RB, Exelsus L

100   the] that RB   make] makes R

101   author] alter R

102   on highe] above R   on (2)] in B   to] *om* B

103   of wine] *om* B

104   amplye] amplifye RB   wise] *om* L

105   did] that did RB

107   worshipfull] worthie B

110   stable] stall B

113   the] the small RB   babes] babes beinge B

114   beinge] *om* B   age] age a most blasfemus thinge B

115   yea] *om* R

117   your] in RB

118   tabrett] tabarte R   flute] harpe B

119   the] *om* RB

120   woulde Criste needes] Christe woulde needes RB, woulde needes Christe L

121   used] *om* R

122   rugged] ragger R, ragged BL

125   pageon] pagente R, pagion B, pagiantes L

127   howe] howe that R

128   full] *om* R

130   true storye] storye true B   of] *om* R

132   and] and his RL

133   with] *om* B   the] *om* L

134   memorall] memoriall RB
135   after ensue] ensue after R
136   these storyes] this storye B   doth] doe RL
137   godes] god R   loves] looves R, loaves B
       accustomed] a R   harte] h B
138   irnemongers] iremongers R, iremongers altogether B
139   oute] of RB
142   consistethe] consisted B
143–45]   *om* R
143   manye yeares soe] so manye yeres BL
144   now] *om* L
146   that] *om* L
149   he dothe] doth he R
150   you] you may L
155   arose] rose R
157   frysers] fusterers R
158   appearance] appearances R   traveyle] travayle R,
       travell B
159   woman] women R   and] and to R
160   agayne] *om* L
162   formallye doe] formablye doe R, formly to B
163   ardente] orient R
166   author] aulter R
167   the (1)] that B   Goaste well] crose will B
169   yet] yt R   author] storie R
171   see] *om* R
172   yow] the L
176   well sett yow] set you well R, well sett B
180   to] for to R
185   benedicitie] benedicti RB
186   joyes] wayes RB
187   us] us all B
Heading]   *om* RB
190–213]   *om* R
193   those] these L
194   cunninge] comyng B
195   this daye] these dayes B   players] preserve B
196–*Finis*]   *om* B

Textual Notes

Manuscript E

12	*fest*: *f* written over another letter
17	*worshipfull*: abbreviated as *wor*ʷ and inserted above line with a caret after *The*
	thys: *y* written over *e*
18	*manshon*: *sh* written over *c*
19–185	Entries occur in left margins as indicated below. Words not italicized in these entries were added later in different ink by the same scribe:

19	*Tanners*
25–26	*Drapers* and hosiers
28–29	waterleaders and *drawers of dee*
33–34	*Barbur* surgions and Tallowchandlors (*Barbur* first had a final *s*, which was changed to a long *s* as first letter of *surgions* when it was added)
38	*Cappers* and linnen drapers
43–44	*wryghts* and slaters
49–50	*Paynters* Imbrautherers and glasiers
54–55	marchants and *vinteners and* (*vinteners* written over another word; that word and *and* (2) blurred)
65	*marcers*
73–74	*Goldsmyths* and masons
81–82	*Smyths* furbors and Pewterers
85	*Butchers*
89	*glovers*
93	*Corvisors* or showmakers (*i* written over *e*?)
97–98	*Bakers* and milners
100–104	Coupers stringers *Flechers Bowyers* and Turners (Inkblot partially obscures first two words)
	Ironmongers and Ropers (dotted line from Ironmongers at 103 to 104)
109	*kookes*

113–14	*Skynners* Cardmakers Poynters and girdlers
116–17	*Sadlers Foysters* (F written over I?)
121	*Taylyers*
125–26	*fysshemongers*
128–29	*wyves*
132	*Shermen* (*n* smudged)
141	*Hewsters* or Diers
145	*wevers* and walkers
159	*erazed in the booke*, with a vertical line to left of 156–63, and a horizontal line above 156 and 157 and beneath 163
167–68	*erazed in the booke*, with a vertical line to left of 164–71 and a horizontal line beneath 171
185	*erazed*, with a vertical line to right of *Marie* and a horizontal line beneath 185

Concerning the entries 19–185, see Greg, *Chester Play Studies*, pp. 123–39, Salter, "The Banns of the Chester Plays," and Clopper, "History and Development."

32	*cheve*: *v* inserted, with caret, above line
33	*barbers*: *r* (2) blurred. *chaunndlers*: *n* (2) above line
42	*of*: lower part of *f* written over another letter
53–127	These lines are in a different hand from the other lines of the Banns. Greg says the different hand is that of Randle Holme II; Salter says RH III.
60	*of* blurred
61	*worshipfull*: abbreviated as *wor*^{tt}
66	*within*: written *wthin*
82	*day*: *a* written over *e*
84	*butchers*: *t* squeezed in
	pagend: *p* written over *b*
105	*the* appears as *ye*
106	*blud*: *b* written over *p*
116	*foysters*: *f* written over *I*?
117	*the* (2): *t* written over another letter
133	*butt*: *b* written over *p*?
135	*prophecied*: *p* (2), downstroke only, squeezed in
144	*very*: seems to be written over *every*, which appeared as *euy̑*)

145   after *well, they* canceled
        spede: sp written over other letters
162   *clergye: g* written over *k*?
165   *marchaunty:* unusual *m*; *a* (2) above *n*
187   *kepe: k* written over *b*

Manuscript R

Content of   1r, 1–31; 1v, 32–69; 2r, 70–106; 2v, 107–42; 3r,
Pages   146–81; 3v, 182–*Finis*
Heading   *iiii June* in margin to left of *The*; *1600* to right of *Chester*;
        4 June 1600 beneath *of Chester*
5   line in red ink
7   *Rondall:* in red ink
After 10   R has the needed line to fill out the stanza: "the olde and
        newe testament with livelye comfort,"
63–180   As each guild is named, an underlined Arabic numeral,
        1–24, appears in the left margin, and the guild-name
        appears in the right margin, as indicated below. A virgule
        in an entry indicates line-division. The guild-names are in
        a nonscribal hand, presumably Holme's.

     1   *worshipfull Tanners*
     2   *drapers*
     3   *water leaders/drawers in dee*
     4   *barbers/wax chaundlers*
     5   *cappers/linen drapers*
     6   *wrights/slaters*
     7   *painters/glassiers*
     8   *merchants/vintners*
     9   *worshipfull Mercers*
   10   *Goldsmiths*
   11   *Smiths*
   12   *Buchers*
   13   *Glovers*
   14   *Corvisors*
   15   *Bakers*
   16   *Flechers/Bowyers/Coopers/Stringers/*
        Ironmongers
   17   *cookes*

18   *skinners*
19   *sadlers/Fusterers*
20   *Taylours*
21   *Fishmongers*
22   *sherman*
23   *diers/Hewsters*
24   *wavers*
99   *Gloria in Excelsis*: in red ink
127   *waye*: *e* in the margin
After 189   *Amen* beneath *laude*
Finis deo gracias: in red ink

Manuscript B

Content of
Pages   1r, 70–95; 1v, 96–135; 2r, 136–75; 2v, 176–95
102   after *peace*: *to God and* canceled and *in earth* written
above line with caret below
114   *towe*: reinked
a most blasfemus thinge: smaller writing and squeezed in
118   after *and*: *flute* canceled
After 135   *the* in bottom right corner as catchword
137   *h—*: rest of word destroyed by damage to manuscript
153   after *skinners*: *sk* canceled
162   after *the* (2): *asse* and downstroke canceled
174   *round*: *d* blotted
183   after *to*: *staye* canceled
185   *venite benedicitie*: different hand

Manuscript Ch

The scribe almost always writes *c* as *ć*
6   *in*: *i* partially covered by ink-blot
20   *deserve*: a final *d* canceled
98   *Paynters*: *P* written over abbreviation for *per*
Glassers: letter canceled after *s* (2)
98–99   pointed bracket to left of these lines
102   *on*: before *o*, letter canceled
107   *worshipfull*: abbreviated *wor*, with *r* above the line

125 *in*: unusual form for capital *I*

160 *to* canceled after *risinge*

185 *venite benedicitie*: different hand; *e* (3) blurred in *benedicitie*

Finis followed by *DR*

Arabic numerals, 1–24, appear as play-numbers to the left of certain lines and to the right of the left marginal rulings, as follows:

1, 66; 2, 71–72; 3, 76; 4, 81–82; 5, 87; 6, 92; 7, 99; 8, 104; 9, 108–9; 10, 112–13; 11, 116–17; 12, 120–21; 13, 125; 14, 129; 15, 134; 16, 141–42; 17, 149–50; 18, 154–55; 19, 158–59; 20, 162–63; 21, 167; 22, 170; 23, 175–76; 24, 182–83

The following entries appear to the left of the lines indicated below and to the left of the left marginal rulings:

1–5 Sir John Arnewaye; the first maior of Chester, first sett oute the Whitson Playes; anno domini 1329, beinge made by a moncke named Rondoll of the Abbey of St. Warburge.

8–9 This moncke was of the most esteimed a godly man and religeose in those dayes.

14–17 The matter of the play he made in xxiiii partes or playes. Here he is commended for his worke.

21–25 This moncke without fere of marterdome sett out in Enlishe the storye of the testament from the Bible, that men mighte understand and beleve.

28–30 These playes weare verye chargeable to the cittee, and had greate labor to make them readye.

35–38 Here he confesseth that he leved in the tyme of Ignorance wantinge knolege to use the holy thinges of God almighte; yet this monke had a good intente to doe good, thoe blyndly he did shew it.

42–47 He sayeth that if neither matter or shewe doe effecte the companye, then his labor was loste, for to please the companye was all his gaine. In antiant tyme there was noe such excellent and curiose wittes.

49–54 He desires that the grosse wordes herein used not (?) to be

condemed, for now in oure age and tyme the seeme
strange and grosse; yet the weare the same wordes which
we now use, thoe with more fine wordes and exellent
speech.

56–61   Sir John Arnewaye, the first maior, set out these playes
and caused the companyes to make the cariges for them to
playe in, every companye at theire owne charges.

64–65   The worshipfull companye of the Taners playe

71   The welthie Drapers playe

75–76   The simple waterleaders and drawers in Dee

80–81   The antient Barbers and Waxe-chandlers playe

86   Cappers and Linandrapers playe

91–92   The lusti wrightes and sclaters playe

98–99   The deckeinge Paynters and Glaseers playe

103   The worthie marchantes and vinteners playe

108   The worshipfull, costely, and fine Mercers playe

112   The Goldesmythes and Massons playe

116   The honest Smythes playe

120   The Butchers playe

124   The wett and dry glovers play

128–29   The Corvysers or shooemakers playe

134   The Bakers playe

140–41   The Fletchars, boyers, cowpers, stringers, and Irnemongers playe

148   The Cookes playe

154   The Skyners play

158   The Sadlers and Frysers playe

162   The Taylors playe

167   The Fishmongers playe

170   The Shermens playe

174   The Diers and Hewsters playe

182–83   The Weavers playe, the laste of all

186–89   The conclusion of Banes. He wisheth heaven to the
beholders of these playes

192–96   He wisheth men not to take the sighte of the playe only,
but to conceave of the matter so as it mighte be profitable
and not offencive.

For the foregoing entries, the following notes are pertinent:

1–5   *named*: unusual abbreviation, *naed* with a long mark over *a*

28–30   *verye*: not fully clear

35–38   *Intente*: *I* written over *e*

49–54   after *that*, a word blotted: *all*?

not and *thoe*: inserted above line, with a caret, and not clear

and (1 and 2): possibly *ad*

64–65   *worshipfull*: abbreviated *wor*, with *r* above the line

108   as for 64–65

Manuscript L

Content of   22r, 1–13; 22v, 14–55; 23r, 56–95; 23v, 96–130; 24r,
Pages   131–64; 24v, 165–201; 25r, 202–Finis

19   *fame*: *a* written above a canceled letter

45   *the* (1): inserted above line, with caret, as y^e

59   *be*: inserted above line, with caret; different ink?

63   *worshipfull*: abbreviated as *worll*, with *r* and crossed *ll* above line

80   *the*: as in 45; after *pagiante*: a letter canceled

97   *shepparde*: *s* canceled after *e* (2)

98–99   pointed bracket to left of lines

107   *worshipfull*: abbreviated as *wor*, with *r* above line

109   after *stable*: word canceled

119   *yow*: abbreviated as y^w, canceled after *And*

133   *you*: appears as *ye* with *e* canceled and *u* above *y*

162   *formallby* canceled after *assention*

164   *the*: inserted with caret above line

175   after *and* (1): word canceled

207   *And*: *A* written over another letter

Finis   followed by *DR*

Arabic numerals, 1–24, appear as play-numbers to the left, with only insignificant differences in their positions from those in Ch (see Textual Notes for Manuscript Ch)

The entries in the left margins listed in Textual Notes for Ch appear in L with only insignificant differences in position and wording. The chief differences—except for variations in spelling—are as follows, with Ch as base:

1–5]   Chester] Chest

21–25]   from] with

28–30]   verye (?)] veri

35–38]   he (1)] *om*   he (2)] the   leved] lived

42–47]   gaine] gayne   excellent and curiose] curiouse and excellent

49–54]   not (?)] not   age and] *om*

71]   playe] *om*

80–81]   playe] *om*

112]   The] The gliteringe

120]   The] The stoute

134]   The] The profittable

182–83]   the laste of all] *om*

186–89]   of] of the

192–96]   not] not only   sighe] sighte   only] *om*

L's entries in the left margin have several textual peculiarities; the line-numbers refer to positions in Ch:

1–5   same unusual abbreviation as Ch: *nāed* for *named*

21–25   *martirdom*: *a* blotted and another *a* written above it

49–54   *wordes* (1): *des* crowded against text and above *r*

64–65   *worshipfull*: abbreviated *wor*, with *r* above the line

108   as for 64–65

Explanatory Notes

The Early Banns

Heading *comen bannes*: the banns for the cycle as a whole. We
          have no record of Banns being presented for plays
          individually.

10 *royall cominaltie*: presumably the Mayor's council, repre-
    senting the commons.

16 The rhyme calls for "a while abyde."

18 *hevenly manshon*: the scene on the carriage will represent
    Heaven.

21 "And after the bright angels are created."

24 *be full prest*: "are strongly urged," or "are quite willing."

27 The Drapers may have used a map of the world as a
    property for their play. Perhaps it was shown when Adam
    and Eve are sent from Paradise to Earth.

45–48 Perhaps the meaning is "As a reward for presenting the
       birth of Christ, I grant all of you, the Wrights and Slaters,
       the blessing of God, including the actors playing Octavian
       and Preco."

55 *Colyn*: Cologne, the shrine of the Three Kings, is in the
    cathedral in that city. In 1322 a new choir was conse-
    crated, and the bones of the Kings were removed to it
    from the place they had occupied in the former cathedral.

61–71 This eleven-line grouping is contrary to the stanzaic
       pattern. 61–64 would have made a regular stanza if
       added to 49–52. A line is needed after 71 to rhyme with
       loke (68).

83 *the find it* means "they willingly provide for it."

119 "see you shall" would fit the rhyme.

126 *frayth*: error for *fayth*.

128–31 The quatrain does not match the stanzaic pattern.

138 Probably *be* should precede *myst*: "shall not be missed."

144 *They*: meaning calls for *The*.

148–49 *feyre companye* would seem more appropriate as an
        addition to *Sovereigne sirs* than *feyre cuntre*.

165 *marchaunty*: final *s* carelessly omitted.

168–69 These churches are still to be seen in Chester. The distance between them is about a third of a mile.

178 *mercy* would be preferable to *merely*.

179 Perhaps *and* should read *to*.

The Late Banns

Heading See the explanatory note for the *Heading* in the Early Banns.

1–7 Unlike E, where the dominant stanzaic pattern is eight lines—aaabcccb—as it is in most of the cycle, the dominant pattern in the Late Banns is rhyme royal—ababbcc—with considerable variation.

8 *not moncke-lyke*: note R's omission of *not*.

8–13 The stanza lacks a line between 10 and 11; cf. Textual Notes for R.

11–13 These lines seem to defend the nonbiblical material in the cycle.

16 The rhyme is faulty.
  the cercumstance to accomplishe: "to give the full story"?

19 R's *deserveth* for *deserued* improves the sense.

20 *professinge the same*: "being Catholic"; note R's variants.

21–22 "These stories from the Bible at that time, you know, [were] never read or heard in English."

24–25 The rhymes are faulty; note R's omission of *noe* in 24.

24–27 "This monk—not the kind of person we associate with monks—could have suffered terrible punishment; but he was not afraid of these punishments and, with true Protestant spirit, went ahead."

27 "and to distribute good doctrine, believe me."

35–39 A plea for historical objectivity.

39 R's *did* improves the sense.

40–41 "Our Chester Cycle is better than Cycles performed in other towns."

43 *gayne*: should be *payne* (effort)? Cf. Textual Note 42–47 for Ch and L.

44–48 "If you present-day watchers of the plays are displeased, then remember that in earlier times your fine wit was lacking."

46 *sayne* would rhyme; R's line fits.

51 R's *lewtie* seems more appropriately archaic.

53 *this* means *that*.

54–55 "If you understand the sound and meaning of the words as archaic, then all is 'well fyne.'"

67–68 The lines seem to mean, "If anyone objects to the content of your play, your defense is that your author did not change the inherited text."

70–77 A shift to two quatrains: abab, abab.

83 *preservation* includes the idea of a continuing Sacrament, as B's *presentacion* does not.

85–88 another quatrain: abab.

94 *In*: should be *If*, as in R and B. "Our author relates his sources—"

97 RB's *sheapeardes* is preferable.

101 R's *alter* does not fit the sense, which requires *author*.

103–6 as for 85–88.

105 *did*: "which did"; cf. R and B.

107–10 as for 85–88.

111–14 another quatrain; shifting *did rage* (112) and *he slewe* (113) to the ends of their lines would correct the rhyme; cf. B.

115–18,

119–22,

123–26,

127–30 as for 85–88.

122 BL's *ragged* is preferable.

136 Presumably the *Trial and Flagellation* and the *Crucifixion* are the "worste."

137 It seems that the Bakers distributed bread customarily from their carriage.

138–45 eight lines instead of seven. Combining 144–45 would provide a kind of rhyme for 143. But 140 has no rhyme for 138: B's *altogether* does not help.

146–50 The lines sound defensive about the "nonbiblical" *Harrowing of Hell*.

153–56 as for 85–88.

153 *before you after*: "in front of you, the audience, next."

156 "The play is little altered from its traditional version."

157–60   as for 85–88.

159   *often speeche*: "Frequent speeches."

    woman: R's *women* improves the sense.

161–64   as for 85–88.

165–66   The plays following the Fishmongers' will be apocryphal.

174   The line can mean "who are Antichrist's followers" or "who are Antichrists—like Antichrist."

175   *walkinge on grownde*: "back on earth from Paradise."

177   The antecedent of *which* is *partes*; that is, "the content of the speeches by Enoche and Hely."

186–89   as for 85–88.

190–95   A line is missing after 193.

191   *the muste*: "they (the plays) must."

193–202   A defense against the charge that impersonating God is sacrilege: the gilt-covered face removes the sacrilege, just as a cloud-covering would.

195   B's *preserve* seems clearly erroneous.

206   *storye*: a poor rhyme for *before* and *doore*.

207   *then open is the door*: The statement seems figurative rather than literal: "then no one is keeping him here." It has been taken as evidence that the performance was to be indoors on a fixed stage rather than outdoors on carriages; but Clopper's argument that it means "open is the door" from the outer Pentice—i.e., "leave if you wish"—makes good sense.

208   *that lett hime into heare*: The last two words can mean "in to listen to the plays," as well as "into here, into this hall."

210–13   Perhaps added by David Rogers: completely different stanzaic form; third line has a faulty rhyme.

APPENDIX:

STANZA-FORMS

IN THE CYCLE

THE FOLLOWING SURVEY of stanza-forms is based on the stanza-divisions in Hm set out in Volume I of our edition. References are to the stanza-numbers in the edition.

In determining stanza-form no attempt has been made to supplement the lines in a Hm form from other manuscripts, but generous allowance has been made for imperfect rhyme and meter. Additionally, a stanza that does not in its Hm form conform to an existing pattern may nevertheless be included under that pattern if a rearrangement of word-order, a change in line-division, or the substitution of a near-synonym for the rhyme-word would produce that pattern; in such cases the stanza is distinguished by an asterisk in the list.

Rhymes in final long -e and rhymes in final -y, -ie, or I have been regarded as distinct and different unless they are clearly combined within the stanza.

The number of syllables in a line and the number of stressed syllables often seem to be a matter of subjective assessment. Many lines have no syllabic regularity. Particular caution should be exercised in interpreting the less frequent stanza-forms used in Plays 1 and 7.

In the lists the stanza-forms appear in order of their frequency within each play, but for convenience variants of a particular stanza-form are listed after the dominant form.

PLAY I [45 stanzas]
The lines of stanzas 2–4 are misdivided to a greater or less extent in all MSS but are here described in their corrected form.
abab^4 [18] 1, 5, 7, 8, 11, 12, 18, 21, 29, 33, 34, *35, 36, 37, 38, 39, 40, 41.
abababab^4 [13] 13, *14, 15, 25, 26, 27, 28, 30, 31, 32, 42, 43, 44.
ababababababab^4 [1] 16.
ababbcbc^4 [3] 17, 22, 23.
ababbaba^4 [1] 19.
ababcbcb^4 [1] 20.
*abababab^6 [3] *2, 3, 4.
aaa^{4}b^3 [1] 6.
abbbcbcb^4 [1] 9.

aa [1] 10.
ab^{4}b^3 [1] 24.
a^{4}b^{3}a^{4}b^3 [1] 45.

PLAY 2 [88 stanzas]
aaa^{4}b^{3}ccc^{4}b^3 [60] 2, 3, 4, 5, 6, 7, 8, 9, 10, 11, 12, 13, *14, *15, 18, 19, 20, 24,
    25, 26, 27, 29, *30, 31, 35, 36, 37, 38, *39, 40, 42, *43, *47, 48, *49, *57, 59,
    60, 61, 62, *63, 66, 67, 68, 69, 71, 72, 73, 74, 75, 76, 78, 79, 81, 82, 83, 84,
    *85, 86, 87.
aaa^{4}b^{3}aaa^{4}b^3 [28] 1, 16, 17, 21, 22, 23, 28, 32, 33, 34, 41, 44, 45, 46, 50, 51, 52,
    53, 54, 55, 56, 58, 64, 65, 70, 77, 80, 88.

PLAY 3 [43 stanzas]
aaa^{4}b^{3}ccc^{4}b^3 [35] 1, 3, 4, *5, 7, 8, 9, 10, 11, 12, 13, 14, 15, 16, 17, 18, 19, 20,
    21, 22, 23, 24, 25, 26, 27, 28, 32, 33, 34, 36, 37, *38, 40, 41, 42.
aaa^{4}b^{3}aaa^{4}b^3 [4] 2, 6, 35, 39.
abab^4 [2] 29, 30.
aaaa^4 [1] 43.
aaab^4 [1] 31.

PLAY 4 [63 stanzas]
aaa^{4}b^{3}ccc^{4}b^3 [46] 1, 2, *4, 5, 6, 8, 13, 14, 15, 16, 17, 20, 21, 23, 24, 26, 27, 29,
    30, 31, 32, *33, 34, 35, 36, 37, 39, 40, 41, 42, *43, 44, 45, 46, 47, 49, 50, 51,
    53, 55, 57, 58, 59, 60, *61, 62.
aaa^{4}b^{3}aaa^{4}b^3 [13] 3, 7, 9, *10, 11, 12, 18, 19, 22, 25, 28, 54, *63.
aaa^{4}b^3 [3] 38, 48, 52.
aaa^{4}b^{3}aa^{4}b^3 [1] 56.

PLAY 5 [59 stanzas]
aaa^{4}b^{3}ccc^{4}b^3 [47] 1, 2, 3, 4, 5, 6, 8, 9, 10, 11, 13, 14, 15, 17, 18, 19, 20, *21, 24,
    25, 26, 27, *28, 29, 30, 31, 32, 34, 37, 38, 39, 40, 42, 43, 45, 46, 47, 48, 50,
    51, 52, 53, 54, 55, 56, 57, 58.
aaa^{4}b^{3}ccc^{4}d^3 [1] 49.
aaa^{4}b^{3}aaa^{4}b^3 [6] 7, 23, 33, 35, 36, 41.
aaa^{4}b^{3}cc^{4}b^3 [1] 12.
aaa^{4}b^3 [3] 16, 22, 44.
aaab^4 [1] 59.

PLAY 6 [92 stanzas]
aaa^{4}b^{3}aaa^{4}b^3 [53] 1, 3, 4, 7, 8, 11, 19, *23, 24, 25, 26, 31, 32, 33, 34, 35, 36, 37,
    38, 39, 40, 41, 42, *43, 44, 45, 46, 48, 49, 50, 51, 52, 53, 54, 55, 56, 59, 60,
    62, 63, 64, 65, 66, 67, 72, 78, 82, 84, 85, 87, *89, 90, 91.
aaa^{4}b^{3}aa^{4}b^3 [2] 29, 69.
aaa^{4}b^{3}ccc^{4}b^3 [30] 2, 5, 6, 9, 13, 14, 15, 16, 17, 18, 20, 21, 22, 57, 58, 61, 68, 70,
    71, 73, 74, 75, 76, 77, *79, 80, 81, 86, 88, 92.

aaa^{4}b^{3}baa^{4}b^3 [1] 30.
*abcb (French) [2] 27, 28.
aaa^{4}b^{3}c^{4}c^3 [1] 10.
abbbb^{4}c^{3}bbb^{4}c^3 [1] 12.
aaa^{4}b^3 [1] 47.
aaaaaa^{4}b^3 [1] 83.

P L A Y 7 [128 stanzas]

abab This is the dominant rhyme-pattern in the play, occurring mainly in
quatrain-stanzas, but it is also found as part of eight-line stanzas. There is,
however, considerable variation within the lines; line-length varies from four to
nine syllables, the number of stressed syllables from two to four, and the
stress-patterns are frequently highly debatable. All examples of the rhyme-
pattern are therefore listed together, with no attempt to distinguish them by
stressed syllables or line-length.
   In the stanza-series 35–41 the additional lines and stanza-division of
H are preferred to those of Hm, giving the familiar abab pattern. H's arrangement, however, also gives an additional stanza in that section.

abab [65] 6, 8, 9, 12, 13, 14, 15, 17, 18, 19, 20, 21, 22, *23, 24, 26, 27, 28, 29,
   30, 32, 33, 34, *35, *36, *37, *38, *39, *40, *41, 43, 44, 55, 56, 57, 74, 75,
   76, 77, *78, 79, 80, 81, 82, 83, 84, 85, 86, 87, 88, 89, 91, 92, 95, *96, 97, 104,
   106, 108, 109, 119, 122, 125, 127, 128.
aaaa [2] 16, 42.
abababab [14] 48, 49, 50, 51, 52, 54, 98, 99, 100, 101, 102, 123, 124, 126.
aaa^{4}b^{3}ccc^{4}b^3 [9] 1, *5, 10, 11, 72, 73, 113, *117, 118.
aaa^{4}b^{3}ccc^{4}d^3 [1] 116.
aaa^{4}b^{3}aaa^{4}b^3 [5] 2, *4, *7, 71, 114.
aaa^{4}b^{3}aaa^{4}c^3 [1] 3.
*aaa^{4}b^3 [1] 110.
aabaab^2 [13] 53, 58, 59, 60, 61, 63, 64, 65, 66, 67, 68, 69, 70.
aaabaaab^2 [6] 45, 46, 47, 90, 93, 94.
aaabaa^3 [1] 121.
aaab^2 [2] 62, 103.
aaab^3 [1] 115.
abab^4 [1] 111.
abcb^4 [1] 31.
aaab (irreg) [1] 25.
aa^{4}bccb^2 [1] 105.
abbbcdddc [1] 107.
abcbc^3 [1] 112.
a^{3}bccb^{4}d^3 [1] 120.

Note. Stanzas 35–41 are included under abab because it is assumed that such a
   stanza-form underlies this section. The division in the edition does not conform
   to this description and would require this section to be listed as containing a
   unique stanza-form.

PLAY 8 [56 stanzas]

aaa⁴b³aaa⁴b³ [33] 1, 5, 6, 8, 11, 12, 13, 14, 15, 16, 17, 18, 19, 22, 23, 25, 27, *28, 29, 30, 31, 32, 33, 34, 35, 47, 49, 50, *51, 52, 53, 54, 56.

ababbcc⁴ [11] 36, 37, 38, 39, 40, 41, *42, 43, 44, 45, 46.

aaa⁴b³ccc⁴b³ [5] 2, 3, 4, 26, 55.

aaa⁴b³ [2] 24, 48.

aaa⁴b³ (French) [2] 9, 10.

aaa⁴b³ccc⁴d³ [1] 7.

ababcbcb⁴ [1] 20.

aaa⁴b³aaa⁴b³ (French) [1] 21.

PLAY 9 [33 stanzas]

aaa⁴b³aaa⁴b³ [27] 1, 2, 3, 4, 5, 7, 8, 9, 10, 11, 12, 13, 15, 16, *17, 18, 19, 21, 22, 23, 24, 25, 26, 27, 28, 29, 30.

aaa⁴b³ccc⁴b³ [3] *20, 32, 33.

aaa⁴b³aa⁴b³ [1] 6.

aaa⁴b³baa⁴b³ [1] 14.

ababccc⁴d³ [1] 31.

PLAY 10 [65 stanzas]

aaa⁴b³ccc⁴b³ [33] 6, 7, 8, 9, 10, 17, 18, 19, 22, 24, *25, 31, 32, 36, 37, 38, 39, 40, *41, 45, 46, 48, 49, 50, 51, 52, 53, 57, 60, 61, 62, 63, 64.

aaa⁴b³aaa⁴b³ [21] 1, 2, 3, 4, 5, 16, 20, 21, 23, 26, 33, 34, 35, *42, 43, 47, 54, 55, 58, 59.

aaa⁴b³ [4] 11, 14, 28, 30.

aabb⁴ [1] 12.

aba⁴b³abab⁴ [2] 27, 29.

abab⁴ [1] 13.

aaa⁴b³bbb⁴a³ [1] 15.

abbb⁴c³ddd⁴c³ [1] 56.

aaa⁴a³bbb⁴a³ [1] 65.

PLAY 11 [48 stanzas]

aaa⁴b³aaa⁴b³ [13] 1, 2, 5, 6, *8, 11, 12, 18, 21, 22, 23, 25, 26.

abab⁴ [11] 28, 30, 33, 34, 38, 39, 42, 44, 45, 46, 47.

aaa⁴b³ccc⁴b³ [9] 3, 9, 10, 13, 15, 16, 17, 19, 48.

ababcdcd⁴ [2] 32, *43.

ababbcbc⁴ [2] 27, *41.

ababacac⁴ [2] 36, 40.

aaa⁴a³bbb⁴a³ [1] 4.

aaa⁴b³aa⁴b³ [1] 7.

aaa⁴b³aaa⁴ [1] 14.

aaa⁴b³aaa⁴c³ [1] 20.

aaa⁴a³aaa⁴a³ [1] 24.

abcbdcdc⁴ [1] 29.

ababcbcb⁴ [1] 35.
abababab⁴ [1] 31.
abcb⁴ [1] 37.

PLAY 12 [39 stanzas]
aaa⁴b³ccc⁴b³ [21] 4, 6, 8, 9, 10, 13, *15, 17, 20, 21, 22, 24, 25, 26, 29, 30, 31, 32, 33, *36, 38.
aaa⁴b³aaa⁴b³ [18] 1, 2, *3, 5, 7, 11, 12, 14, *16, 18, 19, 23, 27, 28, 34, 35, 37, 39.

PLAY 13 [66 stanzas]
aaa⁴b³ccc⁴b³ [24] 7, 9, 10, 12, 14, 15, 20, 22, 23, 25, 26, 34, 36, 40, 42, 47, 49, 50, 52, 55, 58, 59, 60, 61.
aaa⁴b³ccc⁴d³ [1] 21.
aaa⁴b³ccccc⁴b³ [2] 16, 32.
aabbb⁴c³ddd⁴c³ [1] 30.
aaa⁴b³ccddd⁴b³ [1] 19.
aaa⁴b³aaa⁴b³ [17] 13, 17, 18, 33, 41, 43, 44, *45, 46, 48, 51, 53, *56, 57, *62, *64, 65.
aaa⁴b³aaa⁴c³ [1] 63.
aaa⁴b³aaccc⁴b³ [1] 11.
aaa⁴b³ [7] 24, 27, 29, 37, *38, 39, 66.
ababbcc⁴ [5] 1, 2, 3, 4, 5.
abab⁴ [1] 6.
aaa⁴ [1] 8.
aabb⁴ [1] 28.
aabbcc⁴ [1] 31.
aaa⁴b³c⁴b³ [1] 35.
aaa⁴b³c⁴ [1] 54.

PLAY 14 [54 stanzas]
aaa⁴b³aaa⁴b³ [28] 1, 2, 3, 5, 6, 7, 11, 15, 16, 21, 22, 23, 26, 28, 30, *31, 33, 34, 35, 38, 41, 43, 45, 48, 50, 51, 53, 54.
aaa⁴b³ccc⁴b³ [26] 4, 8, 9, 10, 12, 13, 14, 17, 18, 19, *20, 24, 25, 27, *29, 32, 36, 37, 39, 40, 42, 44, 46, 47, 49, 52.

PLAY 15 [46 stanzas]
aaa⁴b³ccc⁴b³ [31] 1, 2, 3, 4, 5, 7, 9, 10, 12, 15, 16, 18, 19, 20, 21, 22, 23, 24, 25, 27, 28, 30, 31, 32, 35, 36, 37, 41, 42, 43, *45.
aaa⁴b³aaa⁴b³ [14] 6, 8, 11, 13, 14, 17, 26, 29, 33, 34, 38, 39, *44, 46.
aabbb⁴c³ [1] 40.

PLAY 16 [52 stanzas]
aaa⁴b³aaa⁴b³ [22] 1, 2, 4, 5, 6, 8, 17, 18, 20, 21, 22, 23, 24, 25, 26, 27, *28, 32, 36, 37, 38, *40.

$aaa^4b^3aaaa^4b^3$ [1] 7.
$aaabaaab^2$ [12] 9, 10, 11, 12, 15, 41, 42, 43, 44, 45, 46, 49.
$aaa^4b^3ccc^4b^3$ [9] 16, 29, 30, 31, 33, 34, *35, 39, *48.
aaa^4b^3 [2] 3, 52.
$aaab^3$ [2] 13, 14.
$aaab^2cc^4d^3$ [1] 19.
$aaaaaaa^4b^3$ [1] 47.
$aabbb^4c^3$ [1] *50.
$aaaaa^4b^3$ [1] 51.

PLAY 16A [61 stanzas]
$aaa^4b^3aaa^4b^3$ [24] 3, 4, 7, 28, 29, *31, 32, 34, 38, 39, 41, 42, 43, 47, 51, 52, 53, 54, 55, 57, 58, 59, *60, 61.
$aaabaaab^2$ [18] *10, 11, 12, 13, 14, 15, 16, 17, 18, 19, 20, 21, 22, 23, 24, 25, 26, 27.
$aaa^4b^3ccc^4b^3$ [16] 1, *2, 5, 6, 8, 9, 30, 33, 35, 36, *37, 40, 48, *49, 50, 56.
$aaabbbc^4$ [1] 44.
aaa^4b^3 [1] 45.
$abab^4$ [1] *46.

PLAY 17 [43 stanzas]
$aaa^4b^3aaa^4b^3$ [23] 1, 2, 3, 4, 6, 8, 9, 15, 16, 21, 22, 23, 24, 26, 27, 28, 29, 30, 31, 32, 33, 34, *35.
$aaa^4b^3ccc^4b^3$ [18] 5, 7, 10, 11, 12, 13, 14, 17, 18, 19, 20, 36, 37, 38, *39, 40, 41, 43.
$abab^4$ [1] 25.
aaa^4b^3 [1] 42.

PLAY 18 [57 stanzas]
$aaa^4b^3ccc^4b^3$ [25] 3, 4, 5, 7, 8, 9, 10, *11, *12, *13, 14, 15, 16, 17, 18, 19, 30, 31, 33, 35, 38, 47, 48, 49, 53.
*$aa^4b^3ccc^4b^3$ [1] *32.
$aaa^4b^3aaa^4b^3$ [17] 24, 25, 26, 27, *28, 29, 40, 41, 42, 43, 44, 46, 50, 51, 52, 54, 57.
$a^4b^3a^4b^3a^4b^3a^4b^3$ [4] 20, 21, 22, *23.
$abab^4$ [2] 34, 36.
aaa^4b^3 [3] 37, 45, 56.
aaabaaab (French) [1] 1.
*$abab^4c^3dd^4c^3$ [1] 2.
$aaaa^4a^3bbb^4a^3$ [1] 6.
$aaa^4b^3ccc^4$ [1] 39.
aab^4c^3 [1] 55.

PLAY 19 [35 stanzas]
$aaa^4b^3aaa^4b^3$ [20] 1, 2, 3, 4, 5, 6, 7, 8, *10, 14, *15, 16, *17, 18, *20, 22, 24, 25, 29, 30.

$aaa^4b^3ccc^4b^3$ [13] 11, 12, 13, 19, 21, *23, 26, 27, 28, 31, *32, 33, 35.
$aaa^4b^3cc^4b^3$ [1] 9.
aaa^4b^3 [1] 34.

PLAY 20 [24 stanzas]
$aaa^4b^3ccc^4b^3$ [15] *2, 4, 5, 7, 8, 9, 10, 11, 13, 14, *15, 16, 18, 19, 21.
$aaa^4b^3aaa^4b^3$ [8] 1, 6, 12, 17, 20, 22, 23, 24.
$aaa^4a^3aaa^4a^3$ [1] 3.

PLAY 21 [49 stanzas]
$aaa^4b^3aaa^4b^3$ [36] 1, 2, 3, 4, 5, 7, 8, 9, 10, 15, 16, 17, 18, 19, 21, 22, 23, 24, 25, 26, 27, 28, 29, 30, *32, 33, 34, 35, 36, 37, 39, 40, 46, 47, 48, 49.
$aaa^4b^3ccc^4b^3$ [10] 6, *11, 12, 13, 14, 41, 42, 43, 44, 45.
$aaa^4a^3bbb^4a^3$ [1] 31.
$aaa^4b^3bbb^4b^3$ [1] *38.
$aa^4b^3aa^4b^3$ [1] 20.

PLAY 22 [43 stanzas]
$aaa^4b^3ccc^4b^3$ [28] 2, 3, 4, 5, 6, *17, *18, 20, 21, 22, 24, 25, 26, 27, 28, 30, 31, 32, 33, *34, 35, 36, 37, 38, 39, 40, 41, 42.
$aaa^4b^3aaa^4b^3$ [14] *1, 7, 8, 9, *10, 11, 12, 13, 14, 16, 19, 23, 29, 43.
aaa^4b^3 [1] 15.

PLAY 23 [98 stanzas]
$aaa^4b^3ccc^4b^3$ [44] 8, 9, 10, 11, 12, 15, 16, *19, 20, 23, 24, 27, 28, 29, 32, 35, 40, 42, 43, 44, *45, 53, 54, *57, 58, 59, *61, 63, 69, 71, 72, 73, 75, 76, 78, 79, 80, 81, 82, 83, *84, *96, 97, 98.
$aaa^4b^3cbc^4b^3$ [1] 25.
$aaa^4b^3aaa^4b^3$ [28] 2, 3, 4, 5, 6, 7, 13, 22, 26, 30, 34, 36, 37, 38, 39, 41, 46, 47, 64, 65, 66, 68, 70, 74, 77, 86, 87, 89.
$aaaa^4b^3aaa^4b^3$ [1] 18.
$aa^4b^3aaa^4b^3$ [4] 21, 52, 55, 67.
$aa^4b^3ccc^4b^3$ [1] 56.
aaa^4b^3 [6] 17, 31, *33, 50, 62, 85.
$abab^4$ [6] 90, 91, 92, 93, 94, 95.
$aa^4b^3aa^4b^3$ [3] 48, 51, *60.
$aa^4b^3cc^4b^3$ [1] 88.
$aaa^4b^3bbb^4b^3$ [1] 14.
$aa^4b^3cc^4b^3$ [1] 49.
Latin stanza [1] 1.

PLAY 24 [89 stanzas]
$aaa^4b^3aaa^4b^3$ [66] 1, 2, 3, 4, 6, 8, 9, 10, 11, 15, 16, 17, 18, 19, 23, 24, 25, 26, 27, 28, 29, 30, 31, 32, 33, 34, 35, 36, 37, 38, 39, 40, 41, 42, 43, 44, 45, 46, 47, 48, 49, 50, 51, 52, 53, 54, 55, 58, 59, 61, 62, 64, 65, 66, 69, 70, 72, *73, 75, 76, *78, 81, 82, 83, 84, 87.

aaa⁴b³ccc⁴b³ [22] 5, 7, 12, 14, *20, *21, 22, 56, 57, 60, 63, 67, *68, 71, *74, 77, *79, 80, 85, 86, 88, 89.
aaa⁴b³ [1] 13.

A NOTE ON THE "CHESTER STANZA"

Of the 1,476 stanzas in this survey, 579 are listed under aaa⁴b³ccc⁴b³ and 538 under aaa⁴b³aaa⁴b³. These two forms together account therefore for 1,117 stanzas in the cycle. But both are clearly variants of a single stanza-form, the "Chester stanza." Moreover, other variations upon this form occur (e.g., aaa⁴a³aaa⁴a³), and a number of aaa⁴b³ quatrains, seven-line stanzas, and other "defective" forms also derive from the same base, often a product of scribal omission or error. Hence the contribution of the stanza-form to the verse in the cycle is even greater than the figure of 1,117 stanzas would suggest. Such metrical consistency is not found in the other extant English cycles and might be held to indicate that Chester, in its extant form, was the result of a single revision.

The aaabaaab and aaabcccb types are fairly evenly distributed in Plays 12, 13, and 14. The aaabaaab type markedly predominates in Plays 6, 8, 9, 11, 16, 16A, 17, 19, 21, and 24; the aaabcccb type markedly predominates in Plays 2, 3, 4, 5, 10, 15, 18, 20, 22, and 23. There are, however, no examples of the form in Play 1 and a negligible number in Play 7, whereas in Play 11 the stanza is a minority form. Plays that show a high proportion of other forms are Plays 8, 13, 16, and 16A. We attach little significance to variations within the "Chester stanza-form." We believe that stylistic considerations could have been the dominant reason for the employment of other stanza-forms.

BIBLIOGRAPHY

Allison, Richard. *The Psalmes of David in Meter*. London: William Barley, 1599. Reprint. Menston: Scolar Press, 1968.

Babington, Churchill, and Lumby, J. R., eds. *Polychronicon Ranulphi Higden*. 9 vols. Rolls Series. London, 1865–86.

Baugh, A. C. "The Chester Plays and French Influence." In *Schelling Anniversary Papers*, edited by A. H. Quinn, pp. 35–63. New York, 1923.

Block, K. S. *Ludus Coventriae, or The Plaie Called Corpus Christi*. London: Early English Text Society, extra series 120, 1922.

Boulton, Helen E. *Chester Mystery Plays*. Chester: Chester Corporation, 1966.

Browe, Petrus, ed. *Textus Antiqui de Festo Corporis Christi*. Fascicule IV of *Opuscula et Textus*. Munich, 1934.

Calendar of State Papers: Domestic. Vol. 1, *1547–80*. London: Longmans and Co., 1856.

Carpenter, Nan Cooke. "Music in the Chester Plays." *Papers on English Language and Literature* 1 (1965):195–216.

———. "Music in the English Mystery Plays." In *Music in English Renaissance Drama*, edited by John H. Long, pp. 1–31. Lexington: University of Kentucky Press, 1968.

———. "Music in the *Secunda Pastorum*." In *Medieval English Drama: Essays Critical and Contextual*, edited by Jerome Taylor and Alan H. Nelson, pp. 212–17. Chicago: University of Chicago Press, 1972.

Cawley, A. C., ed. *The Wakefield Pageants in the Towneley Cycle*. Manchester: Manchester University Press, 1958.

———, and Stevens, Martin, eds. *The Towneley Cycle: A Facsimile of Huntington MS 1*. Leeds Texts and Monographs, Medieval Drama Facsimiles II. Leeds: University of Leeds School of English, 1976.

Charles, Sydney R., ed. *The Music of The Pepys MS 1236*. Corpus Mensurabilis Musicae, 40. Rome: American Institute of Musicology, 1967.

Clopper, L. M. "The Chester Plays: Frequency of Performance." *Theatre Survey* 14 (1973): 46–58.

———. "The History and Development of the Chester Cycle." *Modern Philology* 75 (1978): 219–46.

———. "The Rogers' Description of the Chester Plays." *Leeds Studies in English* 7 (1973–74): 63–94.

———, ed. *Chester: Records of Early English Drama*. Toronto: University of Toronto Press, 1979.

Coussemaker, E. de. *Drames liturgiques du moyen âge*. Rennes: H. Vatar, 1860. Reprint. New York: Broude Bros., 1964.

Craig, Hardin, ed. *Two Coventry Corpus Christi Plays*. London: Early English Text Society, extra series 87 (2d ed.), 1957.

Davis, Norman, ed. *Non-Cycle Plays and Fragments*, with a note on The Shrewsbury Music by F. Ll. Harrison. London: Early English Text Society, supplementary series 1, 1970.

Deimling, Hermann, and Matthews (first name unknown), eds. *The Chester Plays*. 2 vols. London: Early English Text Society, extra series 62 and 115, 1892 and 1916.

Dobson, E. J., and Harrison, F. Ll. *Medieval English Songs*. London: Faber and Faber. 1979.

Dutka, JoAnna. *Music in the English Mystery Plays*. Early Drama, Art, and Music: Reference Series 2. Kalamazoo: Medieval Institute Publications, Western Michigan University, 1980.

————. "Mysteries, Minstrels, and Music." *Comparative Drama* 8 (Spring 1974): 112–24.

————. "The Use of Music in the English Mystery Plays." Ph.D. dissertation, University of Toronto, 1972.

————, ed. *Records of Early English Drama: Proceedings of the First Colloquium*. Toronto: Records of Early English Drama, 1979.

England, George, and Pollard, A. W., eds. *The Towneley Plays*. London: Early English Text Society, extra series 71, 1897.

Foster, Frances, A., ed. *A Stanzaic Life of Christ*. London: Early English Text Society, original series 15, 1926.

Frere, Walter Howard. *Antiphonale Sarisburiense*. London: Plainsong and Mediaeval Music Society, 1901–24. Reprinted in 6 vols. Farnborough: Gregg Press, 1966.

————. *Graduale Sarisburiense*. London: Bernard Quaritch, 1894. Reprint. Farnborough: Gregg Press, 1966.

Frost, Maurice. *English and Scottish Psalm and Hymn Tunes, c. 1543–1677*. London: Society for the Promotion of Christian Knowledge and Oxford University Press, 1953.

Graduale Romanum. Malines: Dessain, 1909.

Graesse, J. G. T., ed. *Jacobi a Voragine: Legenda Aurea*. 3d ed. Vratislaviae: Koebnor, 1890. Reprint. Osnabrück: Zeller, 1969.

Greene, Richard Leighton. *The Early English Carols*. 2d ed. Oxford: Oxford University Press, 1977.

Greg, Sir W. W. "Bibliographical and Textual Problems of the English Miracle Cycles. III. Christ and the Doctors: Inter-Relation of the Cycles." *Library*, 3d series, 5 (1914): 280–319.

————. *The Play of Antichrist from the Chester Cycle*. Oxford: Clarendon Press, 1935.

————. *The Trial and Flagellation with Other Studies in the Chester Cycle*. Malone Society Studies. London: Oxford University Press, 1935.

Harrison, Frank Ll. *Music in Medieval Britain*. London: Routledge and Kegan Paul, 1958.

————, ed. *The Eton Choirbook*. 3 vols. Musica Britannica 10–12. London: Stainer and Bell for The Royal Musical Association, 1956–61.

Horstmann, Carl, ed. *Altenglische Legenden*. Paderborn: Druck und Verlag von Ferdinand Schöningh, 1875.

Ingram, Reginald W. " 'Pleyng geire accustumed belongyng and necessarie': Guild Records and Pageant Production in Coventry." In *Records of Early English Drama: Proceedings of the First Colloquium*, edited by JoAnna Dutka, pp. 60–92. Toronto: Records of Early English Drama, 1979.

Jackman, James L., ed. *Fifteenth-Century Basse Dances*. Wellesley Edition, 6. Wellesley, Mass.: Wellesley College, 1964.

James, Montague Rhodes, trans. *The Apocryphal New Testament*. Oxford: Clarendon Press, 1924. Corrected, 1953. Reprinted, 1963.

Keane, Ruth M. "The Theme of Kingship in the Chester Cycle." M.A. thesis, University of Liverpool, 1977.

Kolve, V. A. *The Play Called Corpus Christi*. Stanford: Stanford University Press, 1966.

Krummel, D. W. *English Music Printing, 1553–1700*. London: Bibliographical Society, 1975.

Liber Usualis. English edition. Tournai: Desclée, 1950.

Lumiansky, R. M., and Mills, David. *The Chester Mystery Cycle*. Vol. 1. London: Early English Text Society, supplementary series 3, 1974.

————. "The Five Cyclic Manuscripts of the Chester Cycle of Mystery Plays: A Statistical Survey of Variant Readings." *Leeds Studies in English*, n.s. 7 (1974): 95–107.

————. "Introduction for *The Chester Mystery Cycle*: A Facsimile of Bodley MS 175." Leeds Texts and Monographs. Leeds: University of Leeds School of English, 1973.

————. "Introduction for *The Chester Mystery Cycle*: A Reduced *Facsimile of Huntington Library MS 2*." Leeds Texts and Monographs. Leeds: University of Leeds School of English, 1980.

McGavin, John J. "Sign and Transition: The *Purification* Play in Chester." *Leeds Studies in English*, n.s. 11 (1980): 90–104.

Mezey, Nicole. "Creed and Prophets Series in the Visual Arts." *Early Drama, Art, and Music Newsletter*, 2, no. 1 (November 1979): 7–10.

Missale Romanum. Tournai: Desclée, 1942.

Morris, Rupert H. *Chester in the Plantagenet and Tudor Reigns*. N.p., 1893.

Nichols, Francis Morgan, trans. *The Marvels of Rome*. London: Ellis and Elvey, 1889.

Paris, Gaston, and Raynaud, Gaston, eds. *Le Mystère de la Passion D'Arnoul Greban*. Paris, 1878.

Parthey, Gustavus, ed. *Mirabilia Romae e codicibus vaticanis emendata*. Berolini: A. Effer and L. Linotner, 1869.

Pickering, O. S., ed. *The South English Nativity of Mary and Christ*. Middle

English Texts 1. Heidelberg: Winter, Universitäts-Verlag, 1975.

Purvis, J. S. *From Minster to Market Place*. York: St. Anthony's Press, 1969.

Pynson, Richard. *Processionale ad Usum Sarum*. London: Richard Pynson, 1502. Reprinted with introduction and indexes by Richard Rastall. Kilkenny: Boethius Press, 1980.

Rastall, Richard. *A Fifteenth-Century Song Book*. Leeds: Boethius Press, 1973.

————. "Music for a Royal Entry, 1474." *Musical Times* 118 (June 1977): 463–66.

————. "Some English Consort-Groupings of the Late Middle Ages." *Music and Letters* 55 (April 1974): 179–202.

————, ed. *Four Songs in Latin from an English Song-Book*. Newton Abbot: Antico Edition, 1979.

Rothschild, Le Baron James de, ed. *Le Mystère du Viel Testament*. Société des Anciens Textes Français. 5 vols. Paris: Firmin Didot, 1878–91.

St. Augustine of Hippo. *Opera*, in *Patrologiae Latinae*, edited by J. P. Migne. Vols. 32–47. Paris: Garnier Fratres, 1877.

St. Bede. *Opera*, in *Patrologiae Latinae*, edited by J. P. Migne. Vols. 90–95. Paris, 1861–62.

Salter, F. M. "The Banns of the Chester Plays." *Review of English Studies* 15 (1939): 432–57 and 16 (1940): 1–17, 137–48.

————. *Mediaeval Drama in Chester*. Toronto: University of Toronto Press, 1955.

Severs, J. Burke. "The Relationship between the Brome and Chester Plays of 'Abraham and Isaac.'" *Modern Philology* 42 (February 1945): 137–51.

Sharp, Thomas. *A Dissertation on the Pageants or Dramatic Mysteries Anciently Performed at Coventry*. Coventry: Merridew, 1825. Reprint. Wakefield: E. P. Publishing, 1973.

Smith, Lucy T., ed. "Abraham and Isaac, a Mystery Play: From a Private Manuscript of the 15th Century." *Anglia* 7 (1884): 316–37.

————. *York Plays: The Plays Performed by the Crafts or Mysteries of York on the Day of Corpus Christi in the 14th, 15th, and 16th Centuries*. Oxford: Clarendon Press, 1885. Reprint. New York: Russell and Russell, 1963.

Steele, Robert. *The Earliest English Music Printing*. 1903. Revised ed. London: Bibliographical Society, 1965.

Stevens, John. *Music and Poetry in the Early Tudor Court*. London: Methuen, 1961.

————. *Music at the Court of Henry VIII*. Musica Britannica 18. London: Stainer and Bell for The Royal Musical Association, 1964.

————. "Music in Mediaeval Drama." *Proceedings of the Royal Musical Association* 84 (1958): 81–95.

————, ed. *Mediaeval Carols*. Musica Britannica 4. London: Stainer and Bell for The Royal Musical Association, 1952.

Trowell, Brian, ed. *Invitation to Medieval Music* 3. London: Stainer and Bell, 1976.

————. *Invitation to Medieval Music* 4. London: Stainer and Bell, 1978.

Utesch, Hans. *Die Quellen der Chester-Plays.* Kiel: Kieler Tagespost, G.m.b.H., 1909.

Whiston, William, trans. *The Works of Flavius Josephus.* London and Edinburgh: William P. Nimmo, n.d.

Wilson, Robert H. "The *Stanzaic Life* of Christ and the Chester Plays." *Studies in Philology* 28 (1931): 413–32.

Woolf, Rosemary. *The English Mystery Plays.* London: Routledge and Kegan Paul, 1972.

Wright, Thomas, ed. *The Chester Plays.* London: Shakespeare Society Publications, 1843 and 1847; reprinted, 1853.

INDEX

A (Additional 10305): and errors of rhyme, 6–9, 23–24, 25, 26, 27, 37, 54–55, 56–57, 60, 78, 80–81; and errors of meter, 11–12, 24, 27, 51, 52, 53, 56–57; and errors of meaning, 14, 25, 49–50, 52, 53; evidence of Exemplar alternatives in, 20, 21, 33, 35, 36; relationship of to R, 23, 26, 36, 53, 55, 57, 59–64, 66, 85, 194; Exemplar derivation of, 23, 49–57, 63–64; evidence of Exemplar alterations in, 24–27; guild-ascription in, 25, 190, 191, 195–202; and errors of stanza-structure, 26, 38; and use of MDs and SDs, 28, 29, 30–31; evidence of censorship in, 37, 38; evidence for dating Exemplar in, 42–46; relationship of to Hm, 57, 62–64; unique readings in, 59; date of, 59, 194; Bellin's practices as scribe of, 59–64, 66; relationship of to C, 64–66; evidence in for use of music, 125, 128, 129–30, 139, 140, 141, 145–46, 156–57; play-headings in, 195–202. *See also* Group (HmARB)
Accipite spiritum sanctum, 141, 143, 153
Act of Supremacy (1534), 189
Act of Uniformity (1549), 144
Acts of Pilate, 108
Aldersley, William, 167
"Ale wife" scene (Play 17), 34, 37, 46–47, 74
Apostles' Creed, 4, 107, 110, 169, 200–201; musical setting and performance of, 116, 129–30, 141, 143, 144, 153
Arneway, John, 166, 167, 168
Ascendo ad patrem meum, 141, 143, 150–52
As I lay upon a night, 162
As I out-rode, 162
Assumption. See Wives' *Assumption*
Augustine, St., 104
Ave regina caelorum, 155

B (Bodley 175): and errors of rhyme, 6–9, 23–24, 25, 26, 27, 37, 50, 54–55, 56–57, 80–81, 83; and errors of meaning, 14, 25, 49, 52, 53; evidence of Exemplar alternatives in, 21, 33, 35, 36–37; and errors of meter, 24, 26–27, 49, 51, 52, 53, 56–57, 83, 84; evidence of Exemplar alterations in, 24–26; guild-ascription in, 25, 48, 190, 191, 195–202; and errors of stanza-structure, 26, 38; and use of MDs and SDs, 28, 29, 30–31; evidence of censorship in, 37, 38; evidence for dating Exemplar in, 42–46, 48; Exemplar derivation of, 49–57, 63–64; date of, 67, 194; Bedford's practices as scribe of, 67–71; unique readings in, 68; evidence in for use of music, 125, 129, 131, 139, 141, 145, 152, 156; play-headings in, 195–202. *See also* Group (HmARB)
Bakers, 170, 174, 175, 190, 191, 199
Bakers' Charter (1462, 1552–53), 169, 170, 175, 190, 206–7